MW01252859

# APPLIED PSYCHOLOGY RESEARCH TRENDS

# APPLIED PSYCHOLOGY RESEARCH TRENDS

## KARL H. KIEFER
### EDITOR

**Nova Science Publishers, Inc.**
*New York*

**NOTICE TO THE READER**

The Publisher has taken reasonable care in the preparation of this book, but makes no expressed or implied warranty of any kind and assumes no responsibility for any errors or omissions. No liability is assumed for incidental or consequential damages in connection with or arising out of information contained in this book. The Publisher shall not be liable for any special, consequential, or exemplary damages resulting, in whole or in part, from the readers' use of, or reliance upon, this material. Any parts of this book based on government reports are so indicated and copyright is claimed for those parts to the extent applicable to compilations of such works.

Independent verification should be sought for any data, advice or recommendations contained in this book. In addition, no responsibility is assumed by the publisher for any injury and/or damage to persons or property arising from any methods, products, instructions, ideas or otherwise contained in this publication.

This publication is designed to provide accurate and authoritative information with regard to the subject matter covered herein. It is sold with the clear understanding that the Publisher is not engaged in rendering legal or any other professional services. If legal or any other expert assistance is required, the services of a competent person should be sought. FROM A DECLARATION OF PARTICIPANTS JOINTLY ADOPTED BY A COMMITTEE OF THE AMERICAN BAR ASSOCIATION AND A COMMITTEE OF PUBLISHERS.

LIBRARY OF CONGRESS CATALOGING-IN-PUBLICATION DATA

Applied psychology research trends / Karl H. Kiefer, editor.
     p. ; cm
Includes bibliographical references.
ISBN: 978-1-60456-372-6 (hardcover)
1. Psychology, Applied—Research. I. Kiefer, Karl H.
BF636.A635 2008
158—dc22

2007052526

*Published by Nova Science Publishers, Inc. ✦ New York*

# CONTENTS

# PREFACE

The basic premise of applied psychology is the use of psychological principles and theories to overcome problems in other areas, such as mental health, business management, education, health, product design, ergonomics, and law. Applied psychology includes the areas of clinical psychology, industrial/organizational psychology, human factors, forensic psychology, engineering psychology, as well as many other areas such as school psychology, sports psychology and community psychology. In addition, a number of specialized areas in the general field of psychology have applied branches (e.g., applied social psychology, applied cognitive psychology). This new book presents the latest reseach from around the world.

Chapter 1 - In Europe, as in the United States, laws ruling alcohol or tobacco advertising have been intensified. The purpose of this chapter is to take an inventory of this evolution and then to analyse the impact of these adverts. In that sense, three methods of analyses are presented in order to appreciate their advantages and limits. Then, the main results will be detailed. This assessment shows that most of the studies intend to demonstrate that advertising has an impact on the consumption of individuals. Nevertheless, only some authors questioned the opposite link between advertising and consumption. In other words, it may be conceivable that exposure to alcohol or tobacco adverts has been caused by people's attitude toward these products. This argument corresponds to the theory of selective exposure (Festinger, 1957). Following this theory, people tend to expose themselves to information which can confirm their positions and avoid the information that could challenge their attitude. In other words, alcohol and tobacco consumers will expose themselves to adverts for these products more than the abstinent ones. In addition, the authors will see that this argument is developed by advertisers. According to them, advertising orientates consumers towards a particular brand but it has no effect on non-consumers who pay little attention to this information. In the same way, the authors will question the impact of prevention campaigns on the people who are the targets. Indeed, the aim is to show that people who are weak consumers of alcohol, or who don't smoke, are, as evidenced by selective exposure theory, more inclined to expose themselves to prevention campaigns to these products. Thus, prevention campaigns maintain the healthy behaviours of non-smokers or occasional drinkers but do not modify the attitudes of heavy drinkers or smokers. Several lines of research linked to modulating factors of selective exposure will be suggested with the idea of improving exposure of the heavy drinkers, or smokers, to prevention campaigns.

Chapter 2 - Previous research on the relationship between organizational commitment and job performance had led researchers to the equivocal conclusion that increased commitment results in higher levels of job performance. In this study, the authors argue that by applying the conservation of resources model of stress, they can better understand the relationship between different types of commitment (affective, continuance, and normative) and different types of job performance (task and contextual) through targeted investment of resources by employees. Two studies provide support for their contention that affective commitment is related to task and contextual performance, continuance commitment is related to task performance, and normative commitment is related to a specific type of contextual performance. The authors discuss the implications of the conservation of resources model in terms of the theory surrounding organizational commitment and managerial practice.

Chapter 3 – The authors examine the effects of demographic diversity, skill diversity, and cultural value diversity (specifically, one's value for collectivism) on group cooperation and group performance. Results from a longitudinal study of 79 work groups show that demographic diversity is the least helpful, whereas collectivistic diversity helps group cooperation and performance. Group cooperation acts as a partial mediator, helping to explain the effects of diversity on performance. As expected, the context of the group does matter; specifically, task interdependence and group norms moderate the relationship between demographic diversity and group cooperation. Implications and several future research directions are discussed.

Chapter 4 – This study analyzed from a semiological framework (Peirce, 1931-1935; Theureau, 1992, 2004, 2006) the affective states and sentiments of three expert table tennis players during international matches. The matches were videotaped and the players' verbalizations while viewing the tapes, as well as their reports of affective states during the matches, were collected a posteriori. The data were analyzed by (a) the construction of graphs to display the evolution in affective states, (b) transcriptions of the players' actions and verbalizations, and (c) identification and categorization of the elements that described the situations in which the players experienced a sentiment. The results showed (a) an evolution in affective states during matches in relation with the score, (b) typical "situation-sentiment" couplings, and (c) the contradictory nature of emotion. The discussion focuses on the relationships between affective states and sentiments and the situated aspect of emotion.

Chapter 5 – Eyewitness identification evidence plays a crucial role in western legal systems. As a result, the consequences of an erroneous identification decision are serious. Specifically, the misidentification of an innocent suspect can, at best, delay the apprehension and conviction of the real offender or, at worst, lead to the conviction of an innocent person and the escape of the offender. Similarly, failure to identify the offender when they are present in the lineup may reduce the chances of a successful conviction. Not surprisingly, psychologists have sought to solve this problem by identifying factors (e.g., confidence) that discriminate correct from incorrect lineup decisions. Recent studies investigating confidence using a calibration approach have found consistent, robust confidence-accuracy calibration for choosers from lineups and positive decisions in face recognition tasks. Although encouraging, the applied usefulness of the calibration approach may be limited by its reliance on numerical, indeed probabilistic, confidence judgments. The use of a numerical confidence judgment stands in contrast with the U.S. Department of Justice's guidelines which suggest eliciting a confidence judgment in the witness's own words. Further, evidence from other areas of psychology suggests that people deal more naturally with verbal rather than numeric labels and struggle particularly with judgments about probabilities. Here the authors present an experimental investigation of these potential limits on the usefulness of confidence. Specifically, they compared confidence itself, and the confidence-accuracy relationship, between responses made on an eleven-point scale with either numeric (0% - 100%) or verbal (e.g., "Impossible" and "Certain") labels. One hundred and ninety two participants made identification decisions about four independent lineups and rated their confidence in the accuracy of each of their decisions. Each participant made two confidence judgments using the verbal scale and two using the numeric scale. Analyses revealed nearly identical confidence distributions for the verbal and numeric scales. Further, examination of the confidence-accuracy relationship revealed negligible differences between responses made on the verbal and numeric scales. These findings suggest that despite problems with numeric judgments in other domains, participants are no better able to provide confidence judgments in verbal than numeric form. Consequently, the reliance of the calibration approach for examining the confidence-accuracy relationship and for using confidence to predict accuracy is not a barrier to its use in eyewitness identification.

Eyewitness identifications are widely accepted as important and convincing evidence in Western legal systems. Often eyewitness testimony is the only evidence available (Cutler & Penrod, 1995) and, in some cases, convictions are based solely, or primarily, on an eyewitness identification or identifications (Wells et al., 1998). Further, eyewitness identifications have been demonstrated to have a consistent and robust impact on the proportion of guilty verdicts in mock-juror studies (Cutler & Penrod, 1995). As a result, the consequences of erroneous identification decisions are considerable. False identifications (i.e., identifying an innocent suspect as the offender) can lead to the prosecution and conviction of an innocent person and incorrect rejections (i.e., failing to identify the offender when they are, in fact, in the lineup) can reduce the ability to successfully prosecute the actual culprit. Unfortunately, in addition to its importance and persuasiveness, the fallibility of eyewitness identification evidence has also been consistently demonstrated in both laboratory experiments and field studies (for review, see Brewer, Weber, & Semmler, 2005; Cutler & Penrod, 1995). For example, the Innocence Project website (2007) reports that mistaken identifications were important in the wrongful conviction of over 75% of the 208 individuals exonerated to date.

Two complementary approaches to the unreliability of eyewitness identifications have been adopted by psychology-law researchers: specifically, identification of (a) a lineup procedure that eliminates false identifications and (b) markers of the accuracy of an identification decision. Here the authors focus on an aspect of the latter approach: namely, the use of confidence as a marker of identification accuracy. Specifically, they present an experiment investigating the impact of verbal versus numeric confidence scales on confidence judgments and the confidence-accuracy (CA) relationship in eyewitness identification.

Chapter 6 - Wine expertise has a long and great tradition, but what is wine expertise? The question, asked 50 years ago by experimental psychologists J.J. Gibson and Eleanor Gibson (1955), remains largely unanswered today. Analytical sensory evaluation of wine involves employing a human observer as an analytical instrument to discriminate and to make judgments about the qualities of wine. Wine sensory evaluation is studied and practiced within the discipline of sensory science and its applied component, sensory evaluation. Despite a proliferation of sensory studies and sensory journals over the last few decades, we still know very little about the cognitive processes involved in both wine sensory evaluation and in wine expertise. The present chapter discusses historical aspects of the discipline of sensory evaluation that can be argued as factors in the neglect of human cognitive processes as an inherent component of wine evaluation behaviour. The chapter then reviews and synthesises recent research that has markedly advanced the field by application of methodology and theory from cognitive psychology. The most significant way in which advancement has occurred involves extension of the research field beyond consideration of the phenomena of sensation alone to systematic study of what is happening in the minds and brains attached to our sense organs. The chapter brings together recent research concerning processes of discrimination, perception, conceptualisation, memory, judgment and language relevant to sensory evaluation of wine conducted by key researchers in the field (e.g., Solomon, 1988; Morrot, Brochet, & Dubourdieu, 2001; Hughson & Boakes, 2002; Parr, Heatherbell, & White, 2002; Ballester, Dacremont, Le Fur, & Etievant, 2005). A particular focus is the concept of wine expertise, addressed by comparing behaviour of wine professionals with behaviour of less-experienced wine consumers, to identify and describe cognitive processes implicated in development of wine expertise. Theoretical and applied implications of recent research findings relevant to wine evaluative behaviour are discussed, along with future research directions.

Chapter 7 - Few studies have examined whether performance feedback on a given task can have implications for motivational processes on an altogether distinct task. The present study proposes and tests a model for motivational spillover in a goal-setting context. Participants (N = 222) were provided with bogus goal-performance discrepancy (GPD) feedback on a creativity-brainstorming task (CBT) and were subsequently asked to set a performance goal for an unrelated stock-predicting task (SPT). Results indicated that individuals receiving negative GPD feedback on the CBTs experienced decreased levels of self-efficacy and set lower goals for themselves for the SPT. This effect was mediated by positive and negative affect. These findings provide initial evidence for the occurrence of motivational spillover and its underlying mechanisms.

Chapter 8 - To better understand what accounts for different responses among individuals in a learning endeavor, the authors investigated general approach-goal orientations as predictors. In particular, they focused on approach-goal orientations, which all entail "approach" motivation or a desire to attain some measure of success. In doing so, the authors adopted a multiple goal orientation perspective, which proposes that high levels of different goal orientations may be adaptive and that multiple pathways from goal orientations to positive outcomes may exist. Although general learning and performance orientations have been researched together in a number of other studies, the authors added achievement orientation because of its likely relevance for engendering performance-enhancing motivational states. They also designated interest and effort as mechanisms through which the three approach-goal orientations would facilitate improved performance in a learning endeavor. They obtained data from first-year students in a freshman-level course at a major university, including SAT scores as a measure of cognitive ability. Participants completed the measures of the approach-goal orientations two weeks after the beginning of the semester. Initial performance was measured four weeks into the semester, and one day later respondents received objective feedback on their first-exam performance. Interest and effort were measured six weeks into the semester. Finally, subsequent performance was measured eight weeks into the semester. The authors obtained complete data from 151 out of 171 potential respondents, for a response rate of 84%. The results of structural equations analyses generally supported their proposed model, in which initial performance was taken into account as a predictor of subsequent performance. Cognitive ability ($\beta = .26$) and achievement orientation ($\beta = .26$) contributed to greater initial performance. Initial performance ($\beta = .24$), achievement orientation ($\beta = .27$), and learning orientation ($\beta = .17$) contributed to greater interest. Then, interest ($\beta = .66$), together with achievement ($\beta = .31$) and performance orientations ($\beta = .19$), was associated with greater effort. Finally, effort was the ultimate mechanism through which all three approach-goal orientations, and interest, were associated with improved performance. Overall, the results support a multiple goal orientation perspective. Yet, among the four exogenous factors, cognitive ability and achievement orientation played the greatest roles in facilitating initial performance and improved performance.

Chapter 9 - A social approach to the study of fires is very necessary in the design and implementation of natural environment and forest programs and policies. Forest fires, and the risk they generate to the ecosystem and to human beings, are not only technical problems that can be solved solely by technical experts and the evaluation they make; they also involve environmental understanding, active commitment of citizens and their participation in land management.

The dramatic situation that was the result of the Galician forest fires, in the summer of 2006, revealed the weakness of this region's ecosystem when exposed to one of the most serious risks affecting this community. Also, it made visible the fact that a complex problem – one that has many causes, among which the most important are perceived to be the intentional and irresponsible actions of people - requires multidimensional strategies.

This chapter analyses the subjective perception that the citizens have of the forests fires, and tries to contribute to the development and improvement of efficient public policies in the fight against fires. The necessity to integrate technical and objective criteria, along with the more subjective ones, in the analysis of fires is discussed; also, the reader is provided with an analysis of the social representations of fires, which contain key information for evaluations related to the decision-making process.

Chapter 10 - We are currently witnessing a growing concern regarding lifestyle and a raised awareness in relation to preserving the threatened natural environment. Through its modes of production and its particular relationship with nature, agriculture is directly affected by these concerns. Farming is not the only source of some environmental matters, but because of this particular relationship with natural environment, the media has held it largely responsible, and therefore, so has society. Out of concern for the environnement as well as to restore public confidence in agricutlure or agricultural practices, pro-environmental approaches have appeared and/or developed (organic farming, integrated farming, territorial farming contracts, watershed operations....). A feature that these voluntary actions in favour of the environment have in common is that they are officially referenced, checked and socially recognized. However, despite the rapid development and improvement of these approaches, changes in farming practices seem difficult to bring about and remain a minority.

In that sense, a psychosociological and environmental study was conducted to understand the sociocognitive processes which would allow to distinguish farmers committed in pro-environmental action from farmers not committed in this kind of action. To understand these processes, the authors were attempting to identify how farmers (committed or not committed in pro-environmental approaches) perceived their environment and their profession. These phenomena were analyzing through the study of the social representations which are defined as modalities of knowledges constructed and shared by a social group. This theoretical approach was privileged especially because of the close relationship between social representations and practices.

In this chapter, the authors would like to show the interest of a collective approach in the explanation of pro-environmental behaviours which takes into account indivduals as "social subjects" (in contrast to an individual approach based on emotions, responsability, individual values...). Thus, after a short presentation of the agriculture-environment relationship to introduce the context of the study, they will present the theoretical approach of social representations and its interest to answer their objective. Finally, they will stress on the main results which highlight that the representation of the environment remains basically identical between farmers, and it is closely bounded to the definition of the profession. In fact, the commitment in pro-environmental action appears to be more reasoned by the need to restore a positve social image of the profession than by the need to protect a threatened natural environment. And in turn, this is this commitment which seems to trigger a more important interest in the environment.

Chapter 11 - For adults, faces encoded using trait judgments (e.g., friendliness of the face) are more likely to be accurately recognized than faces encoded using featural judgments (e.g., the distance between one's eyes). Trait judgments can be likened to holistic encoding whereas, feature judgments can be likened to featural encoding. Thus, adults are likely to use holistic encoding for faces. The research on children's facial processing abilities remains equivocal. It has been argued that children are unable or unlikely to process faces holistically. The current study found that both children (6- to 9-years-old) and adults demonstrated higher identification accuracy rates using eyewitness methodology when making either a single trait judgment or no imposed judgements, compared to single featural judgments. Moreover, making two feature judgments produced accuracy rates at a level comparable to single trait judgments and no imposed judgments for children and adults. These data suggest that children are capable of holistic processing and may be using such a strategy when encoding a face "naturally", similar to adults.

Research has suggested that facial recognition and identification is affected by an individual's ability to encode facial information as well as his/her ability to retrieve that information from memory (Baddeley & Woodhead, 1982; Wells, 1993; Wells & Hryciw, 1984). Encoding refers to "the dual process of forming a representation of a new face and storing that representation in memory" (Carey, Diamond, & Woods, 1980, p. 257). Retrieval or recognition abilities refer to "matching a representation of a new instance with a representation already stored in memory" (Carey et al., 1980, p. 257).

Chapter 12 - The present longitudinal study focuses on interactions between self-awareness, imitation, and language development in young children with autism. 30 children aged 5 years on average participated. The sample was divided into two groups according of a scale-evaluation regarding the variable 'recognition of being imitated' (Group 1: observant children; Group 2: indifferent children). An evaluation of interactions between competences of imitation and of language was then carried out for the two groups. The results show that the children of the two groups develop almost identically with respect to imitation but with important differences regarding language. The results are discussed with a view to typical psychological development.

In: Applied Psychology Research Trends
Editor: Karl H. Kiefer, pp.1-34

ISBN 978-1-60456-372-6
© 2008 Nova Science Publishers, Inc.

*Chapter 1*

# DO ALCOHOL AND TOBACCO ADVERTISEMENTS HAVE AN IMPACT ON CONSUMPTION? CONTRIBUTION OF THE THEORY OF SELECTIVE EXPOSURE

## *Stéphane Perrissol*[1] *and Alain Somat*[2]

[1] CLLE-LTC - University of Toulouse Le Mirail, France
[2] LAUREPS - CRPCC - University of Rennes 2, France

## ABSTRACT

In Europe, as in the United States, laws ruling alcohol or tobacco advertising have been intensified. The purpose of this chapter is to take an inventory of this evolution and then to analyse the impact of these adverts. In that sense, three methods of analyses are presented in order to appreciate their advantages and limits. Then, the main results will be detailed. This assessment shows that most of the studies intend to demonstrate that advertising has an impact on the consumption of individuals. Nevertheless, only some authors questioned the opposite link between advertising and consumption. In other words, it may be conceivable that exposure to alcohol or tobacco adverts has been caused by people's attitude toward these products. This argument corresponds to the theory of selective exposure (Festinger, 1957). Following this theory, people tend to expose themselves to information which can confirm their positions and avoid the information that could challenge their attitude. In other words, alcohol and tobacco consumers will expose themselves to adverts for these products more than the abstinent ones. In addition, we will see that this argument is developed by advertisers. According to them, advertising orientates consumers towards a particular brand but it has no effect on non-consumers who pay little attention to this information. In the same way, we will question the impact of prevention campaigns on the people who are the targets. Indeed, the aim is to show that people who are weak consumers of alcohol, or who don't smoke, are, as evidenced by selective exposure theory, more inclined to expose themselves to

---

[1] Corresponding Author: Email: stephane.perrissol@univ-tlse2.fr
[2] Corresponding Author: Email: alain.somat@uhb.fr

prevention campaigns to these products. Thus, prevention campaigns maintain the healthy behaviours of non-smokers or occasional drinkers but do not modify the attitudes of heavy drinkers or smokers. Several lines of research linked to modulating factors of selective exposure will be suggested with the idea of improving exposure of the heavy drinkers, or smokers, to prevention campaigns.

# 1 THE LEGISLATIVE SITUATION: SOME EXAMPLES

A study[3] conducted by the Centre of Information on Alcoholic Drinks (1996) revealed that out of 101 countries considered, 71 had proposed legislation which restricted advertising for alcoholic drinks and 7 others had completely banned such advertising. Only 23 countries had not imposed any control over advertising. With regard to tobacco, legislation most often takes the form of a total ban. For instance, as early as 1965, advertisements in favor of tobacco were banned in England (Cartwright, 2005). In the United States they have been banned on television and radio since 1971 (Loken & Howard-Pitney, 1988; Klitzner, Gruenewald, Bamberger, 1991), but alcohol advertisements are, like in Canada, only subject to restrictions (Ogborne & Smart, 1980). In Europe several countries are finding themselves in situations close to that of the United States. For example, in Italy, advertisements for tobacco are banned on the radio and in magazines as well as on television or placards. Alcohol advertising is strongly regulated and does not legally have the right to portray its product as having performance or health virtues. Furthermore alcohol promotion is subject to restrictions in order to primarily protect minors (e.g. under-18s). For example, advertisements cannot be shown during television programs, movies or in magazines that are aimed at minors. What is more, posting in public places where youngsters meet is prohibited, in addition to broadcasting on television and radio between 4pm and 7pm. Similarly in Belgium any advertisements favoring tobacco are strictly forbidden. Despite this, the ban resulted in the cancellation of the Spa Francorchamps Formula 1 Grand Prix in 2003 and subsequently led to a modification of the law the following year. Advertisers essentially benefit from an exemption for the Grand Prix. Now the problem is no longer an issue since, in November 2002, the European Union voted for an advertising ban on tobacco. According to specialists on motorsport (otherwise known as motor racing) one of the reasons which led to the creation of the grand prix in China is the fact that tobacco advertising is authorized there. In France, the Evin Law (1991) governs advertisements with regards to alcohol or tobacco. Whilst cigarette promotion is banned it is quite a different story for alcohol advertising since it is allowed on the radio as long as certain restrictions are respected (e.g. no broadcasting in programs for younger audiences, obligation to include the warning "*alcohol abuse is harmful to your health, drink in moderation*" etc.). Only cinema and television have been forbidden to broadcast such advertising. If alcohol benefits from favorable treatment compared to tobacco it is only because it was recognized by members of Parliament, on the one hand, that moderate consumption, especially of wine, has positive effects and, on the other hand, that it is an element that belongs to French culture. However since the adoption of the Evin Law in 1991 the measure was toned down. Thus, the *Charasse amendments* on tobacco allow the broadcast of sports events on television that are happening in foreign countries where tobacco

---

[3] In International Center for Alcohol Policies (2001)

advertising is authorized. These amendments are aimed particularly at competitions organized by the Formula 1 subdivision of the Fédération Internationale de l'Automobile (FIA) for which the tobacco industries contribute very largely (specifically with regards to the promotion and organization). The modification of article L17/1 has led to a return to a complete authorization of posting of alcohol advertisements. Article L18, however, sets out some rules for these advertisements to adhere to: the message must be neutral and informative. The interpretation of this article is therefore left to the legislators' judgment. Finally, since May 2004 an amendment that aimed to moderate this article was discussed and finally adopted on October 13th 2004. This amendment was influenced by the intense pressure put on by the professional wine makers, referred to as the "wine lobby" who, at the time, were encountering some economic difficulties resulting from a decrease in sales. In any case if we take the example of the United States or France, there are numerous advertisements in favor of alcohol. In fact, the amount of advertising expenses in favor of alcohol does not seem to have been affected by the Evin Law. Indeed, in France these expenses amounted to 1.0804 billion francs in 1996 compared to 1.0874 billion in 1991. In the United States, alcohol advertising expenses represents 2.3 billion dollars (Saffer, 1995) of which 1.5 billion is only for television (Slater, Beauvais, Rouner, Van Leuven, Murphy, Domenech-Rodriguez, 1996). Moreover, these advertisements are extremely common in sports programs. In 443.7 hours of sports programs watched, researchers counted 685 advertisements for alcohol which amounted to 77% of the total number of advertisements indexed (Madden & Grube, 1994). Similarly Atkin, Hocking and Block (1984) estimated that one individual was exposed to approximately 2000 alcohol adverts per year. It is evident that advertisements only show the pleasant and relaxing aspects of alcohol and completely gloss over the negative effects (Gerbner, 1995).

# 2 THE CURRENT SITUATION IN COUNTRIES WHERE RESTRICTIONS EXIST

## 2.1. Bypassing the Laws

With the legislative framework being set, the alcohol and tobacco profession had to adapt to all the measures put in place. Thus the banning of tobacco advertisements coincided with the arrival of catalogues that would make it possible to obtain products in exchange for points collected on each cigarette pack. Similarly, there were competitions for holidays or the promotion of new products that would bear the name of the brand but had different purposes. All of these were launched on the European market. This was notably the case with *Marlboro* who set up a chain of agencies that would bear the name of Marlboro Country. The advertisers also became renowned for having advertised for *Marlboro* matches or, recycled the same elements previously used for past cigarette advertising campaigns (i.e. the representation of the lonely cowboy in arid country) to sell other products such as, in Italy, the sale of clothes. In Formula I, *Marlboro* signed a new advertising partnership with the Ferrari team until 2011 and this while many countries had banned advertising. The logo for the brand therefore only appears for the Grand-Prix in countries where tobacco advertising is not banned. It is worth remembering, however, that the World Motor Sport Council was committed, like the World Health Organization, to banning tobacco advertising and sponsorship in motor sports, worldwide, from 2006. Likewise, *Royale* cigarettes had, for a long time, sponsored boat races, the most famous being Quebec – St. Malo. The *Camel* brand became renowned with advertisements for the *Camel trophy*, a rally under extreme conditions, and by selling products with the effigy of the famous camel which was associated with the brand (e.g. on matchboxes, watches etc.). Similarly, in France, advertising bags used by tobacconists were banned and so the advertisers replaced them with transparent bags which would allow all cigarette packs being bought to be seen without it being considered as advertising. In the same endeavor, relying on the example of Marlboro, Slater, Chaloupka and Wakefield (2001) demonstrated that, in the United States, cigarette retail outlets in states that had comprehensive tobacco control programs offered more advertising or gifts with purchases than in other states. In Canada "cigarette-girls", models dressed in the brand's color, offered packs of cigarettes to customers whilst prompting them to smoke during special parties organized by bars.

## 2.2. OMNIPRESENCE OF THE ENCOURAGEMENT TO CONSUME

James Bond (License to Kill, Moonraker), Superman II, Pulp Fiction, Casino, Independence Day etc., are all films that have integrated indirect advertising for tobacco (Basil, 1997; Pechman & Shih, 1999). This method of "product placement" is becoming more and more common even despite fines punishing its practice. For example, in England a fine of £20,000 was enforced against the film Superman II (Basil, 1997). According to Basil (1997), some actors like Sean Connery, Sylvester Stallone, Paul Newman or Clint Eastwood, would smoke some brands of cigarettes rather than others in exchange for a donation in kind from the relevant tobacco company. This practice is not restricted to the tobacco industry and it can be found for many other consumer products (video equipment, cars etc.). Besides this type advertising for targeted brands, alcohol is also very present in daily TV programs, as noted by Gerbner (1995) and in the studies of Dillin (1975) and Signorielli (1987; 1993)[4]. In the United States, for example, Dillin (1975) estimated that 80% of primetime shows were referring to alcohol outside of advertising. For Signorielli (1993) the estimation is still 70% in the 1980s. This same researcher estimated that more than a third of television characters consumed alcohol. Only 2% of these characters were suffering from any negative affects. The characters consuming alcohol or smoking are even portrayed, like Simon Templar (from *The Saint*) or Christian Troy (from *Nip Tuck*), as being attractive and successful and, as such, contribute to social learning, as defined by Bandura (1977), of these two products. *Lucky Luke* is a French-Belgian comic book hero who was also promoting a positive image of the smoker. For example, in one of his adventures, the cowboy participated in a rodeo which he won brilliantly. One of the spectators, following his success, shouted "that's extraordinary for someone who smokes so much" (from *Lucky Luke Western Circus*). It is worth pointing out, however, that there were some attempts from producers and writers to limit this sort of situation in programs, or works generally targeted at young audiences. So *Lucky Luke*, against the opinion of Morris, his creator, has replaced his cigarette with a twig of wheat. Comic

---

[4] In Gerbner, 1995

superheroes never consume tobacco or drink alcohol. Similarly in France when Formula 1 racing cars drive close to the spectator stand, the Marlboro logos on Ferraris are blurred. Nevertheless TV producers neglect to do the same by not obscuring or hiding logos on the drivers' overalls and helmets when they go up onto the podiums. Whilst advertising restrictions are increasing, the debate between the legislators and producers of alcohol and tobacco concerning the impact of advertising persists. According to Aitken, Eadie, Leathar, McNeill and Scott (1988), we can have a hypothesis that alcohol advertisements would have 6 effects:

- Encourage non drinkers to drink,
- Discourage drinkers to abandon,
- Encourage drinkers to increase their consumption,
- Discourage drinkers to diminish their consumption,
- Encourage drinkers to maintain or change their drink preference,
- Encourage drinkers to maintain or change their preference for specific brands.

For the industry, only the last two affirmations are true. As for the legislators, they are focusing on the first four. By modifying the law concerning advertisements for these products, the legislators are considering that advertising has a positive impact on consumption. However the literature is far from unanimous on this subject.

# 3 STUDIES THAT LOOK AT THE LINK BETWEEN ADVERTISING AND CONSUMPTION

The studies that look at the link between advertising and consumption are extremely numerous and diverse especially in the literature specializing in marketing, ranging from the effect of warning messages (Cvetkovitch & Earle, 1995), advert size to the effect of content on consumption. Particular attention is also paid to the effect of adverts on the underage in terms of attitude, expectations and behavioral intentions. Nevertheless, because of publicity bans in favor of tobacco in several countries and especially in the United States, or the tough restrictions depending on the medium, studies dealing with the impact of tobacco advertising on consumption are relatively less numerous than those focusing on alcohol. This explains the obvious imbalance in the following sections. Studies in this domain can be grouped into three categories: econometric studies, field surveys and experimental studies.

## 3.1. Econometric Studies

### 3.1.1 Presentation and Results

Econometric studies rely on the principle that consumption is linked to a large number of factors that could be economic (price, revenue etc.), demographic or social in nature (like information available on the products such as advertisements and prevention campaigns etc.). In other words, for Saffer (1995), one can explain individual consumption via the classic multiple regression model in which consumption would be predicted by a set of variables and their respective weights as well as a part of unexplained variance. For advertising, one would consider the global effects of the advertisements in favor of the product and not the marginal effect of an advertisement. This model attempts also to consider the non-linear relationship between advertising and consumption and the fact that the quantity of advertisements corresponds to a fixed rate depending on consumption. This does not prevent the consideration that the latter could have a positive effect on consumption. This effect could be cumulative with previous advertising which is accepted, in such a model, to be controlled for statistically. Finally it is also necessary to know the number of advertisements to which the group studied was probably exposed. In most of this research authors are crossing annual advertising expenses with consumption (Simon, 1969[5]; Grabowski, 1976; McGuiness, 1980; Duffy, 1987; Selvanathan, 1989 etc.)[6]. Work by Grabowski (1976), Duffy (1991), Wilcox (1987) and Bourgeois and Barnes (1979)[7] fail to show the existence of an effect of advertising on consumption. In contrast, work by McGuiness (1980; 1983) and Duffy, (1981; 1987) tends to demonstrate the existence of such a link. These results depend on the number of variables taken into account and the method of calculation used. In any case, econometric studies reveal that alcohol advertisements have only a limited effect on consumption contrary to the cost of drink sales. Moreover, most of the authors are in agreement in saying that the increase of consumption would have a tendency to boost the number of advertisements and not the reverse. The econometric method is employed to establish the impact of measures put into place to restrict advertising on consumption (Smart & Cutler[8], 1976; Ogborne & Smart, 1980). Laugesen and Meads (1991) have, for example, studied the impact of warnings placed on cigarette packs on the weekly development of tobacco consumption. Ogborne and Smart (1980) have been interested in the impact of restrictions of advertising in favor of alcohol established in 1974. Specifically they have studied the impact on beer consumption in Manitoba compared to the controlled province of Alberta which was not subjected to such a law. For this the authors calculated, for each province, the quantity of alcohol consumed annually compared to each province's population (over 15 years old) between 1970 and 1978. In this study no link could be found concerning advertising and alcohol consumption (Ogborne & Smart, 1980).

### 3.1.2 Concerns and Limitations of the Econometric Method

In the end, econometric studies have not clearly demonstrated that advertising in favor of alcohol has an influence on global consumption since, even in the best cases, only small effects could be highlighted. Smart (1988) remarked that while advertising expenses increased by 400%, the global consumption of alcohol significantly decreased. The advantages of this method is that it considers, not the direct effects of advertising on consumption in the short term, but rather the global effect of advertising on consumption in the long term. Moreover the indicators used constitute measures that are relatively objective. However, the results obtained depend clearly on the methods used and on the variables that are revealed in the multiple regression. This limitation is even more important if you consider that certain elements are not taken into account in different studies. Thus, econometric studies

---

[5] Cited in Smart (1988)

[6] Cited in Saffer (1995) - as for Grabowski, (1976); McGuiness, (1980); Duffy, (1987); Selvanathan, (1989)

[7] All studies cited in Saffer (1995)

[8] Cited in Smart (1988).

are interested in advertising either in favor of alcohol or tobacco or in prevention campaigns. Yet it would seem that the effect of one is not controlled when the effect of the other is studied. So how is it possible to come to a conclusion based on the absence of the effect of a prevention campaign on alcohol consumption if, during the same time, the number of advertisements in favor of alcohol increases? Moreover, econometric studies only study the effect of advertising on the global population. Therefore, it is postulated that the effect will be the same in every layer of population despite the fact that there are inter-individual differences (if only, for example, at the level of exposure to advertising). Children and older people watch more television than an average adult and that could result in higher exposure to advertising in favor of alcohol (Smart, 1988). Similarly this method does not focus on any specific groups (men, women, youngsters, minority etc.) since it is based on aggregated measures on the population as a whole. It, therefore, does not incorporate the fact that some advertising only affects a certain category of people. Finally this method tends to consider only the amount of alcohol consumption. Therefore this prevents the study of the effect of advertising on attitudes or on behavioral intentions of youngsters who have not started to drink. Yet this effect is real. Indeed, 10 year olds are capable of naming more brands of beer than presidents' names (Gerbner, 1995). Brown (1995) also remarked that a third of 3 year olds were able to associate the old Joe Camel (used in the brand campaigns in the form of a drawing) and a pack of cigarettes.

## 3.2 Field Studies

### 3.2.1 Presentation and Results

The survey method is a technique that is more used than the econometric method to verify the plausibility of causal relationships between advertising and consuming behavior. This method consists in verifying the existence of a link between real exposure of the subject to alcohol or tobacco advertising and their level of consumption of the products in question. In other words, these correlation studies try to verify that people who are, for example, most exposed to advertising in favor of alcohol are also those who consume the most alcohol.

It appears that, in this field of study, it is necessary to develop a pattern of indicators likely to provide the best account of the real levels of exposure that subjects have to advertisements during a given period. Two types of indicators are generally used. The first consists of a global statistical evaluation of the number of advertisements which the individual could be exposed to (e.g. Strickland[9], 1983; Atkin, Hocking & Block, 1984; etc., for alcohol, and Aitken, Eadie, Leathar, McNeill & Scott, 1988 for tobacco). Thus Strickland (1983) asked his subjects to report the frequency with which they had watched different programs and for which the researcher knew the average number of alcohol advertisements. This afforded the possibility of estimating the number of televised advertisements to which the individual was exposed. The second indicator is given by asking subjects to remember the past frequency of exposure to advertisements. Furthermore, such a protocol also requires the working out of consumption measures or, for the youngest subjects, the intention to consume. For the latter, an interviewing approach (Aitken, Eadie, Hastings & Haywood, 1991; Aitken & al., 1988) is sometimes preferred to the questionnaire method. Survey studies have also

---

[9] Cited in Adlaf and Kohn (1989).

shown the weak impact of advertising on consumption. So, for example, Strickland (1983) observed a correlation of only 0.12 between the two elements (advertising and consumption). The size of the sample probably explains the fact that the correlation nevertheless had an acceptable threshold of significance. Adlaf and Kohn (1989) used a structural approach on this data and, therefore, obtained a slightly higher correlation of 0.18. The studies of Atkin and Block[10] (1981) ended up with a correlation of 0.28 that was a little bit more substantial especially concerning beer consumption. Similarly, among people who had not started drinking, those who were the most exposed to advertisements had a greater intention to consume alcohol than people who were less exposed. This result is also found in the studies of Kelly and Edwards (1998) and of Grube (1993[11] ; 1994[12]). In these latter studies, aside from a greater intention to consume, those who were the most exposed to advertising knew the brand better and had more positive beliefs regarding the effects of alcohol.

Moreover, Atkin and Block (1981) have also shown that the subjective impact of advertisements exists even if it remains relatively weak. Thus, only 29% of subjects declared that advertising had motivated their alcohol purchase twice or more in the year. Finally, several researchers were interested in the evaluation of these advertisements according to the level of consumption of the subject. Aitken and Eadie (1990) thus showed that smokers appreciated more the advertisements than non-smokers when the effect of certain variables (i.e. gender, age, socioeconomic status and peers attitudes etc.) was controlled for. Similarly Wyllie, Zhang, and Casswell (1998a; 1998b) obtained similar results with alcohol advertising.

### 3.2.2 Concerns and Limitations of the Survey Method

The survey method overcomes the aforementioned problem of people who have not started drinking or smoking. Likewise, as for the econometric method, this method tries to verify the effects of alcohol in the long term. Moreover it relies on real behavior of those who have already consumed (measure of past consumption) and allows for an estimation of differences within specific groups (Atkin, 1995). Moreover resorting to large samples ensures that no factor other than those taken into account modifies the results. Once again the difficulty of obtaining consistent effects from one study to the next was observed. This inconsistency can, in part, be explained by the measures that are used. Thus, the exposure measure consists mostly of evaluating the number of advertisements seen. This is achieved by using a recall task (either by considering the television programs or the number of hours of exposition to television or the magazines usually read etc.). The recall task is problematic because of forgetfulness and selective recall. This is also true for the declaration of alcohol consumption which could suffer from desirability biases. Concerning this latter problem, Atkin, Hocking and Block (1984) objected, however, that consumption scores were in line with the national averages and that there was no reason to think that the strong and the weak consumers differed with regards to the accuracy of their answers. Concerning the estimates of the average number of advertisements to which an individual was exposed, it is problematic to consider that all individuals who were exposed to a particular program including an alcohol advertisement processed the advertisement in the same way. Studies show, on the one hand,

[10] Cited in Atkin (1995), as for Brown.
[11] Cited in Kelly and Edwards (1998).
[12] Cited in Wyllie et al. (1998a).

that a certain number of people leave the room at the time of televised advertisements and, on the other hand, that all individuals do not pay the same amount of attention to advertising. For example, Stewart and Rice (1995) note that children who are aged between 6 and 10 are incapable of differentiating advertisements from a television show and, therefore, are more attentive to television advertising than adults. In the end, surveys that have been carried out do not clearly establish an existing link between alcohol consumption and advertising since the results are inconsistent and the behavioral measures, as well as the exposure cues to advertising, are questionable.

## 3.3 Experimental Studies

### 3.3.1 Presentation and Results

Experimental studies constitute the method most developed in this domain. They are looking to account for the possible impact of advertising in the immediate future. More specifically, this impact is studied in a controlled situation, therefore allowing for the study of the direct effect of an advertisement on consumption in the short term (Atkin, 1995). The dependent variables used in these protocols are generally consumption, the intention of consuming, the appreciation of advertising, the attention that is given to advertisements, recall, etc. Nevertheless, other studies on advertising in favor of tobacco, like that conducted by Fischer, Richards, Berman, and Krugman (1989), have used more modern measures. In this particular study the authors used, besides a recall measure, a measure of eye-movement in order to identify the elements of the advertising on which subjects oriented their attention. The independent variables were the exposure to advertising and the length and frequency of exposure (McCarty & Ewing[13], 1983; Kohn & Smart, 1984; Sobell, Sobell, Riley, Klajner, Leo, Pavan & Cancilla[14], 1986), the manipulation of messages and the type of advertising proposed: the use of celebrities (Atkin & Block, 1981) or of sexual stimuli (Kilbourne, Painton & Ridley, 1985) etc.

Whilst many experimental works used protocols that were quite similar in order to verify the link between advertising and consumption, results that are coming out are quite less homogeneous. Thus, the experiments by Brown (1978) and Kohn and Smart[15] (1987) concluded that advertisements, at least temporarily, boost the consumption of alcohol and this even more so when a celebrity is present in the advertisement (Atkin et al, 1981). Elsewhere, men are more inclined to buy alcohol when the advertising includes a naked woman. Similarly, tobacco advertising which includes top models is judged as being more attractive and more persuasive (Loken & Howard Pitney, 1988). The research conducted by Kohn, Smart and Ogborne[16] (1984), Moschis and Moore (1982), or Sobell, Sobell, Riley, Klajner, Leo, Pavan and Cancilla (1986), does not show a causal relationship between advertising and consumption. The duration of exposure to advertising also does not seem to influence consumption (McCarty et al., 1983). Recall measures, however, are correlated with consumption levels (Willye et al., 1998b). Nevertheless, the effect of recall and the

---

[13] Cited in Atkin (1995).

[14] Cited in Smart (1988) as for Duffy (1981).

[15] Cited in Smart (1988)

[16] Cited in Smart (1988).

appreciation of advertising on consumption was never clearly established (Aitken et al., 1988). Indeed, to our knowledge only Kelly and Edwards (1998) for alcohol, and Aitken et al., (1991) for tobacco, have shown that appreciation of advertising was different among the young who expressed an intention of consuming compared to those who did not have the same craving.

### 3.3.2 Concerns and Limitations of the Experimental Method

Experimental studies do not present the difficulties inherent to other methods in estimating the number of advertisements and alcohol consumption. Contrary to the econometrics and survey methods, the experimental methods are more interested in the effect of advertising in the short term. In making this choice, researchers, therefore, can control the situation and particularly the exposure of subjects to advertisements. For this reason the results obtained are directly attributable to the manipulated variable. The main limitations of this type of study are that they rely on forced exposure to advertising and that, contrary to the other two methods, the samples are rarely representative of the population, making the results very difficult to generalize. Moreover, the measures rely on situations of consumption which are not ecologically valid and raise the likelihood that the subject will not be blind to the theme of the experiment in most experiments. Finally, to consider the impact of an advertisement, or series of particular advertisements, probably leads to an underestimation of the real effect of these advertisements, especially in the long term.

## 3.4 Conclusion on the Link between Advertising and Consumption

Despite the diversity of studies and the methods employed, the impact of advertising on the consumption of alcohol or tobacco could not be clearly established. In fact, as Orlandi, Lieberman and Schinke (1988) pointed out, the studies developed in the domain are producing contradictory results. At best, the impact of advertisements is weak. Thus a decrease of 50% of the quantity of advertisements would only reduce alcohol sales by 5% (Smart, 1988). The inconsistency of the results leads one to question the existence of a direct causal relationship between advertising and consumption and especially as the direction of this causal relationship is, perhaps, inversed. For Stewart and Rice (1995), "individuals tend to give more attention to advertising that is relevant to products and brands that they are using and tend to ignore most of the advertising to which they are exposed" (p. 211). Thus, only a selection of advertisements would affect subjects as a function of their consumption habits. According to the authors, there are four consumer profiles which exist as a function of the different processes they would apply to the same advertisements. Thus, for those who don't use the products, advertising constitutes for them "a waste of money" (p.218). However, loyal users, convinced that their brand is the best, will expose themselves to advertising concerning it thereby upholding this loyalty. Those who change brand, which could be as a result of a number of different criterion (e.g. price, availability etc.), are potentially influenced by a wide number of factors among which is advertising. Finally, among the emerging users, mainly represented by youngsters, advertising is going to have an effect at the moment where they become aware of the product's existence. This inverse causal relationship corresponds to the principal argument of the industry's defense. Given that neither of the first two methods presented allowed for a conclusion to be drawn regarding the direction of this relationship (since they are correlation studies) the position is even more plausible. In fact, for Grabowski (1976), the results obtained in econometric studies are linked to the fact that alcohol sales determine spending for advertising campaigns. Similarly, for surveys, nobody can affirm that the results obtained are not caused by the fact that consumers of alcohol would be more exposed to advertising than others. Indeed, if all the authors are setting out a causal relationship of advertising and consumption as a hypothesis, most of them are actually discussing the inverse possibility. This is true for advertising in favor of tobacco (Aitken et al., 1990; 1991; Klitzner, Gruenewald & Bamberger, 1991) in addition to those working on advertising in favor of alcohol (Grube et al., 1994; Atkin et al., 1984; Atkin, 1995; Saffer, 1995; Grube, 1995; Mazis, 1995; Martin, 1995). Thus, for example, alcohol consumers would be more inclined than non consumers to expose themselves to advertising in favor of alcohol for as long as it constitutes more useful information for the consumers than for the non consumers. In other words, advertising would reinforce consumption behavior, rather than have an initiating effect. Both econometrics and survey methods which are interested in the global effects of advertising, hypothesize such an inverse causal relationship. Thus, in econometric studies an increase in alcohol sales leads generally to an increase in advertising expenses. Likewise, survey methods rely on the result of correlations which means it is impossible to distinguish, with any degree of certainty, the effect from the cause. This is a position supported by the industry because in such a case, and in accordance with the last two suggestions of Aitken (1988), advertising would maintain the level of consumption of drinkers or smokers, even disseminating information on the different brands of product to the consumers. Furthermore, this alternative explanation, within which alcohol consumption predicts exposure to advertising, is echoed in the theory of selective exposure.

# 4 SELECTIVE EXPOSURE

According to Festinger (1957), dissonance corresponds to the co-existence of incoherent cognition. It is worth saying in more detail that opinions and beliefs on someone or something, just like behaviors, can be considered as entering the area of cognitive processes. Incompatibility between the different cognitive processes is going to bring about a state of dissonance. This state will have two consequences:

- Dissonance is a state that is psychologically uncomfortable which motivates a person to reduce it and find a state of consonance again
- When dissonance is present, on top of trying to reduce it, a person will actively search to avoid situations which would be likely to increase it (page 3).

In a dissonant situation the subject is therefore motivated to find again consistency between the different cognitive processes which form his opinion on a given object. Moreover the dissonance that is caused will be stronger when the inconsistent cognitions are important for the individual. Consequently, the pressure to reduce dissonance will be high and the individual will be more inclined to avoid information that would be likely to increase dissonance. Certainly this avoidance behavior is not necessarily going to reduce dissonance if it is already there, but it will, at least, protect against a possible increase in its magnitude.

The classic experimental paradigm used consists of first measuring the attitude of individuals on a given object or in proposing a situation that leads individuals to make a decision. Then, two types of information concerned with the attitude, or the situation connected to the decision making, are proposed. These most often take the form of titles or brief text abstracts. Half of the information is inconsistent with the attitude or the decision taken whilst the other half is consistent. In some cases some neutral information is added also. The subject must then express his desire to expose himself to each of these bits of information. It is advisable to distinguish the phase preceding the decision making, or the attitude formation, from that taking place after the decision making (the phase where the attitude is formed). Before decision making, in order to make an objective evaluation and to help choose the best possible alternative, individuals expose themselves to all the information relevant to the subject. In contrast, once the decision is made the individual commits in a series of processes of dissonance reduction so that there is no regret regarding the choice made. He therefore puts into place a re-evaluation process (Jecker, 1964a; Davidson, 1964). This acts to increase the desirability of the chosen alternative and decrease that of the rejected alternative. To achieve this, not only will he voluntarily expose himself to information in the direction of the chosen alternative, but he will equally also avoid information likely to challenge his choice. This process of re-evaluating the alternatives is only necessary if an individual has made a choice between several alternatives that are all relatively attractive. The more similar the alternatives are in terms of degree of attractiveness, the more intense dissonance becomes. When conflict is considerable one is more inclined to reevaluate the chosen alternative (Frey, 1981b; Greenwald, 1969).

In summary, once the decision is made, selective exposure means an individual increases the proportion of positive elements for a chosen alternative and, for the rejected alternative, increases the proportion of negative elements and avoids an increase in positive elements. For instance, Ehrlich, Guttman, Schonbach and Mills (1957) offered three types of advertisements to recent car buyers. The first concerned the car that they had chosen to purchase. The second concerned cars that they had considered buying for a time and the third concerned cars that they had never considered buying. The authors firstly hypothesized that people would be more inclined to consult brochures that would 'sing the praises' of the vehicle they had chosen to purchase. Secondly, they also predicted a preference for brochures concerning vehicles that were not considered during the buying decision over brochures that contained previous buying alternatives. In other words, they expected that individuals would expose themselves to consonant information by looking in advertising materials that reinforce their buying choice and would avoid dissonance by not consulting advertising for vehicles that they had already rejected.

## 4.1 Selective Exposure and Advertisements

If the principle behind the theory is applied to the advertising domain, we can assume that smokers or consumers of alcohol will expose themselves more to favorable advertising for these products than people who abstain. Indeed, by exposing themselves to the advertising, consumers are reinforcing their consuming behavior. For example, an experiment conducted by Perrissol, Bordel and Somat (submitted), disguised as a survey on mobile phones, asked subjects to make clear which type of advertising they were ready to listen to, in an impromptu manner, in exchange for a reduction on their mobile phone line rental. Among these messages were advertisements for alcohol and tobacco. The more people consumed alcohol or tobacco the more they were ready to be exposed to advertising in favor of alcohol and tobacco. These results were reproduced with different experimental materials (Perrissol, 2004; Perrissol, Boscher, Cerclé & Somat, 2004). In spite of that, in some experiments conducted on selective exposure, subjects do not always avoid the dissonant information. Several explanations have been put forward to account for such inconsistencies. The explanation that is most often proffered is there are factors that are likely to mediate the relationship between attitude and exposure.

## 4.2 The Mediating Factors of Selective Exposure

### 4.2.1 The Utility, Curiosity and Novelty of the Information

The first factor likely to affect selective exposure concerns the utility of the proposed information. An individual would expose himself to inconsistent information if it would show some usefulness. Thus, in studies by Canon (1964), Freedman (1965a) and Chaffee and McLeod (1973), anticipating a public debate made dissonant information appear more useful and reduced avoidance of the information. Similarly, Festinger (1964) remarked that, in the experiment by Mills et al. (1959) and Rosen (1961), the same bias is present since consonant information is also the most useful for individuals. Others like Miller (1977) or Diab (1979) put forward this idea to explain the absence of expected results. Frey (1979) commented that individuals are more inclined to choose consonant information when it comes from credible sources and where it is useful for strengthening their own point of view. When information comes from an unreliable source, individuals will be more tempted to expose themselves to dissonant information with the aim of refuting it.

Moreover, information utility links with factors of novelty and, to a lesser degree, curiosity. Indeed in several studies (Frey & Rosch, 1984; Sears & Freedman, 1965; Sears, 1965), it appears that individuals prefer to choose information that seems new. Sears and Freedman (1965), and Sears (1965), have thus demonstrated that in an artificial judgment situation, subjects preferred to expose themselves to dissonant information if the arguments they were developing appeared to be novel. Similarly in an experiment by Freedman (1965b) all students chose to expose themselves to dissonant information concerning the evaluation of an individual. Thus the 17 experimental subjects systematically chose to expose themselves to information that challenged the positive or negative assessment of a target person. Among all the explanations proposed to account for these results, the author considered that, for some subjects, the suggested counter-evaluation was likely to provide information that was new and, therefore, more useful. What is more, this explanation was given by four of the subjects. Another reason put forward is that a new description that would cast doubt on a previous description could have raised curiosity. This preference for new or curious information gives credence to Klapper's (1960) hypothesis which considers that mass communication is more efficient when it is related to new questions rather than to familiar ones. Moreover, as noted by McGuire (1968b), complex theories give credence to this hypothesis: the "curiosity drive", the need to explore, alternative behavior, stimulus hunger, the need for variety or stimulation, the satiety of the stimulus, and reactive inhibition. These are all theories relying on the principle that the organism is oriented towards the new and unexpected and avoids what is overly familiar.

### 4.2.2 The Effect of the Decision Making

For McGuire (1961)[17], McGuire and Papageorgis (1962), the effects of selective exposure are more apparent when individuals are more familiar with the arguments on both sides. This point is supported by the idea, developed previously, of a preference for novel information. It equally emphasizes the idea of selective exposure processes intervening in the post-decision phase. The study by Ehrlich et al. (1957) illustrates this idea well. In this study, subjects were individuals who had made a decision to purchase a particular car over another. So, at the moment the experiment happened, they were in a post-decisional phase, known to be favorable to the setting up of selective exposure. Since then, this idea has been repeatedly revived (Mills, 1965a; 1965b; 1965c; Sears, 1966; Lowe & Steiner, 1968; Greenwald, 1969; Mann, Janis, & Chaplin, 1969 etc.). In these studies the experimental paradigms consist of letting subjects make a decision and then offering them different consonant and dissonant information. It would be expected that, once the decision was made, individuals would look to reinforce the thought that the chosen alternative was the better one, principally by exposing themselves to supporting information. A confrontation with dissonant information would, in all likelihood, place a person in an awkward position by increasing post-decisional regret. Indeed, according to Festinger (1957; 1964), after decision making, the process of reducing dissonance aims to increase the gap of attractivity between the chosen and rejected alternatives. This point counters that of Janis[18] (1959) who does not make the distinction between the two stages. According to him re-evaluation occurs before, as well as, after the decision. The experiment by Jecker (1964a) shows that the idea proposed by Festinger is the more plausible of the two proposed, provided that the different alternatives preceding a decision have a relatively close level of desirability. Indeed when the situation requires a choice between one element we like and another we don't, there is no dissonance arousal or any regret once the decision is made. However, when the choices are equally attractive an individual should process information objectively until he can make a decision. The quantity of sought-after information becomes more important as the gap of attractivity between the alternatives becomes smaller. This information gathering aims to ensure that adding new information will not affect individual preferences. Braden and Walster (1964) have nevertheless shown that when a choice is too difficult, individuals would anticipate a state of dissonance following the decision and could, therefore, avoid making the choice completely. If an individual makes a decision in such a context, as in the case of Jecker (1964a), re-evaluation of the alternatives would only occur afterwards. Similarly Knox and Inkster (1968) showed that gamblers were more confident after having just gambled compared to just before. There was, therefore, once the decision had been made, a process of reducing dissonance. Jecker (1964b) also demonstrated that the setting up of a process of selective exposure occurs after a decision is made and that it most likely helps increasing the difference between the retained and rejected alternative. The experiment conducted by Walster (1964) on soldiers regarding their future posting shows that, in the post-decisional phase, temporal differences can emerge. Thus, four minutes after the decision is made the subject feels regret. This regret

---

[17] cited in Sears and Freedman (1965).
[18] Cited in Festinger (1964).

diminishes after a period of 15 minutes insofar as the subject has used a process of re-evaluation. Ninety minutes after the decision this dissonance stops decreasing. Walster explained that an individual cannot manage on his own to diminish dissonance beyond a certain threshold. It is probable that if individuals had the possibility to consult information on different possible alternatives, they would preferentially expose themselves to elements that were consonant with the choice they had made.

### 4.2.3 Commitment, Consequences and the Reversibility of the Decision

At the same time that Walster's study (1964), mentioned previously, illustrates the temporal development of the post-decisional processes, it also emphasizes a second important element: the importance of the decision. The decision that soldiers have to take will have important repercussions in their life because they must choose a posting for the following two years. Similarly, in Frey (1979), individuals had to select information related to the work they were thinking of doing once their studies are complete. The consequences of these decisions are therefore a lot more important in this experiment than they might be in others, for example: winning $1.50 (Jecker, 1964b); choosing between two haircuts (Festinger & Walster, 1964); or between two men to spend the evening with (Lowe & Steiner, 1968); or even during mock juries (Sears & Freedman, 1965). Yet, the manipulation of these elements, despite being of little importance, serves to steer the individual to different levels of commitment with the task. It is expected, as in the case of Brock, Albert and Becker (1970) and Chaffee and McLeod (1973) that committed subjects are more inclined to set up processes of selective exposure. The level of commitment is often influenced by the individual's anticipation of the consequences that his or her decision will have. Even though this anticipation is quite real, it is certainly limited. According to Allen (1964) there is dissonance arousal and re-evaluation of the attractiveness of the alternatives only if the subject has made a choice that appears to be irrevocable. Indeed, if this choice is likely to change, the individual will not be in a dissonant state and will therefore not set up a process of reevaluation of the decision. Likewise Frey (1981b), Frey, Kumpf, Irle and Gniech (1984), and Frey and Rosch (1984), show that the processes of re-evaluation take place principally when the decision is irrevocable. This explains why the subjects in Lowe and Steiner (1968) did not always choose consonant information. When the decision is irreversible subjects prefer to expose themselves to consonant information. On the contrary, when the decision is reversible, they do not express a preference in favor of one or other information. Such a result should also be found with attitudes. When an individual has the possibility of changing attitudes, he will be able to face inconsistent information. A contrary case would be an individual who, for example, would be more likely to resort to selective exposure when taking a public stand.

### 4.2.4 Confidence in One's Position, the Refutability of Arguments

Aside from reversibility, the confidence that an individual has in his position seems to influence the type of information he will choose to face. Festinger (1964), based on the study by Canon (1964), suggested that the degree of confidence affects selective exposure. When an individual is not confident he chooses to avoid exposure to inconsistent information. In contrast he could confront inconsistent information providing it appears to him to be easily refutable. Thus, the refuting of arguments that are counter-attitudinal reduces dissonance without requiring outside support. The individual, therefore, will not only be able to confront dissonant information but, what is more, will not feel the need to look for reinforcement through consonant information. Similarly, Rhine (1967a) considers that avoidance of dissonant information will only be useful if the individual feels that they are incapable of refuting it and especially if, as according to Brock (1965), confronting inconsistent information, and managing to eliminate dissonance, is more gratifying for the subject than avoiding it. As well as the experiment by Canon (1964), discussed earlier, a replication carried out by Freedman (1965a) does not show an effect of subject's confidence on information selection. It is worth adding that even in Canon's experiment, whilst confident subjects faced dissonant information to a greater extent, it nevertheless remains true that all the experimental groups would have exposed themselves more to consonant information. In Freedman's (1965b) experiment on the evaluation of a student, to account for the fact that subjects chose dissonant information, he put forward this idea of confident subjects. This is besides the possibility that utility and curiosity would be at the origin of subjects' choice of exposure. He makes clear, nevertheless, that this is a purely speculative explanation (p.289). Indeed, this hypothesis only relies on post experimental statements from the subjects. This speculation is also made by Chaffee and Miyo (1983). Similarly Belhing (1971) shows that subjects express a greater interest for consonant information when their certainty of having made the right choice is weak. He is basing his conclusion, however, using statistical chance higher than the 5% generally applied. The experiments by Thayer (1969) and Schultz (1974) did not reveal an effect of subject's confidence. In the former however, Thayer (1969) was able to verify that the degree of confidence had been manipulated successfully contrary to the studies by Canon (1964) or Mills and Ross (1964).

On the other hand, the study by Lowin (1967) most probably represents a stronger argument on the effect of confidence since, in the first experiment that he conducted, subjects preferred to be exposed to strong consonant messages and weak dissonant messages rather than the inverse. The researcher, however, replicated these results only partially in the second experiment. In the first experiment subjects perhaps estimated the strong dissonant messages to be harder to refute than the weak dissonant ones. As in these aforementioned experiments, it would appear that judging an argument's refutability would be more likely to produce differences in exposure than the confidence of the subjects. Research by Feather (1962, 1963), Wellins and McGinnies (1977), and Kleinhesselink and Edwards (1975) seem to give credence to this hypothesis. Similarly when individuals are knowledgeable about the information that counters their point of view they are less tempted to avoid it. For Frey (1979), arguments that were already known are perceived as easily refutable and therefore less likely to create a strong level of dissonance in subjects and threaten their position. From this standpoint, the theory is in accordance with the theory of positive illusions (Taylor & Armor, 1996): faced with threatening information an individual is likely to set up different cognitive biases in order to put into perspective the threat that constitutes this information. Positive illusions can have two contradictory effects in terms of selective exposure. Firstly, individuals could actively seek information which allows them to put into perspective the threat that constitutes the information. On the contrary a person who is inclined to have positive illusions could also confront information inconsistent with their position while doubting, for example, the credibility of the source or the veracity of the argument. Kunda (1987) shows, for example, that when the dangers of caffeine are presented, consumers doubt more the veracity of the arguments than non-consumers. With such a defense system, one can assume that consumers of caffeine can choose to expose themselves to information on the danger of caffeine in order to later refute it.

### 4.2.5 The Magnitude of Dissonance

Whilst the idea of familiarity with arguments is going partly against that of exposure to novel arguments developed before, the idea of refutability of the argument brings us closer to the idea of dissonance magnitude. Thus Lowin (1967) considered that weak dissonant messages are those considered by subjects as easily refutable. On the contrary, messages that are strongly dissonant are considered as such given the subject's perceived difficulty in trying to refute them. It is therefore expected that messages that are perceived to be harder to refute will give rise to stronger dissonance and more efforts to avoid facing them.

It must be clarified that in some studies the rate of dissonance is manipulated by means other than the refutably of arguments. The use of other methods allowed Frey (1982) to show that, contrary to what one would infer, moderate levels of consonance and dissonance are likely to initiate a selective exposure process. In this experiment dissonance was manipulated by the number of times the subject won money in a card game. This game depended on the decision the subject made before he started to play. If the subject lost a large number of times the dissonance generated would be considered high. If the losses were small the dissonance would then be also weaker. Conversely, if the gains are small, consonance will be weak whereas if the gains are high, consonance will be stronger. It appears that individuals selectively expose themselves to information, insofar as the reinforcement produced by the information strengthens their decision. Though this only occurs in the case of weak consonance or dissonance. In contrast when a subject is in a situation with strong consonance, he will be able to expose himself without fear of inconsistent information as long as the information does not put him in an awkward situation. Finally, in a situation of strong dissonance a subject would be more inclined to admit that it is necessary to change his decision. The information dissonant with his first choice will finally become information consonant with his decision to change. It is advisable not to forget that dissonance in a situation is likely to make a subject's attitude change if the rate of dissonance is too high. Selective exposure would therefore follow logically the curvilinear rate of dissonance: while dissonance increases there is selective exposure. If this becomes too strong, however, to the point of not reducing, an individual would change attitude or decision and will look for information that is more appropriate for his new belief system. In other words, as Cohen, Brehm and Latané (1959) have demonstrated, the exposure of subjects is dependent on the change in attitude that is likely to occur when dissonance becomes too strong for the subject. The information that was consonant before now becomes dissonant and vice versa.

### 4.2.6 The Perception of Information

Postman et al. (1948) thought that selective perception would allow individuals to adapt to their environment. For McGinnies (1949), an individual would set up perceptual filters that would protect them, as much as possible, from becoming aware of information which has, for him, an unpleasant emotional significance. Everything happens as if the individual, without being aware of it, avoids unpleasant or dangerous stimuli with the aim of being protected from them or he gives them meaning in accordance with his belief system. Hastorf and Cantril (1954) took a football match as an object of study with Princeton and Dartmouth as opposing teams. This match was actually won by Dartmouth but there was a controversy about the way it unfolded. In fact the star player from Princeton (it was his last match) was injured during a collision with opposing players. Thus the authors had the idea to show the match to supporters from each team and ask them, not only to record all the infractions committed by both teams, but also to evaluate if the infraction committed was flagrant or not. The results were in line with a selective defense since the supporters of the losing team (Princeton) recorded twice as many faults on the part of Dartmouth compared to Dartmouth supporters. Moreover the supporters from Princeton perceived these faults to be flagrant whereas their counterparts perceived them as conventional. In other words, in attributing the injury of their star, Kazmaier, and the defeat, to the irregularity of the defense practiced by the opposing team, Princeton supporters avoided the thought that Dartmouth players were stronger. This result was replicated by Boon and Davies (1996) and it is also often found in sport since, on the whole, supporters and managers are more inclined to accuse the referee than to blame their team. In the French football championship, a draft agreement had to be found between the body of referees and managers to the extent where the latter were criticizing more and more the work of referees during defeats. Similarly studies by Waly and Cook (1965), Vidmar and Rokeach (1974) and Bothwell and Brigham (1983) all obtained results that agree with those obtained in the football experiment described previously. The first two demonstrated selective perception processes in the domain of racial prejudice. Thus subjects in Bothwell et al. (1983) demonstrated selective perception in relation to a debate between Reagan and Carter. Indeed they judged that the candidate that they supported was the winner of the debate. In a study by Waly and Cook (1965) subjects evaluated arguments consonant with their attitude as being more plausible than counter arguments. Similarly in the Vidmar and Rokeach (1974) study, *Archie Bunker*, hero of the comedy series *All in the Family*, a racist character, was perceived differently depending on the population considered. Thus, minorities did not take the character literally and considered the series as a humorous satire whereas racists thought that he was telling the truth and appreciated him for this. If the study of Vidmar and Rokeach (1974) sheds light on an effect of selective perception it also establishes a link between this latter effect and selective exposure. Indeed by examining the nature of the television audience who were watching *All in the Family*, Klapper[19] (1971) revealed that he would not be surprised if the program audience were more implicated than others in activities fighting racial prejudice. Yet, because of the effect of selective perception, it is worth questioning whether this is plausible. Starting from the principle that the character of *Archie Bunker* is perceived differently depending on whether one is racist or not, we can suppose that the audience is a collection of as many racist as non-racist individuals. The former would take the comments of the character literally and could expose themselves to the series to the extent that it is consonant with their belief system. As for the latter, they would not take the comments literally, considering them as satire, which, as such, would also be consonant with their attitudes. In such a case, where there does not seem to be selective exposure because it is watched by racists and non-racists, the processes of selective perception makes this televised series consonant with the belief system of each of the two groups even though they are opposed. From then on the two groups, by watching the program, are both engaging in a process of selective exposure. The inference from these results is that the absence of effect in some studies on selective exposure comes from the fact that information, supposed to be dissonant for some subjects, is interpreted in a manner to

---

[19] Cited in Vidmar and Rokeach (1974).

make them consonant with the individual's belief system. In the end the subject will expose himself to information perceived as consonant, yet considered dissonant by the experimenter. This possibility is further illustrated by the research from Nadeau, Gidengil, Nevitte and Blais (1998) which compares a group of ordinary citizens to a group of people employed to conduct analysis on the coverage of political campaigns. It emerges that the untrained person tends to perceive media coverage as being favorable to the political candidate that they are supporting. This is, therefore, a real subjective interpretation of political campaign coverage by partisans. This result is supported by the fact that individuals, trained, and therefore likely to be more objective, did not have the same interpretation of the facts. In other words, the perception of coverage of the Canadian electoral campaign of 1997 was influenced by the attitudes of the subjects with regards to the political candidates. The partisans had a tendency to interpret the information in such a way that it corresponded to their attitudes and opinions regarding the candidates. Ditto and Lopez (1992) repeat Kruglanski's (1980, 1990) argument which is that a desire to achieve a particular judgment leads an individual to commit a more serious search for alternative explanations when the information is inconsistent with the desired judgment than when it is consistent. In this research Ditto et al. (*ibid.*) not only find that perception is influenced by the nature of the information but that inconsistent information leads the subject to generate more alternative explanations. To conclude, it appears, therefore, that when the stimuli are dissonant with regard to the individuals they tend to perceive them as consonant with their attitudes. This bias in perception is not without consequence to the subject's selective exposure. Indeed, the interpretation of inconsistent information in comparison to their attitude to consistent information protects the subject from the threat to experience a state of dissonance. Consequently, thanks to this selective interpretation, the individual will be able to expose himself to such apparently dissonant information, however the experimenter will conclude, wrongly, that there was no selective exposure.

### *4.2.7 Information Characteristics*

The characteristics of the information presented can influence a subject's choice as to whether they expose themselves to it or not. According to Freedman and Sears (1963; 1965a), the line of reasoning can be constructed in two different ways: one can bring to the foreground the positive side of the alternative that one is defending or the negative side of the alternative that one is rejecting. In their study, Freedman and Sears demonstrated that subjects preferentially chose information favoring their point of view rather than information that would cast doubt on the opposing position. This tendency would be more pronounced when they have limited knowledge on the subject area (Lazarsfeld et al. 1948).

### *4.2.8 The Cost of Information*

In most experimental paradigms attempting to account for selective exposure, experimenters concurrently offer sets of consonant and dissonant information to the subjects. These subjects must either say whether they want to expose themselves to this information or they must select as many pieces of information as they desire. However, in real settings, it is often costly to consult all this information in terms of time, energy and cognitive resources. The experiment carried out by Frey (1981a) demonstrates that when subjects must take into account the cost of the information (in this particular study subjects had to pay for articles) they select their information more attentively and the preference for consonant, compared to dissonant information, is more marked.

### 4.2.9 The Quantity of Information that can be Selected

Studies carried out on selective exposure rely principally on experiments carried out in the laboratory. These conditions are probably not favorable to the emergence of a process of selective exposure. Indeed, in laboratory contexts an individual has, at his disposal, all information, whether consonant or dissonant, and the possibility is there to consult as much information as he wishes. Yet, in reality, not only is all this information not accessible but, furthermore, an individual generally has limited time and cognitive resources to process the information. Therefore it is probable that these constraints will lead him to be more selective in his choice of information. Therefore, through a series of four experiments, Fischer, Jonas, Frey and Hoffmann (under revision) could demonstrate that an individual was considerably more selective when he was subjected to restrictions on the quantity of information that he could select. Finally, Jonas, Schulz-Hardt, Frey and Thelen (2001) postulated that the search for information is not, as in the experimental paradigm, simultaneous but sequential. Indeed, even if in the previously cited studies subjects were exhibiting a confirmation bias, regardless of the information presentation mode; it appears that as soon as the search for information is sequential, the confirmation bias is more pronounced.

### 4.2.10 Involvement in the Research

Experiments carried out on the theme of selective exposure, especially with a link to decision making, generally use objects of study that are varied but for which the subject does not have high levels of involvement. In fact, such research only produces low levels of involvement in the subject: an error in the choice of a CD, haircut or a potential recruitment situation, etc. These choices have little chance to produce strong levels of dissonance in the subject, even if a debate on the theme is anticipated. This argument is debatable insofar as involvement is not a necessary condition of the phenomenon of selective exposure. Some research appears to show differences in exposure even when the object has no consequences for the subject or does not have any implications for the decision. Otis (1979) has thus managed to show that people who expose themselves to science fiction films would have a higher inclination to believe in the existence of flying saucers. Yet despite the high quantity of research in the domain of selective exposure, few information elements are introduced when a decision has important consequences for the subject.

### 4.2.11 Individual Differences, Personality Factors, the Self Image of the Individual

Apart from the factors induced by the situations presented previously, some authors were also equally interested in personality dimensions likely to play a role in the subject's decision whether to expose himself to given information. Thus, different personality dimensions (introversion, extraversion, dogmatism etc.) have been introduced into research on selective exposure.

#### 4.2.11.1 The Effect of Extraversion/Introversion

In one of his studies concerning exposure to information on the effect of tobacco, Feather (1963) measured not only the subjects' tobacco consumption but also two personality dimensions: neuroticism and extraversion. Subjects with high extraversion scores expressed greater interest in the information discussing the link between smoking and cancer. These same extravert subjects were actually smokers. Extravert subjects would therefore be more inclined to face up to dissonant information. This result is all the more interesting considering that extraversion appears to be a dimension that is relatively stable in a subject's personality. Costa and McCrae[20] (1992) have carried out test-retest correlations between different dimensions of personality (extraversion, agreeableness, openness etc.), with seven year intervals between the two measures, and noted that the correlation on extraversion was about 0.81.

### 4.2.11.2 The Effect of Dogmatism

If few studies looked at the role of extraversion, the effect of dogmatism was studied to a greater extent. Dru (1998) defined dogmatism based on work by Rokeach as "the translation of a general authoritarianism in the structure and organization of beliefs independently of their ideological content" (p. 97). In more concrete terms, this means that the cognitive organization of the belief system of dogmatic people is relatively closed. This is especially revealed by an authoritarian intolerance for information that is not adjusted to the individual's system of thought. Therefore, some authors working on selective exposure have hypothesized that people obtaining high scores on dogmatic scales, thus displaying narrow-mindedness, would tend to avoid exposure to information that would conflict with their system of beliefs to a greater degree than people who were open-minded. Kleck and Wheaton (1967), Donohew and Palmgreen (1971a) and Bertrand (1979) did not succeed in showing such a link between dogmatism and subjects' level of exposure to conflicting information. However, in studies by Feather (1967; 1969), Innes (1978), and Durand and Lambert (1975), those scoring high on dogmatism were less inclined to expose themselves to information that did not support their opinion. Clarke and James (1967) have nevertheless shown that dogmatism only had an effect on exposure in private settings. In other words, when the dissonant information was useful (e.g., when one is anticipating a debate) even relatively narrow-minded people would expose themselves to this information. Finally, dogmatism is likely to provide an explanation for the relative incoherent effects of novelty discussed earlier. On the one hand, new information could be preferred if it arose the curiosity of the individual. Yet, on the other hand, such curious information could be avoided if it resulted in dissonance as it would then be even more difficult to refute and more likely to create a higher level of dissonance. Feather's study (1969a) reconciled these two results by showing that those with high scores on the dogmatism and consistency scales tended to show a lesser preference for new information than those who obtained lower scores on these scales. In other words, it is probable that dogmatism plays a moderating role in exposure to non-familiar information.

### 4.2.11.3 Effect of Gender, Depression and Age

Few studies on selective exposure primarily investigated gender as an independent variable. Nevertheless some have shown that effects of selective exposure could depend on gender. Thus McGinnies and Rosenbaum's (1965) results were in line with the theory's predictions though only for female subjects. Nevertheless this effect was probably due to gender differences for the attitude measured. Bekovitz's (1965) study also showed gender differences that were also probably underpinned by attitudinal differences. As for Brodbeck (1956), he noted differences between men and women concerning their interest for the subject studied. Selective exposure would therefore appear to be equally present in male and in

---

[20] Cited in Huteau (1995).

female subjects. Thus, the study by Rosenbaum, Rosenbaum and McGinnies (1974), which directly studied the effect of gender on selective exposure, did not show any particular difference. It is worth noting, however, that Hammen (1977) managed to bring out such differences. However these only occurred in depressive individuals. The depressed tended to select less positive information than the non-depressed and even less so if they were male. It is also noteworthy, however, that the author's conclusion was based on a .10 statistical level of significance and he himself recognized the necessity to further investigate this effect. Finally, if an eventual effect of age exists, it seems to correspond to the expression of knowledge differences about the object studied. Thus Chaffee and Miyo (1983) and Chaffee, Saphir, Graf, Sandvig and Hahn (2001) showed that individuals selectively exposed themselves to information in the domain of politics and that this tendency is more pronounced in younger individuals. Nevertheless, in all likelihood, this apparent age difference is explained by differences in individuals' knowledge of politics. Greater knowledge in older individuals would generate a stronger confidence. Thus, attention to inconsistent information concerning politics is correlated with curiosity and, above all, with political knowledge, as well as the number of years of education for the older individuals and the number of years of civic instruction for the younger individuals; that is, with different means of knowledge acquisition in the political domain.

### 4.2.11.4 The Effect of Self Esteem and Coping

Some situations can turn out to be threatening to the self esteem of an individual. Thus, failing exercises such as intelligence tests can cause a reduction in self esteem. To prevent this, an individual may search for any information likely to attenuate such a negative feedback. Reading information that casts doubt on the relevance of the test the individual failed is consistent with this endeavor. An individual's level of self esteem is therefore likely to influence his information search. For some individuals, failure on an intelligence test will jeopardize their self esteem whereas others will not perceive failure as a threat because they will have, at their disposal, strategies to cope with their failure: they will engage in rationalization processes such as questioning the validity of these tests etc. Thus, selective exposure can be assimilated to a coping strategy (Lazarus & Launier, 1978) that the individual would be likely to call upon. Coping strategies are defined as "the set of processes that an individual introduces between him and an event perceived as threatening in order to master, tolerate or diminish the impact of this event on his physical or psychological well being" (p. 40, Paulhan & Bourgeois, 1995). Failing an intelligence test constitutes such a threat to an individual. To face this threat, individuals have several strategies at their disposal. Vitaliano, Russo, Carr, Maiuro and Becker (1985) identified two main types of such strategies. The first type (avoidance coping) aims to modify the emotional state of the subjects caused by the threatening elements. The second type (vigilant coping) is focused on problem resolution. Active research of information is a means to put vigilant coping into action whilst avoidance of such information is an example of avoidance coping. This idea of avoidance vs. exposure to the threat can be compared to selective exposure since dissonant information is, by its very nature, a threatening element for an individual's system of beliefs. Adaptive strategies would enable exposure to dissonant information. If we consider that there exist inter-individual differences concerning the use of different strategies, it is then probable that avoidance strategies and information search, as constituted by selective exposure, are used to different degrees depending on the individual, the situation and his evaluation of this situation. In this framework, Olson and Zanna (1979) considered that individuals inclined to use repressive strategies (centered on emotions) instead of sensitive strategies (centered on the problem) would resort more to strategies of avoidance of dissonant information, and even more so when they felt incapable of facing them (Rhine, 1967a). Olson et al. (1979) proposed two possible explanations to account for such results. Firstly, the 'repressives' and the 'sensitives' may have different levels of awareness of dissonance or may react differently to the situation. Moreover, individuals who preferentially use avoidance strategies would be more likely to avoid exposing themselves to dissonant information compared to individuals who use vigilant strategies. Zanna and Aziza (1975) thus showed differences in attitude change between sensitives and repressives. The sensitives shifted their attitude more than the repressives. However, as emphasized by these authors, it is also possible that the two groups of subjects did not feel the same level of dissonance. Besides, Billings and Moos (1981) have demonstrated that individuals who have higher levels of education and social status use more vigilant strategies than people who have a lower level of education and social status. In a similar vein, Star, Hugues and McGill (1950) observed that the poorest and most underprivileged are the least affected by information campaigns. Similarly, Schramm and Carter (1959) account for differences in exposure between Republicans and Democrats by arguing that Democrats generally have lower levels of education. In conclusion, the level of education determines, in part, how individuals are going to face threatening information. Coping therefore appears to play a role in individual exposure, which is mediated by the level of education.

## 4.3 Conclusion on Selective Exposure Factors and Advertisements in Favor of Tobacco and Alcohol

If the idea of selective exposure can appear at first relatively intuitive, the multitude of factors highlighted that are likely to mediate the demonstration of the effect has made the idea developed by Festinger (1957) a little more complex. Despite this complexity, selective exposure brings new light on the impact of advertising on consuming behavior. In arguing that advertising can modify or maintain the preferences of an individual for a brand rather than another, industrialists in the end defend the existence of a selective exposure effect which would only lead existing consumers of alcohol or tobacco to expose themselves to advertisements of the products they are consuming. One can even suppose that individuals are going to expose themselves to a greater extent to alcohol and tobacco advertisements for the brand they are using rather than advertisements for brands that they are not consuming. Of course, the selective exposure effect exists. Nevertheless, as we have seen, it is not systematic. Moreover, selective exposure occurs in individuals who have an established attitude on a given subject. Individuals who do not have an opinion on a given subject will expose themselves to any information on this subject. In other words, for individuals who have not yet started to drink or smoke, advertisements for tobacco or alcohol will constitute information likely to influence their consuming behavior, in the same way that parents' observations will, for example. Advertising concerning alcohol or tobacco is likely to develop positive expectations with regards to alcohol or tobacco and such expectations are known to have an indirect influence on consuming behavior. Nevertheless, this impact is perhaps more indirect. Thus for Wyllie et al. (1998b), advertising would have an effect on consumption if it can modify subjects' beliefs. Based on the alcohol expectations model, itself inspired by the model of reasoned action (Ajzen & Fishbein, 1980), Stacy, Widaman and Marlatt (1990) suggest that positive expectations towards alcohol have an impact on individuals' attitudes, which are known to determine behavioral intention. Positive expectations towards alcohol would also influence behavioral intention directly.

## 4.4 Selective Exposure and Prevention

Aside from its value for studying the link between advertising and consumption, selective exposure is perhaps even more relevant for studying the relationship between prevention and alcohol or tobacco consumption. One can suppose that consumers of these two products would tend to avoid any information likely to question their consumption of alcohol or tobacco. In other words, the probability that an individual exposes himself to a prevention campaign for alcohol or tobacco would be higher for a non-consumer of these products than for a consumer. Accordingly, prevention campaigns would only maintain the healthy behavior of nonsmokers or nondrinkers, and of those who consume alcohol in moderation. Ultimately, this campaign would fail to raise awareness in people whose consumption is more problematic. In his research on tobacco, Feather (1962, 1963) failed to show that smokers avoided the information that smoking provoked cancer. This absence of selective exposure may be explained by the fact that only one category of smoker was considered. Yet some smokers could have developed a negative evaluation towards tobacco but, because of their dependence, continue to smoke. In other words, an individual X, who is at the first stage of Prochaska and DiClemente's (1986) classification, will not, in all likelihood, have the same attitude than an individual Y who has reached the second stage, even if both of them are smokers. Prochaska's model postulates that quitting smoking occurs in five phases. The first phase (pre-contemplation or non-motivation) is characterized by an absence of the smoker's desire to stop smoking. In the second phase (contemplation) the smoker manifests a motivation to stop without, however, putting it into action. The third phase (preparation) is marked by the appearance of minor changes in the smoker's behavior. The fourth (action) and fifth (maintenance) phases corresponds to the effective stopping of the consumption of tobacco, and to the persistence of this stopping, respectively. Individuals targeted by prevention campaigns are those in one of the two first phases. For Noël (1999), individuals in the contemplation phase "tend to express more negative feelings towards their tobacco consumption" (p. 123) than those in the pre-contemplation phase. This implies that an individual in pre-contemplation phase will have a positive attitude towards tobacco whereas one in the contemplation phase would have developed a negative attitude. Thus, in pre-contemplation phase, the smoker will perhaps be more inclined to avoid prevention information because it is in conflict with his attitudes towards tobacco. In contrast, the individual in contemplation phase has, in all likelihood, developed an attitude that is negative towards tobacco. He will, therefore, be inclined to expose himself to information about prevention as such information would be likely to reinforce his motivation to stop tobacco. To examine the impact of a tobacco prevention campaign, for example, or to put into place such a campaign, it is therefore, according to us, necessary to differentiate smokers according to which stages they are in but also to take into account a certain number of factors mentioned previously. Thus, to affect individuals in pre-contemplation phase with prevention information on tobacco, it is necessary to consider their level of confidence concerning their consumption behavior. Indeed, it is probable that confident smokers will confront prevention information because they would have the readily available means to refute this information. For instance, Feather (1962, 1963) mentioned the idea that smokers will expose themselves to information on the risk of throat cancer since they may consider that this information only concerns the category of heavy smokers and that they do not belong to this category. In contrast, individuals who are less confident will be inclined to resort to avoidance strategies with prevention information. To reach such individuals, it may be necessary to arouse their curiosity so that they expose themselves to this information. In France, such a campaign was run. In 2002, a televised advertisement was shown a little before the news with the following message: "Notice to the consumers – a product on the market contains traces of mercury, hydrocyanic acid and acetone – to know more about it, call XXX". This advertisement raised quite a panic amongst the French, inundating the call centre with calls. The National Health Service and the National Institute of Prevention and Education for Health finally stopped their campaign and quickly revealed that the dangerous product was in fact cigarettes. Individuals who are in the contemplation phase have, in all likelihood, developed a negative attitude towards the use of tobacco and a positive attitude towards stopping, which would lead them to consider quitting. Such individuals would be more inclined to expose themselves to prevention information since it would strengthen their attitude. Incidentally, Noël (1999) remarked that the contemplation phase is characterized by vigilance to any information related to quitting smoking. The individual will be more prepared to take into consideration interventions for health education, for example. In accordance with Freedman and Sears (1963; 1965a), however, recall that individuals will rather confront themselves to information that favor their point of view than to information that challenges the opposite point of view. Therefore, for individuals in the first phase, negative effects of tobacco usage (financial costs, health risks, etc.) should be put forward. In contrast, for individuals in the latter phase, what would be needed is a greater insistence on the benefits of quitting smoking (savings, health gain, etc.) and possibly on the information showing that stopping is within their reach. In other words, prevention campaigns cannot reach all individuals. It is therefore necessary to identify the population targeted by the campaign and, consequently, to employ a specific communication strategy to ensure that the targeted individuals will expose themselves to the campaign. Similarly, studies aiming to evaluate the impact of a prevention campaign should also consider the issues related to selective exposure. For example, Netemeyer, Andrews and Burton (2005) attempted to evaluate the impact of a prevention campaign carried out in Wisconsin in 2001. They solicited a representative sample of people living in the States to participate in a telephone survey presented as "a survey on attitudes and opinions towards tobacco". The results obtained spoke in favor of a positive impact of the prevention campaign, which would have particularly encouraged individuals to quit smoking. Nevertheless, from our point of view, it is appropriate to put this result into perspective. In effect, only regular smokers who answered all the questions of the survey and who were capable of remembering the prevention campaign were included in the final analysis. In other words, out of the 327 regular smokers sampled, only 125 could be included in the analysis. It is therefore possible that among the 202 individuals excluded from the analysis, a non-negligible part may not have remembered the campaign because they had actively resorted to selective exposure strategies. Consequently, the prevention campaign had no impact for these individuals.

# 5 Conclusion

While the laws forbidding or restricting the broadcast of alcohol or tobacco advertisements were adopted in several countries, it is, nevertheless, still very difficult today to distinguish what is the real impact of such advertising. Results from various studies failed to clearly establish a positive relationship between advertising and consumption. From our perspective, these inconclusive results should be reconsidered in the light of selective exposure. This being said, the existence of moderating or mediating factors somewhat complicates the situation. In the domain of prevention, these factors represent as many research leads that could increase the impact of prevention campaigns. Certainly, succeeding in exposing individuals to advertising or prevention campaigns does not guarantee that they would adopt a buying behavior or a healthy behavior, respectively. According to McGuire (1968), to have an impact, a persuasive communication must go through two first successive phases, namely, physical exposure to the message followed by attention given to the proposed message. Taking into account selective exposure and factors that are likely to moderate the relationship between attitude and exposure could favor the implementation of this second phase. Whilst we focused on alcohol and tobacco in this chapter, conclusions can be transposed to other objects. For example, it is noteworthy that today, as for alcohol, some countries are adopting legal measures constraining advertising for food products accused to be responsible for the increase in obesity. Yet, in our opinion, before undertaking a repressive approach aiming at forbidding advertising altogether, it would be necessary to start by questioning the real influence of such advertising and, more specifically, the type of population it may affect. The consumer typology proposed by Stewart and Rice (1995) constitutes a relevant and appropriate basis to consider in the light of selective exposure. For the non-consumer, exposure to advertising will depend on the motivations underpinning this absence of consumption. If non-consumers hold a negative attitude towards the product then it is probable that they would avoid exposure to advertising in favor of the product. If, however, non-consumers do not know the product advertised, they would be more likely to expose themselves to such advertising in order to develop knowledge about the products which would ultimately allow them to form an attitude. We have already mentioned the case of loyal users for whom exposure to advertisements for products they already consume will reinforce their consumption behavior. People who switch brands could be considered as individuals whose decision or attitude is not definite. Exposing themselves to advertisements will allow them to build a more definite opinion as it will for the person who is ignorant of the product or brand. Finally, potential users will perhaps expose themselves to advertising to the extent that this will increase their curiosity for a product they did not know about. The situation is therefore more complex than a simple causal relationship between advertising and consumption. In the best of cases, the effect of advertising on consumption will depend on a multitude of variables, at the forefront of which one can find selective exposure and its various mediating factors.

# BIBLIOGRAPHY

Adlaf, E.M., & Kohn, P.M. (1989). Alcohol advertising, consumption and abuse: A covariance-structural modelling look at Strickland's data. *British Journal of Addiction, 84,* 749-757.

Aitken, P.P., & Eadie, D.R. (1990). Reinforcing effects of cigarette advertising on under-age smoking. *British Journal of Addiction, 85,* 399-412.

Aitken, P.P., Eadie, D.R., Hastings, G.B., & Haywood, A.J. (1991). Predisposing effects of cigarette advertising on children's intentions to smoke when older. *British Journal of Addiction, 86,* 383-390.

Aitken, P.P., Eadie, D.R., Leathar, D.S., McNeill, R.E.J., & Scott, A.C. (1988). Television advertisements for alcoholic drinks do reinforce under-age drinking. *British Journal of Addiction, 83,* 1399-1419.

Ajzen, Fishbein M. (1980). Understanding Attitudes and Predicting Social Behaviour. New Jersey: Prentice-Hall.

Allen, V. (1964). Uncertainty of outcome and post-decision dissonance reduction. In L. Festinger (Ed.), Conflict, Decision and Dissonance. (pp. 34-43). Stanford, CA. Stanford University Press.

Atkin, C. (1995). Survey and experimental research on effects of alcohol advertising. In S.E. Martin, P. Mail, (Eds.), *The effects of the mass media on the use and abuse of alcohol. NIAAA Research Monograph No. 28* (pp. 39-68). NIH.Bethesda, MD: NIAAA.

Atkin, C., Hocking, J., & Block, M. (1984). Media effects on the Young. Teenage Drinking: Does Advertising Make a Difference? *Journal of Communication, 34*(2), 157-167.

Bandura, A. (1977). *Social Learning Theory.* New York: General learning press.

Basil, M.D. (1997). The danger of cigarette "special placements" in film and television. *Health Communication, 9*(2), 191-198.

Belhing, C.F. (1971). Effects of commitment and certainty upon exposure to supportive and nonsupportive information. *Journal of Personality and Social Psychology, 19*(2), 152-159.

Berkowitz, L. (1965). Cognitive dissonance and communication preferences. *Human Relations, 18,* 361-372.

Bertrand, J.T. (1979). Selective avoidance on health topics a field test. *Communication Research, 6*(3), 271-294.

Billings, A.G., & Moos, R.H. (1981). The role of coping responses and social ressources in attenuating the stress of life events. *Journal of behavioral medicine, 4,* 139-157.

Boon, J., & Davies, G. (1996). Extra-Stimulus influences on eyewitness perception and recall: Hastorf and Cantrill revisited. *Legal and Criminological Psychology, 1,* 155-164.

Bothwell, R.K., & Brigham, J.C. (1983). Selective evaluation and recall during the 1980 Reagan-Carter debate. *Journal of Applied Social Psychology, 13,* 427-442.

Braden, M., & Walster, E. (1964). The effect of anticipated dissonance on pre-decision behavior. In L. Festinger (Ed.), *Conflict, Decision and Dissonance.* (pp. 145-151-43). Stanford, CA. Stanford University Press.

Brock, T.C. (1965). Commitment to exposure as a determinant of information receptivity. *Journal of Personality and Social Psychology, 2*(1), 10-19.

Brock, T.C., Albert, S.M., & Becker, L.A. (1970). Familiarity, utility and supportiveness as determinants of information receptivity. *Journal of Personality and Social Psychology, 14*(4), 292-301.

Brodbeck, M. (1956). The role of small groups in mediating the effects of propaganda. *Journal of Abnormal and Social Psychology, 52,* 168-170.

Brown (1978). Educating young people about alcohol use in New Zealand: Whose side are we on. *British Journal on Alcohol and Alcoholism*, 13, 199-204.

Canon, L.K. (1964). Self-confidence and selective exposure to communication. In L. Festinger (Ed.), *Conflict, Decision and Dissonance.* (pp. 83-96). Stanford, CA. Stanford University Press.

Chaffee, S.H., & McLeod, J.M. (1973). Individual Vs social predictors of information seeking. *Journalism Quarterly, 50,* 237-245.

Chaffee, S.H., & Miyo, Y. (1983). Selective exposure and the reinforcement hypothesis an intergenerational panel study of the 1980 presidential campaign. *Communication Research, 10*(1), 3-36.

Chaffee, S.H., Saphir, M.N., Graf, J., Sandvig, C., & Hahn, K.S. (2001). Attention to counter-attitudinal messages in a state election campaign. *Political Communication, 18,* 247-272.

Clarke, P., & James, J. (1967). The effects of situation, attitude intensity and personality on information-seeking. *Sociometry, 30,* 235-245.

Cohen, A.R., Brehm, J.W., & Latané, B. (1959). Choice of strategy and voluntary exposure to information under public and private conditions. *Journal of Personality, 27,* 67-73.

Costa, P.T., & McCrae, R.R. (1992). Four ways five factors are basic. *Personality and Individual Differences, 13,* 653-665.

Courtwright, D.T. (2005). 'Carry on somking': Public relations and advertsing strategies of American and British tobacco companies since 1950. *Business History, 47*(3), 421-432.

Cvetkovich, G., & Earle, T.C. (1995). Product warnings and information processing: The case of alcohol beverage labels. *European Review of Applied Psychology, 45*(1), 17-20.

Davidson, J. (1964). Cognitive familiarity and dissonance reduction. In L. Festinger (Ed.), *Conflict, Decision and Dissonance.* (pp. 45-60). Stanford, CA. Stanford University Press.

Diab, L.N. (1979). Voluntary exposure to information during and after the war in Lebanon. *The Journal of Social Psychology*, 108, 13-17.

Ditto, P.H., & Lopez, D.F. (1992). Motivated skepticism: Use of differential decision criteria for preferred and nonpreferred conclusions. *Journal of Personality and Social Psychology, 63(4),* 568-584.

Donohew, L., & Palmgreen, P. (1971a). An investigation of 'mechanisms' of information selection. *Journalism Quarterly, 48,* 627-639.

Duffy, M. (1991). Advertising in Demand Systems: Testing a Galbraithian Hypothesis. *Applied Economics, 23*(3), 485-496.

Durand, R.M., & Lambert, Z.V. (1975). Dogmatism and exposure to political candidates. *Psychological Reports, 36,* 423-429.

Ehrlich, D., Guttman, I., Schonbach, P., & Mills, J. (1957). Post-decision exposure to relevant information. *Journal of Abnormal and Social Psychology*, 54(1), 98-102.

Feather, N.T. (1962). Cigarette smoking and lung cancer: A study of cognitive dissonance. *Australian Journal of Psychology, 14*(1), 55-64.

Feather, N.T. (1963). Cognitive dissonance, sensitivity, and evaluation. *Journal of Abnormal and Social Psychology*, 66(2), 157-163.

Feather, N.T. (1967). An expectancy-value model of information-seeking behavior. *Psychological Review, 74*(5), 342-360.

Feather, N.T. (1969). Preference for information in relation to consistency, novelty, intolerance of ambiguity, and dogmatism. *Australian Journal of Psychology, 21*(3), 235-249.

Festinger, L. (1957). *A Theory of Cognitive Dissonance.* Stanford, CA. Stanford University Press.

Festinger, L. (1964). *Conflict, Decision and Dissonance.* Stanford, CA. Stanford University Press.

Festinger, L., & Walster, E (1964). The temporal sequence of post-decision processes. In L. Festinger (Ed.), *Conflict, Decision and Dissonance.*(pp. 100-112). Stanford, CA. Stanford University Press.

Fischer, P., Jonas, E., Frey, D., & Hoffmann, B. (en revision). Confirmation bias in information seeking: Why does information search adapted to real-life situations increase the confirmation bias?

Fischer, P.M., Richards, J.W., Berman, E.J., & Krugman, D.M. (1989). Recall and eye tracking study of adolescents viewing tobacco advertisements. *Journal of the American Medical Association, 261*(1), 84-89.

Freedman, J.L. (1965a). Confidence, Utility and Selective Exposure: A partial replication *Journal of Personality and Social Psychology, 2*(5), 778-780.

Freedman, J.L. (1965b). Preference for dissonant information. *Journal of Personality and Social Psychology, 2*(2), 287-289.

Freedman, J.L., & Sears, D.O. (1963). Voters preference among types of information. *American Psychologist, 18,* 375.

Freedman, J.L., & Sears, D.O. Selective Exposure (1965a). *Advances in Experimental Social Psychology, 2,* 58-97.

Frey, D. (1979). Postdecisional preference for decision-relevant information as a function of the competence of its source and the degree of familiarity with this information. *Journal of Experimental Social Psychology, 17,* 51-67.

Frey, D. (1981a). The effect of negative feedback about oneself and cost of information on preferences for information about the source of this feedback. *Journal of Experimental Social Psychology, 17,* 42-50.

Frey, D. (1981b). Rerversible and irreversible decisions: Preference for consonant information as a function of attractiveness of decisions. *Alternatives Personality & Social Psychology Bulletin, 7*(4), 621-626.

Frey, D., Kumpf, M., Irle, M., & Gniech, G. (1984). Re-evaluation of decision alternatives dependent upon the reversibility of a decision and the passage of time. *European Journal of Social Psychology, 14,* 447-450.

Frey, D., & Rosch, M. (1984). Information seeking after decisions: The roles of novelty of information and decision reversibility. *Personality and Social Psychology Bulletin, 10*(1), 91-98.

Gerbner, G. (1995). Alcohol in American culture. In S.E. Martin, P. Mail, (Eds.), *The Effects of the Mass Media on the Use and Abuse of Alcohol. NIAAA Research Monograph No. 28* (pp. 3-29).  NIH.Bethesda, MD: NIAAA.

Grabowski, H. G. (1976).The effect of advertising on the inter-industry distribution of demand. *Explorations in Economic Research, 3,* 21–75.

Greenwald, H.J., (1969). Dissonance and relative versus absolute attractiveness of decision alternatives. *Journal of Personality and Social Psychology, 11*(4), 328-333.

Hammen, C.L. (1977). Effects of depression, feedback, and gender on selective exposure to information about the self. *Psychological Reports, 40,* 403-408.

Hastorf, A.H., & Cantril, H. (1954). They saw a game: A case study. *Journal of Abnormal and Social Psychology, 49,* 129-134.

Innes, J.M. (1978). Selective exposure as a function of dogmatism and incentive. *The Journal of Social Psychology, 106*(2), 261-265.

International Center for Alcohol Policies (2001). Self-regulation of beverage alcohol advertising. *Icap Reports, 9,* 1-15.

Jecker, J.D. (1964a). The cognitive effects of conflict and dissonance. In L. Festinger (Ed.), *Conflict, Decision and Dissonance.*(pp. 21-32). Stanford, CA. Stanford University Press.

Jecker, J.D. (1964b). Selective exposure to new information. In L. Festinger (Ed.), *Conflict, Decision and Dissonance.*(pp. 65-81). Stanford, CA. Stanford University Press.

Jonas, E., Schulz-Hardt, S., Frey, D., & Thelen, N. (2001). Confirmation bias in sequential information search after preliminary decisions: An expansion of dissonance theoretical research on selective exposure to information. *Journal of Personality and Social Psychology, 80*(4), 557-571.

Kelly, K.J., & Edwards, R.W. (1998). Image advertisements for alcohol products: Is their appeal associated with adolescents' intention to consume alcohol. *Adolescence, 33*(129), 47-59.

Kilbourne, W.E., Painton, S., & Ridley, D. (1985). The effect of sexual embedding on responses to magazine advertisements. *Journal of Advertising,* 14 (2) 48-55.

Klapper, J.T. (1960). *The effects of mass communication.* Free Press, New York.

Kleck, R.E., & Wheaton, J. (1967). Dogmatism and responses to opinion-consistent and opinion inconsistent information. *Journal of Personality and Social Psychology, 5*(2), 249-252.

Kleinhesselink, R.R., & Edwards, R.E. (1975). Seeking and avoiding belief-discrepant information as a function of its perceived refutability. *Journal of Personality and Social Psychology, 31*(5), 787-790.

Klitzner, M., Gruenewald, P.J., & Bamberger, E. (1991). Cigarette advertising and adolescent experimentation with smoking. *British Journal of Addiction, 86,* 287-298.

Knox, R.E., & Inkster, J.A. (1968). Postdecision dissonance at post time. *Journal of Personality and Social Psychology, 8*(4), 319-323.

Kohn, P.M. & Smart, R.G. (1984). The impact of television advertising on alcohol consumption: An experiment. *Journal of Studies on Alcohol, 45,* 295-301

Kohn, P.M. & Smart, R.G. (1987). Wine, women, suspiciousness and advertising on subsequent consumption. *Journal of Studies on Alcohol, 48,* 161-167.

Kohn, P.M., Smart, R.G. & Ogborne, A.C. (1984). Effects of two kinds of alcohol advertising on subsequent consumption. *Journal of Advertising,*

Kunda, Z. (1987). Motivated inference: Self-serving generation and evaluation of causal theories. *Journal of Personality and Social Psychology, 53*(4), 636-647.

Laugesen, M., & Meads, C. (1991). Advertising, price, income and publicity effects on weekly cigarette sales in New Zealand supermarkets. *British Journal of Addiction, 86,* 83-89.

Lazarsfeld Berelson et Gaudet (1948). The people's choice (2nd edition). New York: Columbia Press.

Lazarus, R., & Launier, R. (1978). Stress-related transactions between person and environment. In L.A. Pervin & M.Lewis (Eds.), *Perspectives in Interactional Psychology* (pp. 287-327). New York : Plenum.

Loken, B., & Howard-Pitney, B. (1988). Effectiveness of cigarette advertisements on women: An experimental study. *Journal of Applied Psychology, 73*(3), 378-382.

Lowe, H.R., & Steiner, I.D. (1968). Some effects of the reversibility and consequences of decisions on postdecision information preference. *Journal of Personality and Social Psychology, 8*(2), 172-179.

Lowin, A. (1967). Approach and avoidance: Alternate modes of selective exposure to information. *Journal of Personality and Social Psychology, 6*(1), 1-9.

Madden, P.A., & Grube, J.W. (1994). The frequency and nature of alcohol and tobacco advertising in televised sports, 1990 through 1992. *Public Health Briefs, 84*(2), 297-299.

Mann, L., Janis, I.L., & Chaplin, R. (1969). Effects of anticipation of forthcoming information on predecisional processes. *Journal of Personality and Social Psychology, 11*(1), 10-16.

Martin, (1995). Alcohol and the mass media: Issues, approaches, and research directions. In S.E. Martin, P. Mail, (Eds.), *The Effects of the Mass Media on the Use and Abuse of Alcohol. NIAAA Research Monograph No. 28* (pp. 277-295). NIH.Bethesda, MD: NIAAA.

Mazis, M.B. (1995). Conducting research on nontraditional media in the marketing of alcoholic beverages. In S.E. Martin, P. Mail, (Eds.), *The Effects of the Mass Media on the Use and Abuse of Alcohol. NIAAA Research Monograph No. 28* (pp. 239-244). NIH.Bethesda, MD: NIAAA.

McGinnies, E. (1949). Emotionality and perceptual defense. *Psychological Review, 56,* 244-251.

McGinnies, E., & Rosenbaum, L.L. (1965). A test of the selective exposure hypothesis in persuasion. *The Journal of Psychology, 61,* 237-240.

McGuiness, T. (1980). An Econometric Analysis of Total Demand for Alcoholic. Beverages in the UK, 1956-1975, *Journal of Industrial Economics, 29*(1), 85-105

McGuire, W.J. (1968a). Selective exposure: A summing up. In R.P. Abelson, E. Aronson, W.J. McGuire, T.M., Newcomb, M.J., Rosenberg, & P.H. Tannenbaum (Eds.), *Theories of cognitive consistencies: A sourcebook* (pp. 797-800). Chicago: Rand McNally.

McGuire, W.J. (1968b). Resume and response from the consistency theory viewpoint. In R.P. Abelson, E. Aronson, W.J. McGuire, T.M., Newcomb, M.J., Rosenberg, & P.H. Tannenbaum (Eds.), *Theories of cognitive consistencies: A sourcebook* (pp. 275-297). Chicago: Rand McNally.

McGuire, W.J., & Papageorgis, D. (1962). Effectiveness of forewarning in developing resistance to persuasion. *Public Opinion Quarterly, 26,* 24-34.

Miller, R.L. (1977). The effects of postdecisional regret on selective exposure. *European Journal of Social Psychology, 7*(1), 121-127.

Mills, J. (1965a). Avoidance of dissonant information. *Journal of Personality and Social Psychology, 2*(4), 589-593.

Mills, J. (1965b). Effect of certainty about a decision upon postdecision exposure to consonant and dissonant information. *Journal of Personality and Social Psychology, 2*(5), 749-752.

Mills, J. (1965c). The effect of certainty on exposure to information prior to commitment. *Journal of Experimental Social Psychology, 1,* 348-355.

Mills, J., Aronson, E., & Robinson, H. (1959). Selectivity in exposure to information. *Journal of Abnormal and Social Psychology, 59,* 250-253.

Mills, J., & Ross, A. (1964). Effects of commitment and certainty upon interest in supporting information. *Journal of Abnormal and Social Psychology, 59,* 250-253.

Moschis, G.P., & Moore, R.L.A. (1982). Longitudinal study of television advertising effects. *Journal of Consumer Research, 9*(3), 279-286.

Nadeau, R., Gidengil E., Nevitte, N., & Blais, A. (1998). Do trained and untrained coders perceive electoral coverage differently? In *Paper prepared for delivery at the annual meeting of the American Political Science Association.*

Netemeyer, R.G., Andrews, J.C., & Burton, S. (2005). Effects of antismoking advertising-based beliefs on adult smokers' consideration of quitting. *American Journal of Public Health, 95*(6), 1062-1066.

Noël, Y. (1999). An ordination approach to the quantification of smokers' readiness to change. *Swiss Journal of Psychology, 58*(2), 123-133.

Ogborne, A.C., & Smart, R.G. (1980). Will restrictions on alcohol advertising reduce alcohol consumption? *British Journal of Addiction, 75,* 293-296.

Olson, J.M., & Zanna M.P. (1979). A new look at selective exposure. *Journal of Experimental Social Psychology, 15,* 1-15.

Orlandi, M.A., Lieberman L.R., & Schinke, S.P. (1988). The effects of alcohol and tobacco advertising on adolescents. *Drugs and Society, 3*(1), 77-97.

Otis, L. (1979). Selective exposure to the film close encounters. *The Journal of Psychology, 101,* 293-295.

Paulhan, I., & Bourgeois, M. (1995). *Stress et coping les stratégies d'ajustement à l'adversité.* Série Nodules, PUF.

Pechmann, C., & Shih, CF. (1999). Smoking scenes in movies and anti-smoking advertisements before movies: Effects on youth. *Journal of Marketing, 63,* 1-13.

Perrissol, S. (2004). Exposition sélective appliquée aux objets alcool et tabac : influence de la structure et de la mesure de l'attitude. Thèse de Doctorat. CRPCC - LAUREPS. Rennes.

Perrissol, S., Bordel, S., & Somat, A. (unpublished). Redefining the Methodological Paradigm of Selective Exposure and Accounting for its Effects.

Perrissol, S., Boscher, G., Cerclé, A., & Somat, A. (2005). Consommation d'alcool, capacité de résistance à la consommation et exposition sélective aux publicités pro alcool. *European Review of Applied Psychology, 55,* 235-243.

Perrissol, S., & Somat, A. (*in press*). L'exposition sélective : bilan et perspectives.

Postman, L., Bruner, J.S., & McGinnies, E. (1948). Personal values as selective factors in perception. *Journal of Abnormal and Social Psychology, 43,* 142-158.

Prochaska, J.O., & DiClemente, C.C. (1986). Toward a comprehensive model of change. In W.E. Miller, N. Heather (Eds.), *Addictive behaviors processes of change.* (pp. 3-27). New York, Plenum Press.

Rhine, R.J. (1967a). Some problems in dissonance theory research on information selectivity. *Psychological Bulletin, 68*(1), 21-28.

Rosen, S. (1961). Critique and notes postdecision affinity for incompatible information. *Journal of Abnormal and Social Psychology, 63*(1), 188-190.

Rosenbaum, W.B., Rosenbaum, L.L., & McGinnies E. (1974). Sex differences in selective exposure? *The Journal of Social Psychology, 92*, 85-89.

Saffer, H. (1995). Alcohol advertising and alcohol consumption: Econometrix studies. In S.E. Martin, P. Mail, (Eds.), *The Effects of the Mass Media on the Use and Abuse of Alcohol. NIAAA Research Monograph No. 28* (pp. 83-99). NIH.Bethesda, MD: NIAAA.

Schramm, W., & Carter, R.F. (1959). Effectiveness of a political telethon. *Public Opinion Quarterly, 23,* 121-127.

Schultz, C.B. (1974). The effect of confidence on selective exposure: An unresolved dilemma. *The Journal of Social Psychology, 94,* 65-69.

Sears, D.O. (1965). Biased indoctrination and selectivity of exposure to new information. *Sociometry, 28*, 363-373.

Sears, D.O. (1966). Opinion formation and information preferences in an adversary situation. *Journal of Experimental Social Psychology, 2*, 130-142.

Sears, D.O., & Freedman, J.L. (1965). Effects of expected familiarity with arguments upon opinion change and selective exposure. *Journal of Personality and Social Psychology, 2*(3), 420-426.

Slater, M.D., Rouner, D., Beauvais, F., Murphy, K., Domenech-Rodriguez, M., & Van Leuven, J. (1996). Adolescent perceptions of underage drinkers in TV beer ads. *Journal of Alcohol and Drug Education, 42*(1), 43-56.

Slater, S. & Chaloupka, & Wakefield, M. (2001). State variation in retail promotions and advertising for Marlboro cigarettes. *Tobacoo Control, 10,* 337-339.

Smart, R.G. (1988). Does alcohol advertising affect overall consumption? A review of empirical studies. *Journal of Studies on Alcohol, 49*(4), 314-323.

Smart, R.G., & Cutler, R.E. (1976). The alcoholic advertising ban in British Colombia: Problems and effects on beverage consumption, British Journal of Addictions, *71*, 13-21

Sobell, L.C., Sobell, M.B., Riley, D.M., Klajner, F., Leo, G.I., Pavan, D. & Cancilla, A.A. (1986). Effect of television programming and advertising on alcohol consumption in normal drinkers. *Journal of Studies on Alcohol, 47*(4), 333-340.

Stacy, A.W., Widaman, K.F., & Marlatt, G.A. (1990). Expectancy models of alcohol use. *Journal of Personality and Social Psychology, 58*(5), 918-928.

Star, S.A., Hughes, H., & McGill, H. (1950). Report of an educational campaign: The Cincinnati plan for the United Nations. *American Journal of Sociology, 55,* 389-400.

Stewart, D.W., & Rice, R. (1995). Nontraditional media and promotions in the marketing of alcoholic beverages. In S.E. Martin, P. Mail, (Eds.), *The Effects of the Mass Media on the Use and Abuse of Alcohol. NIAAA Research Monograph No. 28* (pp. 209-238). NIH.Bethesda, MD: NIAAA.

Taylor, S.E., & Armor, D.A. (1996). Positive illusions and coping with adversity. *Journal of Personality, 64*(4), 873-898.

Thayer, S. (1969). Confidence and post-judgment exposure to consonant and dissonant information in a free-choice situation, *The Journal of Social Psychology, 77,* 113-120.

Vidmar, N., & Rokeach, M. (1974). Archie's Bunker's bigotry: A study in selective perception and exposure, *Journal of Communication, 24,* 36-47.

Vitaliano, P.P., Russo, J., Carr, J.E., Maiuro, R.D., & Becker, J. (1985). The ways of coping checklist: Revision and psychometric properties. *Multivariate Behavioral Research, 20,* 3-26.

Walster, E. (1964). The temporal sequence of post-decision processes, in L. Festinger (Ed.), *Conflict, Decision and Dissonance,* Stanford (CA) Stanford University Press, 112-128.

Waly, P., & Cook, S.W. (1965) Effect of attitude on judgments plausibility, *Journal of Personality and Social Psychology, 2*(5), 745-749.

Wellins R., McGinnies E. (1977) Counterarguing and selective exposure to persuasion, *The Journal of Social Psychology, 103*(1), 115-127.

Wyllie, A., Zhang, J.F., & Casswell, S. (1998a). Responses to televised Alcohol advertisements associated with drinking behaviour of 10-17-year-olds. *Addiction, 93*(3), 361-371.

Wyllie, A., Zhang, J.F., & Casswell, S. (1998b). Positive responses to televised beer advertisements associated with drinking and problems reported by 18 to 29-year-olds. *Addiction, 93*(5), 749-760.

Zanna, M.P., & Aziza, C. (1975). On the interaction of repression-sensitization and attention in resolving cognitive dissonance. *Journal of Personality, 44,* 577-593.

In: Applied Psychology Research Trends
Editor: Karl H. Kiefer, pp.35-58

ISBN 978-1-60456-372-6
© 2008 Nova Science Publishers, Inc.

*Chapter 2*

# CLARIFYING THE RELATIONSHIP BETWEEN ORGANIZATIONAL COMMITMENT AND JOB PERFORMANCE: EXTENDING THE CONSERVATION OF RESOURCES MODEL

## *Jonathon R. B. Halbeslebe[1], Anthony R. Wheeler[2] and M. Ronald Buckley[3]*

[1]Department of Management & Marketing, University of Wisconsin-Eau Clair,
105 Garfield Avenue, PO Box 4004, Eau Claire, WI 54702
[2]University of Rhode Island
[3]University of Oklahoma

## ABSTRACT

Previous research on the relationship between organizational commitment and job performance had led researchers to the equivocal conclusion that increased commitment results in higher levels of job performance. In this study, we argue that by applying the conservation of resources model of stress, we can better understand the relationship between different types of commitment (affective, continuance, and normative) and different types of job performance (task and contextual) through targeted investment of resources by employees. Two studies provide support for our contention that affective commitment is related to task and contextual performance, continuance commitment is related to task performance, and normative commitment is related to a specific type of contextual performance. We discuss the implications of the conservation of resources model in terms of the theory surrounding organizational commitment and managerial practice.

---

[1] Corresponding Author: Tel-(715) 836-2090, Fax -(715) 836-2944, Email- halbesjr@uwec.edu

Over the past five decades, organizational commitment has developed into one of the most researched attitudinal variables in the study of organizational behavior. Organizational commitment is typically seen as an important attitude for organizations to develop in their employees, in part because of its inverse relationship with turnover (Angle & Perry, 1981; Blau & Boal, 1987; Cohen, 1993; Jaros, 1997; Porter, Steers, Mowday, & Boulian, 1974) and positive relationship with job satisfaction (Meyer, Paunonen, Gellatly, Goffin, & Jackson, 1989). Researchers have also correlated commitment with job performance; however, the relationship between those two important constructs is considered equivocal at best (Cohen, 1991; Mathieu & Zajac, 1990). The purpose of this paper is to further explore the complex relationship between three types of commitment, affective, continuance, and normative and two types of job performance, task and contextual. We offer a theoretical framework that allows for predictions with regard to these variables and an empirical test of the proposed theoretical framework.

## ORGANIZATIONAL COMMITMENT AND JOB PERFORMANCE

Commitment scholars agree that the construct of commitment includes three distinct dimensions, affective, continuance, and normative (Keller, 1997; Mathieu & Zajac, 1990). Whereas *affective* commitment taps into an individual's "identification with and involvement in a particular organization" (Porter, Steers, Mowday, & Boulian, 1974, p.604), *continuance* commitment measures an individual's commitment "to engage in consistent lines of activity" (Becker, 1960, p. 33). *Normative* commitment describes an employee's feelings of obligation to remain with an organization (Meyer & Allen, 1991).

Performance scholars also generally agree that the construct of performance is multidimensional. Borman and Motowidlo (1993) describe task performance as behaviors specifically related to performing the required duties of a job, and they describe contextual performance as non-job specific behaviors, such as volunteering for non-job related tasks or cooperating with coworkers to complete tasks. Contextual performance, or extra-role behavior (Borman & Motowidlo, 1997), includes behaviors that are considered discretionary and are not explicitly included in the reward system. This class of contextual performance is commonly called organizational citizenship behaviors (OCB; Organ, 1988; see also Bateman & Organ, 1983). Furthermore, researchers (Organ & Konovsky, 1989; Smith, Organ, & Near, 1983; Williams & Anderson, 1991) have found that employees can direct OCB-type behavior to the benefit of the organization (OCB-O) or to the individual (OCB-I). These distinctions between dimensions of commitment and performance convolute empirical investigations of the link between job performance and organizational commitment and have resulted in equivocal findings.

Randall's (1990) meta-analysis of the consequences of commitment suggested that the relationship between commitment and performance was positive, but weak ($r = .15$, *corrected r = .17*). However, she did not differentiate between dimensions of commitment or performance; which may explain the somewhat the weak relationship. A more recent meta-analysis conducted by Riketa (2002) found similar results, with a corrected correlation coefficient of .20 for overall job performance. Riketa separated out the effects of in-role and extra role performance, finding that the corrected correlation between commitment and extra-role performance to be higher than the relationship with in-role performance (.25 and .18, respectively). However, his analysis was limited to attitudinal (affective) commitment.

A number of studies have found a positive relationship between affective commitment and self-reported performance or work effort (Baugh & Roberts, 1994; Bycio, Hackett, & Allen, 1995; Darden, Hampton, & Howell, 1989; Ingram, Lee, & Skinner, 1989; Johnston & Snizek, 1991; Leong, Randall, & Cote, 1994; Meyer, Allen, & Smith, 1993; Randall, Fedor, & Longenecker, 1990; Sager & Johnston, 1989; Saks, 1995) as well as with supervisor ratings of job performance (Adkins, 1995; Bauer & Green, 1998; Mayer & Schoorman, 1992; Meyer, Paunonen, Gellatly, Goffin, & Jackson, 1989; Moorman, Neihoff, & Organ, 1993; Sager & Johnston, 1989). However, other studies have either found no relationship between commitment and job performance (e.g., Ganster & Dwyer, 1995; Keller, 1997; Williams & Anderson, 1991) or a negative relationship between commitment and performance (Wright, 1997).

To test for the possible incremental predictability of commitment on performance, Meyer et al. (1989) hypothesized that the dimensions of commitment would differentially predict employee performance. In a study of 65 managers of a food service organization, they reported that affective commitment positively predicted supervisor-rated job performance while continuance commitment negatively predicted job performance ratings. These relationships remained when the researchers controlled for the effects of age and tenure. Konovsky and Cropanzano (1991) found similar effects in their study of laboratory employees. However, both Meyer et al. and Konovsky and Cropanzano assessed performance as a unidimensional construct.

Some researchers, on the other hand, have suggested that the dimension of performance being measured is critical to understanding the relationship between commitment and job performance. In a sample of restaurant managers, DeCotiis and Summers (1987) found no relationship between supervisor ratings of performance and affective commitment; however, they found a positive relationship between affective commitment and objective measures of performance (e.g., cost control). Some studies have suggested that considering different dimensions of commitment and different dimensions of performance will lead to better prediction of performance. In their study of employees of a large multinational corporation, Shore and Wayne (1993) found a positive relationship between affective commitment and supervisor-rated OCB and a negative relationship between continuance commitment and OCB. Angle and Lawson (1994) found that affective commitment was unrelated to supervisor ratings of performance but was related to supervisor ratings of dependability and initiative. They found no relationship between continuance commitment and job performance.

Chen and Francesco (2003) conducted a comprehensive study that evaluated the role of all three types of commitment in the prediction of both in-role and extra-role (OCB) job performance. Using a sample of pharmaceutical employees in China, they found that affective commitment was positively associated with task performance and OCB but that continuance commitment was not associated with task performance and negatively related to OCB. Finally, they found that normative commitment moderated the relationship between affective commitment and performance, such that the relationship between affective commitment and in-role performance and OCB was stronger among those employees with lower normative commitment.

Taken together, the literature investigating the relationship between organizational commitment and job performance has led to a number of equivocal conclusions. While there appears to be a relationship between these two variables, the nature of this relationship requires further attention. In order to clarify the relationship, we suggest that a model of stress, the conservation of resources model may provide insight into this relationship.

## THE CONSERVATION OF RESOURCES MODEL

A limitation of the previous work investigating the link between commitment and performance has been the lack of a clear theoretical framework to meaningfully integrate and guide predictions such that one might expect different relationships between different types of commitment and performance. For such a framework, we suggest a stress theory, specifically Hobfoll's (1988, 1989, Hobfoll & Freedy, 1993) conservation of resources (COR) model. Central to the COR model is the notion of resources, which Hobfoll (1988; Hobfoll & Freedy, 1993) defines as any object, condition, characteristic, or energy that we value. Of course, the value of different resources will depend upon the situation encountered; one would expect work-related resources to be relevant to work settings whereas other resources might be relevant to other settings. Examples of resources relevant to the present work include involvement in organizations with others who have similar interests, stable employment, and a sense of commitment (Hobfoll, 1998, 2001).

According to the COR model, employees seek to maintain what social resources they have and engage in behavior to generate more resources (Hobfoll, 1988). The model suggests three ways in which individuals experience stress: 1) loss of resources, 2) threat to current resources, and 3) inadequate return on investments made to maximize resources (e.g., an employee who takes extra courses in management in order to increase the likelihood of promotion, but is passed over in the promotion).

While Hobfoll focused primarily on stress in the form of resource loss, the notion of investment of resources has important implications for organizational commitment. His model suggests that individuals will invest resources, as a coping mechanism, where the greatest potential return on investment is possible (Hobfoll & Freedy, 1993). Based on the theory, we posit that employees will invest resources into the organization in a manner that maximizes the likelihood of a payout. The manner in which those resources are invested depends largely on the employee's perceived relationship with the organization, in terms of their commitment. Figure 1 presents our model of the relationship between the dimensions of commitment and performance.

### Affective Commitment

Affective commitment includes an employee's attachment to and identification with their employer (Meyer & Allen, 1991). The logic underlying the COR model and its relationship to affective commitment is that someone with high levels of affective commitment will have more resources invested in the organization. These resources come in many forms, from social relationships to the personal identity that has developed as a result of working in the organization. Because of this high level of resource investment among those with higher affective commitment, they will work to maximize the investment of their resources (by working harder, including a greater likelihood of contextual performance). Meyer and Allen (1997) suggested that committed employees would be likely to direct their attention to work performance that the employees perceive to be valued by the organization. This suggests that employees are selectively investing their resources in a manner that will be most likely to maximize them, in this case by performing behaviors, whether task or contextual, that are valued by the organization.

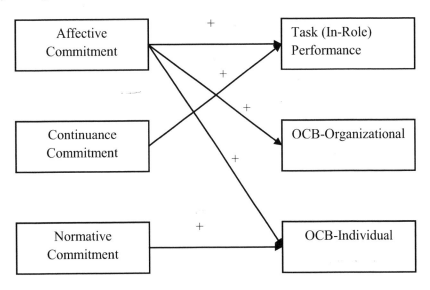

Figure 1. Hypothesized Relationships between Commitment and Performance

As noted earlier, OCB are extra-role behaviors that that are "discretionary, not directly or explicitly recognized by the formal reward system, and in aggregate promotes the efficient and effective functioning of the organization" (Organ, 1988, p. 4; see also Bateman & Organ, 1983). When directed toward the organization (OCB-O), employees engage in behaviors that include actions such as adhering to informal organizational rules and putting in extra effort to aid the company (e.g., working extra hours). On the other hand, when employees direct extra-role behavior toward the individual (OCB-I), sometimes referred to as altruism (Moorman, 1993) or interpersonal citizenship behavior (Settoon & Mossholder, 2003), they engage in behaviors such as helping coworkers after an absence and taking time to listen to coworkers concerns (Williams & Anderson, 1991). OCB-I actions enhance organizational performance indirectly as these actions positively influence coworker and group performance levels. In the case of affective commitment, we expect that increased affective commitment will lead to increases in both OCB-O and OCB-I, as workers seek to invest resources by going above and beyond for those beneficiaries that share their values. Additionally, because task performance is explicitly linked to the reward system in an organization, we would expect that those with affective commitment would be more likely to invest performance resources in task performance as well.

*Hypothesis 1: Increased affective commitment will be associated with higher levels of task performance, OCB-O, and OCB-I.*

## Continuance Commitment

Continuance commitment is commitment that is based on need; those high in continuance commitment stay with organizations for the sake of keeping a job (Meyer & Allen, 1991). In terms of the COR model, one would expect that those employees with only high levels of continuance commitment will minimally invest resources, in the form of task performance, but would not be expected to engage in contextual performance. The COR model is consistent with Becker's (1960) side-bet theory of commitment. Becker argued that commitment develops as a result of side-bets (investments) a person makes. This theory has been most readily applied to continuance commitment, suggesting that employees make investments in organizations (e.g., training for specialized skills) that would lose their value if they left the organization. A number of studies have found empirical support for the notion that side-bets are associated with higher levels of continuance commitment (cf., Allen & Meyer, 1990; Whitener & Walz, 1993).

While both the COR model and side-bet theory rely on the notion of investment, side-bet theory has been primarily utilized to understand the relationship between commitment and turnover. On the other hand, the more general COR model focuses on the manner in which employees invest their resources rather than the outcome of staying on a job or leaving it. As such, the COR model addresses the question of what employees do on the job once they have determined that their side-bets are too great to justify leaving the position. One would expect that those individuals would engage in job performance behaviors that are different from employees who are not staying with the organization simply for the sake of keeping a job. Specifically, based on the COR model, one would expect employees to maintain basic levels of task (in-role) performance, because such an investment would allow the employee to maintain his or her job status. However, one would not expect employees with higher levels of continuance commitment to engage in contextual performance behaviors, since such behaviors would not yield a return in investment that the employee seeks.

*Hypothesis 2: Increased continuance commitment will be associated with higher levels of task performance.*

## Normative Commitment

Normative commitment is based on feelings of obligation to remain with the organization, often because of relationships developed with those in the organization (Meyer & Allen, 1991). The COR model suggests that those employees with increased normative commitment would be associated with more targeted investment in resources, which would lead people to engage in contextual performance in the form of OCB-I (but not necessarily those directed at the organization). The rationale for such behavior is that resources would be best invested in further fostering the relationships developed in the organization. One way to foster such relationships is to engage in behavior that is specifically directed at others in the organization.

*Hypothesis 3: Increased normative commitment will be associated with higher OCB-I.*

# STUDY 1

## Method

### *Participants and Procedure*
The participants in this study were 239 managerial employees at a large, publicly-traded telecommunications firm. The participants worked at two different locations, in one of three company divisions. They represented a variety of pay grades within the organization. Because of strong confidentiality concerns of the telecommunications firm during its performance evaluation process, we were not provided with information regarding gender, age, race, or other demographics from the members of the sample.

The managers were asked to complete the commitment measure in the study during working hours. With their permission, their next supervisory performance appraisal was accessed from their personnel file, which served as the assessment of performance. The time between the collection of the commitment measure and supervisor performance rating was 2-3 days.

## Measures

*Organizational Commitment*. We assessed organizational commitment using the 15-item Organizational Commitment Questionnaire (OCQ; Mowday, Steers, & Porter, 1979). We divided the items of the OCQ into affective and continuance commitment subscales based on the work of Ahktar and Tan (1994).

- **Performance**. Performance was assessed using the supervisory performance appraisal of each manager. The company's performance appraisal system was a multidimensional system that rated performance on decision-making, supervising and developing, performance appraisal and feedback, job responsiveness and flexibility, interpersonal effectiveness, leadership, planning and organizing, communication, job knowledge, and financial management.
- To determine which of the performance dimensions reflected task and contextual performance, we asked three individuals with doctoral degrees in either management (organizational behavior) or industrial/organizational psychology to sort the ten performance dimensions based descriptions of task and contextual performance as provided by Borman and Motowidlo (1993). All three sorters were not directly involved in the research project and did not have prior

knowledge of the research hypotheses. Generally speaking, the initial sort task led to consistent results, with a percentage agreement among the three sorters of 86%. Following the initial sort, the three individuals discussed the differences in their individual sorts and came to a consensus regarding a final grouping of the performance dimensions. Based on this exercise, it was determined that the decision-making, supervising and developing, performance appraisal and feedback, planning and organizing, communication, and job knowledge dimensions were deemed task performance and the job responsiveness and flexibility, interpersonal effectiveness, leadership, and financial management dimensions were deemed contextual performance dimensions.

## Results

The means, standard deviations, internal consistency estimates (Cronbach's $\alpha$), and correlations of variables are reported in Table 1. To test the hypotheses of the study, separate multiple regression analyses for each of the performance types (task and contextual) were undertaken (see Table 2).

**Table 1-Study 1 Descriptive Statistics**

|  | Mean | SD | 1. | 2. | 3. | 4. |
|---|---|---|---|---|---|---|
| 1. Affective Commitment | 5.71 | 1.19 | .84 |  |  |  |
| 2. Continuance Commitment | 5.47 | 1.12 | .53** | .73 |  |  |
| 3. Task Performance | 2.24 | .30 | .21** | .067 | .76 |  |
| 4. Contextual Performance | 2.25 | .34 | .17* | .29*** | .86*** | .70 |

*Note*: Numbers on the diagonal (and in bold font) are internal consistency estimates (Cronbach's alpha).

Hypothesis 1 predicted that affective commitment would be associated with both task performance and contextual performance. In support of that hypothesis, we found that affective commitment was associated both with task performance ($\beta$ = .21, $p$ < .001) and contextual performance ($\beta$ = .08, $p$ < .001). Hypothesis 2 predicted that continuance commitment would be associated with only task performance. In support of that hypothesis, we found that continuance commitment was associated with task performance ($\beta$ = .06, $p$ = .0016) but not contextual performance ($\beta$ = .006, $p$ = .76).

**Table 2- Study 1 Regression Results**

| β | | Standard Error | F | p |
|---|---|---|---|---|
| Criterion: Task Performance ($R^2 = .046$) | | | | |
| *Affective Commitment* | .21 | .020 | 21.31 | <.0001 |
| Continuance Commitment | .06 | .019 | 10.17 | .0016 |
| Criterion: Contextual Performance ($R^2 = .084$) | | | | |
| *Affective Commitment* | .08 | .022 | 14.14 | .0002 |
| Continuance Commitment | .0065 | .021 | 0.0961 | .76 |

## Discussion

Generally speaking, this study supported Hypotheses 1 and 2, with a finding that affective commitment was associated with both task and contextual performance and that continuance commitment was only associated with task performance. Such findings support the notion of targeted investment of resources (in the form of performance behaviors) as a result of different types of commitment to the organization.

## Limitations

We recognize that there are a number of limitations that temper our confidence in the conclusions we can draw from Study 1 alone. First, the data are essentially cross-sectional, as there was a limited time between the assessment of commitment and the performance appraisal process. Second, the post-hoc separation of the performance dimensions into task and contextual performance and the OCQ, while based on previous empirical research, into affective and continuance commitment is not ideal. Third, data concerning normative commitment were not collected; as such, we are unable to draw conclusions with regard to hypothesis 3. Finally, because of the limited demographic information provided and because the participants all held managerial positions at one company, we are limited in the extent to which we can generalize the findings to other workers in other situations. To address these issues, we conducted Study 2.

# STUDY 2

## Method

### Participants and Procedure

- The participants in Study 2 included 395 working adults. The sample included 157 males and 228 females (10 participants did not indicate gender) with a mean age of 38.99 (SD = 10.82) years of age. The participants had held their current positions for an average of 5.05 years (SD = 5.37) and had been working for their current organization for 7.84 years

(SD = 7.59). A wide variety of industries were represented, including education ($n = 51$), health care ($n = 36$), banking or financial services ($n = 28$), government ($n = 24$), manufacturing ($n = 20$), retail ($n = 18$), and telecommunications ($n = 14$). Data from seven participants was not analyzed due to incomplete surveys, leaving a final sample of 388 participants.

- We used a modification of the snowball sampling technique that many organizational scholars have recently used in organizational settings, especially when used in conjunction with samples drawn from a single organization (Ferris, Treadway, Kolodinsky, Hochwarter, Kacmar, & Douglas, in press; Kolodinsky, Hochwarter, & Ferris, in press). As a part of a class assignment meant to integrate the research experience with the classroom experience, management students were given measurement packets to distribute to three working adults at two points during the semester (with approximately two months separating time 1 and time 2 data collection). Along with completing the measurement packet, the participants in this study were also asked to give a short survey to his or her supervisor and his or her closest coworker. The supervisor and coworker surveys were returned directly to the participant in signed and sealed envelopes. Once the survey packet was completed by the participant, coworker, and supervisor, it was returned to the students, who then returned the survey packets to us. To ensure that the surveys were indeed completed by the working adults, we randomly selected 35 percent of the surveys and directly contacted the participant to verify their participation. We asked the participants a series of questions, such as tenure with the organization and the position, to verify the voracity of the data. All of the participants we contacted verified that they had completed the survey (and received surveys from their supervisor and coworker).

## Measures

*Organizational Commitment.* We assessed organizational commitment using the scales created by Meyer and Allen (1997). The scales measure affective (six items), continuance (seven items), and normative commitment (six items).

*Performance.* We assessed different types of performance by utilizing the performance measure developed by Williams and Anderson (1991). It is a 21-item, five-point Likert-scale measure that assesses task performance behaviors and contextual performance behaviors, both OCB-I behaviors and OCB-O behaviors. This measure was completed by the participant, his or her supervisor, and his or her closest coworker. For each seven-question subscale (in-role performance, OCB-I, and OCB-O), we mean aggregated the items to create each performance subscale.

## Results

The means, standard deviations, internal consistency estimates (Cronbach's $\alpha$), and correlations of variables are reported in Table 3. To test the hypotheses of the study, structural equations modeling was performed using PROC CALIS in SAS version 8.

### *Goodness of Fit of Proposed Model and Alternatives*

Several goodness-of-fit indices were used to assess the overall fit of the proposed model: the Comparative Fit Index (CFI; Bentler, 1990), the Tucker-Lewis Index (TLI; Bentler & Bonett, 1980), Akike's Information Criterion (AIC; Akaike, 1987), the Bayesian Criterion (BIC), and the Root Mean Squared Error of Approximation (RMSEA) with confidence intervals. For the CFI, IFI, and TLI, values of .95 or above indicate a model with acceptable fit (Hu & Bentler, 1999; Bentler & Bonett, 1980). For the RMSEA, values of .06 or less indicate a well-fitting model (Hu & Bentler, 1999). The AIC and BIC are used for model comparison purposes, where lower index scores indicate a better fitting model. The fit statistics for the structural models can be found in Table 4.

The proposed model yielded an acceptable degree of fit to the data in (see Table 4). However, to test for the possibility that other structural models would also provide reasonable fit and to rule out possible alternative explanations, we tested three alternative models. The first alternative (Alternative 1 in Table 4) that we tested was a model that included additional paths from all of the forms of commitment to all of the types of performance. The rationale behind this model is that it would provide greater fit to the extent that paths not predicted by the COR model described significant relationships between commitment and performance. A second alternative (Alternative 2 in Table 4) was tested that collapsed OCB-O and OCB-I into one single contextual performance score (through mean aggregation). Paths were then tested from affective commitment and continuance commitment to task performance and affective commitment and normative commitment to contextual performance. The rationale for this model was that the more general conceptualization of contextual performance may be more parsimonious in explaining the effects of commitment than separating the two types of OCB. As indicated by the fit statistics in Table 4, neither of the alternative models provided as strong a fit as did the proposed model.

### *Parameter Estimates*

Hypothesis 1 had predicted that affective commitment would be positively related to task and contextual performance. In support of Hypothesis 1, significant positive relationships were found between affective commitment and task performance (path coefficients of .36, .27, and .25 for self-, supervisor, and coworker ratings, respectively), OCB-O (.25, .28, .12) and OCB-I (.32, .31, .26, see Figure). Specifically, as participants reported higher levels of affective commitment, they were more likely to engage in higher quality task and contextual performance.

## Table 3- Study 2 Descriptive Statistics

| | Mean | SD | 1. | 2. | 3. | 4. | 5. | 6. | 7. | 8. | 9. | 10. | 11. | 12. |
|---|---|---|---|---|---|---|---|---|---|---|---|---|---|---|
| 1. Affective Commitment | 3.36 | .75 | **.79** | | | | | | | | | | | |
| 2. Continuance Commitment | 3.14 | .64 | -.043 | **.70** | | | | | | | | | | |
| 3. Normative Commitment | 3.23 | .75 | .72*** | .14** | **.78** | | | | | | | | | |
| 4. In-Role Performance (Self) | 3.73 | .56 | .36*** | -.12* | .06 | **.69** | | | | | | | | |
| 5. OCB-O (Self) | 4.18 | .63 | .25*** | -.098 | .10 | .62** | **.83** | | | | | | | |
| 6. OCB-I (Self) | 3.84 | .79 | .51*** | -.044 | .44*** | .55*** | .48*** | **.91** | | | | | | |
| 7. In-Role Performance | 3.77 | .63 | .25*** | -.020 | .07 | .46** | .41*** | .37*** | **.74** | | | | | |
| 8. OCB-O (Coworker) | 4.13 | .69 | .12* | .0097 | .13* | .35** | .46*** | .28** | .64*** | **.84** | | | | |
| 9. OCB-I (Coworker) | 3.83 | .85 | .40*** | .044 | .39*** | .34** | .27*** | .69*** | .62*** | .57*** | **.92** | | | |
| 10. In-Role Performance | 3.72 | .64 | .27*** | -.15** | .08 | .35** | .32*** | .26*** | .37*** | .35* | .27*** | **.77** | | |
| 11. OCB-O (Supervisor) | 4.10 | .69 | .18** | -.10* | .15* | .34** | .47*** | .28*** | .34*** | .49*** | .28*** | .64*** | **.84** | |
| 12. OCB-I (Supervisor) | 3.75 | .80 | .41*** | -.062 | .39*** | .31** | .28*** | .70*** | .33*** | .33*** | .69*** | .58*** | .55*** | **.90** |

*Note*: Numbers on the diagonal (and in bold font) are internal consistency estimates (Cronbach's alpha).

**Table 4.-Fit Statistics for Structural Equations Model Comparisons from Study 2**

Self Performance Ratings

| Model | $\chi^2$ | df | GFI | CFI | TLI | AIC | BIC | RMSEA | RMSEA 90% CI |
|---|---|---|---|---|---|---|---|---|---|
| Proposed Model | 4.14 | 4 | .99 | .99 | .99 | -3.86 | -19.67 | .01 | .00-.078 |
| Alternative 1 | 268.29 | 3 | .80 | .66 | .70 | 262.29 | 250.44 | .48 | .43-.53 |
| Alternative 2 | 184.65 | 3 | .87 | .71 | .04 | 178.65 | 166.80 | .40 | .35-.45 |

Supervisor Performance Ratings

| Model | $\chi^2$ | df | GFI | CFI | TLI | AIC | BIC | RMSEA | RMSEA 90% CI |
|---|---|---|---|---|---|---|---|---|---|
| Proposed Model | 4.89 | 4 | .96 | .99 | 1.00 | -5.06 | -20.71 | .01 | .00-.069 |
| Alternative 1 | 383.17 | 3 | .74 | .50 | .52 | 377.17 | 365.42 | .59 | .54-.64 |
| Alternative 2 | 211.67 | 3 | .85 | .64 | .19 | 205.67 | 193.88 | .43 | .38-.48 |

Coworker Performance Ratings

| Model | $\chi^2$ | df | GFI | CFI | TLI | AIC | BIC | RMSEA | RMSEA 90% CI |
|---|---|---|---|---|---|---|---|---|---|
| Proposed Model | 5.59 | 4 | .99 | .99 | .99 | -2.41 | -18.12 | .03 | .00-.089 |
| Alternative 1 | 332.02 | 3 | .77 | .56 | .54 | 326.02 | 314.23 | .54 | .49-.59 |
| Alternative 2 | 129.94 | 3 | .89 | .73 | .12 | 123.94 | 112.20 | .34 | .29-.39 |

Hypothesis 2 predicted that continuance commitment would be positively related to task performance and not related to contextual performance. Contrary to our expectations, significant negative relationships were found between continuance commitment and task performance regardless of rating source (path coefficients of -.04, -.04, and -.04 for self-, supervisor, and coworker ratings, respectively, see Figure 2). This suggests that as participants reported greater levels of continuance commitment, they had lower task performance. The second clause of Hypothesis 2 was supported, however, in our finding that models with paths between continuance commitment and contextual performance provided significantly lower fit than models without such paths, suggesting that there is not a relationship between continuance commitment and contextual performance. Overall, we found partial support for Hypothesis 2.

Finally, Hypothesis 3 proposed that normative commitment would be positively related to organizational citizenship behaviors that are targeted toward individuals within the organization. In support of Hypothesis 3, significant positive relationships were found between normative commitment and OCB-I (.27, .13, and .17 for self-, supervisor, and coworker ratings, respectively, see Figure 2).

## Discussion

- This study found general support for the hypotheses derived from the COR model to explain the relationship between commitment and performance. We found that affective commitment was positively related to task performance and both types of contextual performance (supporting Hypothesis

    i.    Continuance commitment was negatively related to task performance and not related to contextual performance (partially supporting Hypothesis and that

    ii.   Normative commitment was positively related to a specific type of contextual performance, organizational citizenship behaviors targeted toward individuals (supporting Hypothesis

    iii.  3).Interestingly, continuance commitment was not positively related to task performance as had been predicted in Hypothesis 2, particularly given the findings of Study 1 (which found a positive relationship between continuance commitment and task performance).

- While this was unexpected, it is not inconsistent with past literature, which has found variation in the relationship between continuance commitment and job performance (cf., Hackett, Bycio, & Hausdorf, 1994; Konovsky & Cropanzano, 1991; Meyer et al., 1989). This suggests that there are exogenous factors involved in the relationship that have not yet been considered by researchers. The COR model suggests a number of possibilities, including the potential that employees are more selective in how they invest their resources when experiencing continuance commitment. For example, employees may seek to invest resources where they see the most potential for benefit *on their next job*, including investing in training and political relationships. Such activities may (e.g., training) or may not (e.g., networking) be unrelated to task performance, leading to inconsistent results. Future research that explores the specific nature with which employees invest their resources would be valuable in adding clarity to the continuance commitment-performance relationship.

• Study 2 mitigates a number of the limitations in Study 1 (and previous research) to allow for greater confidence in the findings. First, by using multiple sources of performance information, the likelihood of common method bias is significantly reduced. Second, by collecting the data over a two-month period, we have greater confidence in the appropriate causal ordering of the variables. Finally, this study uses different operationalizations of both commitment and job performance.

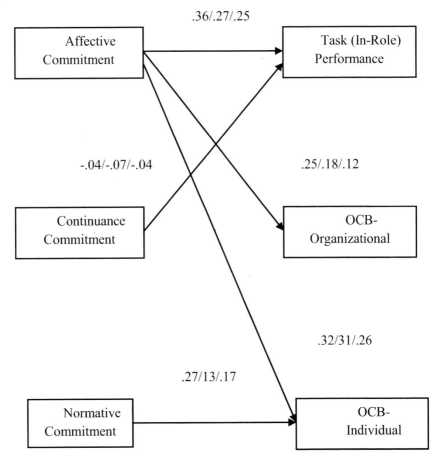

Figure 2-Parameter Estimates from Study 2

*Note*: Parameter estimates are standardized. Estimates are ordered self/supervisor/coworker rated performance.

## General Discussion

In summary, the two studies presented found support for the notion that affective commitment was related to task and contextual performance and moderate support for the prediction that continuance commitment was related to task performance but not contextual performance. Additionally, Study 2 found that normative commitment was related to a specific form of contextual performance that involves citizenship behaviors targeted toward individuals within an organization.

This research extends the literature in a number of important ways. First, it introduces a novel theoretical framework to increase our understanding of the relationship between organizational commitment and performance. The COR model grounds our understanding of commitment in terms of resource investment by employees, leading to important predictions regarding the behavior of employees given their commitment to organizations. While the COR model has its roots in the stress and burnout literature, it clearly has plausible applications in other areas of organizational behavior.

The relationship between the COR model and social exchange theory (e.g., Blau, 1964; Gouldner, 1960) is noteworthy. A number of researchers have considered the relationship between commitment and other important variables (e.g., psychological contracts, perceived organizational support) in terms of social exchange theory (Aselage & Eisenberger, 2003; Fuller, Barnett, Hester, & Relyea, 2003; Ganzach, Pazy, Ohayun, & Brainin, 2002; Johnson & O'Leary-Kelly, 2003). Indeed, the COR model complements and extends social exchange theory by offering a social cognitive explanation (resource investment) for the manner in which individuals develop, maintain, and react to their social exchange relationships. Social exchange theory has typically been utilized to understand the processes leading to the development of commitment (cf., Johnson & O'Leary-Kelly, 2003), but is less precise in predicting the outcomes of commitment. For example, social exchange theory could suggest relationships between all three types of commitment and all three types of performance; in fact, McNeely and Meglino (1994) argued that it is important to consider the complexities of the exchange partnership in understanding the effects of social exchange (see also Settoon, Bennett, & Liden, 1996). On the other hand, when considering the dynamics of resource investment, we can provide a more precise model that underscores the nuanced relationship between different types of commitment and different types of performance.

Second, the present research provided us with more confidence in the causal relationship between variables. Other research in this area has been cross-sectional (cf., Chen & Francesco, 2003) limiting our ability to appropriately order the causal relationship between commitment and performance. We recognize, however, the possibility of a reciprocal relationship between commitment and performance. Meyer and Allen (1997) noted that affective performance develops in part because of positive work experiences at work. To the extent that performance is rewarded at work, it may lead to further development of commitment. Research designs (e.g., time series analyses) that can explore such a relationship are needed to address this important possibility.

Third, Study 2 incorporated coworker ratings of performance; coworkers have been an underutilized source of performance ratings in commitment-performance studies. Given that coworkers are often considered an accurate source of performance information about employees (cf., Yammarino & Atwater, 1997), more research is needed that utilizes coworkers for performance ratings. Moreover, the present research found marked consistency across the three performance rating sources, leading to greater confidence in our findings. Finally, the present study also investigated normative commitment, which has been rare in organizational commitment research, particularly in terms of its influence on performance (Meyer & Allen, 1997). Moreover, the conservation of resources model helps to theoretically integrate the effects of normative commitment with affective and continuance commitment to help explain performance patterns in organizations.

## Implications for Theory and Practice

This research also has a number of important implications for managing employee performance. It suggests that high quality performance can be facilitated through the development of higher affective commitment. Meyer and Allen (1997) have summarized the literature regarding development of affective commitment, concluding that some of the more important antecedents to affective commitment include making an employee feel as though he or she is supported, treated fairly, and valuable to the organization. These antecedents fit with the COR model, which would suggest that to the extent the organization can provide these resources to its employees, the employees will in turn reinvest in the organization through higher performance. Meyer and Allen also noted the importance of fulfillment of personal needs as an antecedent to affective commitment, again consistent with the notion that commitment is the result of accumulating resources within an employee (see also Cook & Wall, 1980).

For practicing managers, this thinking suggests that managers who treat their employees fairly, offer support, and underscore the value of employees to their organization will foster higher levels of affective commitment in their employees. This, in turn, will lead to higher levels of performance, most notably contextual performance behaviors that aid the organization but are not expected of the employee (cf., Settoon et al., 1996). Moreover, it will lead to reduced turnover among employees and lower levels of stress and burnout. (Halbesleben & Buckley, in press)

In an era when organizations and employees both seem increasingly focused on flexibility, mobility, and "rightsizing," this research renews emphasis on the development of commitment and its potential for positive outcomes (Emshoff, 1994). Interestingly, this research brings up an important question of interest to those utilizing contingent workers as a strategy for flexibility. Gossett (2002) recently proposed that developing commitment may lead to wasted resources when utilizing workers (such as contingent workers) that would not remain with the organization in the long-term. In light of the present research, such a conclusion may be premature. To the extent that commitment, particularly affective, is related to job performance, it may be useful to develop some levels of affective commitment in all employees. Future research that explores the nature of commitment and its relationship to the conservation of resources among contingent workers would be particularly useful in addressing this emerging issue.

## Limitations

It is important to note some of the limitations of the present research. First, we did not administer the same commitment scale to both samples. We used the OCQ in Study 1, which does not cleanly differentiate between affective and continuance commitment or measure normative commitment. Although we did separate the OCQ based on the work of Ahktar and Tan (1994), we felt that this separation was not optimal. Therefore, we measured commitment in Study 2 using Meyer and Allen's (1991) multidimensional measure. While we would have liked to administer both commitment measures to each sample, the constraints of conducting field research in an organization (e.g., confidentiality, time, resources) did not afford that opportunity. Thus, the shortcomings of Study 1 provided the impetus for us to conduct Study 2. It is also important to note that we did not collect commensurate indicators of performance in Study 1 and Study 2. While the telecommunications organization that granted us access to participants in Study 1 allowed us to examine employee performance appraisals, the nature of the data collection effort to obtain participants for Study 2 did not afford us the ability to collect actual performance appraisal information. Thus, we used a self-report performance measure to collect this data; however, we mitigated concerns regarding the accuracy of participants' self-reported performance ratings by supplementing the self-report data with peer and supervisor performance ratings of the target employee. We believe that this multisource performance data enhances construct validity in our study and the use of a previously published performance measure allows for some comparison across similar studies conducted in the future.

Second, as an initial test of the COR model, this study has been intentionally kept relatively simple. Certainly, there are myriad variables that influence the processes underlying commitment and performance in organizations. For example, one might expect that social support might moderate the relationship between normative commitment and performance, whereby employees who are high in normative commitment and perceive social support will be more likely to engage in OCB-I. On the other hand, employees who have high normative commitment but perceive low social support would have little reason to invest social resources in OCB-I or other behaviors that would further develop the relationship. Future research should seek to examine commitment and resource investment in the more general literature concerning organizational citizenship and social support networks (e.g., Bowler & Brass, 2003).

One could argue that trust is also likely to play a role in the process. Indeed, a number of researchers (e.g., Aryee, Budwhar, & Chen, 2002; Cook & Wall, 1980) have suggested that trust is an antecedent to organizational commitment. Trust is also likely to play a role in the likelihood of investing resources in performance, particularly in terms of engaging in OCB-I. Whether or not someone invests resources, in the form of performance behaviors, is largely a matter of whether or not they trust that those resources will be reciprocated in kind. As such, future research that incorporates trust as a potential factor in resource investment that stems from commitment will be valuable in expanding our understanding of the relationship between commitment and performance.

In their explication of the concept of normative commitment, Meyer and Allen (1997) noted that normative commitment could be related to individual relationships with employees, as we have focused it, or an obligation to "stick with" an organization. Such an orthogonal relationship between employee-employer exchange and employee-employee exchange has been suggested by prior research in organizational citizenship behavior as well (Bowler & Brass, 2003; Halbesleben & Bowler, in press). As such, one could argue that in the latter form of normative commitment, one might expect higher OCB-O rather than OCB-I. Indeed, the data from study 2 suggest significant correlations between normative commitment and OCB-O; however, the correlations are much lower than those between normative commitment and OCB-I. Moreover, when a path is added to the structural equation models from normative commitment and OCB-O, it has a menial influence on the findings. Research that considers the potential multidimensionality of normative commitment and its relationship with extra-role performance may further inform this issue.

Moreover, researchers (cf., Wright & Bonett, 2002) have noted that organizational tenure plays a key role in the commitment-performance relationship, we did not account for such effects in our study. However, despite the parsimonious nature of this study, its findings are suggestive of the value of the COR model in predicting outcomes of commitment, particularly to the extent that the COR model can integrate the multidimensional characterization of the commitment construct.

## FUTURE RESEARCH & CONCLUSION

An implicit theme in much of the present effort has been the role of political behavior in organizations and its relationship to commitment and performance. Using the COR framework, one might better understand how employees invest their resources in order to maximize outcomes. For example, political skill might serve as an important moderator to the commitment-performance relationship, where those who are politically skilled and committed to their organization (e.g., affective commitment) may engage in behaviors that benefit themselves and the organization (e.g., OCB-O). Conversely, those who are politically skilled and not committed to their organization (e.g., continuance commitment) may engage in behaviors that benefit themselves but not the organization. Finally, those who do not have political skill may not be as effective in resource investment and not see the accompanying return in terms of higher performance ratings.

The study of organizational commitment and its relationship to job performance remains important. Meyer and Allen (1991) encouraged such research, suggesting that the manner in which employees perform on the job is important to understand in terms of commitment, as is at least as important as the relationship between commitment and turnover. We have attempted to provide a new theoretical framework to the relationship between commitment and performance by extending the conservation of resources model from the stress literature to understand commitment and performance in terms of resource investment by employees. Such a theoretical framework, and the accompanying empirical support for it, helps to clarify the relationship between these two important organizational variables. Further, knowledge of these relationships has important implications for managers as they seek to positively influence the performance of individuals in organizations.

# REFERENCES

Adkins, C. L. 1995. Previous work experience and organizational socialization: A longitudinal examination. *Academy of Management Journal,* 38: 839-862.

Akaike, H. 1987. Factor analysis and AIC. *Psychometrika,* 52: 317-332.

Akhtar, S., & Tan, D. 1994. Reassessing and reconceptualizing the multidimensional nature of organizational commitment. *Psychological Reports,* 75: 1379-1390.

Allen, N. J., & Meyer, J. P. 1990. The measurement and antecedents of affective, continuance, and normative commitment to the organization. *Journal of Occupational Psychology,* 63: 1-18.

Angle, H., & Lawson, M. B. 1994. Organizational commitment and employees' performance ratings: Both type of commitment and type of performance count. *Psychological Reports,* 75: 1539-1551.

Angle, H., & Perry, J. 1981. An empirical assessment of organizational commitment and organizational effectiveness. *Administrative Science Quarterly,* 26: 1-14.

Aryee, S., Budhwar, P. S., & Chen, Z. X. 2002. Trust as a mediator of the relationship between organizational justice and work outcomes: Test of a social exchange model. *Journal of Organizational Behavior,* 23: 267-286.

Aselage, J., & Eisenberger, R. 2003. Perceived organizational support and psychological contracts: A theoretical integration. *Journal of Organizational Behavior,* 24: 491-509.

Bateman, T. S., & Organ, D. W. 1983. Job satisfaction and the good soldier. *Academy of Management Journal,* 26: 587-595.

Bauer, T. N., & Green, S. G. 1998. Testing the combined effects of newcomer information seeking and manager behavior on socialization. *Journal of Applied Psychology,* 83: 72-83.

Baugh, S. G., & Roberts, R. M. 1994. Professional and organizational commitment among engineers: Conflicting or complementary? *IEEE Transactions on Engineering Management,* 41: 108-114.

Becker, H. S. 1960. Notes on the concept of commitment. *American Journal of Sociology,* 66: -42.

Bentler, P. M. 1990. Comparative fit indexes in structural models. *Psychological Bulletin,* 107: 238–246.

Bentler, P. M., & Bonett, D. G. 1980. Significance tests and goodness of fit in analysis of covariance structures. *Psychological Bulletin,* 88: 588-606.

Blau, G. J., & Boal, K. B. 1987. Conceptualizing how job involvement and organizational commitment affect turnover and absenteeism. *Academy of Management Review,* 12: 288-300.

Blau, P. 1964. *Exchange and Power in Social Life.* New York, Wiley.

Borman, W. C., & Motowidlo, S. J. 1993. Expanding the criterion domain to include elements of contextual performance. In N. Schmitt and W. Borman (Eds), *Personnel selection in organizations* (pp. 71-98). New York: Jossey-Bass.

Borman, W.C., & Motowidlo, S.J. 1997. Task performance and contextual performance: The meaning for personnel selection research. *Human Performance,* 10: 99-109.

Bowler, W. M., & Brass, D. J. 2003. Relational determinants of interpersonal citizenship behavior: A social network perspective on organizational citizenship behavior. *Best Paper Proceedings of the Academy of Management Annual Meetings, Seattle, WA.*

Bycio, P., Hackett, R. D., & Allen, J. S. 1995. Further assessment of Bass's (1985) conceptualization of transactional and transformational leadership. *Journal of Applied Psychology,* 80: 468-478.

Chen, Z. X., & Francesco, A. M. 2003. The relationship between the three components of commitment and employee performance in China. *Journal of Vocational Behavior,* 62: 490-510.

Cohen, A. 1991. Career stage as a moderator of the relationships between organizational commitment and its outcomes: A meta-analysis. *Journal of Occupational Psychology,* 64: 253-268.

Cohen, A. 1993. Organizational commitment and turnover: A meta-analysis. *Academy of Management Journal,* 36: 1140-1157.

Cook, J., & Wall, T. 1980. New work attitude measures of trust, organizational commitment, and personal need non-fulfillment. *Journal of Occupational Psychology,* 53: 39-52.

Darden, W. R., Hampton, R., & Howell, R. D. 1989. Career versus organizational commitment: Antecedents and consequences of retail salespeoples' commitment. *Journal of Retailing, 65:* 80-106.

DeCotiis, T. A., & Summers, T. P. 1987. A path analysis of a model of the antecedents and consequences of organizational commitment. *Human Relations,* 40: 445-470.

Emshoff, J. R. 1994. How to increase employee loyalty while you downsize. *Business Horizons,* 37: 49-57.

Ferris, G.R., Treadway, D.C., Kolodinsky, R.W., Hochwarter, W.A., Kacmar, C.J., & Douglas, C. In press. Development and validation of the political skill inventory. *Journal of Management.*

Fuller, J. B., Barnett, T., Hester, K., & Relyea, C. 2003. A social identity perspective on the relationship between perceived organizational support and commitment. *Journal of Social Psychology,* 143: 789-791.

Ganzach, Y., Pazy, A., Ohayun, Y., & Brainin, E. 2002. Social exchange and organizational commitment: Decision-making training for job choice as an alternative to the realistic job preview. *Personnel Psychology,* 55: 613-637.

Ganster, D. C., & Dwyer, D. J. 1995. The effects of understaffing on individual and group performance in professional and trade occupations. *Journal of Management,* 21: 175-190.

Gossett, L. M. 2002. Kept at arm's length: Questioning the organizational desirability of member identification. *Communication Monographs,* 69: 385-404.

Gouldner, A. W. 1960. The norm of reciprocity: A preliminary statement. *American Sociological Review,* 25: 161-178.

Hackett, R. D., Bycio, P., & Hausdorf, P. A. 1994. Further assessments of Meyer and Allen's (1991) three-component model of organizational commitment. *Journal of Applied Psychology,* 79: 15-23.

Halbesleben, J. R. B., & Bowler, W. M. In press. Organizational citizenship behaviors and burnout. In D. L. Turnipseed (Ed.). *A handbook on organizational citizenship behavior: A review of 'good soldier' activity in organizations.* Hauppauge, NY: Nova Science Publishers.

Halbesleben, J. R. B., & Buckley, M. R. In press. Burnout in organizational life. *Journal of Management.*

Hobfoll, S. E. 1988. *The ecology of stress.* New York: Hemisphere.

Hobfoll, S. E. 1989. Conservation of resources: A new attempt at conceptualizing stress. *American Psychologist,* 44: 513-524.

Hobfoll, S. E. 1998. *Stress, culture, and community.* New York: Plenum.

Hobfoll, S. E. 2001. The influence of culture, community, and the nested-self in the stress process: Advancing conservation of resources theory. *Applied Psychology: An International Review,* 50: 337-421.

Hobfoll, S. E., & Freedy, J. 1993. Conservation of resources: A general stress theory applied to burnout. In W. B. Schaufeli, C. Maslach, & T. Marek (Eds.). *Professional burnout: Recent developments in theory and research* (pp. 115-129). Washington, DC: Taylor & Francis.

Hu, L-T., & Bentler, P.M. 1999. Cutoff criteria for fit indexes in covariance structure analysis: Conventional criteria versus new alternatives. *Structural Equation Modeling,* 6: 1-55.

Ingram, T. N., Lee, K. S., & Skinner, S. 1989. An empirical assessment of salesperson motivation, commitment, and job outcomes. *Journal of Personal Selling and Sales Management,* 9: 25-33.

Jaros, S. J. 1997. As assessment of Meyer and Allen's (1991) three-component assessment of organizational commitment and turnover intentions. *Journal of Vocational Behavior,* 51: 319-337.

Johnson, J. L. & O'Leary-Kelly, A. M. 2003. The effects of psychological contract breach and organizational cynicism: Not all social exchange violations are created equally. *Journal of Organizational Behavior,* 24: 627-647.

Johnston, G. P., & Snizek, W. 1991. Combining head and heart in complex organizations: A test of Etzioni's dual compliance structure hypothesis. *Human Relations,* 44: 1255-1272.

Keller, R. T. 1997. Job involvement and organizational commitment as longitudinal predictors of job performance: A study of scientists and engineers. *Journal of Applied Psychology,* 82: 539-545.

Kolodinsky, R.W., Hochwarter, W.A., & Ferris, G.R. In press. Nonlinearity in the relationship between political skill and work outcomes: Convergent evidence from three studies. *Journal of Vocational Behavior.*

Konovsky, M. A., & Cropanzano, R. 1991. Perceived fairness of employee drug testing as a predictor of employee attitudes and job performance. *Journal of Applied Psychology,* 76: 698-707.

Leong, S. M., Randall, D. M., & Cote, J. A. 1994. Exploring the organizational commitment-performance linkage in marketing: A study of life insurance salespeople. *Journal of Business Research,* 29: 57-63.

Mathieu, J. E., & Zajac, D. M. 1990. A review and meta-analysis of the antecedents, correlates, and consequences of organizational commitment. *Psychological Bulletin,* 108: 171-194.

Mayer, R. C., & Schoorman, F. D. 1992. Predicting participation and production outcomes through a two-dimensional model of organizational commitment. *Academy of Management Journal,* 35: 671-684.

McNeely, B. L., & Meglino, B. M. 1994. The role of dispositional and situational antecedents to prosocial organizational behavior: An examination of intended beneficiaries of prosocial behavior. *Journal of Applied Psychology,* 79: 836-845.

Meyer, J. P., & Allen, N. J. 1991. A three-component conceptualization of organizational commitment. *Human Resource Management Review,* 1: 61-89.

Meyer, J. P., & Allen, N. J. 1997. *Commitment in the workplace: Theory, research, and application.* Thousand Oaks, CA: Sage.

Meyer, J. P., Allen, N. J., & Smith, C. A. 1993. Commitment to organizations and occupations: An extension and test of a three-component conceptualization. *Journal of Applied Psychology,* 78: 538-551.

Meyer, J. P., Paunonen, S. V., Gellatly, I. R., Goffin, R. D., & Jackson, D. N. 1989. Organizational commitment and job performance: It's the nature of the commitment that counts. *Journal of Applied Psychology,* 74: 152-156.

Moorman, R. H. 1993. The influence of cognitive and affective based job satisfaction measures on the relationship between satisfaction and organizational citizenship behavior. *Human Relations,* 46: 759-776.

Moorman, J. H., & Niehoff, B. P., & Organ, D. W. 1993. Treating employees fairly and organizational citizenship behavior: Sorting the effects of job satisfaction, organizational commitment, and procedural justice. *Employee Responsibilities and Rights Journal,* 6: 209-225.

Mowday, R., Steers, R., & Porter, L. 1979. The measurement of organizational commitment. *Journal of Vocational Behavior,* 14: 79-94.

Organ, D. W. 1988. *Organizational citizenship behavior: The good soldier syndrome.* Lexington, MA: Lexington Books.

Organ, D. W., & Konovsky, M. A. 1989. Cognitive versus affective determinants of organizational citizenship behavior. *Journal of Applied Psychology,* 74: 157-164.

Porter, L. W., Steers, R. M., Mowday, R. T., & Boulian, P. V. 1974. Organizational commitment, job satisfaction, and turnover among psychiatric technicians. *Journal of Applied Psychology,* 59: 603-609.

Randall, D. M. 1990. The consequences of organizational commitment: Methodological investigation. *Journal of Organizational Behavior,* 11: 361-378.

Randall, D. M., Fedor, D. B., & Longenecker, C. O. 1990. The behavioral expression of organizational commitment. *Journal of Vocational Behavior,* 36: 210-224.

Riketa, M. 2002. Attitudinal organizational commitment and job performance: A meta-analysis. *Journal of Organizational Behavior,* 23: 257-266.

Sager, J. K., & Johnston, M. W. 1989. Antecedents and outcomes of organizational commitment: A study of salespeople. *Journal of Personal Selling and Sales Management,* 9:30-41.

Saks, A. M. 1995. Longitudinal field investigation of the moderating and mediating effects of self-efficacy on the relationship between training and newcomer adjustment. *Journal of Applied Psychology,* 80: 211-225.

Settoon, R. P, Bennett, N., & Liden, R. C. 1996. Social exchange in organizations: Perceived organizational support, leader-member exchange, and employee reciprocity. *Journal of Applied Psychology,* 81: 219-227.

Settoon, R. P., & Mossholder, K. W. 2002. Relationship quality and relationship context as antecedents of person- and task-focused interpersonal citizenship behavior. *Journal of Applied Psychology*, 87: 255-267.

Shore, L. M., & Wayne, S. J. 1993. Commitment and employee behavior: Comparison of affective commitment and continuance commitment with perceived organizational support. *Journal of Applied Psychology,* 78: 774-780

Smith, C. A., Organ, D. W., & Near, J. P. 1983. Organizational citizenship behavior: Its nature and antecedents. *Journal of Applied Psychology,* 68: 653-663.

Whitener, E. M. & Walz, P. M. 1993. Exchange theory determinants of affective and continuance commitment and turnover. *Journal of Vocational Behavior,* 42: 265-281.

Williams, L. J., & Anderson, S. E. 1991. Job satisfaction and organizational commitment as predictors of organizational citizenship and in-role behaviors. *Journal of Management,* 17: 601-617.

Wright, T. A. 1997. Job performance and organizational commitment. *Perceptual and Motor Skills,* 85: 447-450.

Wright, T. A., & Bonett, D. G. 2002. The moderating effects of employee tenure on the relation between organizational commitment and job performance: A meta-analysis. *Journal of Applied Psychology,* 87: 1183-1190.

Yammarino, F. J., & Atwater, L. E. 1997. Do managers see themselves as others see them? Implications for self-other rating agreement for human resource management. *Organizational Dynamics,* 25: 35-44.

# AUTHOR NOTE

Thanks to Lynn Weber for her assistance in obtaining part of the dataset used in this research. A version if this paper was presented at the 2004 meeting of the Academy of Management in New Orleans, Louisiana.

In: Applied Psychology Research Trends
Editor: Karl H. Kiefer, pp.59-80

ISBN 978-1-60456-372-6
© 2008 Nova Science Publishers, Inc.

*Chapter 3*

# GROUP DIVERSITY AND PERFORMANCE: THE EFFECTS OF DIVERSITY TYPE, CONTEXT AND GROUP COOPERATION

## *Cynthia Lee[1], Chun Hui[2] and Catherine H. Tinsley[3]*

[1] College of Business Administration, Northeastern University, Boston, MA 02115
[2] Department of Management, The Chinese University of Hong Kong, Shatin, Hong Kong
[3] The McDonough School of Business, Georgetown University, Washington, DC 20057

## ABSTRACT

We examine the effects of demographic diversity, skill diversity, and cultural value diversity (specifically, one's value for collectivism) on group cooperation and group performance. Results from a longitudinal study of 79 work groups show that demographic diversity is the least helpful, whereas collectivistic diversity helps group cooperation and performance. Group cooperation acts as a partial mediator, helping to explain the effects of diversity on performance. As expected, the context of the group does matter; specifically, task interdependence and group norms moderate the relationship between demographic diversity and group cooperation. Implications and several future research directions are discussed.

[1] Correspondence to: College oc Business Administration, Northeastern University, Boston, MA 02115
Tel (617) 373-5146, Fax: (617) 373-2491, E-mail: c.lee@neu.edu
[2] Correspondence to: department of Management, The Chinese University of Hong Kong, Shatin, Hong Kong
Tel: (852) 2609-7825, Fax: (852) 2603-5473, E-mail: huichun@cuhk.edu.hk
[3] Correspondence to: School of Business, Georgetown University, Washington, D.C. 20057
Tel (202) 687-2524,Fax (202) 687-4031, E-mail: tinsleyc@georgetown.edu

Diversity, according to Jackson, Joshi, and Erhardt (2003), refers to the distribution of personal attributes among interdependent members of a work unit. With the increasing use of diverse teams and work groups in organizations (e.g., Eby & Dobbins, 1997), the need to understand how such diversity affects group process and performance becomes critical. This need is exacerbated in organizations that conduct business globally because multinational and multicultural diverse teams are a necessity and their effective functioning is a primary concern (Earley & Mosakowski, 2000; Snow, Davison, Snell, & Hambrick, 1996). According to Jackson and Joshi (2002), globalization means that employees are working among a set of colleagues and customers who are internationally diverse. Therefore, it is important to understand how to manager diversity effectively in global contexts. Both a positive (e.g., Cox, Lobel, & McLeod, 1991) and a negative relationship (e.g., Williams & O'Reilly, 1998) between diversity in a group and group performance have been found, however. We suggest that the inconsistent findings can be attributed to constraints imposed by the work settings (Earley & Mosakowski, 2000; McGrath, 1984).

To understand how group diversity affects group performance, we suggest that we need to take into account the type of diversity, the group process, and the context in which the group performs. Team similarity and differences are relative and their meaning is construed within a larger social context (Jackson & Joshi, 2002). Further, Jackson et al. (2003) note that one of the weaknesses in the research on diversity and performance is that people have mostly ignored skill diversity. Another weakness in the diversity research is that demographic similarity is often measured at the individual level of analysis even though it occurs within a group, including the immediate supervisor. As in Hackman (1983), we define a group as an intact, bounded social system, with interdependent members and differentiated member roles that pursue shared, measurable goals. Additionally, a group consists of members reporting to the same supervisor and who are engaged in tasks requiring some degree of coordination (Chattopadhyay, 1999).

We explore three types of diversity in this study— demographic or surface level diversity, deep level diversity of cultural value and heterogeneity in skill. Teams, especially those in MNCs, commonly involve members with different demographics and value and skill differences. We suggest that these diversity types have differential effects on group process and performance. We examine group process by the extent of a group's cooperation and suggest that group process mediates the relationship between diversity type and group performance (Chatman & Flynn, 2001; Chattopadhyay, 1999; Eby & Dobbins, 1997). We also suggest that task interdependence and group norm would jointly moderate the relationship between diversity and group performance. This is extremely important in international contexts as group norms facilitate task-related information exchange. Specifically, we propose that diversity has positive effects on group performance unless the group has a legitimate shared standard against which the appropriateness of behavior can be evaluated (Birenbaum & Sagarin, 1976). Further, task interdependence is a boundary condition that should be taken into account. To our knowledge, this is the first study to examine three types of diversity, group processes, as well as task characteristic and group norms in a single study.

In line with social categorization and similarity-attraction paradigm, members of a group may perceive members of the same category as in-group members so as to differentiate themselves from out-group members. One purpose is to reduce uncertainty and to maintain perceptions of superiority to dissimilar others in order to create a desired positive social identity (Van der Vegt et al., 2003). Therefore, similarity in a group fosters cooperative behaviors, task and extra-role performance in order to maintain positive social identities. Recently, Joshi and Jackson (2003) suggest that cooperation within teams is a function of the demographic distinctiveness of team members in relation to the immediate environment. In addition to group task performance, we extend the outcomes of diversity to cooperative behaviors and group extra-role behaviors. In the following discussion, we will refer task and extra-role performance as group performance.

## THEORETICAL BACKGROUND AND HYPOTHESES

To build a conceptual model for the relationship between group diversity, process and performance, we synthesize four general research streams in this study. The first stream looks at the effects of similarity on attraction (Byrne, 1971). The similarity-attraction paradigm suggests that those who are similar to each other especially in terms of demographics and appearance are attracted to each other. Such attraction would have implications on both group process and group performance. The second stream is social categorization, which describes the categorization of people based on salient attributes such as age and gender, resulting in stereotyping on the basis of these differences (Turner, 1987). The third stream considers the effects of information distribution on decision-making (Wittenbaum & Stasser, 1996). Teams with knowledge, skill, or ability diversity should have a broader distribution of information than should teams without such diversity. The availability of this broader distribution of information would also have implications on group process and group performance. The third stream emphasizes the importance of group process, especially in terms of cooperation, to group performance (Eby & Dobbins, 1997). Group diversity would affect the degree to which a group can cooperate, which in turn would affect group performance.

The first two theoretical perspectives suggest negative effects of diversity while the third stream suggests positive effects of diversity. In an effort to account for the mixed results of the above research streams, the fourth stream emphasizes the boundary conditions in which a group has to perform (Schippers, Den Hartog, Koopman, & Wienk, 2003; Van der Vegt, Van de Vliert, & Oosterhof, 2003). One such condition is task interdependence-- whether group members depend upon direct support from each other in order to accomplish the task (Thompson, 1967). When tasks are highly interdependent, cooperation should be more important for performance. The second condition is group norms that are used to regulate behavior expected by group members. We shall discuss how each stream of research fits into our model to account for the effects of different types of group diversity on group process and performance.

## DEMOGRAPHIC DIVERSITY

Demographic diversity has been conceptualized as relational demography at the individual level. Tsui and O'Reilly (1989) introduced the term "relational demography" to describe the differences between a manager and his or her subordinates in demographic characteristics such as race, gender, age, and educational or socioeconomic status. They proposed that relational demography could affect work perceptions and attitudes through interpersonal attraction and the frequency of communication. Similarity enhances behavioral predictability (Meglino, Ravlin, & Adkins, 1991) making the "similar" person more likeable and seemingly more reliable (i.e., someone with whom to discuss work matters). Liden, Wayne, and Stilwell (1993) used Byrne's (1971) similarity-attraction paradigm to document that similarity between individuals is related to interpersonal attraction. This is because individuals who have similar backgrounds may share similar life experiences and values and thus find the interaction experience easier, more positively reinforcing and more desirable (Williams & O'Reilly, 1998).

Additionally, social identity theory also explains the negative outcomes of group demography. According to social identity theory, group members will exhibit favorable bias toward similar others, or their in-group members, and will view themselves as being in conflict with out-group or dissimilar others (Turner & Haslam, 2001). According to Joshi and Jackson (2003), in-group members are assumed to have shared interests and goals, and cooperative behavior follows because it is consistent with one's self-interest. Similarity in the so-called readily detectable personal attributes of age, gender, organizational tenure or educational level stimulates in-group membership. In a group of low demographic diversity, in-group identification results in more cooperative behaviors (Kramer, 1991). On the other hand, demographic diversity in a group inhibits in-group identification, which translates into low cooperation among team members (Kramer, 1991). Further, Williams and O'Reilly (1998) also observed that research findings consistently show that demographic diversity often results in group process and performance loss, including less positive attitudes, less frequent communication, less attachment, and greater turnover in the group. Thus, demographic diversity within groups should negatively influence the cooperative relationship between members and group performance.

## DEEP-LEVEL SKILL AND VALUE DIVERSITY

While the similarity/attraction and social identity theories predict negative outcomes for readily detectable dissimilarities or demographic diversity, diversity might enhance outcomes if it influences the breadth of information, perspectives, skills, and insights while also increasing the group's creativity and problem-solving capabilities, thereby enhancing performance (Cox, 1993; Wittenbaum & Stasser, 1996). Diversity can provide competitive advantages for organizations by increasing the skill, knowledge, perspectives and insight diversity members bring to the table (Cox, 1993). It is possible that while there may be a negative relationship between the readily detectable diversity attributes with cooperation and group performance, the relationship between deep-level diversity – differences among group members' personality, values and attitudes – may enhance performance. Nemeth (1986) suggests that heterogeneous (in skills) group members holding unconventional views can lead groups to consider non-obvious alternatives. Depending upon a group's task, heterogeneous groups are more likely to be creative and make higher-quality decisions, and perform better than homogenous groups (Wanous & Youtz, 1986). If members of heterogenous groups can take advantage of their resources by pooling their knowledge and exchanging expertise, then performance should be enhanced. Past empirical work documents that group membership diversity in terms of abilities and experiences has a positive effect on performance (Campion, Medsker, & Higgs, 1993). This is especially true when the tasks require a wide range of competencies (Goodman, Ravlin, & Argote, 1986; Hackman, 1987). Therefore, we predict that group heterogeneity will enhance group cooperation and group performance.

Additionally, we examine collectivism because of its presumed importance for the ability of a group to pull together as a team (Kirkman & Shapiro, 1997)—i.e. cooperate (Eby & Dobbins, 1997). Collectivists tend to be higher among Asians and are concerned with how their actions affect other group members by putting aside their own self-interests in deference to the group's interest and desires (Wagner & Moch, 1986). Cox et al. (1991) found support for their hypothesis that groups composed of people from collectivist cultural traditions display more cooperative behavior than do groups composed of people from individualistic cultural traditions. As discussed by Cox et al. (1991) and Eby and Dobbins (1997), a group's collectivism orientation relates positively to its cooperation and performance. This is especially relevant in Chinese context. Past literature suggests that if group members espouse a high level of collectivist orientation, performance will be enhanced. We further extrapolate that group members' high level of collectivist orientation implies members share similarity in these values, so that members' *similarity* and high levels of collectivist orientation form the basis for group identity and thus enhance group cooperation and group performance. We propose that groups need to be homogeneous in their collectivism orientation to induce cooperation and good performance. Moreover, we assert that group members need to be uniformly high in their collectivism orientation in order to induce cooperation and performance. Formally, we predict that:

H1a: Group demographic diversity will relate negatively to group cooperation and group performance.

H1b: Deep-level diversity of skill heterogeneity will relate positively to group cooperation and group performance.

H1c: Deep-level diversity of collectivistic orientation will relate negatively to group cooperation and group performance.

## GROUP COOPERATION AS A MEDIATOR

Group cooperation is the quality and the reciprocity of relationships between group members. It reflects the perceptions of intra-group willingness to reciprocate information and assistance (Eby & Dobbins, 1997). Exchanging information and assistance clarifies members' expectations and leads teams to strategize and set goals that enhance performance (Eby & Dobbins, 1997; Sundstrom, Busby, McClane, & Bobrow, 1994). While cooperation fosters mutual support and integration of effort, competitive behaviors within a group lead to distrust and frustration (Tjosvold, 1995).

We argue that, to the extent that they are similar to each other in group level demography and collectivistic orientation, group members should be more attracted to each other. This mutual attraction will enhance members' propensity to cooperate with each other. To the extent that group members are heterogeneous and have different skills and abilities, members will have a self-serving interest in exchanging knowledge and expertise, and this interest in exchange will enhance members' motivation to cooperate with each other. Then, as noted above, group cooperation should enhance performance. Chatman and Flynn (2001) found that cooperative norms mediated the effects of demographic similarity on group outcomes. We posit the mediating role of group cooperation between diversity and group performance.

H2: Group cooperation is positively related to group task performance and group extra-role performance.

H3: Group cooperation mediates the relationship between all three types of group diversity (demographic, collectivistic orientation, and heterogeneity) and group task and extra-role performance.

## THE INFLUENCE OF CONTEXT: TASK INTERDEPENDENCE AND GROUP NORMS

As noted in the introduction, the interdependence required of a group to accomplish a task may affect the group's process. Task interdependence is defined as the degree to which an individual is dependent upon and directly supports others in task accomplishment (Thompson, 1967). Hogg and colleagues (Hogg, 2000; Hogg & Mullin, 1999) have proposed that since little interaction is required when task interdependence is low, group members may pay little attention to the demographic information of gender or race of other group members. On the other hand, when task interdependence is high, because of the uncertainty inherent in highly interdependent situations, mutual adjustments and immediate feedback are necessary for effective group process (Thompson, 1967), group members are likely to pay more attention to the demographic characteristics of their group members. Dependency on these members breeds a need to attend to who they are (in terms of demographics, collectivistic orientation, and heterogeneity). Thus, demographic diversity may have a negative effect on group cooperation when task interdependence is high rather than when it is low. Negative effects may be more likely during the early stages of group development (Earley & Mosakowski, 2000; Harrison et al., 1998; 2002) since task type may exacerbate perceived differences among subgroups (Lau & Murnighan, 1998).

Additionally, Williams and O'Reilly (1998) have theorized this moderating effect for interdependency on the relationship between demographic diversity and group process and outcome. Recently, van der Vegt et al. (2003) demonstrated this moderating effect on OCB. In a study of 20 project teams, they found that the relationship between informational differences in educational level, educational background and job functions between a focal person and his or her fellow team members' citizenship behavior and team identification were dependent upon both task and goal interdependence. Specifically, under conditions of congruent low-low and high-high combinations of task and goal interdependence, informational dissimilarity was unrelated to team identification and OCB. However, under incongruent low-high or high-low combinations of task and goal interdependence, informational dissimilarity was negatively related to team identification and OCB. We extend their findings by examining the moderating effects of task interdependence and group norms on other forms of diversity and group cooperation.

Group norm was defined earlier as a legitimate shared standard against which the appropriateness of behavior can be evaluated (Birenbaum & Sagarin, 1976). Shared goals and values among diverse group members can suppress diverse differences by encouraging members to use the group as a whole, rather than their separate group identities, as the basis for identification and perceived similarity (Chatman, Polzer, Barsade, & Neale, 1998). Group norms are different than goal interdependence. While goal interdependence represents the degree to which group members believe that they are assigned group goals or provided with group feedback (Saavedra, Earley, & Van Dyne, 1993), group norms are shared behavioral guidelines, rules and expectations. We suggest that when task interdependence is low or when the task requires very little coordination or communication between group members, group norm is essential for facilitating group performance in demographic diverse teams. When task interdependence is low as in singles in tennis, bowling, wrestling, it is important that each team member shares the same standard since these members can perform independently of each other. In low interdependent task, group norms are also important when groups are diverse in collectivistic orientation and heterogeneity. However, when the task is highly interdependent, the task requires mutual adjustment and coordination among group members, implicit norms may emerge as a result of their frequent interaction and communication. Through the exchange of information or resources required by the task and members' constant interaction and communication, they have come to an understanding of what to do and how to complete their interdependent task for diverse teams. Therefore, group norms are less critical for highly interdependent tasks.

H4a: Task interdependence and group norms jointly moderate the effects of demographic diversity on group cooperation. Specifically, we predict that for low interdependent tasks, group norms should be positively related to group cooperation in demographic diverse groups. On the other hand, group norms would be unrelated to cooperation of demographic diverse groups when task interdependence is high.

H4b: Task interdependence and group norms jointly moderate the effects of heterogeneity on group cooperation. Specifically, we predict that for low interdependent tasks, group norms should be positively related to group cooperation in heterogeneous groups. On the other hand, group norms would be unrelated to cooperation of heterogeneous groups where task interdependence is high.

H4c: Task interdependence and group norms jointly moderate the effects of collectivistic diversity on group cooperation. Specifically, we predict that for low interdependent tasks, group norms should be positively related to group cooperation when collectivistic diversity is high. On the other hand, when task interdependence is high, group norms would be unrelated to cooperation when collectivistic diversity was low.

# METHOD

A total of 288 members of 86 work groups from a highway company with over 600 employees were targeted as participants in the present study. This company manages one of the major expressways in the eastern coastal region of China[*]. Its responsibilities include overseeing the construction and maintenance of the expressway, collection of tolls, and providing and managing the accessory services (e.g., gas stations, restaurants, accommodations, vehicle repairs, and advertisements). The targeted participants were all members of work groups in this organization. The work groups ranged from three to five members in size. Participants were targeted if they belonged to a work group. These groups were identifiable work units in which members understood that they were part of an entity with a specific set of responsibilities. We sent two questionnaires over a six-month period to these 288 participants. We collected 285 questionnaires from wave one of the data collection and 273 from wave two of data collection. A total of 86 supervisors of these work groups were also sent questionnaires during the second wave of data collection, of which 79 returned their questionnaires. A total of 79 groups and 267 matched cases of supervisors and work group members formed the sample for the present study.

## PROCEDURE

We used three questionnaires: two for the participants and the other for the immediate supervisors of their work groups. The first questionnaire (Time 1) measured the demographic, skill heterogeneity and collectivistic diversity variables, group norm as well as task interdependence. The second questionnaire (Time 2) measured group cooperation. The third questionnaire (Time 2) was addressed to the work group supervisor to assess each group's in-role and extra-role performance. Questionnaires were sent to potential respondents through the company's internal mail system. In a cover letter, we explained the purposes of the survey and guaranteed anonymity to the respondents. We asked respondents to mail the completed questionnaires directly to the researcher in a stamped, pre-addressed envelope. We explained to the respondents that the ID number on the survey was for data matching purposes only. Participant responses were anonymous to the researchers and responses from individual employees were kept confidential from the company's management. A follow-up reminder and copies of the questionnaire were sent again to participants two weeks after the questionnaires were first sent out. Six months after the first questionnaire (Time 1) was collected, we disseminated the second and third questionnaires (Time 2). As before, we sent a follow-up reminder letter and an extra copy of the questionnaire after two weeks. Among the respondents who provided complete data, the average age was 28 years; 56 percent were males (coded as 1, and females were coded as 2): and the majority of the respondents were high school graduates. The respondents had worked in the organization for one to 32 years.

## TRANSLATION

To assure equivalence of the measures in the Chinese and the English versions, all the scales used in this study were translated into Chinese and then translated independently back into English (Brislin, 1980). Expert judges in Chinese also examined the questionnaires to ensure that the items were interpretable in Chinese.

## MEASURES

(a) **Demographic diversity**. We used age, gender, educational level and job tenure reported by our respondents at Time 1 as the demographic variables. We used the entropy-based index (Teachman, 1980) for categorical variables, $\Sigma\text{-}P_i(\ln P_i)$, to represent the diversity of gender, educational level and job tenure in every group, respectively. $P_i$ represents the proportion of the group that has each diversity characteristic. The diversity index is the positive value of the sum of the products of each characteristic's proportion in the group and the natural log of its proportion: the higher the diversity index, the greater the distribution of characteristics within the group. Because age is a continuous variable, we used the coefficient of variation (standard deviation divided by mean) as the diversity index. Groups ranged on this measure from a score of 0.0 (homogeneous) to a score of .36 (heterogeneous). To yield an overall diversity index that represents the surface level diversity, we averaged the centralized scores of the Teachman index for gender, education level and job tenure, and for the coefficient of variable for age.

(b) **Group heterogeneity** was measured using the three-item scale developed by Campion et al. (1993) and Campion et al. (1996). We used a five-point Likert scale ranging from 1 (strongly disagree) to 5 (strongly agree). A sample item was "The members of my group vary widely in their areas of expertise." The Coefficient Alpha for this scale was .81. Because group heterogeneity should reflect the skills of the group, it should be a group-level variable and should have agreement between group members. We used James, Demaree, and Wolf's (1984) measure of within-group agreement ($rwg_{(j)}$) to justify the use of aggregated data. Values of .70 or higher are necessary to demonstrate homogeneity within each group (see George, 1990). Agreement between members was mostly acceptable with the median at .82 ($rwg_{(j)}$ ranged from -.57 to 1.00). Thus, we aggregated the ratings from different members into a group score and included all groups in the analyses.

(c) **Collectivistic diversity** was measured using the horizontal collectivism scale developed by Singelis, Triandis, Bhawuk, and Gelfand (1995). Triandis (2002) described individuals who have high horizontal collectivism as those who see the self as an aspect of an in-group. Relationships are of great importance to these individuals and they tend to maintain the relationship. These collectivists view themselves as interdependent with in-group members. They also emphasize giving priority to relationships and taking into account the needs of others, even when such relationships are not advantageous to the individual. This seven-item scale was measured at Time 1 using a five-point Likert scale ranging from 1 (strongly disagree) to 5 (strongly agree). A sample item was "The well-being of my co-workers is important to me." The Coefficient Alpha for this scale was .86. Similar to age diversity, we computed the coefficient of variation for this scale because we are interested in the degree of variation in attitudinal diversity within the groups. Groups ranged on this measure from a score of 0.0 (homogeneous) to a score of .31 (heterogeneous).

**Task interdependence** was measured using the three-item scale developed by Campion et al. (1993; 1996). We used a five-point Likert scale ranging from 1 (strongly disagree) to 5 (strongly agree). A sample item was "I cannot accomplish my tasks without information or materials from other members of my group." The Coefficient Alpha for this scale was .75. Because task interdependence for the group should reflect that of the group, it should be a group-level variable and should have agreement between group members. Agreement between members was mostly acceptable with the median at .72 ($rwg_{(j)}$ ranged from -.83 to 1.00). Thus, we aggregated the ratings from different members into a group score and included all groups in the analyses.

**Group norm** was measured using the three-item scale developed by Cohen, Ledford and Spreitzer (1996). A sample item was "Our group has clear standards for the behavior of group members." This scale was administered using a 5-point strongly disagree to strongly agree format. The Cronbach alpha for this scale was .88 for time 2. We use the James, Demaree, and Wolf's (1984) measure of within-group agreement ($rwg_{(j)}$ to justify the use of aggregated data. Values of .70 or higher are necessary to demonstrate homogeneity within each group (see George, 1990). Agreement between members was mostly acceptable with median at .80 (Rwg ranged from -1.67 to 1). Therefore, there was adequate evidence to justify aggregating individual scores of group norm to the team level.

**Group cooperation.** As in Eby and Dobbins (1997), group cooperation was operationalized using the team-member exchange quality scale developed by Seers (1989). This ten-item scale measured the quality and reciprocity of relationships between team members and the peer group. A sample item was "I often suggest better work methods to others." The items were rated on a five-point Likert scale ranging from 1 (strongly disagree) to 5 (strongly agree). The Coefficient Alpha for this scale was .91. Similar to diversity composition and task interdependence, team cooperation should reflect what happens in the group as a whole and, hence, should be a group-level variable. Agreement between members was mostly acceptable with the median at .80 (Rwg ranged from -1.23 to 1.00). Thus, we aggregated the ratings from different members into a group score and included all groups in the analyses.

**Group task performance.** Immediate supervisors of the groups were asked to evaluate the quality of the group's performance. This three-item scale used a five-point (1=not at all; 5=to a great extent) scale format. The items were: "This group is one of the best in our organization," "This group's performance always exceeded management's expectations," and "This group makes a significant contribution to the overall performance of our organization." The Cronbach alpha was $\alpha$=.91. Since this measure was taken at the group level, no aggregation was required.

**Group extra-role performance.** Extra-role performance was operationalized as organizational citizenship behavior (OCB). The immediate supervisors of each group were asked to evaluate the group's level of OCB performance. We adapted the scale developed by Podsakoff, MacKenzie, Moorman and Fetter (1990) to the group level. This scale was based on Organ's (1988) five dimensions of organizational citizenship behavior. Lam et al. (1999) found this scale to be valid in American, Australian, Chinese and Japanese settings. Previous research, however, has identified etic and emic dimensions of OCB (cf. Farh, Earley & Lin, 1997; Lam et al., 1999). In the present study, we focused on the etic dimensions: (1) altruism — discretionary behavior that has the effect of helping a specific other person with an

organizationally relevant task or problem (Cronbach's alpha=.76); (2) conscientiousness –
discretionary behavior that goes well beyond the minimum role requirements of the
organization (Cronbach's $\alpha$=.84), and (3) civic virtue – discretionary behavior that indicates
that the employee responsibly participates in, is involved in, or is concerned about the life of
the organization (Cronbach's $\alpha$=.85). Three items were used to measure each of the OCB
dimensions. A five-point scale was used for this OCB measure (1=strongly disagree;
3=neither agree nor disagree; 5=strongly agree). The confirmatory factor analysis (CFA)
results were acceptable ($x^2$=126.27 d.f.=24; CFI=.90; IFI=.90). Consistent with the
suggestions of Law and Wong (1999) and LePine, Erez, and Johnson (2002), and because we
were hypothesizing the effects of our antecedent variables on OCB as a whole instead of on
individual dimensions of OCB, we aggregated the three dimensions of OCB into one OCB
score. The Cronbach's alpha for the aggregate scale was .85. Since this measure was taken
at the group level, no aggregation was required.

## RESULTS

   Demographic diversity, heterogeneity, collectivistic diversity, group cooperation, task
and extra-role performance were all treated as group level variables. The descriptive
statistics, scale reliabilities, and intercorrelations are reported in Table 1. In general, the
bivariate correlations were consistent with our expectations.

   To test hypotheses 1 to 4, we used hierarchical multiple regression. To reduce
multicollinearity and standardized the rating scales, we centered all variables in the equations.
Similar to Chatman and Flynn (2001), we used group size as a control variable for all
equations. To test hypothesis 1, after entering the control variables in step 1, we entered the
diversity variables in step 2. Hypothesis 1a predicted that demographic diversity and
collectivistic diversity would relate negatively to group outcomes. However, group
heterogeneity would relate positively to group outcomes. As shown in Table 1, demographic
diversity related negatively to cooperation ($\beta$=-.22, p<.001, group task performance ($\beta$=-.37,
p<.001; and group extra-role performance ($\beta$= -.25, p<.001). Because demographic diversity
was an aggregate of diversity in age, gender, education and job tenure, we conducted a
multiple regression using the diversity index of the four demographic variables as predictors
to examine which specific type of diversity contributed to the effects. This is analogous to
univariate analysis. Results indicated that diversity in age was the only variable that
significantly related to cooperation ($\Delta r^2$=-.46; $\Delta F$=5.31, df=4, 70, p<.001), group task
performance ($\Delta r^2$=.-.74; $\Delta F$=15.28, df=4, 70, p<.001) and group extra-role performance
($\Delta r^2$=-.37; $\Delta F$=4.04, df=4, 70, p<.01). Contrary to hypothesis 1b, group heterogeneity did not
significantly predicted group cooperation ($\beta$=.16, n.s.), group task and extra-role performance
respectively ($\beta$=-.11, n.s.; $\beta$=.22, p<.10). Contrary to H1c that predicted a negative
relationship, collectivistic diversity was related positively to cooperation ($\beta$=.41, p<.01) and
group task performance ($\beta$=.39, p<.01) but did not relate significantly to group extra-role
performance ($\beta$=.25, p<.08).

# Table 1 Descriptive Statistics

| | Mean | SD | 1 | 2 | 3 | 4 | 5 | 6 | 7 | 8 | 9 |
|---|---|---|---|---|---|---|---|---|---|---|---|
| 1 Group Size | 3.38 | 0.61 | -- | | | | | | | | |
| 2 Demographic Diversity | -0.01 | 0.53 | -0.32 | -- | | | | | | | |
| 3 Skill Heterogeneity | 3.55 | 0.53 | 0.19 | -0.01 | (0.81) | | | | | | |
| 4 Collectivistic Diversity | 3.52 | 0.44 | 0.10 | 0.00 | 0.68 | (0.86) | | | | | |
| 5 Cooperation | 3.58 | 0.56 | 0.31 | -0.28 | 0.48 | 0.54 | (.91) | | | | |
| 6 Task Interdependence | 3.25 | 0.47 | 0.13 | 0.09 | 0.31 | 0.25 | 0.22 | (.75) | | | |
| 7 Group Norm | 3.92 | 0.55 | 0.04 | -0.16 | 0.61 | 0.64 | 0.54 | 0.21 | (0.88) | | |
| 8 Group Performance | 3.80 | 0.92 | 0.23 | -0.40 | 0.17 | 0.32 | 0.50 | 0.10 | 0.38 | (.91) | |
| 9 Group OCB | 3.65 | 0.41 | 0.16 | -0.25 | 0.39 | 0.40 | 0.53 | 0.14 | 0.59 | 0.52 | (.85) |

*Note*: Alpha Coefficients are shown in parentheses; N=76-79;

Correlations $\geq$ .29 are significant at the P<.01 level (2-tailed);

Correlations $\leq$ .22 and $\geq$ .28 are significant at the P<.05 level (2-tailed)

## Table 2 Summary of Mediation Analysis

| Dependent Variables | Group Performance | | | Group Citizenship Behavior | | |
|---|---|---|---|---|---|---|
| Independent Variables | β | $\Delta R^2$ | $\Delta F$ | β | $\Delta R^2$ | $\Delta F$ |
| (1) Group Size | -.01 | | | -.05 | | |
| (2) Group Cooperation | .25** | .21** | 21.22*** | .31* | .26** | 26.65*** |
| (3) Demographic Diversity (DD) | -.47** | | | -.26* | | |
| Skill Diversity (SD) | .17 | | | .18 | | |
| Collectivistic Diversity (CD) | -.12 | .19** | 8.24** | .06 | .08** | 2.85** |

To test hypothesis 2, we entered group cooperation in step 2. Results indicated that group cooperation significantly predicted both group task performance ($\Delta r^2$=.21; F=21.22; d.f.=1,75; p<.001; β=.48, p<.001) and group extra-role performance ($\Delta r^2$=.26; F=26.65; d.f.=1,75; p<.001; β=.53, p<.001). Thus, hypothesis 2 was supported.

To test hypothesis 3 (that cooperation mediates the diversity and performance relationship), we entered group cooperation in step 2 of the analysis and the group diversity variables in step 3 of the analysis. We report the results in Table 2. As shown in Table 2, even after group cooperation was entered into the multiple regression equation, demographic diversity still significantly predicted both group task performance ($\Delta r^2$=.19; F=8.242; d.f.=3,75; p<.001; β=-.47, p<.001) and group extra-role performance ($\Delta r^2$=.08; F=2.85; d.f.=3,75; p<.05; β=-.26, p<.05). Thus, we found that group cooperation only partially mediated the effects of demographic diversity on group task and extra-role performance. After cooperation was entered first into the equation, however, collectivistic diversity no longer significantly related to group performance (β=.17, n.s.) or group OCB (β=.06, n.s.). Group heterogeneity did not predict group task or extra-role performance. Thus, cooperation fully mediated the effects of collectivistic diversity on group performance.

Hypothesis 4 suggests that task interdependence and group norm moderate the relationship between group diversity and cooperation. We used moderated hierarchical multiple regression to test this hypothesis. Because we have only limited number of groups, we entered the different diversity variables and their interactions with task interdependence and group norm into separate equations. For all equations, we entered the control variables in step 1. In step 2, we entered the independent variables (diversity, task interdependence and group norm). In step 3, we entered the three interaction terms (diversity * task interdependence * group norm). Consistent with H4, the three-way interaction between demographic diversity, task interdependence and group norm significantly predicted

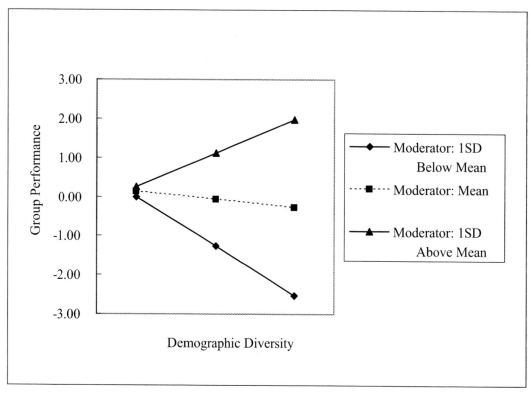

Figure 1A  Low task interdependence: Moderating effects of group norm

cooperation ($\Delta r^2$=.04; F=5.30; d.f.=1,69; p<.05; $\beta$=-.22, p<.05). The three-way interaction between heteroegeneity, task interdependence and group norm did not significantly predict cooperation ($\Delta r^2$=.01; F=.94; d.f.=1,69; n.s.; $\beta$=.12, p<.05), however. The three-way interaction between collectivistic diversity, task interdependence and group norm also did not significantly predict cooperation ($\Delta r^2$=.01; F=1.05; d.f.=1,69; n.s.; $\beta$=.15, p<.05).

We depicted the interaction effects of demographic diversity, task interdependence and group norm on cooperation in Figure 1. As shown in Figures 1a, when task interdependence was low, groups with strong norms increased cooperation as demographic diversity increased. However, weak norms decreased cooperation as demographic diversity increased. Further, group norms did not make a difference to group cooperation when demographic diversity was low. As shown in Figure 1b, when task interdependence was high, norms affected cooperation regardless of demographic diversity.

## DISCUSSION

Hypothesis 1 (that group diversity predicts cooperation, task, and extra-role performance) was a broad hypothesis with multiple parts. Although it was not fully supported, the pieces that were supported tell an interesting story that generally highlights the benefits of diversity. To summarize our findings, it appears that both demographic diversity and deep level diversity variables are quite important in predicting group performance. Contrary to hypothesis, although in the prediction direction, heterogeneity has no significant positive effect on group cooperation ($\beta$=.17, n.s.), task and extra-role ($\beta$=.22, n.s.) performance. Surprisingly, collectivistic diversity, although it appears to have no significant effect on the group's extra-role performance ($\beta$=.25, p<.10.), it has significant positive effect on group cooperation ($\beta$=.41, p<.01) and extra-role performance ($\beta$=.39, p<.01) —a finding about which we speculate below. And as expected, age diversity has a significantly negative impact on group cooperation, task and extra-role performance.

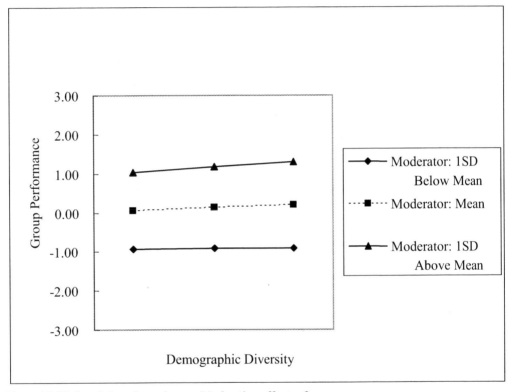

Figure 1B High task interdependence - Moderating effects of group

Our results support our second hypothesis fully. When groups engage in more cooperative interaction processes, there is higher task and extra-role performance. This is not particularly surprising, but does offer further confirmation that cooperative norms and group process help promote group effectiveness (Chatman & Flynn, 2001). Tjosvold, Hui, Ding, Sun, and Hu (2003) found that having cooperative goals between team members helped enhance team performance. Tjosvold, Yu, and Hui (2004) found that having cooperative goals between team members allowed teams to learn from their mistakes more effectively and engage in more effective team problem solving.

Our results further support the findings of Eby and Dobbins (1997) and Sundstrom et al. (1994) that intra-group cooperation contributes to group effectiveness. Contrary to Eby and Dobbins's (1997) finding that group cooperation increased as the proportion of team members' collectivist attitudes increased, our results indicated that diversity in group collectivism contributed to group cooperation, it also contributed to group task and extra-role performance. Thus, it appears that there may be two mechanisms for inducing cooperation—one is that individuals are predisposed to collectivist goals (as in Eby & Dobbins, 1997); the other is that individuals may be enlightened in their "self-interest" and realize that they need to cooperate with other group members because they have complementary values in collectivism, and by cooperating they make everyone's tasks easier. Future research should look further at these two mechanisms for inducing cooperation and whether the resulting cooperation differs either in its nature or duration.

Our results also show that group cooperation mediates between group demographic diversity variables and performance (H3), although cooperation does not fully mediate this relationship. In other words, similarity in demography has a positive effect, beyond cooperation, that leads to quality performance. The additional contribution to cooperation and performance comes, most likely, from collectivistic diversity. Together, these findings are intriguing as they imply that demographic diversity may lead to some difficult group processes. However, differences in collectivistic values are better for group process and outcomes. This speaks to the debate in the conflict literature on whether or not some level and some types of conflict (moderate amounts of task conflict) are functional for groups (for a review see Jehn & Bendersky, 2003). Essentially, De Dreu and Weingart's (2003) meta-analysis showed very little support for the functional properties of conflict, which usually has a harmful effect. Yet, our results show that collectivistic diversity does help group outcomes. Thus, deep-seated collectivistic diversity can help groups as long as it does not disrupt group cooperation.

Since collectivist people care about the group's (rather than an individual's) outcomes, the more collectivist and homogeneous the group, the stronger should be the group's performance. Quite interestingly, what our results show, however, is that groups need variance in this collectivist attitude. That is, the group functions best when it has some members who are collectivist and some who are not. The former members may be those who have a softer attitude, who may accommodate more, and who are the ones responsible for the group maintenance function. The latter members may be those who push the group, who play devil's advocate, and who are more focused on task accomplishment. Thus, one way in which collectivistic diversity may not disrupt cooperation is if it perhaps leads to a division of labor and role-specification with the group.

Our final hypothesis that group norms and task interdependence moderate the effects of group diversity and cooperation was supported for skill diversity. The more interdependent the task, the more group members must meet and communicate to complete the task. The frequency of interaction increases group cooperation to perform their tasks. Our results demonstrate that although norms are important for group cooperation when task interdependence was high, without norms, group cooperation will suffer with demographic diversity when tasks are low in interdependence.

Contrary to prediction, task interdependence and norms did not moderate the relationship between heterogeneity, collectivistic diversity and cooperation. It appears that across all types of tasks, collectivistic diversity helps cooperation and performance. It may be that it is important to have some members who push the group (low in collectivism) and others who take care of the group maintenance function (high in collectivism). Future research should detail the group process more thoroughly to chart if there is such a division of labor and role specification.

# LIMITATIONS

All studies have limitations; ours is no exception. Common method variance is somewhat of a threat. We sampled from multiple data sources with a longitudinal design to reduce common method biases. For example, the demographic diversity, heterogeneity, and task interdependence were measured at Time 1, whereas group cooperation, collectivistic orientation, task and extra-role group performance measures were collected at Time 2. Furthermore, if common method bias was an issue, we might expect more relationships to be significant, rather than primarily the ones we had hypothesized. We would also like to point out that not all our measures came from the same source. Task and extra-role group performance were obtained from independent sources (i.e., supervisors).

Another possible limitation is generalizability. Our sample consisted of 79 groups in one organization in China. A broader and larger sampling of work groups would strengthen statistical power. However, our results are consistent with Tjosvold et al.'s (2003) results from data collected in China and Eby and Dobbins's (1997) results from data collected in the United States. Therefore, cultural context does not appear to threaten the basic findings of our study. It may be that in other cultures other facets of our surface- level demographic characteristics would be salient (such as race). As well, our positive effects for gender diversity on cooperation may be limited to more "masculine" cultures. Masculine cultures (found mostly in Latin American and Asia) are those with pronounced gender differences (Hofstede, 1980). Recently, Chattopadhyay (2003) found that gender diversity had a positive impact on outcomes when individuals had high (rather than low) levels of dogmatism (or belief regarding status hierarchies in society). High-dogmatism employees were more likely to acceptance of the higher status accorded to male employees and may not challenge the domination of male employees in their group. If status differences across genders are accepted in China, this might explain why gender diversity did not hinder group cooperation, and these results may be more generalizable to other masculine cultures. Yet, beyond these specifics, our results appear to be generalizable. Future studies could further replicate our results in other cultures and other organizations.

# IMPLICATIONS FOR MANAGERS

Work groups, and hence organizations, benefit from diversity. Many multinational organizations have branches in Asia employing diverse work groups or project teams as part of their formal organizational structure. It is especially important for multinational managers to understand how to manage these diverse groups and teams. As shown in our study, the most evident beneficial diversity is skill diversity, as it broadens the information, perspectives and ideas considered. Managers should work hard to assure work groups draw members from across functional areas, particularly when task interdependence is high. Moreover, managers should continually mix and train employees with diverse skill sets into work groups. Our results also show that age and job tenure group homogeneity are likely precursors to good performance, so that managers should pay attention towards placing employees into groups. Our data suggest age cohorts may be particularly useful for inducing performance. Moreover, gender diversity appears to induce employees to go the extra mile at work, so that mixed-gender groups should be encouraged. In a study conducted in Hong Kong, Lee and Farh (2004) found that mix-gender groups' performance were higher when the group members feel capable of completing the task (with higher group efficacy). This result is also consistent with a recently released study showing that Fortune 500 companies with a higher percentage of women in top management positions have a higher return on interest than companies with a low percentage of women in top management positions (Kitchen, 2004).

Cooperation helps performance, but the partial mediation of cooperation suggests that managers should seek diversity, rather than cooperation or a harmonious work environment. Diversity in collectivistic orientation helps work group cooperation and performance. Managers should explain to employees the value of diversity as being able to trade off each other's strengths, perhaps by creating roles and dividing the labor. Then, the lower attraction of dissimilar others might be overruled by the usefulness of their heterogeneity and collectivistic orientation differences.

# CONCLUSION

Results of our study appear to provide support to both Cox et al.'s (1991) and Williams and O'Reilly (1998) diversity positions. What is so striking is that demographic diversity appears to be the biggest threat to cooperation and performance, while deep-level collectivism diversity contributes positively to group cooperation and performance. That is, group members continue to be uncomfortable with those around them who "appear" different, especially in age; yet they actually perform better when those around them *are* different—in deep-level ways. Our results are generally consistent with the similarity-attraction paradigm, if we consider similarity to mean the surface-level appearance of similarity. They are also consistent with the information distribution paradigm, where differences in deep-level collectivistic orientation allow for a wider distribution of knowledge and perspectives, which enhances performance. As globalization continues, managers should play close attention to staffing and training policies as well as the role that organizational context can play in shaping the consequences of diversity in multinational firms. Future efforts should be to continue to educate people about the value of diversity.

# REFERENCES

Birenbaum, A., & Sagarin, E. 1976. *Norms and human behavior.* New York: Praeger.
Brislin, R.W. 1980. Translation and content analysis of oral and written material. In Triandis, H. C., & Berry, J. W. (Eds.), *Handbook of Cross-Cultural Psychology:* 339-444. Boston: Allyn and Bacon.
Byrne, D. 1971. *The attraction paradigm.* New York: Academic Press.
Campion, M.A., Medsker, G.J., & Higgs, A.C. 1993. Relations between work group characteristics and effectiveness: Implications for designing effective work groups. *Personnel Psychology*, 46(4): 823-850.

Campion, M.A., Papper, E.M., & Medsker, G.J. 1996. Relations between work team characteristics and effectiveness: A replication and extension. *Personnel Psychology*, 49(2): 429-452.

Chatman, J., Polzer, J., Barsade, S., & Neale, M. 1998. Being different yet feeling similar: The influence of demographic composition and organizational culture on work processes and outcomes. *Administrative Science Quarterly*, 43(4): 749-780.

Chatman, J.A., & Flynn, F.J. 2001. The influence of demographic heterogeneity on the emergence and consequences of cooperative norms in work teams. *Academy of Management Journal*, 44(5): 956-974.

Chattopadhyay, P. 1999. Beyond direct and symmetrical effects: The influence of demographic dissimilarity on organizational citizenship behavior. *Academy of Management Journal*, 42(3): 273-287.

Chattopadhyay, P. 2003. Can dissimilarity lead to positive outcomes? The influence of open versus closed minds. *Journal of Organizational Behavior*, 24(3): 295-312.

Cohen, S.G., & Ledford, G.E., & Spreitzer, G.M. 1996. A predictive model of self-managing work team effectiveness. *Human Relations*, 49(5): 643-676.

Cox, T.H.Jr., Lobel, S., & McLeod, P. 1991. Effects of ethnic group cultural differences on cooperative and competitive behavior on a group task. *Academy of Management Journal*, 34(4): 827-847.

Cox, T.H. Jr. 1993. *Cultural diversity in organizations: Theory, research, and practice*. San Francisco: Berrett-Koehler.

De Dreu, C.K.W., & Weingart, L.R. 2003. Task versus relationship conflict, team performance, and team member satisfaction: A meta-analysis. *Journal of Applied Psychology*, 88(4): 741-749.

Earley, P.C., & Mosakowski, E. 2000. Creating hybrid team cultures: An empirical test of transnational team functioning. *Academy of Management Journal*, 43(1): 26-49.

Eby, L.T., & Dobbins, G.H. 1997. Collectivistic orientation in teams: an individual and group-level analysis. *Journal of Organizational Behavior*, 18(3): 275-295.

Farh, J.L., Earley, P.C., & Lin, S. 1997. Impetus for action: A cultural analysis of justice and extra-role behavior in Chinese society. *Administrative Science Quarterly*, 42(3): 421-444.

George, J.M. 1990. Personality, affect, and behavior in groups. *Journal of Applied Psychology*, 75(2): 107-116.

Goodman, P.S., Ravlin. E.C., & Argote, L. 1986. Current thinking about groups: Setting the stage for new ideas. In P.S. Goodman (Ed.), *Designing effective work groups:* 1-27. San Francisco: Jossey-Bass.

Hackman, J.R. 1983. *A normative model of work team effectiveness*. Technical report no.2, Yale School of Organization and Management, New Haven CT.

Hackman, J.R. 1987. The design of work teams. In J.W. Lorsch (Ed.), *Handbook of organizational behavior:* 315 – 342. Englewood Cliffs, NJ: Prentice-Hall.

Harrison, D.A., Price, K.H., & Bell, M.P. 1998. Beyond relational demography: Time and the effects of surface- and deep-level diversity on work group cohesion. *Academy of Management Journal*, 41(1): 96-107.

Harrison, D.A., Price, K.H., Gavin, J.H., & Florey, A.T. 2002. Time, teams, and task performance: Changing effects of surface- and deep-level diversity on group functioning. *Academy of Management Journal*, 45(5): 1029-1045.

Hofstede, G. 1980. *Culture's consequences*, Beverly Hills, CA: Sage.

Hogg, M.A., & Mullin, B.A. 1999. Joining groups to reduce uncertainty: Subjective uncertainty reduction and group identification. In D. Abrams & M.A. Hogg (Eds.), *Social identity and social cognition:* 249-279. Oxford, England: Blackwell.

Hogg, M.A. 2000. Social identity and social comparison. In J. Suls & L. Wheeler (Eds.), *Handbook of social comparison: Theory and research:* 401-421, New York: Kluwer Academic/Plenum.

Jackson, S.E., & Joshi, A. 2002. Research on domestic and international diversity in organizations: A merger that works? In N. Anderson, & D.S. Ones (Eds.), *Handbook of Industrial, Work and Organizational Psychology:* 206-231. Thousand Oaks, CA: Sage Publications, Inc.

Jackson, S.E., Joshi, A., & Erhardt, N.L. 2003. Recent research on team and organizational diversity: SWOT analysis and implications. *Journal of Management,* 29(6): 801-830.

James, L.R., Demaree, R.G., & Wolf, G. 1984. Mediators, moderators, and tests for Mediation. *Journal of Applied Psychology,* 69(2): 85-98.

Jehn, K.A. & Bendersky, C. 2003. Intragroup conflict in organizations: a contigency perspective on the conflict-outcome relationship. *Research in Organizational Behavior,* 25: 187-243.

Joshi, A., & Jackson, S.E. 2003. Managing workforce diversity to enhance cooperation in organizations. In M.A.West, D. Tjosvold, & K.G. Smith (Eds.), *International Handbook of Organizational Teamwork and Cooperative Working:* 277-296. Hoboken, NJ: John Wiley and Sons, Ltd.

Kirkman,B.L., & Shaprio, D.L. 1997. The impact of cultural values on employee resistance to teams: Toward a model of globalized self-managing work team effectiveness. *Academy of Management Review,* 22(3): 730-757.

Kitchen, P. 2004. Profits bloom with women on top jobs. http://www.newsday.com. *January 26.*

Kramer, R. 1991. Intergroup relations and organizational dilemmas: The role of categorization processes. In L.L. Cummings & B.M. Staw (Eds.), Research *in Organizational Behavior:* 191-228. Greenwich Conn.: JAI Press.

Lam, S.S.K., Hui, C., & Law, K.S. 1999. Organizational citizenship behavior: Comparing perspectives of supervisors and subordinates across four international samples. *Journal of Applied Psychology,* 84(4): 594-601.

Lau, D.C., & Murnighan, J.K. 1998. Demographic diversity and fault lines: The compositional dynamics of organizational groups. *Academy of Management Review,* 23(2): 325-340.

Law, K.S., & Wong, C.S. 1999. Multidimensional constructs in structural equation analysis: An illustration using the job perception and job satisfaction constructs. *Journal of Management,* 25(2): 143-160.

Lee, C., & Farh, J.L. 2004. Joint effects of group efficacy and gender diversity on group cohesion and performance. *Applied Psychology: An International Review,* 53(1): 136-154.

LePine, J.A., Erez, A., & Johnson, D.E. 2002. The nature and dimensionality of organizational citizenship behavior: A critical review and meta-analysis. *Journal of Applied Psychology,* 87(1): 52-65.

Liden, R.C., Wayne, S.J., & Stilwell, D. 1993. A longitudinal study on the early development of leader-member exchange. *Journal of Applied Psychology,* 78(4): 662-674.

McGrath, J.E. 1984. *Groups: Interaction and performance*, Englewood Cliffs, NJ: Prentice-Hall.

Meglino, B.M., Ravlin, E.C., & Adkins, C.L. 1991. Value congruence and satisfaction with a leader: An examination of the role of interaction. *Human Relations*, 44(5): 481-495.

Nemeth, C. 1986. Differential contributions of majority and minority influence. *Psychological Review*, 93(1): 23-32.

Organ, D.W. 1988. *Organizational citizenship behavior: The good soldier syndrome*, Lexington, MA: Heath.

Saavedra, R., Earley, P.C., & Van Dyne, L. 1993. Complex interdependence in task performing groups. *Journal of Applied Psychology*, 78(1): 61-72.

Podsakoff, P. M., MacKenzie, S. B., Moorman, R. H., & Fetter, R. 1990. Transformational leader behaviors and their effects on followers' trust in leader, satisfaction, and organizational citizenship behaviors. *Leadership Quarterly*, 1(2): 107-142.

Schippers, M.C., Den Hartog, D.N., Koopman, P.L., & Wienk, J.A. 2003. Diversity and team outcomes: The moderating effects of outcome interdependence and group longevity and the mediating effect of reflexivity. *Journal of Organizational Behavior*, 24(6): 779-802.

Seers, A. 1989. Team-member exchange quality: A new construct for role-making research. *Organizational Behavior and Human Decision Processes*, 43(1): 118-135.

Singelis, T. M., Triandis, H. C., Bhawuk, D. S. P. & Gelfand, M. 1995. Horizontal and vertical dimensions of individualism and collectivism: A theoretical and measurement refinement. Cross -Cultural Research: The Journal of Comparative Social Science, 29(3): 240- 275.

Snow, C., Davison, S., Snell, S., & Hambrick, D. 1996. Use transnational teams to globalize your company. Organizational Dynamics, 24(4): 50-67.

Sundstrom, E., Busby, P.L., McClane, W.E., & Bobrow, W.S. 1994. Group processes and performance: Interpersonal behaviors in problem solving. Paper presented at the meeting of the Society for Industrial and Organizational Psychology, Nashville, TN.

Teachman, J.D. 1980. Analysis of population diversity. *Sociological Methods and Research,* 8(3), 341-362.

Thompson, J.D. 1967. *Organizations in action*, New York: McGraw-Hill.

Tjosvold, D. 1995. Cooperative theory, constructive controversy, and effectiveness: Learning from crisis. In R. A. Guzzo, E. Sales, & Associates (Eds.), *Team effectiveness and decision making in organizations:* 79 – 112. San Francisco, CA: Jossey-Bass.

Tjosvold, D., Hui, C., Ding, D., Sun, H. & Hu, J.C. 2003. Conflict Values and Team Relationships: Conflict's Contribution to Team Effectiveness and Citizenship in China. *Journal of Organizational Behavior*, 24(1): 69-88.

Tjosvold, D., Yu, Z.Y., & Hui, C. 2004. Team learning from mistakes: The contribution of cooperative goals and problem solving. *Journal of Management Studies*, 41(7), 1223-1245.

Triandis, H.C. 2002. Generic individualism and collectivism. In M.J. Gannon & K.L. Newman (Eds.), *The Blackwell Handbook of Cross-Cultural Management:* 16-45. Oxford, UK: Blackwell Business.

Tsui, A.S., & O'Reilly, C.A. 1989. Beyond simple demographic effects: The importance of relational demography in superior-subordinate dyads. *Academy of Management Journal*, 32(2): 402-423.

Turner, J.C. 1987. *Rediscovering the social group: A social categorization theory*, Oxford, UK: B. Blackwell.

Turner, J.C., & Haslam, S.A. 2001. Social identity, organizations and leadership. In M. Turner (Ed.), *Groups at work: Theory and research:* 25-65. London: Lawrence Erlbaum.

Van der Vegt, G.S., Van de Vliert, E., & Oosterhof, A. 2003. Informational dissimilarity and organizational citizenship behavior: The role of intrateam interdependence and team identification. *Academy of Management Journal*, 46(6): 715-727.

Wagner, J.A. III, & Moch, M.K. 1986. Individualism-collectivism: Concept and Measure. *Group and Organization Studies*, 11(3): 280-304.

Wanous, J.P., & Youtz, M.A. 1986. Solution diversity and the quality of group decisions. *Academy of Management Journal,* 29(1): 149-158.

Williams, K.Y., & O'Reilly, C.A. III. 1998. Demography and diversity in organizations: A review of 40 years of research. In B.M. Staw & L.L. Cummings (Eds.), *Research in Organizational Behavior:* 77-140. Greenwich, CT: JAI Press Inc.

Wittenbaum, G., & Stasser, G. 1996. Management of information in small groups. In J. Nye, & M. Bower (Eds.), *What's social cognition? Social cognition research in small groups:* 3-28. Thousand Oaks, CA: Sage.

## FOOTNOTE

[*]Although data were collected in China, this is not a cross-cultural comparative study, but rather a uni-cultural study similar to those done on strictly U.S. samples. We do discuss the cultural generalizability of our findings, as any uni-cultural study should do.

In: Applied Psychology Research Trends
Editor: Karl H. Kiefer, pp.81-101

ISBN 978-1-60456-372-6
© 2008 Nova Science Publishers, Inc.

*Chapter 4*

# EXPERT TABLE TENNIS PLAYERS' SITUATED SENTIMENTS AND AFFECTIVE STATES DURING MATCHES

### *Germain Poizat[1] and Carole Sève[2]*
University of Nantes Atlantic, Nantes, France

This study analyzed from a semiological framework (Peirce, 1931-1935; Theureau, 1992, 2004, 2006) the affective states and sentiments of three expert table tennis players during international matches. The matches were videotaped and the players' verbalizations while viewing the tapes, as well as their reports of affective states during the matches, were collected *a posteriori*. The data were analyzed by (a) the construction of graphs to display the evolution in affective states, (b) transcriptions of the players' actions and verbalizations, and (c) identification and categorization of the elements that described the situations in which the players experienced a sentiment. The results showed (a) an evolution in affective states during matches in relation with the score, (b) typical "situation-sentiment" couplings, and (c) the contradictory nature of emotion. The discussion focuses on the relationships between affective states and sentiments and the situated aspect of emotion.

**Keywords**: Emotion, Table Tennis, Situated Action.

Emotions are a fundamental part of performance and the focus of considerable research in sports. In most cases, the study of the relationship between emotion and performance has been oriented toward an analysis of the influence of emotion, particularly precompetition emotion, on performance (e.g., Cerin, Szabo, Hunt, & Williams, 2000; Hanin, 2000). Lazarus (2001) distinguished two main approaches to the study of emotion: dimensional and discrete.

---

[1] Correspondence to: 2, Rue du Moineau, 76000 Rouen, France, taziop@libertysurf.fr

[2] Correspondence to: University of Nantes Atlantic, UFR STAPS, Boulevard Guy Mollet, 44300 Nantes, France, carole.seve@univ-nantes.fr

The dimensional approach is centered on the effort to identify a minimum number of factor-analytic-derived basic dimensions of emotion (such as pleasantness-unpleasantness or tension-relaxation) that can statistically account for the greatest quantity of emotion variance. In the field of sports research, the dimensional approach has principally been used to characterize the impact of anxiety on performance. Researchers quickly distinguished several dimensions to anxiety (notably, cognitive and somatic), which were assumed to relate differently to performance (Martens, Vealey, & Burton, 1990). Unfortunately, the studies that tried to assess the effects of anxiety on performance according to the nature of the anxiety yielded contradictory results (for a review see Cerin et al., 2000), and the inconsistencies were explained as other, intervening factors. The discrete approach focuses on discrete categories of emotion based on qualitative content and brings to the fore the concept of appraisal (Scherer, Schorr, & Johnstone, 2001). The dimension of intensity is retained in the discrete approach but is drawn upon only within each emotion category (as, for example, in the intensity of a given experience or display of anger, anxiety, and so forth). In the field of sports research, the discrete approach to emotion is essentially structured around the Individual Zones of Optimal Functioning (IZOF) model proposed by Hanin (2000). This model was built with the aims of (a) characterizing the content and intensity of the categories of emotion experienced before and during competition and (b) identifying the emotional patterns associated with optimal and poor performances. These patterns differ across athletes and sports and are composed of pleasant and unpleasant emotions (Hanin, 2000). In other words, pleasant and unpleasant emotions are expected to produce either a facilitating or debilitating effect on performance (Hanin, 2000; Hanin & Syrjä, 1995).

Although emotions have been classed as either "pleasant" (e.g., happiness, relief, hope) or "unpleasant" (e.g., anger, anxiety, sadness, shame), emotion theorists differ as to how many can be distinguished and which are most worthy of programmatic study. For example, the Positive and Negative Affect Schedule (PANAS; Watson, Clark, & Tellengen, 1988) presents five pleasant and five unpleasant emotions, whereas the Positive Negative Affect list (Hanin & Syrjä; 1995, 1996) presents 77 emotions (40 pleasant and 37 unpleasant). These scales have been used to identify the emotions experienced by athletes before, during and after a poor or optimal performance (e.g., Hanin & Syrjä, 1995, 1996; Robazza, Bortoli, Nocini, Moser, & Arslan, 2000; Robazza, Bortoli, & Nougier, 2000) without, however, precise description of the situations in which they were experienced. Lazarus (2000), on the other hand, insisted on the need for empirical studies in the field of sports to characterize the situations in which emotions occur. He defined emotion "as an organized psychophysiological reaction to ongoing relationships with the environment, most often, but not always, interpersonal or social" (p. 231) but noted that this definition is incomplete. It does not integrate the processes involved in arousing and sustaining an emotion, and he considers these processes to be part of the emotion. In other words, without the continuation of causal thoughts about an ongoing relationship with the environment, emotion disappears or changes, and each discrete emotion tells a different story about a person's adaptational struggle (Lazarus, 1991). To understand emotion, it must be studied in its ecological situation and in close relationship with the judgments of the actors involved in the situation.

The situated-cognition approach, which is the framework for this study, was designed to analyze the affective and cognitive processes of individuals in context (e.g., Clancey, 1997; Goodwin & Goodwin, 2000; Hutchins, 1995; Kirshner & Whitson, 1997; Lave, 1988; Suchman, 1987). This approach is organized around one key idea: affective and cognitive processes are inseparable from the situation in which they take place. These processes participate in the structural coupling of the actor with his or her environment (Varela, 1980) and emerge from the effort to adapt to a context whose significant elements function as resources that the actor can use to act (Hutchins, 1995; Lave, 1988; Norman, 1993). This interaction is asymmetric in that the actor interacts only with those elements of the situation that are relevant to his or her point of view. A study by Saury, Durand, & Theureau (1997) introduced a research perspective in sports based on the assumptions of the situated-cognition approach; this perspective was, more specifically, grounded in the semiological framework called the course of action (Theureau, 1992, 2004, 2006). This theoretical framework is particularly well-suited to investigating the relationships between psychological processes and situations. One of the strengths of course-of-action theory is that it provides a means to access to (a) the emotions experienced in situ in relation with the other components of the activity (e.g., preoccupations, interpretations) and (b) the situations both experienced by the actors and constructed by their activity. This approach is thus a complement to the studies that describe and explain the impact of emotions on performance. The course-of-action theory is itself based on Peirce's semiotics (1931-1935) and focuses on the level of activity that is meaningful for the actor: that which can be shown, told and commented on by the actor a posteriori. This theory is founded on the postulate that the level of activity that is meaningful to the actor has a relatively autonomous organization compared with other possible levels of analysis and can therefore result in valid and useful observations, descriptions and explanations (Theureau, 1992). When actors are asked to describe their activity, they spontaneously break down a continuous stream of actions into discrete units that have meaning for them. These discrete units are called elementary units of meaning (EUMs) and may be physical actions, communicative exchanges, interpretations, or sentiments: they constitute the EUMs of the course of action and are analyzed in relation with situational variables. In sports, the course of action theory offers the possibility of studying psychological processes based on the reconstruction of the natural and sport-specific conditions of athletic activity. Numerous recent empirical studies in the field of expertise in sport have demonstrated the power of this semiological framework (D'Arripe-Longueville, Saury, Fournier, & Durand, 2001; Hauw, Berthelot, & Durand, 2003; Poizat, Sève, & Rossard, 2006; Sève, Saury, Ria, & Durand, 2003; Sève, Saury, Theureau, & Durand, 2002a, 2002b; Sève & Poizat, 2005; Sève, Poizat, Saury, & Durand, 2006).

Ria and Durand (2001) adopted this approach to study the emotion of actors engaged in teaching sports. Borrowing from Peirce's semiotics (1931-1935) and the course-of-action framework, Ria (2001) proposed to study emotion by differentiating affective states, sentiments, and emotion-types. Peirce (1931-1935) distinguished three categories of experience: "firstness", "secondness", and "thirdness". Firstness is the category of experience as it simply is without reference to anything else. It is characterized as an immediate revelation of self in the world (e.g., the simple sensation of being wet without anything else). Secondness is the category of experience during the concretization of a fact. It reflects a particular interaction with the actor's world (e.g., the sensation of being wet might be related to the fact that it is raining). Thirdness is the category of experience that gives rise to reasoning, to generalization. It is the mode of knowledge construction (e.g., the recognition of the experience-type of being in a bad mood when it rains, thus confirming the regularity of the actor's experience in similar situations). Thirdness allows the discovery of typicality in our relationships with the world from past and present experiences. Affective states were defined as arising from the "firstness" of experience; that is to say, from a syncretic sensation experienced by the actor. These states constitute the continuous emotional flow linked to the actor's adaptation to his or her social or physical environment. They are immediate and diffuse revelations of personal engagement in the world; for example, they may be the diffuse sensation of feeling "good" or "bad", comfortable or uncomfortable, pleasant or unpleasant. These states are rooted in the body, can be verbalized only with difficulty, and present with different intensities. Sentiments[3] arise from the "secondness" of experience and translate an actor's particular interaction with the world. Sentiments are the salient moments of affective states, can be told and commented on, and present distinctive content. An example would be the transient irritation experienced when one has made a poor move in sports. Emotion-types are related to the thirdness of experience. They correspond to the typicalization of actors' emotional experience in the light of personal history and contribute to the construction of proven regularities in situations that are similar to the actor's eyes. An example would be the knowledge -more or less implicit- of typically being nervous as the end of a match draws near). The distinction between affective states, sentiments, and emotion-types proceeds from the effort to distinguish the different contents of emotion (emotion's qualitative content) while simultaneously taking into account the emotional flow that permanently accompanies all activity (emotion's intensity dimension). Affective states can be documented with the Estimation of Affective States (EAS) scale. This scale helps actors to estimate and express synthetically the positive or negative character of their experiences. Fluctuations in this estimation reflect the fundamental adaptability of human activity toward positive, pleasant and comfortable states and the anticipation or avoidance of those that are negative, unpleasant or uncomfortable. Sentiments and emotion-types can be documented from verbalized data collected in interviews during which the actor watches a video recording of his or her activity and is invited to comment.

In previous research, we used the framework of course-of-action theory to analyze the activity of expert table tennis players during international matches. The main results showed that (a) players' actions are organized to form sequences dividing a match into phases of exploration, execution, and deception (Poizat et al., 2006 ; Sève et al., 2003), (b) they construct new knowledge during matches (Sève et al. 2002a, 2002b), and (c) their interpretations are embedded in a dynamic of constructing meaning (Sève, Saury, Leblanc, & Durand, 2005). The present study focused on players' emotion. We used this semiological framework to study affective states and sentiments simultaneously in ecological situations in order to describe the dynamics of affective states during the course of matches and the typical couplings between situations and sentiments.

---

[3] This use of "sentiment" differs from Peirce's that he defined it as being of the order of firstness; that is, as a state or revelation of the world without present. Ria (2001) uses "affective states", which is close to the "background emotions" of Damasio (1994), to refer to continuous emotional flow (firstness) and "sentiment" to describe the presentness of the emotional experience (secondness).

# Method

## Participants

Three top-level table tennis players from the French Men's Table Tennis Team volunteered to participate in the study. At the time, the players were European Team Champions and World Team Vice-Champions, and they had participated in the Olympic Games in Atlanta. They were 25, 29, and 30 years old, respectively.

Although the players did not ask to remain anonymous, they were given the following pseudonyms to guarantee some degree of confidentiality: Luc, Jacques, and Marc.

## Procedure

The players' activity was studied in four matches: two for Luc (Match A and Match B), one for Jacques (Match C), and one for Marc (Match D) (see Table 1). These matches were chosen because the competitive stakes were high: they took place during two international qualifiers for the Olympic Games in Sydney. Match A was held in October 1997 during the table tennis World Cup, and Matches B, C, and D were held in January 1999 during the International Table Tennis Federation Pro-Tour finals.

**Table 1. Characteristics of matches**

| Match | Player's name | Player's world ranking | Opponent's world ranking | Match duration (in min) | Result |
|-------|---------------|------------------------|--------------------------|-------------------------|--------|
| A | Luc | 14 | 7 | 48 | Won 3 sets to 2 |
| B | Luc | 17 | 9 | 37 | Lost 3 sets to 1 |
| C | Jacques | 14 | 2 | 35 | Lost 3 sets to 1 |
| D | Marc | 16 | 2 | 25 | Lost 3sets to 0 |

*Note.* The players' world rankings were the ones held at the time of the competition

## Data Collection

Three types of data were gathered: (a) recordings of the matches, (b) verbalizations during post-match interviews, and (c) self-estimations of the players' affective states during the matches while they watched themselves on the video recording, using a 7-point scale.

The matches were recorded on an 8-mm video camera. The camera was positioned above and behind the table and was set for a wide-angle, fixed, overhead view that framed the table and the movements of both players. This setup allowed for continuous recording of the players' actions during the matches.

The verbalization data were collected from interviews with the players two to four days after the meet. The average interview lasted 130 minutes. No competitions took place between the matches and interviews. During the interviews, the players viewed the videotape together with one of the present authors (himself a table tennis expert) and were asked to describe and comment on their activity. The videotape was stopped after each point. The interviewer's prompts were related to descriptions of the actions, sentiments and events as experienced by the players. Requests for interpretations and generalizations were avoided (Theureau, 1992). The interviews were recorded in their entirety using an 8-mm video camera and a tape recorder.

Affective states were documented from the Estimation of Affective States (EAS) scale that had previously been validated by correlation between the estimation of affective state and recorded heart rate as a biological indicator of emotion (Ria, 2001). The EAS scale has 7 points ranging from +3 (very pleasant or very comfortable) to −3 (very unpleasant or very uncomfortable). The estimated tone of an affective state on this scale corresponds to an immediate and syncretic feeling; this level of emotion can only be shown. The estimation of the positive or negative character of the players' experience over the course of the match was made immediately after the interview while watching the videotape again. The players estimated their affective state after each point. They were allowed to modify their estimated scores on the EAS scale at any time without justification or explanation.

## Data Processing

The data were analyzed in five steps by: (a) constructing graphs, (b) generating match logs, (c) labeling the EUMs, (d) specifying the data relative to sentiments, and (e) categorizing the elements.

*Constructing graphs.* This step consisted of constructing graphs to depict the evolution of affective states over the course of a match based on the players' estimations.

*Generating match logs.* In this step, a summary table or log was generated, which contained the data collected for each match (see Table 2). The videotapes were viewed to draw up an inventory of the actions of the two opponents. Reports of the players' actions were as objective as possible (i.e., without interpreting their intentions). The verbal exchanges between the player and the researcher during the interview were recorded and fully transcribed.

*Labelling the EUMs.* This step involved drawing up a summary presentation or condensed narrative of each course of action (see Table 3). The match log was first broken down into EUMs and each narrative was then defined as a chain of EUMs. The EUMs were labelled by simultaneously analyzing the match log and the videotapes while asking questions about the player's actions (What is he doing?), his interpretations (What is he thinking?), and his sentiments (What sentiment is he feeling?) as they appeared in the log. This analysis was done step by step for each instant of each course of action and allowed us to reconstruct a chain of EUMs for each match. The name of each EUM was a phrase that specified the player's physical action, interpretation, and/or sentiment. A total of 1491 were identified (501 for Match A, 380 for Match B, 356 for Match C, and 254 for Match D).

*Specifying the data.* In line with our objective of identifying the typical couplings between sentiments and situations, this step consisted of selecting the EUMs relative to a sentiment (sentiment-EUM) and the extracts from the match log corresponding to these EUMs. A total of 147 sentiment-EUMs were identified (57 for Match A, 36 for Match B, 29 for Match C, and 25 for Match D). This step provided the basis for defining a new corpus of sentiments.

## Table 2. Excerpt from Match A Log, Set 4

| Score | Players' actions | Luc's verbalizations |
|---|---|---|
| [4th set]<br>Luc<br>0-0 | Luc serves long to Peter's backhand side. Peter attacks to Luc's backhand side. Luc blocks to Peter's backhand side and scores the point. | So here I'm doing a long serve. He's attacking but I'm doing a stroke I like: a sideway backhand block on his backhand. I know the ball will come back to my forehand side. It's a game configuration that I know and like. |
| 1-0 | | Here I'm pleased. I did a nice stroke to start the set and I can feel that I'm hitting the ball just right. |
| | Luc serves short to Peter's backhand side. Peter returns a short ball. Luc attacks and scores the point. | Here is a stroke I don't often do: smash when he returns a short ball. Attacking the ball like that gives me confidence. I don't often pull off strokes like that. |
| 2-0 | Luc serves long to Peter's backhand side. Peter attacks to Luc's backhand side. Luc attacks to Peter's forehand side and scores the point. | Here it's perfect. I'm serving like I should. He attacks slowly and I can counter-attack on his forehand side without risk. 3-0, and I feel confident, I'm ahead, and |
| 3-0 | | I'm telling myself to keep going like that. |

Note. Descriptions of the players' actions and verbalizations were placed side-by-side in three-column tables. The first column gives the score and the server's name. The second column lists the actions of the two opponents. The third column gives the verbatim transcription of the verbalizations produced during the self-confrontation interviews. The score of the study participant is given first, followed by that of his opponent.

## Table 3. Excerpt from the condensed narrative of Match A, Set 4

| Score | Elementary Units of Meaning |
|---|---|
| 0-0 | EUM 1. Serves long to Peter's backhand side |
| 1-0 | EUM 2. Blocks sideway to Peter's backhand side |
| | EUM 3. Content; pleased to have made a nice stroke and to have good sensations from the ball |
| | EUM 4. Serves short to Peter's backhand side |
| 2-0 | EUM 5. Attacks |
| | EUM 6. Confident that he's made a difficult stroke |
| | EUM 7. Serves long to Peter's backhand side |
| 3-0 | EUM 8. Counter-attacks to Peter's backhand side |
| | EUM 8. Confident to be ahead in score |

*Categorizing the elements.* In this last step, any elements mentioned by the players to describe the situation in which they had experienced a sentiment were categorized in the new corpus. These elements were grouped into larger units on the basis of three criteria: (a) the nature of these elements mentioned by the players, (b) a comparable level of generality across categories, and (c) the use of category definitions that were discriminating enough to avoid overlapping. The categories were defined step by step, that is, a new category was created for each element that did not fit into an already existing category. The elements were classified into six specific categories

## Assuring Credibility

Several measures were taken to enhance the credibility of the data (Lincoln & Guba, 1985). First, the transcripts were given back to the participants to ensure the authenticity of their commentary and to allow them to make any changes to the text. Minor editorial comments were made regarding confrontational responses. Second, the data were coded independently by two trained investigators who reached a consensus on the number and names of the EUMs. These two researchers had already coded protocols of this type during previous studies, had previous experience in table tennis, and were familiar with the framework of course-of-action theory. The initial agreement rate was 85% for the EUMs. Any initial disagreements about EUMs were resolved by discussion among the researchers until a consensus was reached. The elements of the new corpus (relative to sentiments) were then grouped by these two researchers. The initial agreement rate was 90% for category coding. The researchers discussed any disagreements until a consensus was reached.

## RESULTS AND DISCUSSION

The results are presented in four stages: (a) the evolution of affective states during the matches, (b) typical "situation-sentiment" couplings, (c) the histories in which these couplings were embedded, and (d) the contradictory nature of emotion.

### The evolution of affective states during matches

The players' affective states varied during sets and matches (see Figures 1, 2, 3 et 4). At the start of sets, their affective states were neutral or slightly positive (at a score of 0-0, the players estimated +2 on the EAS scale once, +1 nine times, 0 five times, and -1 once). Only Set 2 of Match C and Set 3 of Match D began with values other than 0 or +1. These states were related to players' judgments regarding the situation. Jacques had won Set 1 of Match C and thought he had played very well. He thus estimated +2 on the EAS scale for the start of Set 2: "Right at this moment, I feel sure. I'm calm and in fighting form. I feel good and I'm focused. In my head I'm ready to go!" [Match C, Set 2, 0-0, +2 on the EAS]. Marc had lost the first two sets of Match D and thought he had little chance of winning the match. He estimated -1 on the EAS scale at the start of Set 3: "Here, I start the third set without really thinking I'll do OK. He's playing really well. The second set has really hurt me" [Match D, Set 3, 0-0, -1 on the EAS].

At the end of sets, the players' affective states were positive or negative (they estimated -3 twice, -2 three times, -1 five times, +1 three times and +2 three times).Whether a state was positive or negative depended principally on the set results. Eleven of the 16 sets were lost and six were won. At the end of winning sets, the players always estimated positive values.

At the end of losing sets, they estimated a negative value ten times. The only losing set with a positive value was Set 2 of Match A: "For those last points, he really played well. There's just nothing to say. But I still found a serve that bothered him. I was hoping I could still maybe win the match" [Match A, Set 2, 18-21, +1 on the EAS].

The affective states changed progressively over the course of the sets and matches. Of the 596 EAS evaluations, 457 successive evaluations were identical, 136 showed a 1-point difference, two showed a 2-point difference, and one showed a 4-point difference. This last difference was seen in Set 2 of Match D. At a score of 19-20, Marc estimated +1 and then -3 went the score changed to 19-21: "I am really disappointed here because it's the turning point of the match. Even though I'd been trailing in the set, I brought the score up to 19-20 and then I lost. By losing two sets to zero, I had almost no chance of winning the match" [Match D, Set 2, 19-21, -3 on the EAS].

Analysis showed that 32.6 % of the estimations were made when the players were ahead, 14.2 % when the score was equal, and 53.2 % when they were trailing. The estimations were positive 53.8 % of the time, neutral 21 %, and negative 25.2%. The positive or negative character of the estimations was linked to the score (see Table 4) ($\chi^2$ (8, $N = 3$) = 160, $p <$ .001).

**Table 4. Repartition of positive, neutral and negative affective states based on score**

| Score position | EAS < 0 | EAS = 0 | EAS > 0 |
|---|---|---|---|
| Leading in score | 8 | 11 | 175 |
| Score equal | 8 | 26 | 51 |
| Trailing in score | 134 | 88 | 95 |

The affective states were in great part positive or neutral during the matches (75% of the EAS estimations were > 0). Negative states were essentially noted when the players were behind in the score (in 89% of the negative estimations, the players were trailing).

### Typical "situation-sentiment" couplings

The players experienced different sentiments during matches, which were labeled on the basis of their verbalized content (e.g., pleasure, confidence, relief, worry, disappointment, irritation). They were felt at different moments and were always expressed in relation to meaningful elements in the situation in which the players were engaged. Certain were relative to events that were perceptible to outside observers (e.g., the difference in scores) and others to the players' judgments (e.g., sensations experienced while making a stroke). Six categories of elements mentioned by the players to describe situations in which they experienced a sentiment were identified: (a) the status and evolution of the score, (b) the win or loss of a point based on numerous rallies, (c) judgments about the adversarial relationship, (d) judgments about the opponent's sentiment of self-confidence, (e) judgments about the strokes performed, and (f) judgments about the making of a point. The identification of these elements provided the means to identify typical "situation-sentiment" couplings, that is, the families of situations (or situation-types) in which players experienced a sentiment. For each category, we identified several situation-types. An example of a "sentiment-situation" coupling for each is illustrated using excerpts from the match logs.

*The status and evolution of the score.* Analysis showed four situation-types in reference to the status and evolution of the score. The players (a) were ahead in the score and maintained their advantage, (b) had been trailing in the score and were catching up, (c) had been trailing in the score and were unable to catch up, or (d) had been ahead but the opponent had caught up to them. A sentiment of confidence or satisfaction was experienced during couplings between the players and one of the first two situations; a sentiment of impatience, agitation, worry, irritation or even discouragement -when they judged that the score was such that they would not be able to win the match- was experienced during couplings with either of the last two situations.

> Overcoming two sets of 0 and 5-10...I didn't think I could win. I'm a little discouraged here. [Match D, Set 3, 5-10, -1 on the EAS]

*The win or loss of a point based on numerous rallies.* Analysis distinguished two situation-types. The players (a) won the point after a high number of rallies (at least four), or (b) lost the point after a high number of rallies. A sentiment of satisfaction, confidence, or pleasure was experienced during couplings between players and the first situation, and a sentiment of disappointment or irritation was experienced during couplings with the second.

> Here I'm really disappointed. I had worked hard for the point, I was ready to counter-attack and I missed the defense. It's never easy to lose points after a long rally...it always brings you down. [Match C, Set 3, 14-17, 0 on the EAS]

*Judgments about the adversarial relationship.* Analysis distinguished two situation-types. The players judged that (a) they had the initiative in the game (e.g., they had identified the most effective strokes in the game or the ones that would limit the opponent's range of responses), or (b) they did not have the initiative (e.g., they could not effectively counter the opponent's strokes or they perceived that the strokes that earlier had been effective were no longer so). A sentiment of relief, confidence, or satisfaction was experienced during couplings between players and the first situation, and a sentiment of worry or irritation was experienced during couplings with the second.

> Here I'm already worried. He's not making any mistakes when he returns the serve. He's returning the ball really nicely even though he had been upset by these serves in Italy. [Match D, Set 1, 2-2, +1 on the EAS]

*Judgments about the opponent's sentiment of self-confidence.* Analysis distinguished two situation-types. The players estimated that either (a) the opponent was agitated, discouraged or irritated, or (b) he had a sentiment of high confidence. A sentiment of confidence was experienced during couplings with the first situation and sentiments of agitation or worry during couplings with the second.

> Here I can feel that he's agitated. From the minute I see that, I'm in good shape, I'm confident. [Match A, Set 5, 4-2, +3 on the EAS]

*Judgments about the strokes performed.* Analysis distinguished six situation-types. The players (a) judged that the opponent was making unusual mistakes, (b) judged that they themselves had succeeded at very difficult strokes, (c) experienced sensations that they qualified as "good" (e.g., they had "felt" the ball, perceived themselves as moving very rapidly), (d) judged that the opponent had made very difficult strokes, (e) estimated that they themselves had made unusual/unexpected mistakes, or (f) experienced sensations that they qualified as "bad" (e.g., they could not really feel the ball, had the sensation of "heavy legs"). A sentiment of pleasure, satisfaction or confidence was experienced during couplings with one of the first three situations and sentiments of doubt, disappointment or irritation during couplings with one of the last three.

> Here I'm happy, I made a beautiful stroke to start the set and I can feel that I'm really connecting with the ball. [Match A, Set 4, 0-0, + 2 on the EAS]

*Judgments about the making of a point.* Analysis distinguished two situation-types. The players (a) won a point and judged that they had been lucky (they made a lucky shot) or (b) they lost a point and judged that their opponent had been lucky (he made a lucky shot). A sentiment of relief or satisfaction was experienced during couplings with the first situation and irritation during couplings with the second.

> Here I'm a little lucky and I'm relieved that the ball was good. [Match B, Set 3, 9-10, 0 on the EAS]

### The histories in which the "situation-sentiment" couplings are embedded

The same events were not always coupled with the same sentiments and affective states. During Set 2 of Match B, with the score 12-11, the opponent got the point with a trajectory that caused the ball to hit the net before bouncing on the table (which prevented Luc from returning it). This event was not coupled with a modification in Luc's affective state (he indicated 0 on the EAS scale for scores of 12-11 and 12-12): "Here I'm trying a new serve, a long fast serve to his backhand side. He 'stole' the ball. It's really too bad because that's how he caught up to me in the score—but, that's part of the game. I would have preferred winning the point but I'm happy to have tried the serve. Sometimes I have to serve long so that he doesn't get too used to returning my short serves" [Match B, Set 2, 12-12, 0 on the EAS].

During Set 4, with the score 18-18, the opponent got the point by producing another trajectory that caused the ball to hit the net before bouncing on the table. This event was coupled to a sentiment of irritation and a modification in Luc's affective state (he estimated 0 on the EAS scale with the score 18-18 and -2 with the score 18-19): "Here I attacked really well and the worst thing happened: he 'stole' the ball. He got the lead in the score by pure luck. Right there I had the impression that the match was starting to turn because I was leading 16-9, I was playing with my second racket, and he steals the ball to take the lead. That was too much, and I got mad" [Match B, Set 4, 18-19, -2 on the EAS].

These extracts show that emotion was coupled with a complex network of events that influenced the judgments made by the table tennis players *in situ*. The "situation-sentiment" couplings were embedded in match histories comprising several points. These histories were linked to the evolution in the players' concerns during the matches. During Set 2, Luc had identified the serves (short serves with varying direction) that bothered his opponent.

Although he used these serves at the start of the set, Luc knew that he was reproducing them too often and that his opponent was going to find an effective response. With the score 12-11, he at last decided to perturb his opponent's game by making a serve he had not yet made. The opponent won the point with a trajectory that Luc described as lucky. Luc's affective state was not modified, however, and he was satisfied to have tried this serve. He felt that this move was going to help preserve the effectiveness of his short serves. When the score was 18-18 in Set 4, Luc tried exclusively to score points. His opponent was winning, two sets to one, and would win the match if he won Set 4. When Luc had been leading 16-9 in Set 4, he thought he had a good chance to win the set. Over the next few points, he varied his strokes and his opponent began to catch up. When the score was 18-16, Luc broke his racket and had to use his spare. At 18-18, his opponent pulled ahead with a shot that Luc again described as lucky. But this event in combination with others (the perception of having lost points foolishly, his opponent catching up in the score, the broken racket) modified his affective state and he now felt irritated.

### The contradictory nature of emotion

The contradictory nature of emotion was revealed when: (a) affective states and sentiments experienced at the same instant did not present with the same tone and (b) the display of sentiments did not correspond to their actual experience (i.e., what was in fact felt). The players sometimes felt sentiments described as pleasant by Hanin (2000) (e.g., pleasure, satisfaction) although they had indicated a negative value for their affective state, and sometimes felt sentiments qualified as unpleasant (e.g., irritation, annoyance, disappointment) although they had indicated a positive value for their affective state.

> Right here I'm happy with the shot I made. Even though I know I can't win the set, it still feels good to make a great shot like that. [Match C, Set 2, 10-20, -1 on the EAS]
> Here I decided to vary the serve and I missed. That really got to me. At 20-17, I'm not worried, but missing a serve is always hard. [Match A, Set 3, 20-17, +3 on the EAS]

The expression of sentiments differed with content. Sometimes the players publicly displayed a sentiment of satisfaction or confidence to influence the opponent and reduce his feeling of confidence. In contrast, they masked sentiments of irritation and agitation. They judged that showing these sentiments could increase their opponent's confidence level.

> Here I made a good shot. This is the first time in the match that I was able to attack like that. I'm happy; it's the first time I'm ahead in this set and so I'm showing my satisfaction—to put pressure on him, to show him that I'm still here and I haven't yet lost. [Match B, Set 3, 11-10, +1 on the EAS]
> Here I'm beginning to get a little irritated. I really feel like I can't counter his game. This is really getting to me but I don't show it. If I do, he'll get even more confident and, for him, the more confident he gets, the easier it is to make really hard shots. [Match D, Set 1, 7-13, -1 on the EAS]

In table tennis, the expression of emotion is intrinsic to the interaction with an opponent. The stakes of competition and the antagonistic objectives of the two adversaries are such that players may exaggerate or mask their emotion in order to mislead the other. They know that the opponent is assessing and judging their emotion and that these judgments will influence their own feelings of self-confidence They thus will look for opportunities to display or, conversely, mask their emotion, and the expression of an emotion will not always be concordant with its experience. Table tennis players face their opponents not only through action but also through the display of emotion. They try to determine the affective states and sentiments of their opponent to improve their own control of the competitive situation, while they hide or misrepresent their own emotion to influence the judgments that their opponent will make.

## CONCLUSION

In this study, emotion was approached from two angles: (a) the dynamics of emotion, and (b) the time frame in which emotion occurs.

### *Emotional Dynamics*

During the matches, the players' emotions developed from two dynamics: one arising from the firstness of experience (Peirce, 1931-1935) and the other from its secondness. These two dynamics were deployed on different time scales, as well. The emotional dynamics defined as affective states could be characterized as a relatively stable, continuous emotional flow against which more ephemeral sentiments were displayed. Important features of affective states were their endurance over time and a certain inertia. Fluctuations were progressive and depended mainly on changes in score. During the matches, the tone of this emotional flow was generally positive. Although three of the four matches studied were lost and 53% of the estimations occurred when the players were trailing, only 25% of the EAS estimations were negative. The players experienced the matches as rather pleasant and, as is the case with most high level athletes, they appreciated the tension of a high-stakes match (Jones & Swain, 1992; Kerr, 1997). This positive tone can also be interpreted as the search for an affective state that favorizes performance. Our method of analyzing our data did not allow us to confirm or disprove the hypothesis of Individual Zones of Optimal Functioning (Hanin & Syrjä, 1995). However, we can note that the players began their sets with either a neutral or positive affective state. By the end of the sets, this state was positive in the case of a win and negative for a loss. At the start of a set, the players presented an affective state that they judged to be favorable for optimal performance. The events encountered during the set and the evolution in score progressively influenced this state in a positive or negative manner.

The second dynamic concerned sentiments and was closely associated with the judgments made by the players during actual situations of play. The sentiments were more labile; they appeared with the unfolding of certain events but did not endure. They had specific content (e.g., pleasure, satisfaction, confidence, relief, impatience, worry, agitation, disappointment, irritation, or discouragement), the tone of which could be classified as pleasant or unpleasant, according to Hanin (2000). This tone, however, was at times in contradiction with the tone of the affective state, probably because the two dynamics did not evolve in the same fashion. The affective states presented an inertia: they were modified only progressively and essentially as a function of the score. We can speak here of the persistence of these states. Sentiments, on the other hand, were coupled to specific situations. They were experienced transiently and instantly in relation to diverse interpretations and events (making a difficult stroke, identifying a disturbing stroke by the opponent, the sensation of having been lucky making a point). This contradictory nature reinforces the idea that emotion cannot be reduced to only its tone and intensity (Hanin, 2000) and explains in part the observation in other studies that the same emotion will, depending on the situation, be associated with optimal or poor performance (e.g., Hanin & Syrjä, 1995; Robazza, Bortoli, Nocini et al., 2000).

### Time Frameworks of Emotion

We observed typical "situation-sentiment" couplings; that is, categories of situations in which the players felt a sentiment. The emotion-arousing nature of a situation was linked to the elements in the situation that had immediate meaning for the players and that formed the basis on which they made judgments. The same elements were not always coupled with the same interpretations and, consequently, were not always coupled with the same sentiments. Interpretations followed from judgments made over the course of different time spans and followed from both (a) the elements taken into account and mentioned as being meaningful by the players in the current situation (which depended on past and present events) and (b) the players' concerns that were woven into a much wider time span covering a succession of several points (Sève et al., 2002b). These concerns arose from both past activity and past judgments. They evolved and contributed to the construction of a progressive and situated history of the match that took shape over the course of strokes performed, points won and lost, choices made, and knowledge built (Sève et al., 2003). "Situation-sentiment" couplings were embedded in this history as salient moments.

Emotion, as well, participated in the construction of this history. Depending on their affective state and the sentiments experienced, the players performed more or less difficult strokes, prolonged or shortened the rest periods between points, displayed, or masked their emotion. Emotion evolves during competition with actions and judgments made *in situ*. It is experienced and expressed in relation to the subjective appropriation of the events encountered (which depends on both present and past events and the player's involvement mode in the situation) and influences in turn the judgments made about the situation. The relationships among emotion, action and cognition were co-definitional: interpretation of the current situation influenced the emotion that was experienced, which in turn influenced the actions and judgments that followed. Although all emotion is relative to a specific state in a situation that will never be identically reproduced, it is the source for the construction of elements of knowledge for the actor (Ria, Sève, Saury, & Durand, 2003).

The players had a general awareness of the satisfactions or resistances that would come, and at times they anticipated, avoided, or controlled the agreeable or disagreeable character of their experience. They tended to reproduce effective strokes and to look for situations that had been coupled to a positive affective experience; they likewise tended to avoid strokes and situations that had been coupled to negative affective experience (Sève et al., 2002a). This typicalization of emotions constitutes an important facet in the development of expertise (Hanin & Syrjä, 1995; Ria et al., 2003).

# REFERENCES

Arripe-Longueville, F.(d'), Saury, J., Fournier, J., & Durand, M. (2001). Coach-athlete interaction during elite archery competitions: An application of methodological frameworks used in ergonomics research to sport psychology. *Journal of Applied Sport Psychology, 13*, 275-299.

Cerin, E., Szabo, A., Hunt, N., & Williams, C. (2000). Temporal patterning of competitive emotions: A critical review. *Journal of Sports Sciences, 18*, 605–626.

Clancey, W.J. (1997). *Situated cognition.* Cambridge UK: Cambridge University Press.

Damasio, A.R. (1994). *Descartes' Error: emotions, reason and the human brain.* New York: Grosset & Putman Books.

Goodwin, M.H., & Goodwin, C. (2000). Emotion within situated activity. In A. Duranti (Ed.), *Linguistic anthropology: A reader* (pp. 239-257). Malden, MA: Blackwell.

Gould, D., Eklund, R.C., & Jackson, S. A. (1993). Coping strategies used by U.S. Olympic wrestlers. *Research Quarterly for Exercise and Sport, 64*, 383-402.

Hanin, Y. (Ed.). (2000). *Emotions in sport.* Champaign, IL: Human Kinetics.

Hanin, Y., & Syrjä, P. (1995). Performance affect in junior ice hockey players: An application of the Individual Zones of Optimal Functioning model. *The Sport Psychologist, 9*, 167-187.

Hanin, Y., & Syrjä, P. (1996). Predicted, actual, and recalled affect in Olympic-level soccer players: Idiographic asseements on individual scales. *Journal of Sport and Exercise Psychology, 18*, 325-335.

Hauw, D., Berthelot, C., & Durand, M. (2003). Enhancing performance in elite athletes through situated-cognition analysis: Trampolinists' course of action during competition activity. *International Journal of Sport Psychology, 34*, 299-321.

Hutchins, E. (1995). *Cognition in the wild.* Cambridge, MA: MIT Press.

Jones, J.G., & Swain, A. (1992). Intensity and direction as dimensions of competitive state anxiety and relationship with competitiveness. *Perceptual and Motor Skills, 74*, 467-472.

Kerr, H.J. (1997). *Motivation and emotion in sport: Reversal theory.* East Sussex, UK: Taylor & Francis.

Kirshner, D., & Whitson, J.A. (Eds.) (1997). *Situated cognition. Social, semiotic, and psychological perspectives.* Mahwah, NJ: Lawrence Erlbaum Associates.

Lave, J. (1988). *Cognition in practice. Mind, mathematics and culture in everyday life.* Cambridge UK: Cambridge University Press.

Lazarus, R.S. (1991). *Emotion and adaptation.* New York: Oxford University Press.

Lazarus, R.S. (2000). How emotions influence performance in competitive sports. *The Sport Psychologist, 14*, 229-252.

Lazarus, R.S. (2001). Relational meanings and discrete emotions. In K.R. Scherer, A. Schorr & T. Johnstone (Eds.), *Appraisal processes in emotion* (pp. 37-67). New York: Oxford University Press.

Lincoln, Y.S., & Guba, E.G. (1985). *Naturalistic inquiry.* Beverly Hills, CA: Sage.

Martens, R., Vealey, R.S., & Burton, D. (1990). *Competitive anxiety in sport.* Champaign, IL: Human Kinetics.

Norman, D.A. (1993). *Things that make us smart. Defending human attributes in the age of the machine.* New York: Addison-Wesley.

Peirce, C.S. (1931-1935). *The collected papers of Charles Sanders Peirce* (Vols. 1-6, C. Hartshorne & P. Weiss Eds.). Cambridge, MA: Harvard University Press.

Poizat, G., Sève, C., & Rossard, C. (2006). Influencer les jugements de l'adversaire au cours des interactions sportives compétitives: Un exemple en tennis de table [Influencing opponent's judgments during competitive interaction: an example in table tennis]. *Revue Européenne de Psychologie Appliquée, 56*, 167-178.

Ria, L. (2001). *Les préoccupations des enseignants débutants en Education Physique et Sportive. Etude de l'expérience professionnelle et conception d'aides à la formation.* [Beginning teachers' preoccupations in Physical Education. Study of professional experience and conception of training aids]. Unpublished doctoral thesis, STAPS, Université de Montpellier 1, France.

Ria, L., & Durand, M. (2001). Les préoccupations et la tonalité émotionnelle des enseignants débutants lors de leurs premières expériences en classe [Beginning teachers' preccupations and emotionnal flow during their first classroom experiences]. *Les Dossiers des Sciences de l'Education, 5*, 111-123.

Ria, L., Sève, C., Saury, J., & Durand, M. (2003). Beginning teachers' situated emotions: A study of first classroom experiences. *Journal of Education for Teaching, 29*, 219-234.

Robazza, C., Bortoli, L., & Nougier, N. (2000). Performance emotions in an elite archer: A case study. *Journal of Sport Behavior, 23*, 144-163.

Robazza, C., Bortoli, L., Nocini, F., Moser, G., & Arslan, C. (2000). Normative and idiosyncratic measures of positive and negative affect in sport. *Psychology of Sport and Exercise, 1*, 103-116.

Saury, J., Durand, M., & Theureau, J. (1997). L'action d'un entraîneur expert en compétition: étude de cas. Contribution à une analyse ergonomique de l'entraînement. [Action of an expert competition coach: Case study. Contribution to an ergonomic analysis of training]. *Science et Motricité, 21*, 21-35.

Scherer, K.R., Schorr, A., & Johnstone, T. (2001) (Eds.). *Appraisal processes in emotion. Theory, methods, research.* New York: Oxford University Press.

Sève, C., & Poizat, G. (2005). Table tennis scoring systems and expert players' exploration activity. *International Journal of Sport Psychology, 36*, 320-336.

Sève, C., Poizat, G., Saury, J., & Durand, M. (2006). A ground theory of elite male table tennis players' activity during matches. *The Sport Psychologist, 20*, 58-73.

Sève, C., Saury, J., Leblanc, S., & Durand, M. (2005). Course-of-action theory in table tennis: A qualitative analysis of the knowledge used by three elite players during matches. *European Review of Applied Psychology, 55*, 145-155.

Sève, C., Saury, J., Ria, L., & Durand, M. (2003). Structure of expert table tennis players' activity during competitive interaction. *Research Quarterly for Exercise and Sport, 74*, 71-83.

Sève, C., Saury, J., Theureau, J., & Durand, M. (2002a). La construction de connaissances chez les sportifs au cours d'une interaction compétitive [Knowledge construction by athletes during competitive interaction]. *Le Travail Humain, 65*, 159-190.

Sève, C., Saury, J., Theureau, J., Durand, M. (2002b). Activity organization and knowledge construction during competitive interaction in table tennis. *Cognitive Systems Research, 3*, 501-522.

Suchman, L. (1987). *Plans and situated action*. Cambridge, UK: Cambridge University Press.

Theureau, J. (1992). *Le cours d'action: Analyse sémiologique. Essai d'une anthropologie cognitive située.* [The course of action: semiological analysis. Essay on situated cognitive anthropology]. Berne, Switzerland: Peter Lang.

Theureau, J. (2004). *Le cours d'action: Méthode élémentaire* [The course of action: Basic methods]. Toulouse, France: Octarès.

Theureau, J. (2006). *Cours d'action: Méthode développée* [Course of action: Developed Method]. Toulouse, France: Octarès.

Varela, F. (1980). *Principles of biological autonomy.* New York: Elsevier North Holland.

Watson, D., Clark, L. A., & Tellengen, A. (1988). Development and validation of brief measures of positive and negative affect: The PANAS scales. *Journal of Personality and Social Psychology, 54*, 1063-1070.

*Figure 1* **Players' estimation of his affective state on the EAS scale as a function of score during Match A**

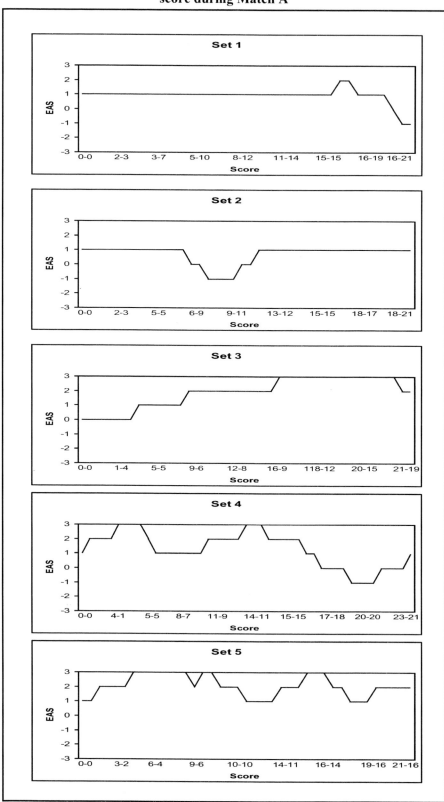

***Figure 2* Players' estimation of his affective state on the EAS scale as a function of score during Match B**

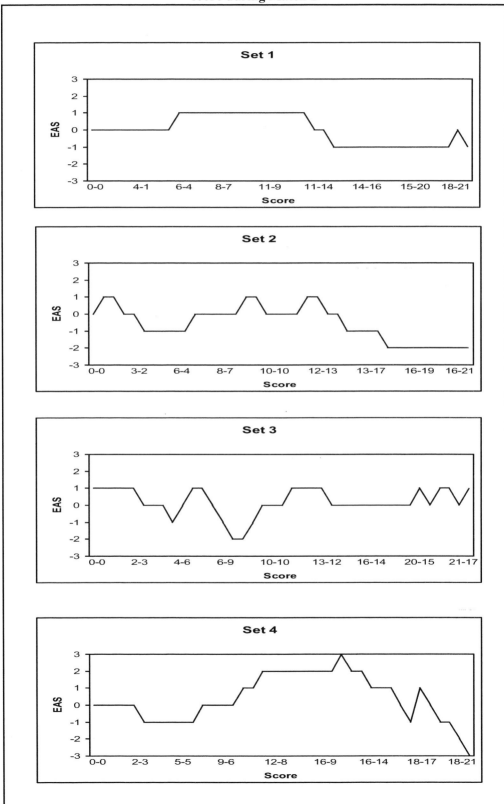

*Figure 3* **Players' estimation of his affective state on the EAS scale as a function of score during Match C**

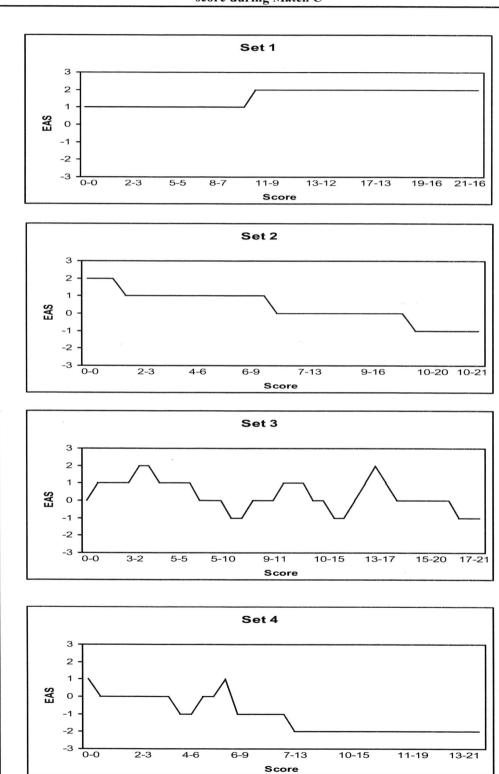

*Figure 4* **Players' estimation of his affective state on the EAS scale as a function of score during Match D**

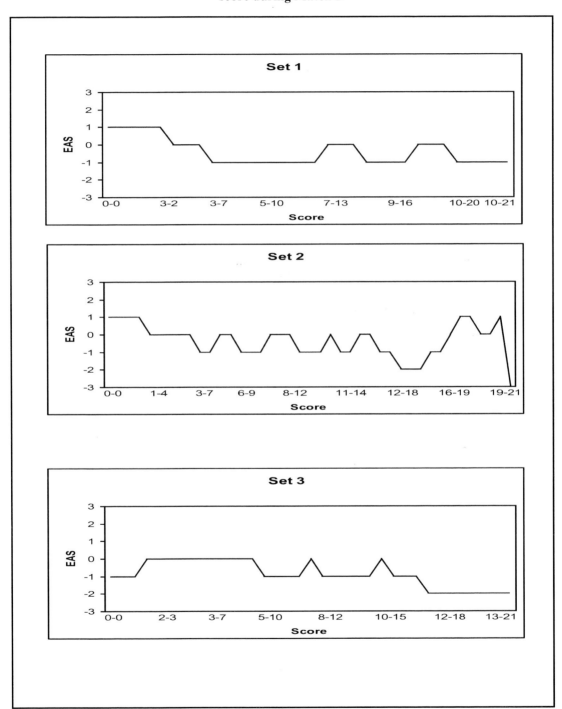

In: Applied Psychology Research Trends
Editor: Karl H. Kiefer, pp.103-118

ISBN 978-1-60456-372-6
© 2008 Nova Science Publishers, Inc.

*Chapter 5*

# THE CONFIDENCE-ACCURACY RELATION IN EYEWITNESS IDENTIFICATION: EFFECTS OF VERBAL VERSUS NUMERIC CONFIDENCE SCALES

## *Nathan Weber[1], Neil Brewer[1] and Scott Margitich[1]*
[1]School of Psychology, Flinders University
[1]GPO Box 2100, Adelaide,S. Aust 5001,Australia

## ABSTRACT

Eyewitness identification evidence plays a crucial role in western legal systems. As a result, the consequences of an erroneous identification decision are serious. Specifically, the misidentification of an innocent suspect can, at best, delay the apprehension and conviction of the real offender or, at worst, lead to the conviction of an innocent person and the escape of the offender. Similarly, failure to identify the offender when they are present in the lineup may reduce the chances of a successful conviction. Not surprisingly, psychologists have sought to solve this problem by identifying factors (e.g., confidence) that discriminate correct from incorrect lineup decisions. Recent studies investigating confidence using a calibration approach have found consistent, robust confidence-accuracy calibration for choosers from lineups and positive decisions in face recognition tasks. Although encouraging, the applied usefulness of the calibration approach may be limited by its reliance on numerical, indeed probabilistic, confidence judgments. The use of a numerical confidence judgment stands in contrast with the U.S. Department of Justice's guidelines which suggest eliciting a confidence judgment in the witness's own words. Further, evidence from other areas of psychology suggests that people deal more naturally with verbal rather than numeric labels and struggle particularly with judgments about probabilities. Here we present an experimental investigation of these potential limits on the usefulness of confidence. Specifically, we compared confidence itself, and the confidence-accuracy relationship, between responses made on an eleven-point scale with either numeric (0% - 100%) or verbal (e.g., "Impossible" and "Certain") labels. One hundred and ninety two participants made identification decisions about four independent lineups and rated their confidence in the accuracy of each of their decisions. Each participant made two confidence judgments using the verbal scale and two using the numeric scale. Analyses revealed nearly identical confidence distributions for the verbal and numeric scales. Further, examination of the confidence-accuracy relationship revealed negligible differences between responses made on the verbal and numeric scales. These findings suggest that despite problems with numeric judgments in other domains, participants are no better able to provide confidence judgments in verbal than numeric form. Consequently, the reliance of the calibration approach for examining the confidence-accuracy relationship and for using confidence to predict accuracy is not a barrier to its use in eyewitness identification.

Eyewitness identifications are widely accepted as important and convincing evidence in Western legal systems. Often eyewitness testimony is the only evidence available (Cutler & Penrod, 1995) and, in some cases, convictions are based solely, or primarily, on an eyewitness identification or identifications (Wells et al., 1998). Further, eyewitness identifications have been demonstrated to have a consistent and robust impact on the proportion of guilty verdicts in mock-juror studies (Cutler & Penrod, 1995). As a result, the consequences of erroneous identification decisions are considerable. False identifications (i.e., identifying an innocent suspect as the offender) can lead to the prosecution and conviction of an innocent person and incorrect rejections (i.e., failing to identify the offender when they are, in fact, in the lineup) can reduce the ability to successfully prosecute the actual culprit. Unfortunately, in addition to its importance and persuasiveness, the fallibility of eyewitness identification evidence has also been consistently demonstrated in both laboratory experiments and field studies (for review, see Brewer, Weber, & Semmler, 2005; Cutler & Penrod, 1995). For example, the Innocence Project website (2007) reports that mistaken identifications were important in the wrongful conviction of over 75% of the 208 individuals exonerated to date.

Two complementary approaches to the unreliability of eyewitness identifications have been adopted by psychology-law researchers: specifically, identification of (a) a lineup procedure that eliminates false identifications and (b) markers of the accuracy of an identification decision. Here we focus on an aspect of the latter approach: namely, the use of confidence as a marker of identification accuracy. Specifically, we present an experiment investigating the impact of verbal versus numeric confidence scales on confidence judgments and the confidence-accuracy (CA) relationship in eyewitness identification.

## CONFIDENCE IN EYEWITNESS IDENTIFICATIONS

A large body of research has investigated the CA relationship in eyewitness identification using the point-biserial correlation as the index of this relationship. A number of researchers have reviewed this work (e.g., Bothwell, Deffenbacher, & Brigham, 1987; Sporer, Penrod, Read, & Cutler, 1995; Wells & Murray, 1984), coming to the generally consistent conclusion that confidence and accuracy are, at best, only weakly correlated. The average coefficients identified in these reviews range from .07 to .28. Not surprisingly, based on this evidence the conclusion of the field has been that confidence is not a useful indicator of accuracy in the eyewitness identification context, a conclusion that has been offered by many expert witnesses in the courtroom (Cutler & Penrod, 1995).

Despite the early preponderance of negative evidence, more recent research suggests that the CA relationship may, at least in some circumstances, have been underestimated. Sporer et al. (1995) meta-analysed 30 identification experiments and found overall results consistent with those described above ($r = .28$). However, in addition to investigating the overall relationship, Sporer et al. also explored the CA correlation for choosers (i.e., participants making an identification from the lineup) and non-choosers (i.e., participants who responded that the offender was not present in the lineup) separately. They found a stronger association between confidence and accuracy for choosers ($r = .37$) than for non-choosers ($r = .12$) and concluded that, when investigation is confined only to witnesses who make positive identifications, confidence is a stronger predictor of accuracy than originally thought.

Much stronger evidence for the efficacy of confidence as a predictor of accuracy has been reported by D. S. Lindsay, Read, and colleagues (Lindsay, Nilsen, & Read, 2000; Lindsay, Read, & Sharma, 1998; Read, Lindsay, & Nicholls, 1998). They argued that in typical eyewitness identification experiments all participants are (a) exposed to very similar stimuli under the same viewing conditions, and (b) make their identification decisions from the same lineup in identical testing conditions. Such conditions constrain the variability in confidence judgments, leading to the low CA correlations typically observed. Data from three experiments supported this argument, with CA correlations of, for example, $r = .72$ and $r = .69$ (Read et al.) observed under encoding and retrieval conditions producing variable performance, but more typical correlations of $r = .18$ and $r = .26$ when performance was more homogenous. As real world conditions are likely to produce a large amount of variability in performance, these studies suggest that the CA relationship in the applied setting has been grossly underestimated.

*Confidence-accuracy calibration.* Recently, Juslin, Olsson, and Winman (1996) argued that the point-biserial correlation is not the most appropriate index of the CA relationship in eyewitness identification. Instead, they argued for the use of calibration. Calibration, an analysis technique common in decision research, is a measure of the association between objective and subjective probabilities. For a sample of observations to be well calibrated, the subjective judgments of the probability of an event occurring must correspond with the objective probability of that event occurring. In the case of the CA relationship then, calibration refers to the extent to which confidence judgments on a proportional or percentile scale (i.e., the subjective probability judgments) correspond to the proportion of correct decisions made with a particular level of confidence (i.e., the objective probability). Specifically, in a perfectly calibrated sample, all of the decisions made with 100% confidence would be correct, 90% of the decisions made with 90% confidence would be correct, 80% of the decisions made with 80% would be correct, and so on for every confidence level.

Calibration is typically assessed in three ways. The major method is the plotting of a calibration curve: specifically, a plot of proportion correct against confidence for each confidence level. Examination of the calibration curves allows a visual assessment of the extent to which a sample deviates from perfect calibration. This deviation from perfect calibration can also be indexed numerically by the calibration statistic (C) which is calculated as the weighted average of the squared difference between proportion correct and confidence (as a proportion) at each confidence level. It ranges from 0 (perfect calibration) to 1 (worst possible calibration). The third measure, over/underconfidence (O/U), is not technically a measure of calibration. Rather, it is an index of the overall tendency of a participant (or participants) to respond with confidence that is more (i.e., overconfidence) or less (i.e., underconfidence) than is warranted by their accuracy. Its calculation simplifies to the difference between mean confidence (again, as a proportion) and overall proportion correct. Over/underconfidence ranges from -1 (extreme underconfidence) to +1 (extreme overconfidence). Another measure associated with calibration is resolution. Resolution refers to the extent to which confidence judgments discriminate correct from incorrect decisions. Resolution is typically indexed by the normalized resolution index (NRI), which is equivalent to eta-squared. It ranges from 0 (no discrimination between correct and incorrect decisions) to 1 (perfect discrimination). For a detailed discussion and formal development of these indices, see, for example, Baranski and Petrusic (1994) or Yaniv, Yates, and Smith (1991).

In addition to a number of statistical reasons, a key point in Juslin et al.'s (1996) argument against the correlation coefficient was that calibration provides exactly the type of information required by the police and in the courtroom. For example, if a witness makes an identification with 80% confidence, knowledge that confidence and accuracy are correlated at 0.3 (or any other value) does not help a police officer make a judgment about the likely accuracy of that decision. However, if the police officer is aware that confidence and accuracy are well calibrated, they know that an identification made with 80% confidence has an 80% chance of being accurate. Thus, knowledge of the situations in which confidence and accuracy are well calibrated is the type of information that can help law enforcement and judicial officials weigh the evidential value of an individual identification decision.

Support for the strong theoretical and statistical reasons for adopting calibration as the index of the CA relationship in eyewitness identification has also been provided empirically. Studies employing both eyewitness identification (Brewer, Keast, & Rishworth, 2002; Brewer & Wells, 2006; Juslin et al., 1996) and face recognition (Weber & Brewer, 2003, 2004, 2006) have identified robust, positive, linear calibration curves for choosers (or positive recognition decisions) for confidence judgments made immediately after the identification or recognition decision. Further, there is consistent evidence of highly confident decisions being indicative of the most accurate group of decisions in a sample (Brewer & Wells, 2006; Weber, Brewer, Wells, Semmler, & Keast, 2004). Thus, in contrast with conclusions based on CA correlations, the calibration research suggests that there is a meaningful CA relationship and that confidence has some promise as a practical marker of identification accuracy.

## MEASUREMENT OF CONFIDENCE

Although results from early research on CA calibration are promising for the practical use of confidence as a marker of eyewitness identification accuracy, a potential problem exists. Specifically, the calibration approach relies on the elicitation of confidence as a probabilistic, numerical response. This reliance on numerical, and particularly probabilistic, responses presents a potential barrier to the successful use of calibration for a number of reasons. First, the elicitation of numeric confidence judgments stands in stark contrast with the recommendation of the US Department of Justice for the collection of eyewitness evidence. In their guide for law enforcement, the Technical Working Group on Eyewitness Evidence (1999) recommended that witnesses be asked to express their confidence in the accuracy of their identification decision in their own words. Although this recommendation may simply represent a continuation of existing practice rather than a deliberate recommendation against numerical confidence judgments, it likely reflects the belief that witnesses will be most able to express their confidence without being restricted to a specific confidence scale.

A second potential problem with the elicitation of probabilistic confidence judgments is highlighted by decision making research on probabilistic reasoning. A large body of work suggests that people's probabilistic reasoning is affected by a number of biases or reasoning errors (see, e.g., Tversky & Koehler, 1994) that impair their ability to make probabilistically appropriate use of evidence. This research raises the possibility that, at least in some situations, the use of a probabilistic confidence scale my produce biased or erroneous confidence judgments. The third, and most important, concern regarding numeric confidence judgments is raised in the research of Windschitl and Wells (1996). They found that verbal scales were more sensitive to manipulations of uncertainty and better predictors of preferences and behavioural intentions than numeric, probabilistic confidence scales. If this relative insensitivity of numeric confidence scales generalises to the eyewitness identification context, the use of calibration may be fundamentally flawed. In other words, if the measurement of confidence necessary for calibration analysis is insensitive to factors that should affect confidence judgments, the CA relationship will likely be distorted in some situations. Consequently, if the use of a numeric confidence scale presented a trade-off between accurately estimating accuracy and the provision of probabilistic information, the practical usefulness of calibration would be diminished considerably.

Accordingly, we investigated the nature of confidence judgments for eyewitness identification decisions using both verbal and numeric confidence scales. Participants completed four independent eyewitness identification decisions and rated their confidence in the accuracy of each decision on either a numeric, probabilistic scale or a scale with verbally labelled response options. The distribution of confidence judgments and their association with accuracy was compared across the two scales.

# METHOD

## Participants

The experiment was completed by 192 people (87 males and 105 females) drawn from the local community around Flinders University. Participants had a mean age of 27.5 years (SD = 11.7 years) and all had normal or corrected to normal vision.

## Materials

All stimuli and instructions were presented on computer with the 15 inch monitor set to a resolution of $1024 \times 768$ pixels. Four films depicting simulated, non-violent crimes were used as stimuli. For each film an eight-person lineup was constructed by selecting eight photographs matching the description of the offender. For each lineup, one of the eight filler photographs was designated as the target's replacement to be used only in target absent lineups. Lineups were displayed in two rows of four photos, each displayed at $200 \times 200$

pixels. A button labelled "Not present" was displayed, centred horizontally beneath the lineup.

Film 1 depicted a young male delivering a pizza to a house. After attempting, and failing, to open the front door he removed the screen, opened a window and climbed into the house. After a short delay he emerged from the window carrying a video cassette recorder. He then left the yard through the open front gate. The duration of the entire video was 29 s with the offender's face in full or profile view for 18 s.

Film 2 showed a bank robbery being committed by two young male offenders. The film started by displaying one of the robbers at the back of the bank, apparently threatening customers and staff with a concealed weapon. The other robber, the target who participants were asked to identify, was at the counter and demanded money from the bank teller. She emptied the contents of her money drawer into a bag and handed it over to the robber. Upon receiving the money, the robbers fled the bank and ran outside to a waiting getaway car. The film ends with the getaway car driving away. The duration of the film was 39 s and the target was in view for 16 s, with a full or partial view of his face for 8 s.

Film 3 also depicted a bank robbery, this time committed by a middle-aged man. The film initially showed the offender walking towards the bank's counter, apparently from the point of view of a teller. Upon reaching the counter, the offender handed a note to the teller and demanded cooperation. The teller handed over a bag of money and the offender walked from the bank. He was visible for the entire 42 s duration of the film and his face was completely or partially visible for 37 s.

Film 4 depicted a break-in committed by three young men. The scene began with the arrival of the offenders' car. The offenders got out of the car and began examining the door of a shop or warehouse. The target offender retrieved a bag from the car and used a screwdriver, taken from the bag, to open the locked storeroom door. The robbers then ferried goods from the building into their car until a police car arrived, causing the robbers to run, and the scene ended. The film lasted for 115 s. The target offender was visible for 50 s, with a full or partial view of his face available for this entire time.

The two confidence scales used in this experiment were created by presenting a column of 11 buttons centred vertically on the screen. The button indicative of the highest degree of confidence (i.e., the 100% or "Certain" buttons) was displayed at the top of the column. The numeric scale presented participants with response options ranging from 0% to 100% with decile response options. In contrast, the verbal scale, developed by Windschitl and Wells (1996), presented participants with 11 words ranging from "Impossible" to "Certain". The scale was developed using the words "likely" and "unlikely" as bases, combined with a series of qualifiers. The ordering of the qualifiers (e.g., "somewhat" and "extremely") was based on responses of 284 participants (Windschitl & Wells, 1996). From the lest confident option, the entire scale was: "Impossible", "Extremely unlikely", "Quite unlikely", "Rather unlikely", "Somewhat unlikely", "As likely as is unlikely", "Somewhat likely", "Rather likely", "Quite likely", "Extremely likely", "Certain".

**Table 1. Identification Response Frequencies by Target Presence and Confidence Scale for Each Film**

| Target Presence | Film | Confidence Scale | Correct Identification | Incorrect Identification | Rejection |
|---|---|---|---|---|---|
| Present | 1 | Numeric | 39 (81.3%) | 3 (6.3%) | 6 (12.5%) |
| | | Verbal | 30 (62.5%) | 8 (16.7%) | 10 (20.8%) |
| | 2 | Numeric | 9 (18.8%) | 12 (25.0%) | 27 (56.3%) |
| | | Verbal | 12 (25.0%) | 8 (16.7%) | 28 (58.3%) |
| | 3 | Numeric | 15 (31.3%) | 23 (47.9%) | 10 (20.8%) |
| | | Verbal | 18 (37.5%) | 17 (35.4%) | 13 (27.1%) |
| | 4 | Numeric | 9 (19.1%) | 17 (36.2%) | 21 (44.7%) |
| | | Verbal | 7 (14.6%) | 22 (45.8%) | 19 (36.9%) |
| Absent | 1 | Numeric | | 22 (45.8%) | 26 (54.2%) |
| | | Verbal | | 20 (41.7%) | 28 (58.3%) |
| | 2 | Numeric | | 17 (35.4%) | 31 (64.6%) |
| | | Verbal | | 17 (35.4%) | 31 (64.6%) |
| | 3 | Numeric | | 33 (68.8%) | 15 (31.3%) |
| | | Verbal | | 34 (70.8%) | 14 (29.2%) |
| | 4 | Numeric | | 28 (58.3%) | 20 (41.7%) |
| | | Verbal | | 19 (39.6%) | 29 (60.4%) |

## Procedure

A 2 (confidence scale: verbal, numeric) × 2 (target presence: present, absent) within-subjects design was used. Participants viewed each of the four films in one of the four conditions. Assignment of the conditions to films and the order of their presentation was counter balanced across participants. Participants responded to the lineup and associated questions for one film before being presented with the next stimulus film. After completing the lineup and questions, participants were informed that they would no longer need to remember any information about that film. For each stimulus, participants viewed the film and were immediately asked to make an identification from an eight-person target-present or –absent lineup (depending on condition). For multiple-offender films, participants were asked to identify one specific offender. In all cases participants were explicitly informed that the person they were looking for may or may not be present in the lineup and that they should use the "Not present" response option if they thought the offender was indeed not in the lineup. Immediately after indicating their decision, participants were asked to rate how confident they were that their decision was correct. Responses were made on either the verbal or numeric confidence scale (depending on condition).

## Results

One identification response was recorded with a latency of less than 50 ms. As this latency is indicative of an inadvertent double-click of the mouse, this response was excluded from all analyses. An alpha level of $\alpha = .05$ was used for all inferential analyses and Cohen's $f$ as the effect size measure for all ANOVAs. Cut-off values for Cohen's $f$ are 0.10, 0.25, and 0.40 for small, medium, and large effects, respectively.

## Accuracy

Identification response frequencies for each film are displayed in Table 1. As suggested by Rosenthal and Rosnow (2008), the impact of confidence scale condition on identification accuracy was examined for each film using a 2 (Confidence Scale) × 2 (Choosing Status) between-subjects ANOVA with accuracy, coded as correct or incorrect, as the dependent variable (Table 2). The ANOVAs revealed no significant effects including confidence scale for any film. Further, all of the main effects of confidence scale and the Confidence Scale × Choosing Status interactions displayed negligible effect sizes, indicating that the failure to find significant effects was not due to a lack of power. In sum, as expected, the confidence scale had no impact on identification decision accuracy.

## Confidence

To allow comparison of responses on the verbal and numeric confidence scales, numeric responses were recoded as percentage values. Specifically, the response "Impossible" was recoded to 0% and "Certain" to 100% and all intermediate responses in 10% intervals between the scale end-points. In light of the accuracy differences between stimuli, confidence analyses were conducted separately for each film. Further, given the consistent observation of differences in CA relationships between choosers and non-choosers (e.g., Brewer & Wells, 2006; Sporer et al., 1995; Weber & Brewer, 2004), choosing status was included as a factor in all confidence analyses. The impact of scale type on mean confidence was investigated using a series of 2 (Scale Type) × 2 (Choosing Status) ANOVAs. Additionally, a Levene's test of equality of variances was conducted for each 2 × 2 model to investigate the variability of confidence responses. Descriptive statistics are presented in Table 3, inferential statistics from the ANOVAs in Table 4 and the Levene's tests in Table 5.

## Table 2. Between-Subjects ANOVAs on Accuracy

| Film | Source | df | F | p | f |
|------|--------|-----|------|------|-------|
| 1 | Scale (S) | 1 | 1.40 | .24 | 0.083 |
|   | Choosing (C) | 1 | 8.85 | < .01 | 0.217 |
|   | S × C | 1 | 0.01 | .91 | 0.007 |
|   | Error | 188 | (0.22) | | |
| 2 | S | 1 | 0.30 | .59 | 0.040 |
|   | C | 1 | 12.11 | < .01 | 0.254 |
|   | S × C | 1 | 0.45 | .50 | 0.049 |
|   | Error | 188 | (0.24) | | |
| 3 | S | 1 | 0.05 | .83 | 0.016 |
|   | C | 1 | 19.64 | < .01 | 0.323 |
|   | S × C | 1 | 0.81 | .37 | 0.066 |
|   | Error | 188 | (0.20) | | |
| 4 | S | 1 | 0.57 | .45 | 0.055 |
|   | C | 1 | 38.16 | < .01 | 0.451 |
|   | S × C | 1 | 1.18 | 0.28 | 0.079 |
|   | Error | 187 | (0.19) | | |

## Table 3. Confidence Means and Standard Deviations by Film, Choosing Status, and Confidence Scale

| Film | Choosing Status | Numeric | | Verbal | |
|------|-----------------|---------|------|--------|------|
|      |                 | M | SD | M | SD |
| 1 | Chooser | 78.91 | 17.74 | 76.21 | 17.45 |
|   | Non-chooser | 74.69 | 20.63 | 78.95 | 14.29 |
| 2 | Chooser | 65.53 | 19.82 | 71.08 | 13.29 |
|   | Non-chooser | 75.00 | 17.50 | 76.27 | 18.56 |
| 3 | Chooser | 67.75 | 17.74 | 68.55 | 18.33 |
|   | Non-chooser | 56.00 | 25.33 | 65.19 | 21.73 |
| 4 | Chooser | 60.37 | 19.81 | 63.13 | 18.12 |
|   | Non-chooser | 70.00 | 26.55 | 67.92 | 21.03 |

The ANOVAs revealed no significant main effects of scale on confidence judgments. Further, the effect size measures for three of the films are negligible, indicating that even a study powerful enough to detect all meaningful effects (i.e., $f \geq .1$) would not have revealed significant effects of confidence scale on mean confidence judgments. For Film 3 a small, yet non-significant, effect was detected suggesting that the verbal scale produced, on average, slightly higher confidence judgments. Similarly, for the interaction effects including confidence scale, there was no evidence of any significant effects and none of the effect size measures suggested a meaningful effect. The Levene's tests revealed a significant difference in variances for only one of the four stimuli. Examination of the descriptive statistics suggests that this was due to a difference in variance of confidence judgments for choosers and non-choosers, not between confidence judgments on the verbal and numeric scales. Two Levene's tests comparing verbal and numeric confidence variability separately for choosers, $F(1,190) = 0.01$, $p = .92$, and non-choosers, $F(1,190) = 0.87$, $p = .35$, revealed no evidence of differing variance, confirming this explanation.

**Table 4. Between-Subjects ANOVAs on Confidence**

| Film | Source | df | F | p | f |
|------|--------|----|----|----|----|
| 1 | Scale (S) | 1 | 0.09 | .77 | 0.022 |
| | Choosing (C) | 1 | 0.08 | .78 | 0.021 |
| | S × C | 1 | 1.74 | .19 | 0.096 |
| | Error | 188 | (308.21) | | |
| 2 | S | 1 | 1.72 | .19 | 0.095 |
| | C | 1 | 7.92 | .01 | 0.205 |
| | S × C | 1 | 0.68 | .41 | 0.060 |
| | Error | 188 | (310.24) | | |
| 3 | S | 1 | 2.45 | .12 | 0.114 |
| | C | 1 | 5.60 | .02 | 0.173 |
| | S × C | 1 | 1.72 | .19 | 0.096 |
| | Error | 188 | (386.00) | | |
| 4 | S | 1 | 0.01 | .91 | 0.007 |
| | C | 1 | 5.40 | .02 | 0.169 |
| | S × C | 1 | 0.61 | .44 | 0.057 |
| | Error | 187 | (455.70) | | |

In sum, there is no evidence that confidence scale had a significant impact on either the central tendency or variability of confidence judgments.

**Table 5. Levene's Tests for Equality of Variances on Confidence**

| Film | df | F | p |
|------|-----|----|----|
| 1 | 3, 188 | 1.93 | .13 |
| 2 | 3, 188 | 1.09 | .36 |
| 3 | 3, 188 | 2.78 | .04 |
| 4 | 3, 187 | 1.54 | .21 |

# CONFIDENCE-ACCURACY RELATIONSHIP

The difference in CA relationships between verbal and numeric confidence scales was examined both graphically and statistically. As a large number of observations are required to establish a stable estimate of CA calibration (for discussion of sample requirements for calibration see, e.g., Brewer & Wells, 2006; Weber & Brewer, 2003) these analyses were conducted on data collapsed across stimuli. Not only does this ensure sufficient data to reliably index the CA relationship, it provides the variability in witnessing conditions necessary to reflect the real-world CA relationship (Lindsay et al., 2000; Lindsay et al., 1998; Read et al., 1998).

**Table 6. Confidence-Accuracy Calibration Statistics by Choosing Status and Confidence Scale**

| Choosing Status | Stat. | Numeric | | | Verbal | | |
|---|---|---|---|---|---|---|---|
| | | Value | SE | CI | Value | SE | CI |
| Choosers | C | .14 | .04 | .08 – .20 | .15 | .04 | .09 – .21 |
| | O/U | .37 | .03 | .33 – .41 | .38 | .03 | .34 – .43 |
| | NRI | .14 | .04 | .09 – .19 | .11 | .03 | .06 – .15 |
| Non-choosers | C | .06 | .02 | .03 – .08 | .03 | .01 | .01 – .05 |
| | O/U | .12 | .04 | .06 – .18 | .13 | .04 | .08 – .19 |
| | NRI | .01 | .01 | .00 – .03 | .03 | .02 | .00 - .07 |

Note. SE = jackknife standard error; CI = inferential confidence interval ($\alpha$ = .05).

Calibration curves (i.e., plots of proportion correct against confidence) for verbal and numeric confidence scales are presented, separately for choosers and non-choosers, in Figure 1. To ensure a sufficient number of observations at each point, the 11 confidence levels were collapsed into 4 levels (0 – 40, 50 – 60, 70 – 80, & 90 – 100) and the overall proportion correct plotted against the weighted mean confidence. The curves for choosers demonstrate the typically observed positive, monotonic functions that, generally, parallel the identity line. The vertical position of the curves below the identity line is indicative of over-confidence. For non-choosers, the generally flat calibration functions are indicative of a weaker CA relationship. Comparison of the curves for the verbal and numeric confidence scales reveals nearly identical curves for choosers and a difference only at the lowest confidence point for non-choosers. In other words, the calibration curves suggest that CA calibration is unaffected by the scale used to elicit confidence judgments.

This conclusion is supported by examination of calibration statistics. Table 6 displays C, O/U, and NRI, calculated separately for choosers and non-choosers, for both verbal and numeric confidence scales. As these statistics are calculated on the entire sample, a conventional estimate of standard error, and consequently the use of standard parametric analyses, is not possible. Following Weber and Brewer (2006), we overcame this problem by using the jackknife procedure developed by Tukey (1958) to estimate standard errors (for a complete mathematical discussion, see Efron & Gong, 1983). We then used these jackknife standard errors to calculate inferential confidence intervals (Tryon, 2001) for each of the calibration statistics. Inferential confidence intervals are calculated for specific pairwise comparisons of means. When the inferential confidence intervals do not overlap, we can conclude that the means differ at the $\alpha$ = .05 level. As the verbal and numeric confidence intervals overlap for all three calibration statistics for both choosers and non-choosers, there is no evidence of any meaningful between verbal and numeric confidence scale for any aspect of the CA relationship.

Choosers

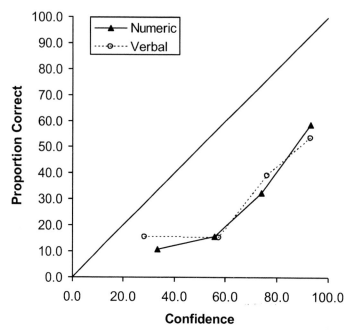

Non-choosers

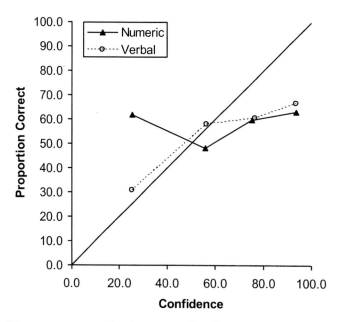

Figure 1. Confidence-accuracy calibration curves for choosers (upper panel) and non-choosers (lower panel) by confidence scale type. Confidence levels were collapsed to ensure at least 20 observations at every point. For each of the collapsed levels, overall proportion correct was plotted against weighted mean confidence

# DISCUSSION

This experiment contrasted numeric confidence judgments about the accuracy of eyewitness identification decisions with confidence judgments elicited on a verbal scale. For four independent sets of stimuli, we observed no evidence of significant differences in the distribution of confidence judgments made on the verbal and numeric scales. Further, evidence of negligible effect sizes for differences in central tendency suggests that even a study powerful enough to detect the smallest of meaningful effects would have found a difference in means for only one of the four stimuli. Examination of the data from the stimulus for which a small, yet non-significant, effect of scale was observed suggests that the difference was largely due to disparate means for non-choosers rather than choosers. As meaningful CA relationships have only been observed for choosers (Brewer et al., 2002; Brewer & Wells, 2006; Sporer et al., 1995), slight differences in the performance of verbal and numeric scales for non-choosers does not represent a meaningful difference in the practical usefulness of the scales. Perhaps more importantly, there was no evidence of any CA relationship difference between judgments elicited on verbal and numeric scales for either choosers or non-choosers. Although not proof of equivalence, these findings provide no support for the argument that numeric confidence judgments are a potential barrier to the practical and research use of calibration, as there is no evidence that verbal scales produce more realistic confidence judgments.

Importantly, the lack of difference in CA relationship between the verbal and numeric scales does not appear to be the result of a floor effect or, in other words, the result of the lack of a relationship for both scales. Considering only choosers, both scales produced overconfident judgments. Given the overall low accuracy of choosers (48.3%), these stimuli can be considered to have produced a difficult identification task (indeed, extremely difficult for three of the four sets of stimulus materials). Consequently, the observation of overconfidence is in line with research on the hard-easy effect (Juslin, Winman, & Olsson, 2000; Weber & Brewer, 2004) and basic theories of confidence (Gigerenzer, Hoffrage, & Kleinbölting, 1991). Further, despite the severe overconfidence, highly confident decisions, regardless of the scale on which they were elicited, did identify a group of decisions markedly more likely to be accurate than the less confident decisions. Thus, consistent with existing calibration data from eyewitness identification studies (Brewer et al., 2002; Brewer & Wells, 2006; Juslin et al., 1996) involving adults (though not children; Keast, Brewer, & Wells, 2007), these data provide evidence of a meaningful CA accuracy relationship for eyewitness identification choosers.

In contrast, the results for non-choosers, while consistent with extant research (Brewer et al., 2002; Brewer & Wells, 2006; Sporer et al., 1995), are indicative of no meaningful CA relationship. Despite the low values of the C statistics for non-choosers, examination of the resolution statistics indicate that confidence judgments were not able to provide any information that distinguished correct from incorrect decisions. In sum, consistent with the existing eyewitness identification and face recognition literature on CA calibration, meaningful CA relationships were observed, regardless of confidence scale, for choosers but not for non-choosers.

The lack of difference between verbal and numeric scales appears to contradict the decision making research on errors and biases in probabilistic reasoning (Tversky & Koehler,

1994). However, the verbal scale used in this experiment employed labels based on the likelihood of the decision being accurate. In other words, it used verbal probabilistic statements. Consequently, one explanation for the apparent disparity is that the biases in probabilistic reasoning apply regardless of the format in which the final probability judgment is conveyed. An alternative approach, suggested by theories of confidence in perceptual (Vickers, 1979) and recognition memory (Van Zandt, 2000) decisions, is that confidence judgments about such decisions are not arrived at through probabilistic reasoning. These theories hold that confidence judgments are based on an interrogation of the amount of evidence for the selected response. This evidential value is then internally scaled to fit onto the specified response scale. Thus, the confidence judgment is not derived through a process of reasoning, rather from the simple scaling of an internal index of certainty. Given that both scales presented participants with 11 options ranging from complete certainty in accuracy to complete certainty in inaccuracy, the use of an identical scaling procedure regardless of confidence scale is not unlikely.

The failure to identify differences between verbal and numeric confidence scales also conflicts with the findings of Windschitl and Wells (1996). Specifically, our data suggest that verbal and numeric confidence scales were equivalently sensitive to the factors affecting likely accuracy of identification decisions. In contrast, Windschitl and Wells found that verbal scales were more sensitive to manipulations affecting uncertainty. However, the sources of variation in uncertainty here and in the Windschitl and Wells experiment are quite different. They used framing and context manipulations to change judgments of certainty even when the objective probability of an event was identical. In other words, the greater sensitivity of the verbal scale was due to a greater propensity for verbal certainty judgments to be distorted by manipulations. In contrast, in this experiment there were no distorting manipulations of certainty through framing or context. Rather, uncertainty presumably varied with changes in memory strength (Van Zandt, 2000), ability to fluently recognize a lineup member (cf. Kelley & Lindsay, 1993), and heuristic judgments about memory quality (cf. Busey, Tunnicliff, Loftus, & Loftus, 2000). In other words, variation in the source of uncertainty in this experiment was directly related to the objective probability of accuracy. Thus, our results reflect a failure to find any difference in sensitivity of verbal and numeric scales to factors that affect the likelihood of making an accurate decision. Thus, taken together, the results from this experiment and those presented by Windschitl and Wells suggest that numeric measures may actually be preferable to verbal measures: (a) there is no evidence that they are less sensitive than verbal scales to factors that actually affect the accuracy of identification decisions, and (b) there is evidence that responses on verbal scales are more likely to be distorted by factors unrelated to the likely accuracy of a decision.

In sum, this experiment provides further evidence of a consistent CA relationship for choosers in eyewitness identification. Further, we found no evidence of significant differences between confidence judgments elicited on verbal versus numeric scales. When considered with the usefulness of probabilistic information gained through calibration and the propensity of verbal scales to be distorted (Windschitl & Wells, 1996), these results provide further support for the potential practical usefulness of confidence and for the ongoing investigation of factors that influence CA calibration and its underlying cognitive processes.

# REFERENCES

Baranski, J. V., & Petrusic, W. M. (1994). The calibration and resolution of confidence in perceptual judgments. *Perception & Psychophysics*, 55, 412-428.

Bothwell, R. K., Deffenbacher, K. A., & Brigham, J. C. (1987). Correlation of eyewitness accuracy and confidence: Optimality hypothesis revisited. *Journal of Applied Psychology*, 72, 691-695.

Brewer, N., Keast, A., & Rishworth, A. (2002). The confidence-accuracy relationship in eyewitness identification: The effects of reflection and disconfirmation on correlation and calibration. *Journal of Experimental Psychology: Applied*, 8, 44-56.

Brewer, N., Weber, N., & Semmler, C. (2005). Eyewitness identification. In N. Brewer & K. D. Williams (Eds.), *Psychology and law: An empirical perspective* (pp. 177-221). New York: Guilford.

Brewer, N., & Wells, G. L. (2006). The confidence-accuracy relationship in eyewitness identification: Effects of lineup instructions, foil similarity and target-absent base rates. *Journal of Experimental Psychology: Applied*, 12, 11-30.

Busey, T. A., Tunnicliff, J., Loftus, G. R., & Loftus, E. F. (2000). Accounts of the confidence-accuracy relation in recognition memory. *Psychonomic Bulletin & Review*, 7, 26-48.

Cutler, B. L., & Penrod, S. D. (1995). *Mistaken identification: The eyewitness, psychology, and the law.* New York: Cambridge University Press.

Efron, B., & Gong, G. (1983). A leisurely look at the bootstrap, the jackknife and cross-validation. *The American Statistician*, 37, 36-48.

Gigerenzer, G., Hoffrage, U., & Kleinbölting, H. (1991). Probabilistic mental models: A Brunswikian theory of confidence. *Psychological Review*, 98, 506-528.

Innocence, P. (2007). Innocence project. Retrieved November 23, 2007, from *http://www.innocenceproject.org/understand/Eyewitness-Misidentification.php*

Juslin, P., Olsson, N., & Winman, A. (1996). Calibration and diagnosticity of confidence in eyewitness identification: Comments on what can be inferred from the low confidence-accuracy correlation. *Journal of Experimental Psychology: Learning, Memory, & Cognition*, 22, 1304-1316.

Juslin, P., Winman, A., & Olsson, H. (2000). Naive empiricism and dogmatism in confidence research: A critical examination of the hard-easy effect. *Psychological Review*, 107, 384-396.

Keast, A., Brewer, N., & Wells, G. L. (2007). Children's metacognitive judgments in an eyewitness identification task. *Journal of Experimental Child Psychology*, 97, 286-314.

Kelley, C. M., & Lindsay, D. S. (1993). Remembering mistaken for knowing: Ease of retrieval as a basis for confidence in answers to general knowledge questions. *Journal of Memory & Language*, 32, 1-24.

Lindsay, D. S., Nilsen, E., & Read, J. D. (2000). Witnessing-condition heterogeneity and witnesses' versus investigators' confidence in the accuracy of witnesses' identification decisions. *Law & Human Behavior*, 24, 685-697.

Lindsay, D. S., Read, J. D., & Sharma, K. (1998). Accuracy and confidence in person identification: The relationship is strong when witnessing conditions vary widely. *Psychological Science*, 9, 215-218.

Read, J. D., Lindsay, D. S., & Nicholls, T. (1998). The relation between confidence and accuracy in eyewitness identification studies: Is the conclusion changing? In C. P. Thompson, D. J. Herrmann, J. D. Read, D. Bruce, D. G. Payne & M. P. Toglia (Eds.), *Eyewitness memory: Theoretical and applied perspectives* (pp. 107-130). Hillsdale, NJ: Lawrence Erlbaum.

Rosenthal, R., & Rosnow, R. L. (2008). *Essentials of behavioral research: Methods and data analysis.* New York: McGraw-Hill.

Sporer, S. L., Penrod, S., Read, D., & Cutler, B. (1995). Choosing, confidence, and accuracy: A meta-analysis of the confidence-accuracy relation in eyewitness identification studies. *Psychological Bulletin*, 118, 315-327.

Technical Working Group for Eyewitness Evidence. (1999). *Eyewitness evidence: A guide for law enforcement.* Washington, DC: U.S. Department of Justice, Office of Justice Programs.

Tryon, W. W. (2001). Evaluating statistical difference, equivalence, and indeterminancy using inferential confidence intervals: An integrated alternative method of conducting null hypothesis statistical tests. *Psychological Methods*, 6, 371-386.

Tukey, J. W. (1958). Bias and confidence in not-quite large samples. *Annals of Mathematical Statistics,* 29, 614.

Tversky, A., & Koehler, D. J. (1994). Support theory: A nonextensional representation of subjective probability. *Psychological Review*, 101, 547-567.

Van Zandt, T. (2000). ROC curves and confidence judgments in recognition memory. *Journal of Experimental Psychology: Learning, Memory, & Cognition*, 26, 582-600.

Vickers, D. (1979). *Decision processes in visual perception.* New York: Academic Press.

Weber, N., & Brewer, N. (2003). The effect of judgment type and confidence scale on confidence-accuracy calibration in face recognition. *Journal of Applied Psychology,* 88, 490-499.

Weber, N., & Brewer, N. (2004). Confidence-accuracy calibration in absolute and relative face recognition judgments. *Journal of Experimental Psychology: Applied,* 10, 156-172.

Weber, N., & Brewer, N. (2006). Positive versus negative face recognition decisions: Confidence, accuracy, and response latency. *Applied Cognitive Psychology*, 20, 17-31.

Weber, N., Brewer, N., Wells, G. L., Semmler, C., & Keast, A. (2004). Eyewitness identification and response latency: The unruly 10-12 second rule. *Journal of Experimental Psychology: Applied*, 10, 139-147.

Wells, G. L., & Murray, D. M. (1984). Eyewitness confidence. In G. L. Wells & E. F. Loftus (Eds.), *Eyewitness testimony: Psychological perspectives* (pp. 155-170). New York: Cambridge University Press.

Wells, G. L., Small, M., Penrod, S., Malpass, R. S., Fulero, S. M., & Brimacombe, C. A. E. (1998). Eyewitness identification procedures: Recommendations for lineups and photospreads. *Law & Human Behavior*, 22, 603-647.

Windschitl, P. D., & Wells, G. L. (1996). Measuring psychological uncertainty: Verbal versus numeric methods. *Journal of Experimental Psychology: Applied,* 2, 343-364.

Yaniv, I., Yates, J. F., & Smith, J. E. K. (1991). Measures of discrimination skill in probabilistic judgment. *Psychological Bulletin*, 110, 611-617.

In: Applied Psychology Research Trends

Editor: Karl H. Kiefer, pp.119-140

ISBN 978-1-60456-372-6

© 2008 Nova Science Publishers, Inc.

*Chapter 6*

# APPLICATION OF COGNITIVE PSYCHOLOGY TO ADVANCE UNDERSTANDING OF WINE EXPERTISE

## *Wendy V. Parr*

Lincoln University, Canterbury, New Zealand

## ABSTRACT

Wine expertise has a long and great tradition, but what is wine expertise? The question, asked 50 years ago by experimental psychologists J.J. Gibson and Eleanor Gibson (1955), remains largely unanswered today. Analytical sensory evaluation of wine involves employing a human observer as an analytical instrument to discriminate and to make judgments about the qualities of wine. Wine sensory evaluation is studied and practiced within the discipline of sensory science and its applied component, sensory evaluation. Despite a proliferation of sensory studies and sensory journals over the last few decades, we still know very little about the cognitive processes involved in both wine sensory evaluation and in wine expertise. The present chapter discusses historical aspects of the discipline of sensory evaluation that can be argued as factors in the neglect of human cognitive processes as an inherent component of wine evaluation behaviour. The chapter then reviews and synthesises recent research that has markedly advanced the field by application of methodology and theory from cognitive psychology. The most significant way in which advancement has occurred involves extension of the research field beyond consideration of the phenomena of sensation alone to systematic study of what is happening in the minds and brains attached to our sense organs. The chapter brings together recent research concerning processes of discrimination, perception, conceptualisation, memory, judgment and language relevant to sensory evaluation of wine conducted by key researchers in the field (e.g., Solomon, 1988; Morrot, Brochet, & Dubourdieu, 2001; Hughson & Boakes, 2002; Parr, Heatherbell, & White, 2002; Ballester, Dacremont, Le Fur, & Etievant, 2005). A particular focus is the concept of wine expertise, addressed by comparing behaviour of wine professionals with behaviour of less-experienced wine consumers, to identify and describe cognitive processes implicated in development of wine expertise. Theoretical and applied implications of recent research findings relevant to wine evaluative behaviour are discussed, along with future research directions.

# INTRODUCTION

"The man who is discriminating about his wine shows a high specificity of perception, whereas the crude fellow who is not shows a low specificity. A whole class of chemically different fluids is equivalent for the latter individual; he can't tell the difference between claret, burgundy, and chianti; his perceptions are relatively undifferentiated. What has the first man learned that the second one has not? Memories? Attitudes? Inferences?"
    Gibson and Gibson, 1955

Wine expertise has a long tradition, but what is wine expertise? The question was asked in the above quotation nearly 50 years' ago by experimental psychologists J.J. Gibson and Eleanor Gibson (1955), yet today it remains largely unanswered. In short, when we use a human observer as an analytical tool to gather *information*[1] about a wine sample (i.e., to employ their senses to examine and make judgments about the qualities of a wine), we know very little about what they are actually doing.

Wine expertise has not so much remained elusive; rather, it has been relatively neglected in the realm of scientific enquiry. Conceivably, a major source of this neglect has been the model of human behaviour adopted last century, and still perpetuated today, by many practitioners in the discipline of sensory evaluation.

## Sensory Evaluation

Evaluation of the complex beverage known as wine is studied and practiced within the umbrella discipline of sensory science and its applied component, namely sensory analysis or sensory evaluation. The term sensory evaluation is typically used interchangeably with sensory analysis in the literature. Some authors however distinguish sensory evaluation from sensory analysis in that the word 'value' is part of the former, and involves giving a mark/grade (as in evaluating a student's exam paper) to the product. This is what formal wine judges are typically asked to do. However, it is not necessarily a component of most other wine-evaluation situations (e.g., when evaluating wines to determine which fining agent best produces the desired result). Therefore, the terms sensory analysis and sensory evaluation are used interchangeably in this chapter.

There is no standardised definition of the term "sensory evaluation". One frequently cited definition is "a scientific method used to evoke, measure, analyse, and interpret those responses to products as perceived through the senses of sight, smell, touch, taste, and hearing" (Stone & Sidel, 1993). In other words, sensory evaluation refers to using the senses, in controlled conditions, to answer a question (e.g., Morrot, 1999). The phrase "controlled

---

[1] The concept of "information" refers to a stimulated receptor *informing* the organism, via encoding processes, about characteristics of a wine sample (Norwich, 1991).

conditions" makes explicit that whilst keeping ecological validity in mind, many informal wine appreciation situations lack the necessary controls to constitute sensory evaluation as the term is employed in this chapter.

## History

Central to the difficulties associated with sensory evaluation methodologies and theory, and to understanding the relation between chemical and sensory analyses of wine, is employment of the adult human as an analytical instrument. The "man as machine" model of human behaviour was adopted by the budding discipline of sensory evaluation after the Second World War. This was a time when the schools of thought that dominated Psychology were Behaviourism and Psychophysics. In practice, what occurred was application of the tools of psychologists by sensory practitioners and researchers, but with the methods largely stripped of their underlying theory. Although psychophysicists made a bold attempt to introduce theory in the 1970s (Moskowitz, 2003), the virtually a-theoretical approach adopted by sensory evaluation practitioners in the 1950s continues to influence methodology and practice in sensory evaluation today.

Adoption of a virtually a-theoretical approach was aimed at giving scientific credibility to the new discipline of sensory evaluation, whose history until that point had been industry (e.g., where a company "expert" graded tea or coffee), rather than science. To improve objectivity in the research field, the "expert taster" of old became a panel of people, trained to function as well-calibrated machines (Stone, Sidel, Oliver, Woolsey, & Singleton, 1974).

The problem with the machine model of human behaviour has not so much been its initial adoption by the budding discipline; the field of sensory evaluation was advantaged by an increased focus on scientific methodology. The problem has been subsequent retention of what the majority of psychologists now consider a relatively contrived view of human behaviour. Long after mainstream Psychology relegated the approach as inappropriate for all but a limited sub-section of human behaviour (e.g., in 1956 at what has become known as the "cognitive revolution": see Reisberg, 1997), the fundamental model of human behaviour underlying the majority of sensory evaluation studies continues to be a variant of the "black box" school of thinking (see Reisberg, 1997): a panel of tasters is rigidly "trained" so that panel members function together as a "well-calibrated machine".

The machine model views consensus responding as the major aim: individual differences among panellists that cannot be ironed out are seen as error in the system, or nuisance variables, rather than as interesting data in their own right that may in fact tell us something about the panellists' underlying mental processing in a particular task. The machine model thus endorses neglect of the complex mental processes that occur between sensory receptor cell stimulation (e.g., a sniff of a wine sample) and a person giving a verbal judgment (e.g., saying "yes, that is acetic acid"). One result is that theoretical development has been slow to accrue in the discipline of sensory evaluation. Despite having sixty years of fundamental research from Experimental Psychology and Sensory Science to draw upon since its adoption of the machine model, the discipline of sensory evaluation currently more closely resembles a tool kit of techniques than a systematically developed, scholarly knowledge base.

A related outcome is that after sixty years of research, what is actually being measured in many sensory evaluation tasks, in terms of human behaviour, is not at all clear. Construct validity has not been an important consideration for many researchers. Validity is a social science term that is close to the concept of accuracy in physical sciences. Validity refers to meaningfulness: Is the task measuring what we think it is measuring? In many sensory evaluation studies, this question cannot be answered easily; we therefore do not know what the resulting data actually mean, even if they are highly replicable.

Several authors have recently argued that ensuring validity of the consensus techniques that currently dominate sensory evaluation practice is beyond the capabilities of present methodologies, and that a new approach is required (Brochet & Dubourdieu, 2001) for sensory evaluation of complex stimuli such as wine. The new approach acknowledges the cognitive component of a sensory evaluation. Moskowitz (2003) comments that the current trend to integrate cognition into psychophysics and sensory analysis is "an emerging trend of potentially great significance" (p. 97).

## A Cognitive Approach to Wine Sensory Evaluation with Focus on Olfaction

Sensation as a process within an information-processing view of human olfactory behaviour (i.e., smelling) involves interaction of odorous molecules with olfactory receptors at the top of the nasal cavity. This generates a signal about quantity and quality of the molecules. It is far from clear at the present time just how our olfactory receptors allow us to discriminate among thousands of different odours with only a few hundred different receptors (e.g., Thorngate, 1997).

Sensation is an important stage with respect to the science of olfaction, but in an information processing analysis, it is merely the first stage in models of how people process information in real time. Olfactory-guided judgments are determined not only by how well the nose is working, but also by what is going on in the brain attached to the particular nose (Lawless, 1997, p. 167). The name given to processes that result in a stimulus becoming meaningful to an organism is perception. For example, a sensory signal is transformed via perceptual processes to give a representation of odour. However, this subjective representation is unlikely to faithfully reflect the objective stimulus because it has been encoded in keeping with a person's current knowledge, language, value judgments, expectations, motivations, mood, and so on. In other words, the ability to identify a smell (e.g., to say "that smells like chlorine") is not as clear-cut as re-playing a video tape, but has automatically involved several processes that are highly dependent upon a person's prior history with respect to olfactory stimuli. These cognitive processes include perception, memory, classification, judgment, and language.

A cognitive analysis demands that researchers note key issues such as (i) cognitive processes will be affected by inherent limits to the capacity of the human information-processing system (e.g., Miller, 1956); (ii) cognitive processes may be influenced by emotions (e.g., Herz & Engen, 1996); and (iii) many of the phenomena concerning olfaction and cognition may occur outside a person's conscious awareness; that is, a judge may not be aware that a particular odour is influencing their behaviour in systematic ways (e.g., Degel & Koster, 1999). The lack of self-awareness of much of our cognitive processing means that rigid controls to minimise cognitive and emotional influences (e.g., by forcing consensus on a profiling panel) are unlikely to be feasible, and will produce data low on both internal and ecological validity.

# KEY CONCEPTS IN A COGNITIVE ANALYSIS OF WINE SENSORY EVALUATION

## Representation:

The concept central to any psychological analysis of wine evaluation is the notion that a wine itself does not have a taste, smell, or mouth-feel: That is, tastes, smells, and tactile sensations are percepts and as such, inherently part of the perceiver. In other words, the representation of a wine, including its visual, tactile, and flavour components, is inherently subjective and as such, "will never be consensual" (Brochet, 1999, p. 22) but will be an individual's interpretation based on his or her physiological and psychological status at any particular time. In short, "The taste of wine is not in the bottle, it is in your mind" (Brochet, 1999, p. 22). The wine composition places limits on any potential sensory experience, but interaction with a perceiving organism is the foremost requirement.

## The Human as an Information Processor:

A second important notion is that it is necessary to move beyond the sensory (receptor cell) level of responding, and to consider the human evaluator of wine as an information processor, rather than as a machine to be rigidly calibrated. At a more global level, this requires consideration of the newer and broader philosophies of science that value qualitative as well as quantitative research; at a specific level, it requires a move beyond the conditioning approaches that force conceptual uniformity (or at least linguistic uniformity, as few researchers have actually studied panellists' conceptual behaviour) among people to ensure repeatability of results.

Within a cognitive framework, the interesting aspects of human behaviour that will tell us *what* humans are actually doing when they evaluate wines come into focus. That is, what happens between a sensation (e.g., an olfactory receptor being stimulated by a volatile compound) and a response (e.g., a wine judge saying "too much sulphur in this wine") can be investigated.

One way in which this has been achieved historically in experimental psychology has been to consider how perceptions, memories, concepts and judgments of an expert differ, both qualitatively and quantitatively, from those of a less-experienced wine taster. The major precedent in the literature for such an approach involved elucidation of the ways in which perceptual and memorial processes of Master chess players differ from those of novice chess players (de Groot, 1965; Chase & Simon, 1973). These classic studies found that the expertise of chess Masters, rather than being based in fundamentally superior perceptual or memorial abilities, resulted from the way in which chess experts organised their perceptions to subsequently retrieve specific, meaningful information from memory.

## Top-down and bottom-up Cognitive Processes:

A third key concept concerns the notion of top-down and bottom-up cognitive processes (see Reisberg, 1997, pp. 77-78). Perception of a wine sample contains variable proportions of sensory and cognitive components, often separated as bottom-up (data-driven) and top-down processes, depending on the exact context. The distinction between cognitive processes that are "bottom up" and those that are "top-down" is important. When our responding on a task is primarily driven/guided by what is already in our head (e.g., judging an odour as "berry" on the basis of a prior experience with red wines, rather than on the phenomenological properties of the wine in the glass), such cognitive processing is referred to as primarily "top-down". Conversely, tasks with tight experimental control such as detecting a subtle change in odour as a function of change in chemical concentration would be argued as primarily bottom-up or data-driven cognitive processing. Top-down and bottom-up processes are assumed to integrate within the brain, to aid our performance on any particular task (Dalton, 2000). However, the weight accorded each type of processing varies across tasks: When weight is given to attending to the stimulus input (e.g., a sample of wine in a glass), the predominant cognitive processing is bottom up; conversely, when previous experience (e.g., expectations; motives; knowledge) plays a large role in the way we perform on a task, the cognitive processing is argued as primarily top-down.

Research with the visual sense (e.g., Loftus & Palmer, 1974; Wells, 1993) has demonstrated via several clever paradigms the importance of top-down processes. Studies show how, from the process of perception to the retrieval of memories, an individual imposes expectations, motives, desires, prior experience and so forth onto their perception such that their subjective representation may deviate substantially from the objective stimulus. There is every reason to think that what we smell in a wine will be as subject to fallacious memories and judgments as that which we see.

# WINE EXPERTISE

Wine experts are expected to have a range of skills associated with evaluating wine quality. They need to be able to recognise and identify specific notes in a wine (e.g., a fault), identifying such notes even when the notes are subtle components of what is a very complex mixture. To be effective, wine judges also need to be able to verbally label the components they identify. Further, to be reliable they must be able to consistently apply the same verbal label to a particular component of a wine sample (i.e., they must demonstrate repeatability).

In a psychological analysis, inherent in expertise in any domain is superior knowledge and experience in the domain. It follows that the question of interest with respect to understanding wine expertise is "what changes when a person develops wine expertise?" Presumably those deemed to have wine expertise have developed richer, domain-specific cognitive processes as a function of their experience (e.g., olfactory images of wine-relevant odorants; semantic memories; autobiographical memories).

A psychological analysis provides a framework in which what changes can be considered in terms of what happens in the mind or brain that is attached to the data-collecting instrument (i.e., the nose or mouth of the wine professional). For example, wine expertise was recently defined as "a superior ability to discriminate between, recognise and describe different wines" (Hughson & Boakes, 2002, p. 463) by researchers who had employed models from psychological science. In other words, to understand how the senses are "educated" with respect to wine sensory analyses requires investigations of perceptual, learning, memorial (e.g., episodic and semantic memory) and thinking processes (conceptualisation; inference; imaging) within the specific domain.

In attempts to understand wine expertise, a few researchers have rejected the consensus, machine model of behaviour dominating mainstream sensory evaluation research and have studied wine sensory evaluation and wine expertise by employing methodologies that highlight individual differences (e.g., Solomon, 1988; 1990; 1991; Hughson & Boakes, 2002; Morrot, 1999; Morrot, Brochet, & Dubourdieu, 2001; Valentin, Chollet, & Abdi, 2003). The major focus of much of the research has been wine-relevant verbal abilities, namely semantic memory and language (e.g., Solomon, 1988; Gawel, 1997; Brochet & Dubourdieu, 2001). Other work has extended the cognitive analyses to consideration of human conceptual behaviour (e.g., Morrot, Brochet, & Dubourdieu, 2001; Ballester et al., 2005; Parr, Green, White, & Sherlock, 2007) and types of memory (e.g., Parr, Heatherbell, & White, 2002), including perceptual or sensory-based memory (e.g., Bende & Nordin, 1997).

## Nature Versus Nurture

The degree to which superior abilities with respect to wine evaluation are predetermined (e.g., genetically based) versus learned is still an open question, and one that is particularly difficult to test empirically. In other words, the degree to which those our societies designate to be "wine experts" are naturally better able to achieve relevant tasks of discrimination, recognition and verbal labelling is an interesting but unanswered question. Research to date appears to suggest that inherently superior sensory abilities do not underlie wine expertise (Morrot, 1999).

Basic olfactory sensitivities do differ among people, the situation with olfaction, especially retronasal olfaction, being more complex than the situation with taste (Lawless, 1997). Further, some people have specific anosmias (inability to smell a particular chemical compound when it is at a supra-threshold concentration). Despite these differences among people, the major contributor to sensory expertise is assumed learned (Morrot, 1999). Even then, it is not our basic sensitivities that change with experience and learning; that is, training with olfactory stimuli appears to have little influence on olfactory sensitivity (the sensory component of perception) (Morrot, 1999, p. 32; Parr et al., 2002). It is the cognitive component of perception that is modifiable by training and experience. The dominant influence is assumed to involve domain-specific experience that in turn leads to changes in cognitive processes such as perception, conceptualisation, and memory (Hughson & Boakes, 2002).

## Cognitive Styles of Wine Evaluation

A wine judge may take several approaches to the task of evaluating a wine. There are two major, qualitatively different evaluative styles that are often referred to as an "Old-world" (synthesis) approach or a "New-world" (analytical) style (Gawel, 1997). In practice, wine professionals presumably employ a combination of the analytical and synthetic approaches, depending on the task to be achieved in any particular situation. The Old-world approach involves combining the flavour notes and mouth-feel characteristics of a wine sample to form a synthesis before commenting on the wine's quality. The evaluation is likely to reflect a holistic assessment of the wine or a Gestalt (e.g., "the wine is clumsy and rather common").

In support of an Old-world approach, Brochet and Dubourdieu (2001) argue that wine tasters' linguistic representations are organised around prototypes and are not in analytical form. On the basis of their data from experienced wine judges, they suggest that analytical procedures such as quantitative descriptive analysis (QDA) may not be appropriate for use in evaluating complex beverages like wine. Evidence from an Australian research group comes to a similar conclusion. Studies of human identification of odours in mixtures (Livermore & Laing, 1996; Jinks & Laing, 2001; Marshall, Laing, Jinks, & Hutchinson, 2006) have demonstrated that people, including expert perfumers, have a limited capacity to identify more than three or four components at any one time, irrespective of whether the odours are single molecules (e.g., ethanol) or complex ones (e.g., a smoky note). Laing and colleagues have recently concluded from their data that the processes underlying human analysis of odour mixtures (such as wine) are analogous to those for facial and object recognition (Jinks & Laing, 2001, p. 51). In keeping with the Gestalt or holistic notion, Jinks and Laing (2001) reported data where identification of most of the prominent qualities of an odorant was not sufficient to ensure identification of the odorant itself. In contrast, failure to identify all prominent features of an odorant did not necessarily result in failure to identify the odorant in a mixture. In other words, the 'whole' does appear to be more than a sum of the parts. This gives a degree of validity to the use of an holistic or configurational approach (Jinks & Laing, 2001) to evaluation of a beverage as complex as wine.

The major alternate evaluative style is an explicitly analytical style. This method is typically adopted in New-world winemaking regions (e.g., California; Australia; New Zealand), especially in teaching institutions. The analytical strategy involves decomposing the flavour notes and other characters of a wine (e.g., textural features) into individual characteristics or chemical compounds, and attempting to attach a verbal label to each component (e.g., by attempting to match the perceived note with an established lexicon such as Noble, Arnold, Buechsenstein, Leach, Schmidt, & Stern's (1987) Wine Aroma Wheel). Despite the fact that analytical strategies involving forced verbalisation (i.e., attempts to identify and give names to separate components) often underlie current training methods for sensory panellists, to my knowledge there is no direct evidence that they enhance a person's ability to identify and remember smells in a specific domain such as wine.

To summarise, although wine professionals' evaluative styles may vary, it is reasonable to assume that their skills are primarily learned, rather than innate, and that the task of any professional wine evaluator has analytical and synthetic components. The analytical component is explicit when a wine judge is challenged to determine whether a specific odour component is present such as a recognised fault (e.g., cork taint; hydrogen sulphide). On the other hand, when a judge is asked which of several wines is the "best" example of a wine style (e.g., of barrel-fermented Chardonnay), the judgment presumably may be made on either an analytical or a synthetic analysis. The latter type of judgment is also likely to involve hedonic (preference) aspects of which a judge may, or may not, be consciously aware. In support of this statement, several researchers have shown that even judgments of odour intensity (intensity is the psychological correlate of concentration) are biased (i.e., influenced) by whether a person likes the smell or not (Richardson & Zucco, 1989; Distel, Ayabe-Kanamura, Martinez-Gomez, Schicker, Kobayakawa, Saito & Hudson, 1999). What is important to note is that an analytical judgment may be no more objective, due to a myriad of factors, than either a synthetic judgment or a judgment that is accepted as containing a hedonistic component (e.g., a preference judgment).

## Wine Complexity and Wine Expertise

Within the study of food and beverages, wine is typically considered a complex mixture (e.g., Marshall et al., 2006). If one uses a quantitative definition, based on the nature of the objective stimulus (e.g., the number of dimensions or factors on which the stimulus may vary), wine is complex relative to the monomolecular stimuli often used in discrimination studies involving the chemical senses (e.g., sucrose). Chemically, wine includes hundreds of volatile, or potentially volatile, substances (Thorngate, 1997).

Psychologically, wine is complex in its non-verbalisable nature. One psychological definition of wine complexity, employed in studies of human perception and memory, relates degree of complexity to the difficulty of capturing the stimulus in words (Melcher & Schooler, 1996). This is a less straightforward definition to work with and open to philosophical debate. However, its advantage is that it brings into focus the person receiving the stimulus input (e.g., a wine judge) as well as the stimulus itself (i.e., the chemical and physical composition of the wine). The non-verbalisable nature of a stimulus is assumed to vary as a function of a person's expertise with the stimulus in question (Melcher & Schooler, 1996; Parr et al., 2002; 2004).

## EMPIRICAL EVIDENCE

The majority of the published empirical work investigating wine expertise and cognitive processing has considered the topic in relation to knowledge (e.g., semantic memory) and language. Solomon (1988), in a doctoral thesis, reported results that could be taken as supporting a linguistic emphasis to wine expertise. In his first experiment, three experts and three novices tasted wines and then generated descriptions about them. Subsequently, a larger group of experts and novices attempted to match the descriptions that had been generated to the wines by the previous experts and novices. The major result from the study was that experts were better able to match wines to descriptions generated by other experts than were the novices, suggesting that wine experts share something of a similar conceptual structure. Subsequent studies, including a psychophysical study, provided data that to variable degrees supported the notion that wine expertise is dependent on categorisation and language processes that develop as a function of experience. Solomon argued that wine experts' knowledge about wines is more structured (e.g., organised in more differentiated categories) than that of novices, and that this allowed the experts to match wine samples to verbal descriptions of wines whereas the novices could not.

Hughson and Boakes (2002) took a somewhat different approach to study similar phenomena, that is, knowledge and linguistic skill in wine expertise. They argued that experience and long-term memory, in the specific field of wine, were important components of wine expertise. Hughson and Boakes undertook several experiments modelled on the chess-playing studies of Chase and Simon (1973). In the first experiment, the procedure was aimed at determining whether their 8 wine experts would have superior recall for meaningful descriptions of wines (i.e., descriptions that could be authentic) than the 21 novices. They also employed a "shuffled" description condition that was an analogy of the random placing of pieces on a chessboard in the chess-playing studies (Chase & Simon, 1973). Hughson and Boakes were therefore able to investigate whether wine experts would recall "shuffled" wine descriptions (i.e., random descriptions that were not likely to fit a typical wine style) as poorly as novices. Results showed that indeed wine experts could recall more varietal than shuffled wine descriptions, and that experts' superiority over novices was limited to the varietal description condition. The results were interpreted in terms of the wine experts' advantage being in their having a knowledge base that included descriptions of typical wine styles (prototypes) stored in memory.

Gawel (1997) also reported work that involved matching wine descriptions generated by other people. Gawel's study was unique in relation to the wine-description matching studies described above in that Gawel differentiated wine experts into two groups, those with formal training and those without. The other major way in which Gawel's task differed from that of the above two studies was in choice of stimulus wines. Gawel employed wines from a single varietal and wine style, namely Australian full-bodied Chardonnay, presumably making the task somewhat more difficult than when matching descriptions across varietals (e.g., Chardonnay, Riesling, Shiraz, and so forth as employed by Hughson & Boakes, 2002). Gawel's results showed that both expert groups could match the wines to wine descriptions provided by others better than chance would predict. However, the expert group without formal training were less successful at matching descriptions generated by their peers (i.e., others without formal training) than the formally trained wine tasters. Gawel interpreted his results in terms of prototype theory (Rosch & Mervis, 1975) within the broader topic of categorisation theory. Specifically, he argued that the wine experts in his study appeared to be matching the wine descriptions by interpreting them as a whole or Gestalt (i.e., as prototypes), rather than being analytical and focusing on individual attributes of a wine (Gawel, 1997, pp. 282-283).

Several other studies have supported the major findings from the studies described above with respect to enhanced verbal efficiency and accuracy in wine experts when describing wine varieties (Chollet & Valentin, 2000; Valentin, Chollet, & Abdi, 2003). In a programme of research concerning conceptual behaviour (Ballester, Dacremont, Le Fur, & Etievant, 2005), the study of wine experts' mental representations was recently extended to investigate the separate contributions of perceptual and conceptual processes to performance on particular tasks. Ballester, Patris, Symoneux, and Valentin (in press) reported data where wine experts and wine novices were compared on tasks that involved olfactory-driven categorisation of two white wines from Burgundy. The tasks were a typicality-rating task (i.e., assessing each wine in terms of how well it exemplified the wine style of interest such as Burgundy Chardonnay), a hedonic rating task, and a sorting task. Their data showed that wine experts categorised the wine types in a similar way, agreeing on what constituted a good example of Burgundy Chardonnay. On the other hand, no such agreement was demonstrated by wine novices in terms of what exemplified a good example of Burgundy Chardonnay. When they considered their data from the sorting task together with the rating-task data (typicality scores and hedonic ratings), the authors argued that both perceptual skill and higher-order cognitive processing were implicated in the performance differences demonstrated between wine experts and novices.

On the other hand, not all studies have shown consensus amongst wine experts when they describe and judge wines. Large variability, both within and between wine experts, has been shown in both wine description tasks (Sauvageot, Urdapilleta, & Peyron, 2006) and in simulated wine judging (Parr, Green, & White, 2006). Neither of these latter studies however included a novice group for comparison. Sauvageot et al. described a study where nine wine experts were permitted to freely describe Chardonnay and Pinot noir wines that had been subjected to different oak treatments. The purpose of the study was to examine wine experts' mental representations of the two wine types. The verbal data underwent lexical analysis. The authors were surprised at the degree of both between-expert and within-expert variability demonstrated, making it difficult to find consensus (i.e., shared patterns) with respect to mental representation of the wines. Experts varied not only in the specific terms they employed to describe the wines but there was large between-expert variability in quantity of text used, and in evaluative style (analytical versus more global and hedonic approaches to describing the wines). Sauvageot et al. qualified their results by pointing out that the differences amongst the wines within a group (i.e., white or red) in this study were small, thus making the task very difficult, even for those experienced with the wine types.

The issue of variability in performance both between and within wine experts has received little experimental attention. In practice, consistency of wine experts when formally judging wines is often assumed and is very important to the wine industry (e.g., to ensure validity of results from formal wine shows). Parr, Green, and White (2006) reported a study that investigated both within-judge variability and between-judge variability when wine experts judged New Zealand Sauvignon blanc wines in a simulated wine show context. Parr et al. reported averaged data showing high variability both between and within judges. Of particular interest, when the data were looked at in terms of individual judges, it was clear that some wine experts were remarkably consistent in rating wines, whilst others were highly variable. In other words, wine judges varied greatly in terms of their internal consistency. Further, those judges who demonstrated the most consistency (i.e., very low within-subject variability) also tended to be the most discriminating.

In summary, the above studies concerning wine expertise demonstrate that wine experts have a structured knowledge base (e.g., in terms of categorical structure) that novices lack, and that experts are able to employ this wine-relevant knowledge to match (Solomon, 1988; Gawel, 1997) and recall (Hughson and Boakes, 2002) wine descriptions. However, there is a dearth of evidence to date concerning the perceptual skills (e.g., sensory-based memory) of wine experts as separate from conceptual skills (i.e., knowledge in the form of semantic memory; categorisation processes). Several experiments to address this gap in knowledge were recently performed in our laboratory. Our overall aim was to investigate whether some form(s) of perceptual advantage or disadvantage could also be contributing to the performance of wine experts.

## EMPIRICAL STUDIES FROM OUR LABORATORY

We recently explored several aspects of wine evaluation that at face value have relevance to wine expertise, employing methodologies from cognitive psychology that emphasise, rather than iron out, individual differences among people. The underlying model of human behaviour that we employed was that pertaining to cognitive change as a function of expertise. Thus, a major methodology was comparison of performance by those assumed to have expertise (e.g., established wine judges) with performance of relative novices (e.g., wine consumers). By employing participants with varying degrees of wine expertise, we aimed to provide evidence concerning how perceptual and memorial processes can both facilitate and inhibit judgments made by novice and expert wine judges.

We investigated olfactory-driven recognition memory, odour identification, semantic memory, and the concept of perceptual bias. The work was limited to the study of ortho-nasal olfaction; that is, to the aromatic characters of a wine that people experience via the sense of smell. This limitation was imposed for several reasons. First, the volatile component of wine, producing aromas that are detected both ortho-nasally (smelling) and retro-nasally ("tasting") is extremely important in wine quality evaluation. Second, the work was limited to ortho-nasal olfaction because complex interactions between taste and smell could serve to confound the issues under investigation (see Dalton, Doolittle, Nagata, & Breslin, 2000) at this early stage of enquiry.

## Perceptual Skill and Semantic Memory in Expert and Novice Wine Judges

Two experiments investigated the relation between memory for smells (perceptual skill) and memory for the names of smells (semantic memory and verbal skill). More specifically, we compared memorial and language processes in wine "experts" (e.g., wine judges; winemakers; Masters of wine) with those of wine novices. The novices were people who drank wine regularly (at least once per month) but had no formal wine training.

In the first study (Parr et al., 2002), 11 wine experts and 11 wine novices participated in tasks measuring olfactory threshold, odour recognition (episodic memory), odour identification, and consistency of odour naming (semantic memory). The tasks were undertaken in that order, in purpose-built sensory facilities (see ASTM, 1986). The olfactory stimuli employed for the olfactory threshold task were various concentrations of 1-butanol, and the stimuli employed for all other tasks were 28 wine-relevant odorants (e.g., Lenoir, 1995; ASTM, 1985). The odorants employed included wine faults (e.g., over-ripe/rotting apple: ethanal), primary characters (e.g., leafy/vegetal: trans-2-hexenal), and maturation characters (e.g., vanilla/oak: ethylvanillin prop. glycol acetate).

Consistent with several previous reports (e.g., Bende & Nordin, 1997), olfactory detection thresholds did not differ between wine experts and novices, $t(20) = 0.31$, $p = 0.76$ (see Table 1). There was however a significant difference in odour recognition, as measured by the discriminability index $d'$, as a function of domain-specific expertise, $t(20) = 2.13$, $p < 0.05$. Table 1 shows that wine experts not only demonstrated superior recognition of the odorants, but also showed less within-group variability. The detection model bias measure did not differ as a function of expertise. Table 1 also shows the "mirror effect" where wine experts' Hit rates were overall higher and their False Alarm (FA) rates lower compared to those of novices. This result is similar to that found in both human and non-human research where increasing task difficulty can result in increased FA rate (Wixted, 1992).

**Table 1. Summary of olfactory performance as a function of expertise. Identification of odorants and consistency of naming are reported as proportions correct. Sensitivity to 1-butanol is reported in dilution steps, where a higher number represents a lower threshold. [Table first published in Parr et al., Chemical Senses, 27, p. 752]**

| 8.5 | Wine | Experts | Wine | Novices |
|---|---|---|---|---|
| **Olfactory performance** | M | *SD* | *M* | *SD* |
| Odour memory ($d'$) | 2.26 | 0.49 | 1.63 | 0.85 * |
| Hit rate | 0.86 | 0.10 | 0.77 | 0.17 * |
| False alarm rate | 0.17 | 0.10 | 0.24 | 0.10 * |
| Response criterion ($C$) | 0.08 | 0.42 | 0.05 | 0.35 |
| Identification of odorants | 0.51 | 0.12 | 0.45 | 0.10 |
| Consistency of naming | 0.55 | 0.14 | 0.53 | 0.22 |
| Sensitivity to 1-butanol (threshold) | 8.18 | 1.40 | 8.36 | 1.36 |

* Denotes a significant difference between groups ($p < 0.05$)

The relations between measures of episodic memory (odour recognition) and semantic memory (identification and consistency of naming) are presented in Table 2. The table shows that there was no significant correlation between odour recognition and odour identification, or between odour recognition and consistency of naming odorants for either wine experts or wine novices. There was a trend toward a positive association between odour recognition and consistency of naming for wine experts which could be interpreted as suggesting that consistent use of a name to label a smell is more important than correct identification. That is, a personally-meaningful term such as a favourite confectionery may be more useful than the objectively 'correct' name for an odorant (see Lehrner et al., 1999 for a similar result).

**Table 2. Correlations of olfactory threshold, odour recognition, odour naming, and consistency of odour naming in expert and novice wine judges. [Table first published in Parr et al., Chemical Senses, 27, p. 753]**

Experts

| Variables | 1 | 2 | 3 | 4 | 5 | 6 |
|---|---|---|---|---|---|---|
| (1) Threshold | | | | | | |
| (2) Odour recognition | -0.82 * | | | | | |
| (3) Hit rate | -0.24 | +0.41 | | | | |
| (4) False alarm rate | +0.42 | -0.44 | +0.59 * | | | |
| (5) Odour identification | -0.24 | -0.09 | +0.36 | -0.49 | | |
| (6) Consistency of naming | -0.41 | +0.30 | -0.54 | -0.01 | +0.17 | |

Novices

| Variables | 1 | 2 | 3 | 4 | 5 | 6 |
|---|---|---|---|---|---|---|
| (1) Threshold | | | | | | |
| (2) Odour recognition | -0.21 | | | | | |
| (3) Hit rate | -0.23 | +0.86 * | | | | |
| (4) False alarm rate | -0.15 | -0.55 | -0.11 | | | |
| (5) Odour identification | -0.60 * | +0.43 | +0.53 | -0.04 | | |
| (6) Consistency of naming | -0.26 | +0.33 | +0.65 * | +0.27 | +0.38 | |

* Denotes a significant difference between variables ($p < 0.05$)

The major result from this study was that perceptual skill, rather than the ability to name odours, advantaged those with wine expertise. We interpreted this result in terms of verbal overshadowing (e.g., Melcher & Schooler, 1996). A prior body of research, including data from electrophysiological studies (Lorig, 1999), supports the argument that perceiving smells and vebalising (as occurs when one is asked to try and identify and label a smell) are cognitive processes that can interfere with one another, rather than be mutually facilitative. Further, the degree of interference appears to interact with one's domain-specific expertise (Melcher & Schooler, 1996). Wine experts, with skill in both perceptual and verbal aspects of wine evaluation, would be expected to be less susceptible to verbal overshadowing than wine novices.

Failure to demonstrate superior verbal abilities in odorant naming in wine experts was unexpected. We reasoned that the result could, at least in part, reflect the emphasis given to wine-relevant language skills in many New World wine regions (e.g., New Zealand; Australia; California) for those developing formally-trained wine expertise (e.g., use of linguistic tools such as a variant of the Wine Aroma Wheel (Noble, Arnold, Masuda, Pecore, Schmidt, & Stern, 1984). An obvious application from the current data is caution when educating people to characterise wine varietals: emphasis on language (e.g., matching perceived smells to a name such as "canned plums", especially when early in a wine professional's training, should not be at the expense of focus on the smell itself. An accumulating body of evidence suggests that verbal codes are not essential to, or even necessarily activated (Herz, 2000), for successful odour-guided cognition. As Schooler & Engstler-Schooler reported (1990), some things may be better left unsaid.

A second experiment investigated the locus of the perceptual recognition memory advantage that the above study had demonstrated in wine experts (Parr, White, & Heatherbell, 2004). We did this by varying the type of encoding of to-be-remembered odorants. Fourteen wine experts and 14 wine novices participated in odour recognition and identification tasks similar to those described above. Type of encoding was varied in the odour recognition task with semantic (odour identification) and hedonic (rating odour pleasantness) encoding conditions undertaken by each participant (repeated measures design). The aim of this was to investigate whether verbalisation per se, or verbalisation specific to odorant naming, influenced recognition accuracy as a function of wine expertise.

Results again showed superior odorant recognition in wine experts, despite olfactory sensitivity, bias measures, and odour identification ability being similar between experts and novices. This replication of the major result of the prior study further supported the argument that superior odour recognition memory in wine experts has its locus in perceptual skill (e.g., olfactory imaging), rather than in superior semantic memory and linguistic skill. The manipulation of type of odorant-encoding task failed to provide any further insight into the specific cognitive processes underlying experts' odour recognition advantage. Type of encoding influenced recognition performance, with both wine experts' and wine novices' odorant recognition facilitated by odorant naming relative to pleasantness rating of the odorants.

## Investigation of Perceptual Bias

Previous experience, now stored as memories, has potential to give rise to expectations, ideas, images, motives, emotions and so forth that can influence our chemosensory perception. For example, the label on a wine bottle may serve as a cue to recall experience of an earlier vintage of the same wine. This in turn can give rise to expectations regarding the flavour characteristics one might expect in the wine. Presumably, such expectations can serve to facilitate and/or inhibit wine evaluation performance, depending on any particular situation.

In two experiments, we investigated olfactory perceptual bias, a cognitive construct concerned with how what we already know influences what we smell. Perceptual bias refers to erroneous judgments that result from influence of knowledge and prior experience on perceptual processing, such as smelling. It is interesting to note that the type of odour-judgment error known as perceptual bias has much in common with demonstrations of faulty eye-witness testimony when visual 'misinformation cues' (i.e., a misleading change in colour) are employed (see Loftus, 1993).

Renowned oenologist, the late Emile Peynaud, is reported to have once said "blind tasting is often disappointing" (Brochet, 1999, p. 21). This comment presumably refers to the notion that much of what we perceive when we sniff or sip a wine has very little to do with what is in the actual glass. Formal wine evaluation is analogous to other diagnostic problems that involve judgment under uncertainty. A fundamental characteristic of these diagnostic situations is that factors other than the objective stimulus (i.e., the physical and chemical characteristics of the wine sample) can contribute to the 'evidence' on which we base our decision. Top-down cognitive processes (see earlier discussion) can influence perception to bias us to smell something that in fact is not present in the wine sample (e.g., Morrot et al., 2001).

Two studies in our laboratory investigated influence of wine colour on judgments of wine aroma. Twenty-nine wine experts (established wine judges; Masters of wine; winemakers) and 23 wine novices (wine consumers) in six geographical locations around New Zealand took part in the studies. Each person undertook ortho-nasal tasks where they (i) self-generated descriptors to each of a Chardonnay and a Pinot noir wine, and (ii) subsequently gave intensity ratings to their self-generated descriptors to the same Chardonnay and Pinot noir wines when they were in opaque (black) glasses and when the samples were presented in standard ISO (ISO, 1977) glasses. Of major interest, some samples of the Chardonnay wine were coloured with odourless anthocyanin to simulate a red wine (called wine "white-red"), while others were coloured with odourless turmeric and natural caramel to simulate an aged Chardonnay (called wine "white-gold").

Results showed that for wine experts, red colour did indeed serve as a visual mis-information cue, biasing wine experts' judgments. Figure 3 shows that while wine experts rated wines appropriately under all conditions (i.e., they gave higher intensity ratings to white-wine descriptors than to red-wine descriptors when a wine was white (and vice versa when a wine was red), they did succumb to a statistically significant degree of perceptual bias. The Chardonnay wine that was coloured red received higher intensity ratings to red-wine descriptors when the artificially coloured wine was presented in clear glass than when presented in opaque glass (see panel 3 of Figure 1).

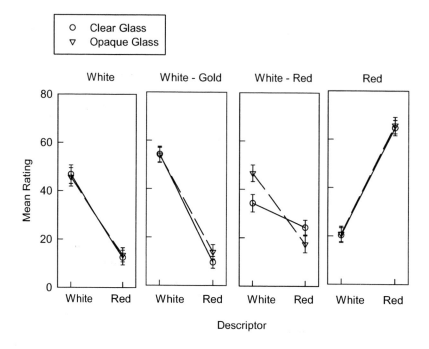

Figure 1. Mean aroma intensity ratings as a function of descriptor, wine sample, and glass colour (clear or opaque) for wine experts. [Figure first published in Parr et al., *Journal of Wine Research,* 2003, *14*, p. 95]

Absence of the requisite wine-relevant knowledge in wine novices was hypothesised to make it less likely that their top-down processes would over-ride data-driven (bottom-up) processing. However, the above study was not entirely effective in testing this hypothesis. Wine novices in general found the task difficult, resorting to indiscriminate judging in some conditions. Novices' ratings to the white wine that was coloured red showed indiscriminate use of descriptors relative to their ratings given to the other wine samples. We interpreted this result as wine novices being influenced by the artificially coloured red wine via top-down cognitive processes, but not in the same way as the wine experts. That is, wine novices, who were social drinkers, were not so much driven by bottom-up processes in the present study, but appeared to have sufficient top-down knowledge to find the situation (a white wine that was coloured red) ambiguous, and to make inappropriate judgments. When the data from the experts and novices were considered together, analyses showed that contrary to the competence of the wine experts, novices showed poorer performance under several opaque-glass conditions than when they could see the wine (standard glass conditions). It is conceivable that the novices' relative lack of knowledge, compared with that of the experts, reduced their confidence, producing indiscriminate judging behaviour.

In summary, results showed wine experts to be more data-driven than wine novices. However, the experts were still seduced to a significant degree by the artificially coloured red wine. Wine novices' performance on the other hand suffered in the opaque-glass condition, possibly due to ambiguity and loss of confidence due to the difficulty and novelty of the task (Parr, White, & Heatherbell, 2003).

## A COGNITIVE MODEL OF WINE EXPERTISE

The expectation of cognitive psychology that it will eventually provide an understanding of complex aspects of human behaviour such as wine expertise is being rewarded with recent progress in the field. The studies from our laboratory described above, along with work by others (e.g., Hughson and Boakes, 2002; Gawel, 1997; Solomon, 1988; Morrot et al., 2001; Brochet & Dubourdieu, 2001; Ballester et al., 2007), are beginning to give some indication as to the ways in which relevant cognitive processes in wine experts differ from those in less-experienced wine consumers.

Conceptual knowledge, such as knowing the typical features that go together in a specific wine style, appears more structured in wine experts than in novices. Data reported to date suggest that such categorical structure assists wine experts to recall (Hughson & Boakes, 2002) and match (Solomon, 1988) wine descriptions, and to judge typicality of wine styles (Ballester et al., 2007). The theory drawn upon to interpret these results includes top-down cognitive processes of semantic memory and language, including a wine-appropriate vocabulary, and a conceptual system that includes prototypes of wine types or styles (Brochet & Dubourdieu, 2001). Gawel's work (1997) has added to the picture by reporting results that implied that formal training in wine enhanced an expert's skills relative to experience of wines without formal training.

The studies from our own laboratory extend the current state of knowledge about wine expertise by moving the information processing emphasis from conceptual and language aspects to focus on perceptual processes. At a more specific level, the studies described in this chapter provide data relevant to three aspects of a cognitive model of wine expertise. First, neither basic olfactory sensitivity, as measured by detection of 1-butanol, nor motivation, as measured within a signal detection model as the tendency to say "yes" in the task, can account for the reported differences between experts and novices on the cognitive tasks. In other words, the differences between experts and novices that are reported in our studies reflect true differences in cognitive processing. Further, the cognitive differences are presumably learned.

The second way in which our recent work extends the research area concerns perceptual mechanisms and their relation to the top-down processes of semantic memory and language. Wine experts, as well as having superior knowledge, exemplified in tasks that require top-down processing, have superior recognition memory skills. Superior olfactory recognition memory, in the absence of superior odour-naming ability, presumably reflects superior olfactory perceptual ability such as enhanced ability for forming olfactory images (e.g., being able to image/imagine the smell of cloves). From a theoretical perspective, this perceptual superiority could conceivably have assisted the wine experts to avoid verbal overshadowing (Melcher & Schooler, 1996). That is, interference between the perceptual (the smell) and the verbal (locating the name of the smell from memory) aspects of the task was rendered less likely due to the experts' well-developed perceptual skill (e.g., recalling the *smell* of anise) as well as their well-developed verbal skills (knowing the *name* "anise"). When judging complex stimuli, interference has been argued as more likely to occur when a person's perceptual and verbal abilities in a particular skill domain are unequal (Melcher & Schooler, 1996).

The third way in which our studies allow elaboration of a cognitive model of wine expertise is to demonstrate the fallibility of humans as judges (Kahneman, Slovic, & Tversky, 1982) within the world of wine. The specific cognitive processing that has been implicated in demonstrating colour-induced, olfactory bias in wine judges concerns the interaction between top-down cognitive processes (previous experience and knowledge) and bottom-up processing (emphasis on the phenomenological properties of the wine sample such as its specific aroma notes). In the case of perceptual bias, domain-specific expertise was shown to be a variable that may not always facilitate a wine expert's performance, but that could lead the expert astray. Wine industry professionals, by becoming aware of the existence of such biases, presumably will be able to limit damage resulting from the types of systematic cognitive biases that have been demonstrated when people make probabilistic judgments across a range of fields such as medicine, economics and political decision-making (Kahneman, Slovic, & Tversky, 1982). Perceptual bias is of major significance in that misidentification of odorants in wine samples could result in a wine being inappropriately categorised in a formal judging. Further, perceptual bias is particularly dangerous in that it is apparently accompanied by marked confidence that the erroneous judgment is in fact correct (e.g., Cain & Potts, 1996).

## CONCLUSION

In summary, to understand wine expertise, differences among people need to be investigated, rather than seen as experimental error or as nuisance variables within a consensus model of sensory responding. Recalling the chess-playing analogy, systematic research concerning wine expertise should not only assist us to understand the cognitive processes implicated in development of wine expertise, but should eventually be able to delineate the ways in which humans differ from physical instruments, and continue to surpass in some situations (e.g., in olfactory detection of methoxypyrazines: Allen, Lacey, & Boyd, 1996), even the best machine or instrument.

Despite its relative neglect, an understanding of sensory phenomena with respect to wine evaluation is important from both theoretical and practical perspectives. Chemical analyses can be accurate and consistent, but there are still odours that neither chemical nor instrumental analyses can detect or identify, but that the human nose can at least detect. Further, recent evidence of the complexity of interactions between tastes and smells which, although individually present at sub-threshold level, can combine to produce a detectable stimulus (Dalton, Doolittle, Nagata, & Breslin, 2000), demonstrates how far we still have to progress with respect to instrumental simulation of human processing in the chemical senses. For the majority of wine connoisseurs and everyday consumers of wine, it doesn't matter what a machine says or what a chemical analysis says. They will be driven by what their senses tell them.

## Future Research

There are likely to be differences between a wine expert's behaviour when going about his or her usual activities on the one hand and their taking part in controlled, scientific investigations on the other. None-the-less, in the present era of accountability, and where formal wine judgements (e.g., awards of gold medals) and wine comment (e.g., written critiques of wines by critics such as Robert Parker) carry enormous weight in terms of wine-consumer behaviour, some attempt to delineate the mechanisms underlying wine expertise appears called for.

Future research has an infinite number of paths to travel, given the relatively untapped nature of research to date. There are some particularly fruitful areas for future study. The first concerns analytic and synthetic analysis of wines, and the relevant underlying theories, in particular, prototype theory. My hypothesis would be that although analytic evaluation appears at face value to be more "objective", and is easier to teach because the task can be broken down into concrete steps, synthetic (holistic or configurational) evaluation is not only likely to be more often employed in everyday wine-evaluation situations, but it may also prove to be as objective and effective (i.e., accurate) in the hands of experts. My hypothesis is based on previous research that has demonstrated a qualitative difference in cognitive processing between experts and novices in other areas of expertise. For example, junior medical doctors have been shown to follow rules (i.e., be more analytic) and, for example, look for the presence of 3 out of 5 symptoms in a list to make a diagnosis. On the other hand, experienced consultants, who give the impression of standing at the end of the bed and producing a diagnosis synthetically, have been argued as having such a developed knowledge base that their associative memory processes and the categorical structure of their semantic memory allow them to rapidly recognise a complex stimulus (the person's ailment) with almost the same degree of accuracy as an expert system (i.e., computer programme developed for diagnosis).

A second area of research that could advantage the field concerns further elaboration of the relation between perceptual experience and language. Extensive use of verbal tools such as Noble et al.'s (1987) Wine Aroma Wheel to match perceived wine characters with names has been called into question by several recent studies, as well as by work in our own laboratory. Why wine professionals can typically list large numbers of component features of a wine sample when outside the laboratory, and yet perform no better than a social drinker at naming smells in the first two studies of the present work, is something of a mystery. A similar mystery relates to how wine connoisseurs appear able to distinguish a large number of individual notes/characters from a sniff or a sip, and yet the work of David Laing and colleagues (e.g., Livermore & Laing, 1996) in the psychological laboratory argues that humans, including expert perfumers, can at most detect three or four components of a complex mixture. Future research that can close the divide between "real life" wine evaluation and the psychological laboratory is needed. Clearly, this will require development of tasks with high ecological validity, and situations where wine professionals feel comfortable and motivated to participate.

## ACKNOWLEDGEMENTS

The work was funded by Lincoln University, Lincoln University Fund for Excellence, and New Zealand Winegrowers. I thank David Heatherbell, Geoff White, James Green, and Andy Frost for valued comment.

## REFERENCES

Allen, M., Lacey, M., & Boyd, S. (1996). Methoxypyrazines: New insights into their biosynthesis and occurrence. *Proceedings for the 4th International Symposium on Cool Climate Viticulure and Enology.*

ASTM (1985). *Atlas of Odor Character Profiles.* Philadelphia: ASTM publications.

ASTM (1986). *Physical Requirement Guidelines for Sensory Evaluation Laboratories, ASTM STP 913.* Philadelphia: ASTM publications.

Ballester,.J., Patris, B., Symoneaux, R., & Valentin, D. (in press). Conceptual versus perceptual wine spaces: does expertise matter? *Food Quality and Preference.*

Ballester, J., Dacremont, C., Le Fur, Y., & Etievant, P. (2005). The role of olfaction in the elaboration and use of the Chardonnay wine concept. *Food Quality and Preference, 16,* 351-359.

Bende, M. & Nordin, S. (1997). Perceptual learning in olfaction: professional wine tasters versus controls. *Physiology & Behavior, 62,* 1065-1070.

Brochet, F. (1999). The taste of wine in consciousness. *Journal International des Sciences de la Vigne et du Vin: Special Issue Wine Tasting,* 19-22.

Brochet, F., & Dubourdieu, D. (2001). Wine descriptive language supports cognitive specificity of chemical senses. *Brain and Language, 77,* 187-196.

Cain, W. & Potts, B. (1996). Switch and bait: Probing the discriminative basis of odor identification via recognition memory. *Chemical Senses, 21,* 35-44.

Chase, W.G., & Simon, H. (1973). Perception in chess. *Cognitive Psychology, 4,* 55-81.

Chollet, S., & Valentin, D. (2000). Le degré d'expertise a-t-il une influence sur la perception olfactive? Quelques éléments de réponse dans le domaine du vin. *L'Année psychologique, 100,* 11-36.

de Groot, A.D. (1965). *Thought and choice in chess.* The Hague: Mouton.

Dalton, P. (2000). Fragrance perception: From the nose to the brain. *Journal of Cosmetic Science, 51,* 141-150.

Dalton, P.,Doolittle, N., Nagata, H., & Breslin, P. (2000). The merging of the senses: integration of subthreshold taste and smell. *Nature neuroscience, 3,* 431-432.

Degel, J., & Koster, E. (1999). Odors: Implicit memory and performance effects. *Chemical Senses, 24,* 317-325.

Distel, H., Ayabe-Kanamura, S., Matinez-Gomez, M., Schicker, I., Kobayakawa, T., Saito, S., & Hudson, R. (1999). Perception of everyday odors -- correlation between intensity, familiarity and strength of hedonic judgement. *Chemical Senses, 24,* 191-199.

Gawel, R. (1997). The use of language by trained and untrained experienced wine tasters. *Journal of Sensory Studies, 12,* 267-284.

Gibson, J.J., & Gibson, E.J. (1955). Perceptual learning: Differentiation or enrichment? *Psychological Review, 62*, 32-41.

Herz, R.S. (2000). Verbal coding in olfactory versus nonolfactory cognition. *Memory & Cognition, 28*, 957-964.

Herz, R.S., & Engen, T. (1996). Odor memory: Review and analysis. *Psychonomic Bulletin & Review, 3*, 300-313.

Hughson, A., & Boakes, R.A. (2002). The knowing nose: the role of knowledge in wine expertise. *Food Quality and Preference, 13*, 463-472.

ISO (1977). Sensory analysis – apparatus – wine-tasting glass. Geneva, Switzerland: ISO

Jinks, A., & Laing, D.G. (2001). The analysis of odor mixtures by humans: evidence for a configurational process. *Physiology & Behavior, 72*, 51-63.

Kahneman, D., Slovic, P., & Tversky, A. (1982*). Judgment under uncertainty: heuristics and biases*. Cambridge: Cambridge University Press.

Lawless, H.T. (1997). Olfactory psychophysics. In G.K. Beauchamp & L. Bartoshuk (Eds.) *Tasting and smelling*. San Diego: Academic Press.

Lehrner, J.P., Gluck, J., & Laska, M. (1999). Odor identification, consistency of label use, olfactory threshold and their relationships to odor memory over the human lifespan. *Chemical Senses, 24*, 337-346.

Lenoir, J. (1995*). Le nez du vin*. France: editions Jean Lenoir.

Livermore, A., & Laing, D. (1996). Influence of training and experience on the perception of multi-component odor mixtures. *Journal of Experimental Psychology: Human Perception and Performance, 22*, 267-277.

Loftus, E. (1993). Psychologists in the eyewitness world. *American Psychologist, 48*, 550-552.

Loftus, E., & Palmer, J. (1974). Reconstruction of automobile destruction: An example of the interaction between language and memory. *Journal of Verbal learning and Verbal Behavior, 13*, 585-589.

Lorig, T.S. (1999). On the similarity of odor and language perception. *Neuroscience and Biobehavioral Reviews, 23*, 391-398.

Marshall, K., Laing, D.G., Jinks, A.L., & Hutchinson, I. (2006). The capacity of humans to identify components in complex odor-taste mixtures. *Chemical Senses, 31*, 539-545.

Melcher, J., & Schooler, J. (1996). The misremembrance of wines past: Verbal and perceptual expertise differentially mediate verbal overshadowing of taste memory. *Journal of Memory and Language, 35*, 231-245.

Miller, G.A. (1956). The magical number seven, plus or minus two: some limits on our capacity for processing information. *Psychological Review, 63*, 81-97.

Morrot, G., Brochet, F., & Dubourdieu, D. (2001). The color of odors. *Brain and Language, 79*, 309-320.

Morrot, G. (1999). Can we improve taster performance? *Journal International des Sciences de la Vigne et du Vin: Special Issue Wine Tasting*, 29-35.

Moskowitz, H.R. (2003). The intertwining of psychophysics and sensory analysis: Historical perspectives and future opportunities – a personal view. *Food Quality and Preference, 14*, 87-98.

Noble, A., Arnold, R., Buechsenstein, J., Leach, E., Schmidt, J., & Stern, P. (1987). Modification of a standardized system of wine aroma terminology. *American Journal of Enology & Viticulture 38*, 143-146.

Nowrich, K.H. (1991). Toward the unification of the laws of sensation: Some food for thought. In H.T. Lawless and B.P. Klein (Eds.), *Sensory science theory and application in foods*, pp. 151-183. Marcel Dekker Inc.: N.Y.

Parr, W.V., Green, J.A., White, K.G., & Sherlock (2007). The distinctive flavour of New Zealand Sauvignon blanc: Sensory characterisation by wine professionals. *Food Quality and Preference, 18*, 849-861.

Parr, W.V., Green, J.A., & White, K.G. (2006). Wine judging, context, and New Zealand Sauvignon blanc. *European Review of Applied Psychology, 56*, 231-238.

Parr, W.V., White, K.G., & Heatherbell (2004). Exploring the nature of wine expertise: what underlies wine experts' olfactory recognition memory advantage? *Food Quality and Preference, 15*, 411-420.

Parr, W.V., White, K.G., & Heatherbell (2003). The nose knows: Influence of colour on perception of wine aroma. *Journal of Wine Research, 14*, 79-101.

Parr, W.V., Heatherbell, D.A., & White, K.G. (2002). Demystifying wine expertise: Olfactory threshold, perceptual skill, and semantic memory in expert and novice wine judges. *Chemical Senses, 27*, 747-755.

Reisberg, D. (1997). *Cognition: Exploring the science of the mind.* NY: W.W. Norton & Co.

Rosch, E., & Mervis, C. (1975). Family resemblances: studies in the internal structure of categories. *Cognitive Psychology, 7*, 573-605.

Richardson, J.T.E. & Zucco, G.M. (1989). Cognition and olfaction: A review. *Psychological Bulletin, 105*, 352-360.

Sauvageot, F., Urdapilleta, I., & Peyron, D. (2006). Within and between variations in texts elicited from nine wine experts. *Food Quality and Preference, 17*, 429-444.

Schooler, J.W., & Engstler-Schooler, T.Y. (1990). Verbal overshadowing of visual memories: Some things are better left unsaid. *Cognitive psychology, 22*, 36-71.

Solomon, G. (1991). Language and categorization in wine expertise. In H.T. Lawless & B.P. Klein (Eds.) *Sensory Science Theory and Applications in Foods, 269-294.* N.Y.: Marcel Dekker, Inc.

Solomon, G. (1990). The psychology of novice and expert wine talk. *American Journal of Psychology, 103*, 495-517.

Solomon, G. (1988). *Great expectorations: The psychology of wine talk.* Ph. D. dissertation, Harvard University.

Stone, H., & Sidel, J.L. (1993). *Sensory evaluation practices, 2nd ed.* San Diego: Academic Press.

Stone, H., Sidel, J., Oliver, S., Woolsey, A., & Singleton, R.C. (1974). Sensory evaluation by quantitative descriptive analysis. *Food Technol., 28*, 24-34.

Thorngate, J.H. (1997). The physiology of human sensory response to wine. *American Journal of Enology & Viticulture, 48*, 271-279.

Valentin, D., Chollet, S., & Abdi, H. (2003). Les mots du vin: experts et novices diffèrent-ils quand ils décrivent des vins? *Corpus, 2*, 183-199.

Wells, G.L. (1993). What do we know about eyewitness identification? *American Psychologist, 48*, 413-424.

Wixted, J.T. (1992). Subjective memorability and the mirror effect. *Journal of Experimental Psychology: Learning, Memory & Cognition*, 18, 681-690.

In: Applied Psychology Research Trends
Editor: Karl H. Kiefer, pp.141-159

ISBN 978-1-60456-372-6
© 2008 Nova Science Publishers, Inc.

*Chapter 7*

# A MODEL OF MOTIVATIONAL SPILLOVER

## *Yvette Quintela[1] and John J. Donovan[2]*
[1] Sirota Survey Intelligence
[2] Rider University

## ABSTRACT

Few studies have examined whether performance feedback on a given task can have implications for motivational processes on an altogether distinct task. The present study proposes and tests a model for motivational spillover in a goal-setting context. Participants (N = 222) were provided with bogus goal-performance discrepancy (GPD) feedback on a creativity-brainstorming task (CBT) and were subsequently asked to set a performance goal for an unrelated stock-predicting task (SPT). Results indicated that individuals receiving negative GPD feedback on the CBTs experienced decreased levels of self-efficacy and set lower goals for themselves for the SPT. This effect was mediated by positive and negative affect. These findings provide initial evidence for the occurrence of motivational spillover and its underlying mechanisms.

## A Model of Motivational Spillover

Theories of work motivation have long recognized the importance of discrepancies between one's goal and actual performance in determining behavior. Proponents of social cognitive theory and control theory suggest that it is not an individual's performance level per se that is important, but rather it is the discrepancy between the person's performance and their performance goal (termed a goal-performance discrepancy; GPD) that affects motivation (e.g., Bandura, 1991; Campion & Lord, 1982; Carver & Scheier, 1981; Locke & Latham, 1990). These theories propose that people monitor the occurrence of these discrepancies and when faced with discrepancies that indicate that their performance is below their goal level (i.e., a negative GPD), engage in behavior aimed at reducing or eliminating this discrepancy. In support of this proposition, numerous studies have found that individual's experiencing negative GPDs tend to engage in discrepancy reduction behaviors such as downward goal revision, increasing effort, or altering their performance strategies (e.g., Bandura & Cervone, 1983; Campion & Lord, 1982; Donovan & Williams, 2003; Williams, Donovan, & Dodge, 2000).

However, it is important to realize that much of this research to date examining the impact of negative GPDs has focused on the role of these GPDs in subsequent motivational processes for *similar* or *identical* tasks (Austin & Vancouver, 1996; Kluger & DeNisi,1996). In other words, research has shown that GPDs on a particular task can influence goal revision, effort expenditure, and performance strategies on the same exact task. Very few studies have examined how the effects of negative GPDs might carry over across *different* tasks. Current self-regulation frameworks have not yet explicitly addressed the possibility that motivational processes for a particular task may effectively "spillover" to affect motivation for an unrelated or distinct task. The present study extended the existing self-regulation research by examining whether the effects of goal failure on a given task can spillover to influence self-efficacy and goal-setting on a subsequent distinct task.

## Motivational Spillover

Motivational spillover (alternatively termed "transfer of motivation"; Festinger, 1942) refers to situations in which motivational processes and outcomes on an initial task impact motivational processes on a subsequent, distinct task (cf., Williams & Alliger, 1994). Motivational spillover can be both positive and negative. For example, an individual experiencing success on a particular task may exhibit an enhanced sense of efficacy for a subsequent, distinct task (positive spillover), which may lead the individual to establish a more challenging goal for themselves on the second task. Similarly, an individual experiencing failure on a particular task may demonstrate a decrease in self-efficacy for a separate task (negative spillover), resulting in the establishment of a less challenging goal for this second task.

Despite the potential importance of motivational spillover for models of motivation and task performance, surprisingly little work has been done to examine this phenomenon. Initial evidence of motivational spillover was obtained by Jucknat (1937) and Festinger (1942) who observed that performance outcomes on one task "transferred over" in such a way to affect levels of aspiration (i.e., goals) for a subsequent task, although this spillover appeared to be dependent on the similarity of the tasks being performed (Jucknat, 1937). More recent research on the phenomenon of motivational spillover has revealed that failure on an initial task can lead to a motivational decline for a second task for both similar and dissimilar tasks. For example, research has demonstrated that task failure can lead to decreased motivation (Carver, Blaney, & Scheier, 1979) and lowered expectations for performance (Kernis, Zuckerman, Cohen, & Spadafora, 1982) on a subsequent, distinct task. These initial studies clearly indicate that motivational processes on a task may be influenced by previous success/failure on a distinct task. Unfortunately, there has been no empirical work on this phenomenon conducted since this initial body of work. This omission is somewhat surprising given the potentially important implications that motivational spillover would have for current models of motivation and their application. The present study sought to remedy this omission by providing an empirical examination of a model of motivational spillover that not only seeks to replicate the initial evidence of this phenomenon, but also to delineate the mechanisms by which spillover occurs.

## Mechanisms of Spillover

Although the previously mentioned studies provided evidence of motivational spillover, they are less informative in terms of the mechanisms by which this spillover occurred. While work by Carver et al. (1979) and Kernis et al. (1982) has indicated that failure/success on one task influences subsequent motivation primarily though its impact on expectancies for future performance, there is no explicit explanation given for how these motivational processes transfers across tasks. That is, why does success on one task influence expectancies for success on a completely different task? The present study represents an initial attempt to provide a model of this spillover process. The conceptual model for this study (provided in Figure 1) argues that (a) goal failure[1] may spillover to a distinct task through its impact on positive and negative affect, (b) positive and negative affect will influence self-efficacy perceptions for the second, distinct task, and (c) self-efficacy will impact the goals individuals set for this second task.

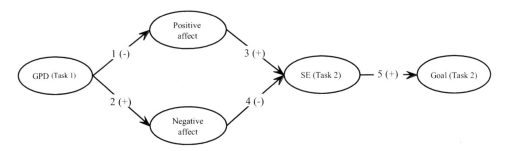

*Figure 1.* Proposed model of motivational spillover.

*Goal failure and affect.* Affect refers to the mood states experienced by individuals, which can be characterized by the levels of positive and negative affect they experience. Positive affect can be defined as the extent to which a person feels enthusiastic, active and alert, while negative affect is defined as the extent to which a person feels displeased, distressed, and aversive (Watson, Clark, & Tellegen, 1988)[2]. Many of the currently accepted models of self-regulation acknowledge that negative GPD states (i.e., goal failure) are likely to bring about increases in negative affect and decreases in positive affect (e.g., Bandura, 1986; Locke & Latham, 2002). In fact, one of the primary tenets of Bandura's (1986) social cognitive theory is that performance below one's goal leads to self-dissatisfaction, which in turn sets off a series of self-regulatory mechanisms aimed at removing this self-dissatisfaction. In support of this link between goal failure and affect, numerous studies have shown that goal failure is typically associated with increases in negative affect and decreases in positive affect (e.g., Bandura & Cervone, 1983; Goldstein & Strube, 1994; Mikulincer, 1988; Mone & Baker, 1992; Pittman & Pittman, 1979; Woo & Mix, 1997). For example, Bandura and Cervone (1983) found that individuals experiencing a large, negative GPD exhibited higher levels of self-dissatisfaction than individuals who experienced smaller discrepancies. Similarly, Mone and Baker (1992) found that students who experienced large, negative GPDs on an exam reported higher levels of negative affect and lower levels of positive affect. In line with this research, the proposed model suggests that a negative GPD would be positively related to negative affect (Path 1) and negatively related to positive affect (Path 2).

*Affect and self-efficacy.* Although there have been relatively few studies examining the link between positive and negative affect and self-efficacy, there is some indication in the literature that affective reactions to failure feedback on a task are directly related to an individual's level of self-efficacy for that task. More specifically, two theoretical perspectives in the current literature on affect support the proposition that affective states impact motivation. The affect priming model (Bower, 1981, 1991; Forgas, 1995; George & Brief, 1996; Isen, Shalker, Clark, & Karp, 1978) suggests that affect influences the type of information that is recalled or attended to as individuals evaluate their own capabilities for a task. Positive affect prompts positive self-relevant information to be recalled, while negative affects prompts negative self-relevant information to be recalled. This affect dependent recall of information subsequently impacts efficacy levels in that positive self-relevant information serves to enhance levels of self-efficacy whereas negative self-relevant information serves to diminish levels of self-efficacy. Although somewhat different in nature, the affect-as-information perspective (Schwarz & Clore, 1983, 1988) also asserts that affective states are likely to influence perceptions of task-related capabilities. This perspective posits that affective states have a more direct influence on perceptions such that they serve as *actual input* for self-efficacy formation. That is, individuals may simply ask themselves how they *feel* about a certain task or activity and in turn rely on these emotional states to establish self-efficacy perceptions. According to this perspective, positive affective states provide the basis for high levels of efficacy, while negative affective states provide the basis for low levels of self-efficacy.

Empirical support for the link between affect and self-efficacy can be seen in the work of researchers such as Saavedra and Earley (1991), who found that students who experienced negative affect after receiving substandard performance feedback on an employee performance evaluation task had unfavorable self-efficacy expectations for the same task on a subsequent trial. Similarly, other research has demonstrated that affect is linked to self-efficacy beliefs for health related behaviors (e.g., Cinciripini et al., 2003; Kavanagh & Bower, 1995; Williams, 2002), academic and non-academic self-efficacy among students (e.g., Forgas, Bower, & Moylan, 1990; Tillema, Cervone, & Scott, 2001), and self-efficacy beliefs for various experimental tasks (Baron 1988, 1990).

Although this body of literature supports the link between affective states and self-efficacy, it is important to realize that the evidence described above simply indicates that affect may impact efficacy perceptions for future performance of the *same* task. It does not indicate whether or not performance-related affect will impact self-efficacy for a *distinct* task. There have been no studies conducted to date that have examined this possibility. However, based upon the mechanisms described by the affect priming perspective and the affect-as-information perspective, it is possible that residual affective states from a given task domain could prime informational cues or actually function as information that could impact self-efficacy associated with a distinct task domain. The present study represents the first research attempting to link affect stemming from performance of an initial task to self-efficacy perceptions for a distinct, subsequent task. We hypothesized that negative affect would be negatively related to self-efficacy for the second, distinct task (Path 3), while positive affect would be positively related to self-efficacy for this second task (Path 4).

*Self-efficacy and goal-setting.* In contrast to the somewhat limited empirical support for the affect-self-efficacy linkage, the relationship between self-efficacy and goal-setting is one of the more well established findings in the motivational literature (for reviews see Bandura, 1986, 1991; Bandura & Locke, 2003; Locke, 2001; Locke & Latham, 1990). Individuals that are highly efficacious with respect to a task tend to set more challenging or difficult goals for themselves than individuals who are less efficacious. In their review of the goal setting literature, Locke and Latham (1990) report an average correlation of .39 between an individual's self-efficacy associated with a given task and his/her personal performance goal. As such, we propose that self-efficacy will be positively related to the goals that individuals set for themselves (Path 5).

## Summary

In summary, the present study proposes a model of motivational spillover in which goal failure on an initial task impacts affective states, which in turn influence efficacy perceptions and goal setting on a subsequent, distinct task.

# METHOD

## Participants

Two hundred and twenty two undergraduates from a large southeastern university participated in the present study in exchange for receiving extra-credit toward their course grade.

## Procedure

Upon arrival at the study, participants were seated at a computer station and were asked to complete a baseline measure assessing affect. Following completion of this measure, participants were told that they would be asked to perform two computer-based tasks during the course of the study: a stock predicting task (SPT), and a creative brainstorming task (CBT). Participants were then told that they would be completing two practice trials for each task, resulting in four total practice trials which alternated among the two tasks (CBT, SPT, CBT, SPT). Prior to actually completing these practice trials, participants were presented with a tutorial for each task describing the nature of the tasks. Participants received actual performance feedback across all four practice trials. Following the practice trials, individuals completed a measure of self-efficacy for the SPT and were then asked to complete three performance trials of the CBT. For each of these trials, participants were assigned a goal which increased in difficulty across the three trials and were presented with performance feedback following the completion of each trial. However, this feedback was not a true representation of the participant's performance, but rather was bogus feedback provided as a part of the experimental GPD manipulation (see below). Following the CBT performance trials, participants completed measures assessing their affective states and their perceptions concerning the feedback they received (see Manipulation Check below), and were told that they would now be asked to perform the SPT they practiced earlier. Next, they completed measures assessing both their self-efficacy and their self-set performance goal for the upcoming SPT trial. Upon completing these measures, participants were informed that they would not be performing the SPT, and that they had reached the end of the study.

## Experimental Tasks

*Creativity brainstorming task (CBT).* Each CBT presented participants with an overall target category, and individuals were asked to name as many members of this category as possible. For example, the first practice trial of the CBT was named "Locks", and participants were told that their objective was to name as many "locks" as possible. Participants were told that they would receive points for each answer based upon the creativity of their response: one point for a common response (e.g., door lock), five points for a creative response (e.g., Goldilocks), and zero points for an invalid response. The second CBT practice trial and the three CBT performance trials followed the same procedure with different categories ("Bears", "Generals", "Slowpokes", and "$H_2O$", respectively).

*Stock predicting task (SPT).* The SPT was adapted from Earley, Connolly, and Ekegren (1989) and consisted of predicting stock prices for fictitious companies based on the performance of three divisions of each company (marketing, research and development, and production) relative to their own division goals. These performance cues were given to the participants in the form of percentages (e.g., "marketing = 100%, research and development = 120% and production = 60%"). Based on this information, participants were asked to predict the value of each company stock within $25 of the correct stock value. Participants were allotted ten seconds to make each prediction, and after each prediction, feedback was provided indicating whether or not the predicted stock price fell within $25 of the correct stock value. One point was awarded for each correct prediction.

In order to test the hypothesis that spillover occurs from one task to an altogether separate and distinct task, it was important to choose two tasks that were distinct from one another. The creativity and stock predicting tasks were chosen based on the different skills necessary to perform well on each task. The stock predicting task is analytical in nature in that individuals must process information based on informational cues about a company to make quick decisions about a stock value. On the other hand, in order to perform well on the creativity tasks, individuals must generate innovative ideas and produce creative responses. Huffcutt, Conway, Roth, and Stone (2001) assert that "creativity" reflects the capability to generate innovative solutions. In addition, many argue that creativity is different from the concept of analytic capabilities because it requires the flexibility of thought, originality, and the ability to see beyond current structures (e.g., Cohen & Swerdlik, 1999).

Nonetheless, to ensure that these tasks were considered to be distinct by participants, a pilot study was conducted prior to the focal study. A total of 54 individuals participated in this pilot study. Participants were asked to perform 2 practice trials for each task and were then asked to respond to 4 questions assessing the extent to which they perceived the experimental tasks to be distinct. A sample question is "The Creative Brainstorming Task and the Stock Predicting Task are very different from one another." Responses were made on a five-point scale ranging from (1) "strongly disagree" to (5) "strongly agree". Higher scores for each item indicate higher levels of perceived dissimilarity between the two tasks. The responses to this scale were summed across the four items (coefficient alpha = .69), resulting in a scale with a possible range of 4 (indicating the tasks are very similar) to 20 (indicating the tasks are very dissimilar). The mean for this scale was 15.96 (SD = 2.82) and was significantly different than the mid-point ($t[53] = 3.43$, $p < .05$), suggesting that individuals perceived these two tasks to be quite distinct from one another.

*Negative GPD Feedback Manipulation.* Feedback on the three CBT performance trials was manipulated such that individuals were always told that they failed to reach their assigned goal, regardless of actual performance. Individuals were randomly placed into one of two conditions: (1) a small, negative GPD condition, or (2) a large, negative GPD condition. Individuals in the small, negative GPD condition were told that they failed to reach the assigned goal by 10% or less for each performance trial, while participants in the large, negative GPD condition were told that they missed reaching the assigned goal by 20% or more for each performance trial. These cut-offs were derived from work by Bandura and Cervone (1986), who found that GPDs of 10% or lower were perceived as "small" by participants, while GPDs of 20% or higher were perceived as "large".

The purpose of providing bogus feedback to participants was to ensure that individuals received either consistently large, negative GPDs or consistently small, negative GPDs. Since research has shown that individuals are more likely to attend to multiple failures than a single failure (e.g., Campion & Lord, 1982), the bogus feedback was administered across all performance trials to ensure that participants had sufficient exposure to the negative GPD. As previously noted, goals were assigned to each group such that they increased in difficulty across the three trials. This was done to help ensure that the negative GPD feedback would be perceived as believable by the participants. As individuals performed multiple trials of this task and gained experience with the elements of the task, it is likely that they would experience an enhanced sense of proficiency. As such, these individuals may have rejected performance feedback indicating that they consistently failed to reach their goal and that their performance was not improving (i.e., they were not reducing their GPD). By increasing the difficulty of the goal in each trial, we hoped to increase the likelihood that individuals would perceive the repeated negative GPD feedback across trials as an accurate representation of their performance.

# MEASURES

*Manipulation check.* Following the completion of the CBT performance trials, participants responded to 4 questions assessing the extent to which they believed the feedback that they had received. A sample question is "The feedback I received was an accurate evaluation of my performance." Responses were made on a two-point scale (1 = disagree, 2 = agree). Coefficient alpha for this scale was .81.

*Performance goal.* Participants set a performance goal for the SPT by indicating how many company stock values (out of 25) they thought they could predict within $10 of the correct stock value. This task required that participants be more accurate in their predictions (within $10) of the company stock values compared to when they performed the task in the practice trials (within $25). Given that participants had the opportunity to get familiar with the SPT across two practice trials and performed at high levels in both trials[3], this was not considered to be an unreasonably challenging task.

*Self-efficacy.* Self-efficacy was assessed using a 10-item scale adapted from Phillips and Gully (1997). A sample item is "I feel confident in my ability to perform well on the upcoming stock-predicting task." Responses were made on a 5 point scale ranging from (1) "strongly disagree" to (5) "strongly agree" and were summed to compute self-efficacy scores. Coefficient alpha was .81 for the baseline administration and .84 for the post-manipulation administration.

*Affect.* The Positive and Negative Affect Schedule (PANAS; Watson, Clark, & Tellegen, 1988) was used to measure positive and negative affect at baseline, as well as after the CBT performance trials. The PANAS consists of 20 feelings or emotions reflecting positive and negative affect. Participants were instructed to indicate the extent to which each item characterized how they felt at that moment. Responses for each scale were made on a five-point scale (1= very slightly or not at all; 5 = extremely) and were summed to form negative and positive affect scores. According to factor-analytic findings, positive and negative affect consistently emerge as two dominant and orthogonal dimensions (e.g., Diener & Iran-Nejad, 1986; Diener, Larsen, Levine, & Emmons, 1985; Gotlib & Meyer, 1986; Watson et al., 1988). As such, positive and negative affect were treated as independent dimensions in the present study. Coefficient alpha for the two administrations of the negative affect scale was .75 and .81, while coefficient alpha for the positive affect scale was .87 and .90, respectively.

## ANALYSIS

To evaluate the proposed model, LISREL 8.54 (Jöreskog & Sörborm, 2003) was used to calculate all parameter estimates based upon the study covariance matrix. To accomplish this, a model was constructed in which each latent variable was represented by a single indicator and all parameter estimates were corrected for measurement error utilizing the obtained reliability estimates and observed variances for all variables. More specifically, the path from each latent variable to its single indicator was fixed at a value of 1.0, while the error variance estimates were fixed to equal one minus the reliability estimates multiplied by the observed variance of each variable (cf. Bollen, 1989; Hayduk, 1987). Following the recommendations of Anderson and Gerbing (1988) and past research (e.g., VandeWalle, Cron, & Slocum, 2001), we set the reliability of performance goals at .95, and the reliability of the GPD manipulation at 1.00. Although this model could have been analyzed using a multiple indicator approach, we decided to use a single indicator model for two reasons. First, the measurement properties of the scales utilized in this study have been demonstrated in previous research (e.g., Watson et al., 1988) and were not of primary interest in the present research. Second, the use of a single indicator model allowed us to correct for measurement error in our model while limiting the number of paths being estimated, thereby reducing the sample size required for obtaining a stable solution.

The fit of the proposed theoretical model was evaluated following Bollen's (1990) recommendation to interpret multiple indices of model fit. Thus, LISREL fit statistics such as the chi-square test, the root mean-mean-square error of approximation (RMSEA), the standardized root-mean-square residual (SRMR), the goodness-of-fit index (GFI; Bollen, 1990), adjusted goodness-of-fit index (AGFI; Bentler, 1983), normed fit index (NFI; Bentler & Bonett, 1980), and the comparative fit index (CFI; Bentler, 1990) were estimated to assess how well the proposed model fit the data. According to Hu and Bentler (1995), good model fit is represented by RMSEA values below .05 and values above .95 for the GFI, AGFI, NFI, and CFI. It is important to note that the fit indices reported in the present study were interpreted with some caution, as the degrees of freedom associated with the hypothesized model were small. Greater emphasis was placed on the significance, direction, and magnitude of the parameter estimates, as they assess the hypothesized relationships between study variables.

## RESULTS

### Initial Analyses

Table 1 reports the means, standard deviations, and correlations for all study variables. Prior to testing the proposed model, we examined responses to the manipulation check items to determine how individuals perceived the performance feedback they received. The results indicated that participants generally perceived that the feedback was an accurate representation of their actual performance ($M = 6.26$, $SD = 1.59$), suggesting that they did not suspect that the feedback was bogus. We then examined our baseline measures of positive and negative affect, self-efficacy, and ability on the SPT to ensure that there were no significant differences among the small and large GPD groups. The results of these analyses indicated that there were no significant differences on any of these variables between the two conditions.

**Table 1. Means, Standard Deviations, and Intercorrelations Among Study Variables**

| Variable | M | SD | 1 | 2 | 3 | 4 | 5 |
|---|---|---|---|---|---|---|---|
| 1. GPD (Task 1) | 1.50 | .50 | - | | | | |
| 2. Positive affect | 25.36 | 8.23 | -.17** | (.90) | | | |
| 3. Negative affect | 15.21 | 5.10 | .21** | -.05 | (.81) | | |
| 4. SSE (Task 2) | 34.68 | 6.10 | -.13* | .25** | -.20** | (.84) | |
| 5. Goal (Task 2) | 17.34 | 5.52 | -.02 | .18** | -.06 | .42** | - |

*Note.* $N = 222$. Values on the diagonals represent internal consistency estimates. GPD (Task 1) = Goal Performance Discrepancy (1 = small negative GPD on CBT; 2 = large negative GPD on CBT). All estimates corresponding to GPD (Task 1) are point biserial correlations. SSE (Task 2) = Specific Self-Efficacy associated with the SPT, Goal (Task 2) = Performance Goal set for the SPT.
*correlation is significant at the .05 alpha level (1-tailed)
**correlation is significant at the .01 alpha level (1-tailed)

***Test of Hypothesized Model***

The results of the analyses for the hypothesized model revealed that the data fit the model very well ($\chi^2$ [5] = 1.78, *ns*, RMSEA = .00, SRMR = .019, GFI = 1.00, NFI = .98, AGFI = .99, CFI = 1.00). In addition, the completely standardized parameter estimates (Figure 2) for the individual paths were all significant and in the expected direction, providing support for the hypothesized model. GPDs were positively related to negative affect (.24) and negatively related to positive affect (-.18), indicating that large goal failures provoked an increase in negative affect and a decrease in positive affect. These positive and negative affective states were subsequently related to self-efficacy for the second task (.28 and -.23, respectively) such that higher levels of positive affect were associated with higher levels of efficacy and higher levels of negative affect were associated with lower levels of efficacy. Finally, the results indicated that self-efficacy was significantly related to performance goals for the second task (.47) such that high levels of self-efficacy were associated with higher performance goals than low levels of self-efficacy.

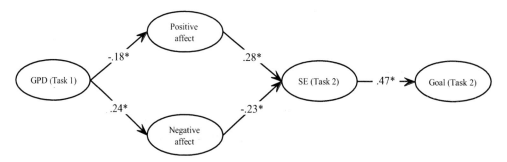

*Figure 2.* Proposed model with standardized path coefficients.
* denotes a path coefficient that is significant at the .05 level.

Taken as a whole, the path coefficients and indices of model fit provide strong support for the proposed theoretical model. However, consistent with the recommendations of numerous researchers (e.g., Hoyle & Panter, 1995; MacCallum et al., 1993), we examined two alternative models to determine if our model could be improved through modifications made on a theoretical basis. Our first alternative model sought to determine if GPD exerted a direct effect on self-efficacy (in addition to its indirect effect through affect) by adding a path between GPD and self-efficacy. This alternative model was based on previous studies that have suggested that negative GPDs may have a direct negative effect on an individual's level of self-efficacy (e.g., Bandura & Cervone, 1983; Thomas & Mathieu; 1994; Williams et al., 2000). The results for this model indicated that the added path was not significant and failed to improve model fit ($\Delta\chi^2$[1] = .16, ns), suggesting that the relationship between GPD and self-efficacy was completely mediated by positive and negative affect. The second alternative model tested the possibility that positive and negative affect exerted a direct influence on goal-setting by adding a direct path between the affect variables and performance goals. This alternative model was tested based upon previous research by Hom and Arbuckle (1988) and Davis, Kirby, and Curtis (2007) who found that individuals in a positive affective state reported setting higher goals for themselves on a task and individuals in a negative affective state reported setting lower goals for themselves. The results of this analysis showed that neither of these paths were significant and the addition of these paths did not improve model fit ($\Delta\chi^2[2] = 1.19$, ns.), indicating that the relationship between affect and goal setting was fully mediated by self-efficacy.

## DISCUSSION

Altogether, the findings obtained in the present study provide strong evidence for the proposed model of motivational spillover. Large, negative GPDs on the creativity task were associated with an increase in negative affect and a decrease in positive affect. These affective states, in turn, influenced self-efficacy perceptions for a second, distinct task, ultimately leading to a decrease in the magnitude of performance goals established by these individuals. In other words, large failure feedback on the creativity tasks effectively "spilled over" to negatively impact motivation for a second, distinct task. Although prior research has provided evidence of motivational spillover (Jucknat, 1937; Festinger, 1942; Carver et al, 1979; Kernis et al., 1982), this study is the first to not only provide evidence of such spillover, but also to delineate the mechanisms by which this spillover may occur.

In addition to providing support for the existence of motivational spillover effects, the results of this study also provided some interesting insights into the self-regulatory processes that span task boundaries by highlighting the role of positive and negative affect in such processes. In the present study, positive and negative affect were identified as important mechanisms by which motivation spills over across task boundaries such that they completely mediated the relationship between task failure and self-efficacy for a distinct task. This mediated relationship not only provides us with an explanation of how spillover occurs, but also highlights the influential role that affective states exert on perceptions of task related capabilities. Although the relationship between affect and self-efficacy has received relatively little attention (with the exception of Erez & Isen, 2002; Scott & Cervone, 2002), the presence of such a relationship is consistent with the theoretical perspectives of both the affect-as-information and affect priming models. These models maintain that affect influences a wide variety of cognitive and behavioral responses that may not be connected to the original source of affect. As such residual affective states from a given task domain could prime informational cues or actually function as information that could impact self-efficacy associated with a distinct task domain. In line with these theoretical perspectives, participants in the present study exhibited a clear link between affective states (Task 1) and self-efficacy perceptions (Task 2). It is this relationship that provides a foundation for the occurrence of motivational spillover across task boundaries.

Given the important role that affective states may play in the process of positive and negative spillover, it is surprising that affect has not received more attention in the research conducted on work motivation. As pointed out by Ilies and Judge (2005), part of the reason for this lack of attention is because current self-regulation frameworks offer cognitive explanations of action but do not recognize affective states as potential agents in the self-regulation process. These researchers recommend that current self-regulation frameworks incorporate theories of affect because they have much to offer in explaining motivational self-regulation. More specifically emotional and affective processes may serve to fill a missing link in the causal chain of self-regulation between task related outcomes and cognitive processes that drive behavior. For example, these theorists draw upon the cognitive-affective personality system theory (Mischel & Shoda, 1995; 1998), affective events theory (Weiss & Cropanzano, 1996), and behavioral motivation theory (Gray, 1981; 1990), to suggest that experienced affect plays a major role in goal-related processes. These affect-based theories argue that affective states have a critical role in linking performance outcomes to future goals such that performance feedback influences individuals' momentary affective states, which in turn influence goal and behavioral regulation. In their study Illies and Judge (2005) found that positive affect partly mediated the relationship between performance feedback and personal goals at the within-individual level of analysis, such that goal failure/success was positively related to positive affect, which in turn influenced goal-setting on the same task. These findings further highlight the need for conceptual frameworks to recognize the importance of affective mechanisms in self-regulation and motivational theories.

At this point, it is worth noting that the present study focused exclusively on the motivational processes that occurred *across* task boundaries, rather than the processes unfolding *within* a single task (i.e., across the successive performance trials on the creativity task). This was done for two reasons. First, although there are several studies that have examined motivational processes as they unfold over the successive performance episodes for a single task (e.g., Campion & Lord, 1982; Donovan & Williams, 2003; Williams et al., 2000), there have been virtually no studies conducted to examine these processes (i.e., the mechanisms of spillover) as they occur when individuals are switching between tasks. As such, we focused our attention on motivational spillover across tasks in order to address this gap in the research literature. Second, we feel that the processes that are likely to unfold *within* a task, where individuals have concrete information on their performance in the previous task performance episode, are likely to be much more cognitive in nature, rather than being based in affective responses (although affect is likely to be involved to some degree). It is when individuals are switching to a new task where they do not have recent performance information that the affective mechanisms proposed and supported in this study become dominant. Support for this proposition that motivational processes involved in successive performance trials for the same task are more cognitive in nature can be seen in the work highlighting the important role that cognitive processes such as causal attributions for performance hold in determining subsequent motivational processes (e.g., Donovan & Williams, 2003; Mone & Baker, 1992; Thomas & Mathieu, 1994; Williams et al., 2000). In sum, our focus on motivation across tasks was a function of the observed gaps in our research literature and an interest in examining the role of affect more closely, rather than an indication that motivational processes within tasks are unimportant.

## Implications

Given the results of the present study and past research demonstrating the existence of motivational spillover effects, one clear implication of this research is that the concept of motivational spillover should be directly incorporated into current models of self-regulation. The notion that perceptions of task related capabilities can be influenced by performance in separate task domains is not explicitly acknowledged in current depictions of self-regulation, which tend to focus on self-regulatory processes within a given task. By ignoring the impact that GPDs in distinct task domains have on efficacy perceptions for a given task, current models may be underestimating the importance of the GPD, as well as providing a somewhat limited perspective on the self-regulation of task performance.

At this point, it is worth noting that several models of self-regulation actually do allow for the *possibility* of motivational spillover, albeit in a much more indirect and time consuming form than what was observed in the present study. More specifically, models of self-regulation that employ a goal hierarchy framework (e.g., Bandura, 1986; Kluger & DeNisi, 1996; Lord & Levy, 1992, 1994) would suggest that the goals being pursued by individuals (and their feedback loop systems) in any given situation can be conceptualized as a hierarchy of goals ranging from higher order goals (e.g., goals regarding self-concept) to lower order goals (e.g., task related goals). Within these frameworks, feedback loop systems among the goals in a given hierarchy are interconnected such that feedback regarding progress towards a lower order goal (or lack thereof) actually serves as input into higher order goals (i.e., "bottom-up" processing), while feedback regarding progress towards higher order goals can potentially serve as input into lower order goals (i.e., top-down processing). With respect to motivational spillover, these interconnected feedback loops suggest the possibility that feedback encountered regarding progress towards a specific task performance goal could work its way up the goal hierarchy to the self-concept level ("bottom-up" processing), which may result in a shift in these higher order goals. Any shift that occurs in these higher order goals would then likely filter down the goal hierarchy to influence the lower order goals being pursued by an individual ("top-down" processing), including performance goals held for altogether distinct tasks. However, we see two primary problems with using this theoretical model as an explanation for the motivational spillover observed in the present study. First, as noted by Lord and Levy (1994), the processing of feedback at the higher levels of a goal hierarchy is a slow and time consuming process (see also Johnson, Chang, & Lord, 2007). Therefore, it is unlikely that the process depicted in the goal hierarchy explanation for motivational spillover above would completely unfold within the time frame of a single one hour performance episode. In other words, the motivational spillover observed in the present study was a much quicker process than would be expected based on this sort of goal hierarchy explanation. Second, these theoretical explanations forwarded in these goal hierarchy models do not explicitly incorporate the constructs of positive and negative affect, which were the critical links in the motivational spillover process demonstrated in this study. Based upon these two issues, we feel that current motivational frameworks do not suitably explain the motivational spillover effects we observed, and therefore return to our previous suggestion that these frameworks should be modified to account for motivational spillover processes in a task performance environment.

Given the novelty of the findings of the present study, a second implication is that future research should seek to replicate these results and determine if there are boundary conditions that limit these effects. Although earlier studies suggest that motivational spillover is largely dependent on task similarity (Jucknat, 1937; Festinger, 1942), the findings from the present study reveal that this is not necessarily the case. However, it is likely that there may be other boundary conditions that exist, such as task familiarity/experience. In addition, although this study focused on affective states as the primary mechanisms of motivational spillover, future research should seek to identify other possible mechanisms by which failure on one task spills over to distinct tasks. For example, generalized self-efficacy (Brockner, 1998), emotionality (Fry & Heubeck, 1998), behavioral inhibition and activation systems (Gray, 1981; 1990), or state-like manifestations of the goal orientation construct (Breland & Donovan, 2005) may provide insights into how goal success/failure on one task may influence motivational processes related to distinct tasks. Further, although the main focus of the present study was to investigate negative spillover, future research should examine the model of motivational spillover model under conditions where positive GPDs (i.e., goal success) are experienced.

Finally, from an applied perspective, the present findings indicate that organizations should be aware that motivational processes are not isolated within the parameters of a given task. Feedback that is perceived as largely negative and indicating goal failure can be detrimental to performance in other task domains. Given that many employees execute multiple tasks of varying nature in a given day, the potential for motivational spillover in organizational settings is substantial. As such, managers may need to monitor employees' task performance and provide assistance and/or skill training when employees repeatedly fail to reach their goals. However, it is worth noting that the performance of multiple tasks in the present study occurred sequentially (i.e., the first task was completed before participants were asked to perform the second task). An interesting question to be addressed by future research would be whether these same processes operate if participants were asked to perform these tasks *simultaneously*, since it could be argued that the simultaneous juggling of multiple tasks more closely resembles the work activities encountered in a typical job (Schmidt & DeShon, 2007). In these situations, tasks are competing for the worker's attention, so it is possible that the processes observed in this situation might be somewhat different than what we observed in the present study.

## Study Limitations

Although the findings and implications are both novel and intriguing, there are several limitations in the present study that should be noted. The primary limitation of the present study is the reliance upon bogus feedback to induce negative GPD states. However, the results of the manipulation check indicated that individuals found this feedback to be believable, suggesting that individuals were not disregarding this feedback. In addition, similar GPD manipulations have been used successfully in previous studies of self-regulatory mechanisms (e.g., Bandura & Cervone, 1986), suggesting that the use of such GPD manipulations may not be problematic. Further, a follow up study conducted using natural performance feedback (rather than manipulated feedback) essentially replicated the results obtained in our study (Quintela & Donovan, 2007), suggesting that the use of manipulated feedback in this study did not impact the outcomes observed. Investigating the motivational spillover concept in a controlled experimental setting was critical to observing the manifestation of the phenomena and understanding the mechanisms by which it occurred. Our recommendation is that future research be conducted in more natural performance settings to expand our understanding of motivational spillover.

A second limitation is the relatively small number of practice trials offered in the present study. Participants had no previous knowledge of the tasks and were only granted a limited number of trials to become familiar with tasks. It is possible that individuals with substantial experience with a given task may be more cognizant and certain of their capabilities and therefore less susceptible to the influence of performance outcomes from a previous task (i.e., previous experience may serve as a buffer against the likelihood of motivational spillover).

Future research should address this possibility by examining the process of spillover as it pertains to both novel and more familiar tasks.

A third limitation is that the current study design did not allow us to assess the stability or longevity of these motivational spillover effects. In this study, the self-efficacy and goal assessments for our second task took place immediately after they received the negative feedback from the first task. It is possible that the effects observed in the present study may be due in part to the temporal proximity of these events. It could be the case that somewhat weaker spillover effects would be observed if goal setting were delayed for a significant period of time. However, it could also be argued that if GPDs associated with a previous task are sufficiently intense (e.g., resulting in hopelessness) that the effects of spillover would persist, even though individuals find themselves currently engaged in performance episodes on an unrelated task (Kluger & Denisi, 1996; Mikulincer, 1988). Future research should be directed towards providing evidence of the longevity of the spillover effects demonstrated in this study. On a related note, the nature of the data collected in our study did not allow us to follow the spillover phenomenon a step further to determine if performance feedback administered for the second task would create motivational spillover if participants were asked to return to the initial task. Clearly, this information would be useful in assessing the overall strength of the motivational spillover effect observed in our study, but was not possible given our research design. Future research should incorporate this possibility with the hopes of providing the field with a more detailed understanding of motivational spillover.

## CONCLUSION

In conclusion, the results of the present study provide strong support for a model of motivational spillover in which goal failure for a given task impacts self-efficacy and goal-setting for a distinct task through its effects on positive and negative affect. Given these results, along with previous research demonstrating the existence of motivational spillover, future research should focus on exploring the mechanisms involved in this process and the conditions that facilitate or hinder the spillover process.

## FOOTNOTES

[1] Although the present model for motivational spillover focuses on goal failure, it is also possible that goal success may spillover to impact motivation on a distinct task (Carver et al., 1979; Festinger, 1942, Jucknat, 1937; Kernis et al., 1982).

[2] Although some have argued that positive and negative affects are simply opposite ends of a single continuum, work by Watson and colleagues (e.g., Watston, Clark, & Tellegen, 1988; Watson & Tellegen, 1985) has suggested that positive and negative affects represent independent dimensions of affect.

[3] Results indicated that out of 25 possible stock predictions, individuals predicted the majority of stock values correctly for the first and second SPT practice trials ($M = 17.25$, $SD = 3.05$ and $M = 17.70$, $SD = 2.85$, respectively).

# REFERENCES

Anderson, J., & Gerbing, D. (1988). Structural equation modeling in practice: A review and recommended two-step approach. *Psychological Bulletin, 103*, 411–424.

Austin, J.T., & Vancouver, J.B. (1996). Goal constructs in psychology: Structure, process, and content. *Psychological Bulletin, 120,* 338-375.

Bandura, A. (1986). *Social foundations of thought and action.* Englewood Cliffs, NJ: Prentice Hall.

Bandura, A. (1991). Social cognitive theory of self-regulation. *Organizational Behavior and Human Decision Processes, 50,* 248-287.

Bandura, A., & Cervone, D. (1983). Self-evaluative and self-efficacy mechanisms governing the motivational effects of goal systems. *Journal of Personality and Social Psychology, 45,* 1017-1028.

Bandura, A., & Cervone, D. (1986). Differential engagement of self-reactive influences in cognitive motivation. *Organizational Behavior and Human Decision Processes, 38,* 92-113.

Bandura, A., & Locke, E.A (2003). Negative self-efficacy and goal effects revisited. *Journal of Applied Psychology, 88,* 87-99. Baron, R.A. (1988). Negative effects of destructive criticism: Impact on conflict, self-efficacy, and task performance. *Journal of Applied Psychology, 73,* 199-207.

Baron, R.A. (1990). Countering the effects of destructive criticism: the relative efficacy of four interventions. *Journal of Applied Psychology, 75,* 235-245.

Bentler, P.M. (1983). Some contributions to efficient statistics for structural models: Specification and estimation of moment structures. *Psychometrika, 48,* 493-571.

Bentler, P.M. (1990). Comparative fit indices in structural equation models. *Psychological Bulletin, 107,* 238-246.

Bentler, P.M., & Bonnet, D.G. (1980). Significance tests and goodness of fit in the analysis of covariance structures. *Psychological Bulletin, 88,* 588-606.

Bollen, K.A. (1989). *Structural equation models with latent variables.* New York: Wiley.

Bollen, K.A. (1990). A comment on model evaluation and modification. *Multivariate Behavioral Research, 25,* 181-185.

Bower, G.H. (1981). Mood and memory. *American Psychologist, 31,* 129-148.

Breland, B. T., & Donovan, J. J. (2005). The role of state goal orientation in the goal establishment process. *Human Performance, 18,* 23-53.

Brockner, J. (1988). *Self-esteem at work: Research, theory, and practice.* Lexington, MA: Lexington Books.

Campion, M.A., & Lord, R.G. (1982). A control systems conceptualization of the goal-setting and changing processes. *Organizational Behavior and Human Performance, 30,* 265-287.

Carver, C.S., Blaney, P.H., & Scheier, M.F. (1979). Reassertion and giving up: The interactive role of self-directed attention and outcome expectancy. *Journal of Personality and Social Psychology, 37,* 1859-1870.

Cinciripini, P.M., Wetter, D.W., Fouladi, R.T., Blalock, J.A., Carter, B.L., Cinciripini, L.G., & Baile, W.F. (2003). The effects of depressed mood on smoking cessation: Mediation by postcessation self-efficacy. *Journal of Consulting & Clinical Psychology, 71,* 292-301.

Davis, M. A., Kirby, S. L., & Curtis, M. B. (2007). The influence of affect on goal choice and task performance. *Journal of Applied Social Psychology, 37,* 14-42.

Deiner, E., & Larsen, R.J. (1984). The independence of positive and negative affect. *Journal of Personality and Social Psychology, 47,* 1105-1117.

Deiner, E., Larsen, R.J., Levine, S., & Emmons, R.A. (1985). Intensity and frequency: The underlying dimensions of positive and negative affect. *Journal of Personality and Social Psychology, 48,* 1253-1265.

Donovan, J. J., & Williams, K. J. (2003). Missing the mark: Effects of time and causal attributions on goal revision in response to goal-performance discrepancies. *Journal of Applied Psychology, 88,* 379-390.

Earley, P.C., Connolly, T., & Ekegren, G. (1989). Goals, strategy, and task performance: Some limits on the efficacy of goal setting. *Journal of Applied Psychology, 74,* 24-33.

Festinger, L. (1942). Wish, expectation, and group standards as factors influencing level of aspiration. *Journal of Abnormal Social Psychology, 37,* 184-200.

Forgas, J. P. (1995). Mood and judgment: The affect infusion model (AIM). *Psychological Bulletin, 117,* 39-66.

Forgas, J. P., & Bower, G. H. (1987). Mood effects on person-perception judgments. *Journal of Personality and Social Psychology, 53,* 53-60.

Forgas, J. P., Bower, G. H., & Moylan, S. J. (1990). Praise or blame? Affective influences on attributions for achievement. *Journal of Personality and Social Psychology*, 59, 809–818.

Forgas, J.P., George, J.M. (2001). Affective influences on judgments and behavior in organizations: An information processing perspective. *Organizational Behavior and Human Decision Processes, 86,* 3-34.

George, J.M. (1991). State or trait: Effects of positive mood on prosocial behaviors at work. *Journal of Applied Psychology, 76,* 299-307.

George, J.M. (1995). Leader positive mood and group performance: the case of customer service. *Journal of Applied Social Psychology, 25,* 778-794.

George, J. M., & Brief, A. P. (1996). Motivational agendas in the workplace: The effects of feelings on focus of attention and work motivation. In B.M. Staw & L.L. Cummings (Eds.), *Research in organizational behavior* (Vol.18, pp.75-109). Greenwich, CT: JAI.

Goldstein, M.D., & Strube, M.J. (1994). Independence revisited: The relation between positive and negative affect in a naturalistic setting. *Personality and Social Psychology Bulletin, 20,* 57-64.

Gotlib, I.H., & Meyer, J.P. (986). Factor analysis of the Multiple Affect Adjective Check List: A separation of positive and negative affect. *Journal of Personality and Social Psychology, 50,* 1161-1165.

Hayduk, L.A. (1987). *Structural equation modeling with LISREL: Essentials and advances. Baltimore*: John Hopkins University Press.

Hom, H.L., & Arbuckle, B. (1988). Mood induction effects upon goal setting ad performance in young children. *Motivation and Emotion, 12,* 113-122.

Hoyle, R.H. & Panter, A.T. (1995). Writing about structural equation models. In R. H. Hoyle (Ed.), *Structural equation modeling concepts, issues, and applications* (pp.76-99). Thousand Oaks, CA: Sage.

Hu, L.T., & Bentler, P.M. (1995). Evaluating model fit. In R.H. Hoyle (Ed.), *Structural equation modeling: Concepts, issues, and application* (pp.76-99). Thousand Oaks, CA: Sage.

Isen, A.M. & Baron, R.A. (1991). Positive affect as a factor in organizational behavior. In B.M. Staw & L.L. Cummings (Eds.), *Research in organizational behavior,* (Vol. 13, pp.1-54). Greenwich, Ct: JAI Press.

Johnson, R. E., Chang, C., & Lord, R. G. (2006). Moving from cognition to behavior: What the research says. *Psychological Bulletin, 132,* 381-415.

Jöreskog, K. G., & Sörbom, D. (2003). *LISREL 8.54.* Chicago: Scientific Software International.

Jucknat, M. (1937). Leistung, Anschpruchsniveau und Slebstbewusstsein. (Untersuchunguen zur Handlungs- und Affectpsychologie: XX. Ed. By Kurt Lewin.) *Psychologie Forsch., 22,* 89-179.

Kavanagh, R., & Bower, G. H. (1985). Mood and self-efficacy: Impact of joy and sadness on perceived capabilities. *Cognitive Therapy and Research, 9,* 507-525.

Kernis, M.H., Zuckerman, M., Cohen, A., & Spadafora, S. (1982). Persistence following failure: The interactive role of self-awareness and the attributional basis for negative expectancies. *Journal of Personality and Social Psychology, 43,* 1184-1191.

Kluger, A.N., & DeNisi, A.S. (1996). The effects of feedback intervention on performance: A historical review, a meta-analysis, and a preliminary feedback intervention theory. *Psychological Bulletin, 119,* 254-284.

Locke, E.A. (2001). Motivation by goal setting. In Golembiewski, Robert T. (Ed.), *Handbook of organizational behavior* (2nd. ed, pp. 43-56). New York: M. Dekker

Locke, E.A., & Latham, G.P. (1990). *A theory of goal-setting and task performance.* Englewood Cliffs, NJ: Prentice-Hall.

Locke, E.A.& Latham, G.P. (2002). Building a Practically Useful Theory of Goal Setting and Task Motivation: A 35-Year Odyssey. *American Psychologist, 57,* 705-717.

MacCallum, R. C., Wegener, D. T., Uchino, B. N., & Fabrigar, L. R. (1993). The problem of equivalent models in applications of covariance structure models. *Psychological Bulletin, 114,* 185-199.

Mayer, J.E., Gayle, M., Meehan, M.E., & Harman, A.K. (1990). Toward a better specification of the mood-congruency effect in recall. *Journal of Experimental Social Psychology, 26,* 465-480.

Mikulincer, M. (1988). Reactance and helplessness following exposure to unsolvable problems: The effects of attributional style. *Journal of Personality and Social Psychology, 54,* 679-686.

Mone, M.A., & Baker, D.D. (1992). A social-cognitive attributional model of personal goals: An empirical evaluation. *Motivation and Emotion, 16,* 297-321.

Phillips, J.M., & Gully, S.M. (1997). Role of goal orientation, ability, need for achievement, locus of control in the self-efficacy and goal-setting process. *Journal of Applied Psychology, 82,* 792-802.

Pittman, N.L., & Pittman, T.S. (1979). Effects of amount of helplessness training and internal-external locus of control on mood and performance. *Journal of Personality and Social Psychology, 37,* 39-47.

Quintela, Y. & Donovan, J. J. (April, 2007). Feedback spillover: When one thing leads to another. Paper presented at the 22nd Annual Conference of the Society for Industrial and Organizational Psychology, New York, NY.

Saavedra, R., & Earley, P.C. (1991). Choice of task and goal under conditions of general and specific affective inducement. *Motivation and Emotion, 15,* 45-65.

Schmidt, A.M. & DeShon, R. P. (2007). What to do? The effects of discrepancies, incentives, and time on dynamic goal prioritization. *Journal of Applied Psychology, 92,* 928-941.

Schwarz, N. (1990). Feeling as information: Informational and motivation functions of affective states. In E.T. Higgins and R. Sorrentino (Eds.), *Handbook of motivation and cognition* (Vol. 2, pp.527-561). New York: Guilford.

Schwarz, N., & Clore, G.L. (1983). Mood, misattribution, and judgments of well-being: Informative and directive functions of affective states. *Journal of Personality and Social Psychology, 45,* 513-523.

Scott, W.D. & Cervone, D. (2002) The impact of negative affect on performance standards: Evidence for an affect-as-information mechanism. *Cognitive Therapy & Research, 26,* 19-37.

Thomas, K.M., & Mathieu, J.E. (1994). Role of causal attributions in dynamic self-regulation and goal processes. *Journal of Applied Psychology, 79,* 812-818.

Tillema, J.L., Cervone, D., & Scott, W.D. (2001). Negative mood, perceived self-efficacy, and personal standards in dysphoria: The effects of contextual cues on self-defeating patterns of cognition. *Cognitive Therapy and Research 25,* 535-549.

VandeWalle, D., Cron, W.L., Slocum, J.W. (2001). The role of goal orientation following performance feedback. *Journal of Applied Psychology, 86,* 629-640.

Watson, D., Clark, L. A., & Tellegen, A. (1988). Development and validation of brief measures of positive and negative affect: The PANAS scales. *Journal of Personality and Social Psychology, 54,* 1063-1070.

Watson, D., & Tellegen, A. (1985). Toward a consensual structure of mood. *Psychological Bulletin, 98,* 219-235.

Williams, K.J., & Alliger, G.M. (1994). Role stressors, mood spillover, and perceptions of work-family conflict in employed parents. *Academy of Management Journal, 37,* 837-868.

Williams, K.J., Donovan, J.J., & Dodge, T.L. (2000). Self-regulation of performance: Goal establishment and goal revision processes in athletes. *Human Performance, 13,* 159-180.

Williams, P.A. (2002). Self-efficacy and affect: Their influences on health-related behaviors.Unpublished manuscript.

Woo, T.O., & Mix, P. (1997). Self-enhancing reactions to performance feedback in an academic setting. *Journal of Social Behavior and Personality, 12,* 481-500.

***Reviewed by:***

Dr. Robert G. Lord

Department of Psychology - University of Akron

In: Applied Psychology Research Trends
Editor: Karl H. Kiefer, pp.161-182

ISBN 978-1-60456-372-6
© 2008 Nova Science Publishers, Inc.

*Chapter 8*

# IMPROVING PERFORMANCE IN AN ONGOING LEARNING ENDEAVOR: THE COMPLEMENTARY ROLES OF APPROACH-GOAL ORIENTATIONS AS EXPLAINED BY INTEREST AND EFFORT

## *Robert R. Hirschfeld[1] and D. Brian McNatt[2]*

[1]University of Colorado at Colorado Springs, CO
[2]Old Dominion University, Norfolk, VA

## ABSTRACT

To better understand what accounts for different responses among individuals in a learning endeavor, we investigated general approach-goal orientations as predictors. In particular, we focused on approach-goal orientations, which all entail "approach" motivation or a desire to attain some measure of success. In doing so, we adopted a *multiple goal orientation* perspective, which proposes that high levels of different goal orientations may be adaptive and that multiple pathways from goal orientations to positive outcomes may exist. Although general learning and performance orientations have been researched together in a number of other studies, we added achievement orientation because of its likely relevance for engendering performance-enhancing motivational states. We also designated interest and effort as mechanisms through which the three approach-goal orientations would facilitate improved performance in a learning endeavor. We obtained data from first-year students in a freshman-level course at a major university, including SAT scores as a measure of cognitive ability. Participants completed the measures of the approach-goal orientations two weeks after the beginning of the semester. Initial performance was measured four weeks into the semester, and one day later respondents received objective feedback on their first-exam performance.

[1] Department of Management and Quantitative Methods, College of Business and Administration, University of Colorado at Colorado Springs, 1420 Austin Bluffs Parkway, Colorado Springs, CO 80933-7150. Electronic mail may be sent to rrhirschfeld@gmail.com. Phone: (719) 262-3777. Fax: (719) 262-3494.

Interest and effort were measured six weeks into the semester. Finally, subsequent performance was measured eight weeks into the semester. We obtained complete data from 151 out of 171 potential respondents, for a response rate of 84%. The results of structural equations analyses generally supported our proposed model, in which initial performance was taken into account as a predictor of subsequent performance. Cognitive ability ($\beta = .26$) and achievement orientation ($\beta = .26$) contributed to greater initial performance. Initial performance ($\beta = .24$), achievement orientation ($\beta = .27$), and learning orientation ($\beta = .17$) contributed to greater interest. Then, interest ($\beta = .66$), together with achievement ($\beta = .31$) and performance orientations ($\beta = .19$), was associated with greater effort. Finally, effort was the ultimate mechanism through which all three approach-goal orientations, and interest, were associated with improved performance. Overall, the results support a multiple goal orientation perspective. Yet, among the four exogenous factors, cognitive ability and achievement orientation played the greatest roles in facilitating initial performance and improved performance.

**Keywords:** Goal Orientation, Achievement Motivation, Cognitive Ability, Interest, Effort, Learning, Academic Performance, Performance Improvement.

The extent to which people continually learn and effectively adapt to situational demands has become increasingly relevant to attaining success in achievement-related endeavors (Bandura, 1997; Chan, 2000; London & Mone, 1999; Ryan & La Guardia, 1999). In situations that require personal development and adaptation, some individuals interpret their experiences and level of initial performance as useful guidance and work to improve their performance. Yet, others may respond to the same circumstances with diminished effort and focus. To better understand what accounts for individuals' different responses, it is relevant for researchers to explore the role of individuals' propensities in shaping interactions with and responses to their feedback environment (Herold & Fedor, 1998; Sansone & Smith, 2000).

In particular, goal-directed propensities, referred to here as *goal orientations*, are likely to be especially relevant for predicting how individuals respond to their initial experiences with a learning endeavor (Button, Mathieu, & Zajac, 1996; Dweck, 1999; VandeWalle, Cron, & Slocum, 2001). Any particular goal orientation represents a *cognition-based* motivational orientation, in that it entails the volitional propensity to pursue a particular type of goal when encountering task endeavors (Brett & VandeWalle, 1999; Fisher & Ford, 1998). Two primary examples are an orientation toward learning and one toward performing. As explained further below, scholars originally designated orientations toward learning and performing as "competing" motivational propensities, which would be mutually exclusive in promoting adaptation or success. In fact, learning and performance orientations have sometimes been theorized as having opposing relationships (positive and negative, in turn) with various expressions of motivation and performance.

More recently, however, researchers have proposed a *multiple goal orientation* perspective (Barron & Harackiewicz, 2000). This framework posits that high levels of different goal orientations may be adaptive and that multiple pathways from goal orientations to positive outcomes may exist (e.g., Barron & Harackiewicz, 2000; Linnenbrink & Pintrich, 2000; Payne, Youngcourt, & Beaubien, 2007). For the present study, we focus specifically on approach-goal orientations, proposing that several may contribute simultaneously, in slightly different ways, to performance improvement in a learning endeavor. What approach-goal orientations have in common is that they entail "approach" motivation or a desire to attain some measure of success (see Elliot, 1999; Higgins, 1997).

Although learning and performance orientations have usually been researched together, we include achievement orientation as well because of its likely relevance for engendering performance-enhancing motivational states. Therefore, this study investigated a unique combination of approach-goal orientations (i.e., learning, performance, and achievement orientations), along with cognitive ability. As such, the results should provide important evidence concerning the unique contributions of approach-goal orientations to adaptive responses, and thereby enhance the understanding of individual differences in learning performance.

Finally, we also investigated interest and effort as motivational states through which general approach-goal orientations are linked to performance improvement. Much of the existing theory and research on interest, and the effort that stems directly from it, has centered on identifying and understanding situational factors that are conducive to experiencing interest and enthusiasm (Henderlong & Lepper, 2002; Larson, 2000; Ryan & Deci, 2000; Van Yperen & Hagedoorn, 2003). In this study, we explored differences among individuals (encountering the same circumstances) in their interest and effort, positing that such differences are predictable from approach-goal orientations (even when controlling for initial performance). In the next section, we first explain the constructs included in the model, and then provide rationale for the proposed relationships.

Constructs and Development of the Theoretical Model

Goal orientations range from general propensities, which individuals possess across different domains of activity and over time, to situation-specific approaches, which represent the specific goals that individuals choose to pursue in connection with a given task at a distinct point in time (Payne et al., 2007). Lee, Sheldon, and Turban (2003) suggested that because general propensities apply to a variety of life domains, they may be viewed as a starting point for considering individuals' behavior in connection with a specific endeavor. Empirically, individuals' general propensities have been shown to be useful constructs in the study of behavior (Fleeson, 2001; Funder, 2001; Shiner, 2000). Thus, for this study we focus on general goal orientations, insofar as such orientations engender predictable response patterns and should have relevance for predicting improved performance in a given endeavor.

Much of the recent research involving general approach-goal orientations has, based largely on the work of Dweck (Dweck, 1986, 1989; Dweck & Leggett, 1988), focused on two types. One is a general *learning orientation*, which represents an overall desire to engage oneself in challenging endeavors with the goal of learning for its own sake. The second is a general *performance orientation*, which represents an overall desire to perform well relative to external norms, without stretching one's capabilities (e.g., Bell & Kozlowski, 2002; Button et al., 1996; Chen, Gully, Whiteman, & Kilcullen, 2000). Scholars have now widely adopted the notion that general learning and performance orientations are relatively independent (Payne et al., 2007). Nevertheless, much of the research on general learning and performance orientations has designated them as "competing" propensities, posited to have opposing relationships with self-regulation and performance variables (e.g., Bell & Kozlowski, 2002; Chen et al., 2000; Ford, Smith, Weissbein, Gully, & Salas, 1998; Fisher & Ford, 1998; Phillips & Gully, 1997).

A "multiple goal" perspective suggests that learning and performance goals (rather than propensities) can both be beneficial (Barron & Harackiewicz, 2000; Linnenbrink & Pintrich, 2000; Pintrich, 2000). By extension, a *multiple goal orientation* perspective embraces the notion that several approach-goal orientations may be jointly adaptive in connection with a given endeavor. Barron and Harackiewicz enumerated four patterns specifying how both learning and performance goals may be adaptive: (1) an *additive* goal pattern, in which both learning and performance goals independently contribute to the same positive outcome, (2) an *interactive* goal pattern, in which learning and performance goals interact, multiplicatively, to promote a positive outcome, (3) a *specialized* goal pattern, in which learning and performance goals are each related to different outcomes of benefit, and (4) a *selective* goal pattern, in which circumstances determine the best type of goal on which to focus as a means of realizing a personally beneficial outcome.

The premise for our study corresponds to the third pattern; namely, a *specialized* goal pattern. This idea is consistent with the theorizing of Kozlowski et al. (2001), in which general learning and performance orientations were posited to each have an adaptive role within the context of a multi-stage training and performance endeavor, yet each predict different desirable outcomes. In particular, Kozlowski et al.'s model designated general learning orientation as a predictor of greater self-efficacy, and general performance orientation as a predictor of greater training performance. We extend the logic of a specialized goal pattern to include achievement orientation, along with learning and performance orientations. In doing so, we submit that all three approach-goal orientations may be jointly adaptive.

*Achievement orientation* represents a desire to consistently attain and surpass one's internal standards of performance excellence (Kanfer & Heggestad, 1997; Pinder, 1998). Although the term "mastery" is also used at times to describe a learning orientation, the latter is not synonymous with a focus on achievement (Payne et al., 2007). A learning orientation represents a willingness to take on difficult tasks for the sake of learning, and not a focus on achieving excellence in connection with that learning. This distinction is consistent with the work of Kanfer and Ackerman (2000), who distinguished between a general desire for learning opportunities and a general desire to attain task excellence in one's endeavors. Likewise, whereas the focus of achievement orientation is on high levels of attainment by one's internal standards, the focus of performance orientation is on performing sufficiently by external comparisons or norms. Given that achievement orientation entails striving to fulfill one's potential in terms of task mastery, we believe it should be included in models designating goal orientations as predictors of performance improvement in a learning endeavor.

Researchers have also suggested that more empirical work is needed to better understand *how* individuals' general goal orientations are linked to their ongoing acquisition of knowledge and skill (Chen et al., 2000). Indeed, in their recent meta-analytic summary of goal orientation research, Payne et al. (2007) suggested that a primary need for future research is to identify and explore mechanisms that mediate relationships of goal orientations with distal outcomes such as learning and academic performance. Payne and colleagues examined a number of self-regulatory constructs that have been proposed as explanatory mechanisms through which goal orientations are related to distal outcomes. These mediators included task-specific self-efficacy, self-set goal level, learning strategies, feedback seeking, and state anxiety. Notably, however, Payne et al. did not include *interest* or *effort* among the list of proximal mechanisms shaped by goal orientations, presumably because these factors have not been well represented in the literature to date. In the present study, we explore interest and effort as mechanisms through which three approach-goal orientations play distinct roles in performance improvement.

Pinder (1998) suggested that interest is a major factor in explaining the behavior of individuals in organizational settings. A principal marker of interest is enjoyment in connection with a specific endeavor at a particular point in time (Barron & Harackiewicz, 2000; Harackiewicz & Sansone, 2000; Hidi, 2000; Sansone & Smith, 2000), and interest activates intrinsic motivation (Krapp, 2005; Renninger, 2000; Schiefele, 1999). A main reason why interest would play a meaningful role in performance improvement is its association with the phenomenon of flow, a state of optimal experience or involvement in which one's actions feel effortless (Csikszentmihalyi, 1990). Although sustained mental concentration normally requires great effort, it feels relatively effortless when interest is high (Hidi, 2000). Therefore, our model places interest and effort as central motivational states in the process of improving performance.

*Cognitive ability* is the final predictor included in our model of performance improvement. Insofar as cognitive ability represents the capacity to process information and learn, it should contribute independently of motivational propensities to the acquisition of knowledge or skill (Schmidt & Hunter, 2004; Kanfer & Ackerman, 1989). The rationale for this is that individuals' cognitive capacity differs qualitatively from how they use their capacity. Accordingly, we explore the role of cognitive ability in predicting an improvement in performance.

## Development of the Theoretical Model: Proposed Relationships

The theoretical model is presented in Figure 1. Although general learning and performance orientations are usually not empirically related, Kozlowski et al. (2001) reported a correlation of .53 ($p < .01$) between the two orientations. In light of this finding, we allowed for a correlation between learning and performance orientations. Given that general learning and achievement orientations are both conceptualized to engender interest, we allowed for a correlation between these two orientations as well. Because cognitive ability is typically unrelated to motivational propensities (Dweck, 1989; Hirschfeld, Lawson, & Mossholder, 2004; Payne et al., 2007; Spence, Pred, & Helmreich, 1989), our proposed model did not include a correlation between cognitive ability and any of the three goal orientations.

### Predicting Initial Performance

Given the relevance of *cognitive ability* to predicting performance in endeavors that involve knowledge or skill acquisition (Schmidt & Hunter, 2004; Kanfer & Ackerman, 1989), we hypothesized that cognitive ability is positively related to initial performance. Because general *achievement orientation* encompasses plunging into tasks immediately for the sake of achieving and surpassing personal standards of performance excellence (Kanfer & Heggestad, 1997; Pinder, 1998; Spence & Helmreich, 1983), we hypothesized that it is positively related to initial performance.

## *Predicting Interest*

In general, interest in an endeavor is enhanced by events that positively influence individuals' experience of competence (Barron & Harackiewicz, 2000; Sansone & Smith, 2000). When people receive feedback indicating proficiency, they are likely to experience a sense of competence and consequently have higher levels of interest in the given endeavor (Harackiewicz & Sansone, 2000). Accordingly, our model proposes that *initial performance* is positively related to subsequent interest.

Scholars have suggested that *achievement orientation* engenders interest toward endeavors that involve competence development, and that the generated interest in the task at hand is what then promotes greater performance in such endeavors (e.g., Spence & Helmreich, 1983). In this vein, Bandura (1997) reasoned that demanding personal standards (a hallmark of achievement orientation) generate sustained interest that fosters the development of greater competence. It is plausible, therefore, that interest is a phenomenon through which achievement orientation is associated with improved performance. Researchers have also argued that a *learning orientation* should be linked to experiencing interest in endeavors that present opportunities for personal development, such as an academic course (e.g., Pintrich, 2000; Sansone & Smith, 2000).

Pinder (1998) suggested that personal interest is associated with attempts to find a challenge and attempts to conquer a challenge. We suggest that learning orientation parallels the former, while achievement orientation corresponds to the latter. As such, we propose that general achievement and learning orientations each explain unique variance in subsequent interest.

## *Predicting Effort*

Effort is a broad concept encompassing spontaneous thought and action stemming from enjoyment and interest, in addition to deliberate practice and repetition for the purpose of performing well (Ericsson, Krampe, & Tesch-Römer, 1993). When individuals possess greater interest or involvement in an endeavor, they are likely to exert greater effort because doing so is experienced as pleasurable in its own right (Csikszentmihalyi, 1990; Hidi, 2000). Accordingly, our model proposes that *interest* promotes a high level of effort. Further, we expect that the positive relationship between interest and effort is a strong one. Therefore, as portrayed in Figure 1, our model proposes that interest completely mediates the relationships of achievement and learning orientations and effort.

Inasmuch as *performance orientation* represents a desire to perform well for the external reason of demonstrating normative competence, we believe it may predict greater effort even when interest is taken into account. It is reasonable to expect that individuals wanting to demonstrate normative competence would put forth deliberate effort in preparing to perform sufficiently. In providing indirect support for this notion, Fisher and Ford's (1998) results indicated that general performance orientation predicted students' rehearsal of subject matter in an academic course. Similarly, Zusho, Pintrich, and Coppola (2003) found that performance goals led to more rehearsal strategies. Such repetitive practice would seemingly involve effort and should facilitate greater performance on a structured assessment of learning. Given its substantive nature, we propose that performance orientation accounts for a portion of effort that is not explained by interest.

### Predicting Subsequent Performance

To investigate an improvement in performance, our model includes *initial performance* as a predictor of subsequent performance. The effect of including initial performance as a predictor of subsequent performance is to cause the residual variance in subsequent performance to represent *a change in performance*; that is, the variance in subsequent performance that is not explained by initial performance (Blanton, Buunk, Gibbons, & Kuyper, 1999).

Inasmuch as *cognitive ability* encompasses the capacity to learn from experience, we propose that it is related to *a positive change in performance*. At the same time, meta-analytic results found that goal orientations can predict learning and academic performance even when cognitive ability has been taken into account (Payne et al, 2007). The rationale for this is that how individuals typically use their cognitive resources is qualitatively different than the level of cognitive resources they possess. As portrayed in Figure 1, we propose that effort is the ultimate mechanism through which the goal orientations and interest are related to a positive change in performance. This proposition is congruent with Brown and Leigh's (1996) designation of effort as the mediating linkage between psychological involvement in a domain of activity and actual performance in that domain. In support of their proposition, Brown and Leigh found that job involvement predicted greater job-directed effort, and that effort, in turn, predicted greater job performance. Finally, they reported that no direct relationship between job involvement and job performance existed when effort was included as a mediator in their model.

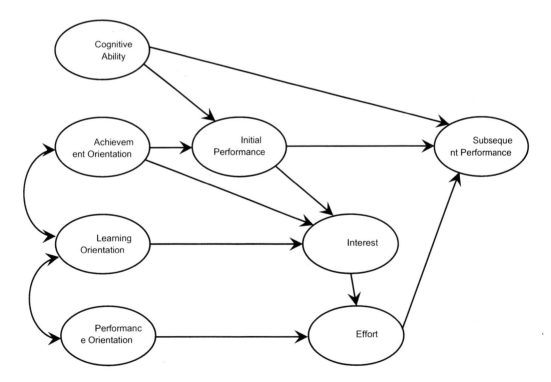

*Figure 1.* Proposed model; all of the depicted relationships are hypothesized to be positive.

# METHOD

## Setting

A college class is a useful setting in which to test a model of performance improvement because performance requires knowledge acquisition and the measures used to evaluate performance (i.e., exams) are composed of identical content across individuals (Chen et al., 2000; Lee & Klein, 2002; Lee et al., 2003). Further, a college class represents an endeavor that has inherent incentives for individuals to perform their best on an initial assessment of learning. As such, improving upon initial performance is likely to be a challenge, which creates a desirable circumstance for examining the predictive efficacy of goal orientations (VandeWalle et al., 2001). Finally, to explore predictors of a change in performance, it is useful to focus on settings in which individuals encounter relatively new challenges (Bandura, 1997). Accordingly, we used a sample of 151 first-year university students enrolled in a freshman-level introductory business course at a major university. The respondents were relatively inexperienced in a university setting as they had completed only between 6 and 18 semester hours and were enrolled in a course that was new to them (one that does not have a prerequisite). Therefore, students would have been developing skills for studying, test preparation, and test taking. In preparing for the second performance episode, students had an opportunity to adapt their goals and strategies in response to their initial performance.

## Procedures and Respondent Sample

Participants completed the goal-orientation measures two weeks after the beginning of the semester, and initial performance was measured four weeks into the semester. Respondents received objective feedback on their first-exam performance in the form of raw and percentage scores in addition to information summarizing the distribution of scores within the class. Interest and effort were measured six weeks into the course. Finally, subsequent performance was measured eight weeks into the semester. Individuals missing scores on any measure were eliminated from the sample. This resulted in a usable sample size of 151 out of 171 potential respondents, representing a response rate of 84%.

On average, respondents were 18.9 years of age and had completed 13.4 semester hours prior to the given semester. Ethnic composition of the sample was as follows: 127 respondents were Caucasian (84.1%), 11 were Hispanic (7.3%), 6 were African American (4.0%) and 7 were either Asian American or Native American (4.6%). In addition, 96 of the participants (63.6%) were female. The results of a multiple analysis of variance indicated that respondents in the final sample were not significantly different from non-respondents with respect to age, sex, and official SAT scores.

## Measures

To limit the potential of response sets associated with priming and consistency, the self-report surveys were designed so that the items measuring each construct were intermingled with items measuring other constructs. All self-report variables were measured using 5-point Likert-type response scales.

*Cognitive ability.* A number of scholars have concluded that standardized aptitude tests, such as the Scholastic Aptitude Test (SAT), largely assess general cognitive ability (Gottfredson & Crouse, 1986; Hunter, 1986). Therefore, we used SAT scores obtained from official university records (with participants' permission). According to The College Board (1998), the stability of SAT scores over repeated testing for high school juniors and seniors is .92.

*General learning and performance orientations.* We used Button et al.'s (1996) eight-item measures to assess general learning and performance orientations. Sample items for general learning orientation are "I prefer to work on tasks that force me to learn new things" and "The opportunity to extend the range of my abilities is important to me." Sample items for general performance orientation are "I like to work on tasks that I have done well on in the past" and "I feel smart when I do something without making any mistakes." Coefficient alphas were .71 and .77 respectively.

*General achievement orientation.* We used the 10-item achievement striving measure from Goldberg's (1999) International Personality Item Pool. Goldberg has provided evidence of reliability and validity for the achievement orientation measure. As is true of the other goal orientation measures used in this study, the achievement orientation items do not refer to a specific context. Respondents indicated the extent to which the items were descriptive of them. Sample items are: "Set high standards for myself and others" and "Plunge into tasks with all my heart." Alpha was .84.

*Interest.* To measure respondents' interest toward the course content, we used four items that parallel those used by Elliot and Church (1997). Sample items include "The subject matter in this course is interesting" and "I am really enthusiastic about this class." Alpha was .83.

*Effort.* We used three items to measure the overall level of effort respondents were devoting to performing well in the class. The items are consistent with Kanfer's (1990) conceptualization of intensity of effort, which reflects how much effort a person is directing toward a particular aim. The items composing the measure are "I am striving as hard as I can to be successful in this class," "I am determined to do my best work in this class," and "In this class, I am giving a lot of effort toward the goal of performing well." Alpha was .75.

*Performance.* To assess initial performance, we used respondents' scores on the first multiple-choice exam in the course; to assess subsequent performance, we used respondents' scores on the second multiple-choice exam. Each exam consisted of 50 items (2 points each) that assessed mastery of subject matter for that segment for the course. Scores were obtained from the course instructor, with participants' permission, after the semester was completed.

## RESULTS

Table 1 presents the means, standard deviations, reliability estimates, and zero-order correlations for the manifest variables. To test our theoretical model, we used structural equations modeling. Consistent with the procedures advocated by Landis, Beal, and Tesluk (2000), we created composite indicators of the three goal orientations, as well as interest, by randomly combining items from each of the multiple-item measures. We formed two composite indicators for interest and three composite indicators for achievement, learning, and performance orientations. However, we used each of the three items measuring effort as separate indicators of that factor. Because cognitive ability and the two performance factors were each represented by one indicator, we fixed the lambda (factor→indicator parameter) and theta (random error variance) coefficients for each of these variables. Lambdas were fixed to equal 1.0 and thetas were fixed to equal 1.0 minus the estimated reliability of the manifest variable multiplied by the variance of the observed score. We tested the measurement model before testing the structural model, and we used four fit indices to assess model fit: the comparative fit index (CFI), goodness-of-fit index (GFI), adjusted goodness-of-fit index (AGFI), and root mean square error of approximation (RMSEA). A model offers an acceptable fit to the data when CFI, GFI, and AGFI values are roughly .90 or higher (Mulaik et al., 1989), and when the RMSEA value is roughly .08 or lower (Browne & Cudeck, 1993).

**Table 1.  Manifest Variable Means, Standard Deviations, Alphas, and Correlations**

| Manifest Variable | M | SD | 1 | 2 | 3 | 4 | 5 | 6 | 7 | 8 |
|---|---|---|---|---|---|---|---|---|---|---|
| 1. Cognitive ability | 10.91 | 1.12 | — | | | | | | | |
| 2. Achievement orientation | 3.85 | .57 | .10 | **.84** | | | | | | |
| 3. Learning orientation | 3.50 | .51 | .02 | .30 | **.71** | | | | | |
| 4. Performance orientation | 3.63 | .60 | −.02 | .08 | .18 | **.77** | | | | |
| 5. Initial performance | 84.86 | 9.17 | .26 | .24 | .10 | .15 | — | | | |
| 6. Interest | 4.18 | .67 | −.01 | .34 | .24 | .10 | .28 | **.83** | | |
| 7. Effort | 3.90 | .75 | −.10 | .42 | .23 | .24 | .30 | .55 | **.75** | |
| 8. Subsequent performance | 85.19 | 9.66 | .26 | .35 | .02 | .09 | .41 | .28 | .32 | — |

*Note.* $N = 151$. Cognitive ability scores were divided by 100 in reporting the mean and standard deviation. Correlations of |.18| or greater are significant at $p < .05$, two-tailed; correlations of |.23| or greater are significant at $p \leq .01$, two-tailed. Alphas are in bold, located on the diagonal. Dashes are inserted for single-item variables.

## Tests of the Measurement Model

An analysis of the hypothesized eight-factor measurement model revealed that the model fit the data adequately, $\chi^2$ (94, $N$ = 151) = 122.06, $p$ < .05; CFI = .96; GFI = .91; AGFI = .86; RMSEA = .045. Because interest and effort are closely linked, we tested an alternative measurement model that specified one factor as underlying their indicators. The fit of the data to this seven-factor (alternative) measurement model was inferior to that of the hypothesized measurement model, as chi-square for the alternative model was considerably higher, $\Delta\chi^2$ (7, $N$ = 151) = 32.55, $p$ < .001. Given that these results supported the validity of the measurement model, we then tested the structural model.

## Test of the Structural Model

The hypothesized structural model, shown in Figure 1, fit the data sufficiently, $\chi^2$ (110, $N$ = 151) = 151.33, $p$ < .01; CFI = .95; GFI = .89; AGFI = .85; RMSEA = .050. In accordance with James, Mulaik, and Brett (1982), we tested two alternative theory-based structural models (that were less constrained than the hypothesized model). To explicitly test whether interest does not entirely account for the link between achievement orientation and effort, the first alternative model included a direct path from achievement orientation to effort; if a relationship existed, it would be expected to be positive. The fit of the model improved, as chi-square decreased, $\Delta\chi^2$ (1, $N$ = 151) = 10.97, $p$ < .001. Moreover, the values of the fit indices were favorable, CFI =.96; GFI =.90; AGFI =.86; RMSEA =.044. For a second alternative model, we then added a direct path from interest to subsequent performance; if a relationship existed, it would be expected to be positive. This explicitly tested whether effort does not entirely account for the link between interest and a positive change in performance. The fit of the model did not improve, as chi-square did not decrease, $\Delta\chi^2$ (1, $N$ = 151) = .24, $p$ > .50. Therefore, we retained the first alternative model as our final structural model, given that it represents a theoretically meaningful model that provided the best fit to the data.

Finally, a chi-square test indicated that the final structural model did not fit the data worse than the measurement model did; that is, the chi-square increase from the measurement model to the final structural model was not significant, $\Delta\chi^2$ (15, $N$ = 151) = 18.30, $p$ > .20. This provides further evidence that the data fit the final structural model quite well. The structural equations results support the proposed model, except for the addendum of the direct relationship between achievement orientation and effort. Next, we report path coefficients, as well as the effects of factors in the model. Given that the hypothesized relationships were directional (i.e., we expected any relationship that existed to be positive), one-tailed significance levels are reported for the path values and factor effects.

## Path Coefficients for the Final Structural Model

The standardized path coefficients for the final structural model are presented in Figure 2. As hypothesized, all relationships are positive. *Initial performance* ($R^2$ = .13) was directly predicted by cognitive ability ($\beta$ = .26, $p$ < .005) and achievement orientation ($\beta$ = .26, $p$ <

.005). *Interest* ($R^2$ = .24) was directly predicted by initial performance ($\beta$ = .24, $p$ < .005), achievement orientation ($\beta$ = .27, $p$ < .005), and learning orientation ($\beta$ = .17, $p$ < .05). *Effort* ($R^2$ = .74) was directly predicted by interest ($\beta$ = .66, $p$ < .0005), achievement orientation ($\beta$ = .31, $p$ < .0005), and performance orientation ($\beta$ = .19, $p$ < .01). Finally, *subsequent performance* ($R^2$ = .31) was directly predicted by cognitive ability ($\beta$ = .21, $p$ < .01), initial performance ($\beta$ = .30, $p$ < .0005), and effort ($\beta$ = .30, $p$ < .005).

Table 2 summarizes the "effects" of the exogenous predictors on the endogenous factors. In particular, it shows the direct and indirect effects of achievement, learning, and performance orientations, along with cognitive ability, on the four endogenous factors: initial performance, interest, effort, and subsequent performance. In the remainder of this section, we detail the various direct and indirect effects of importance.

*"Effects" of Initial Performance on Interest, Effort, and Subsequent Performance*

Initial performance had a direct effect on *interest* of .24 ($p$ < .005), and an indirect effect on *effort* of .16 ($p$ < .01) by way of a path through interest to effort. Finally, initial performance had a total effect on *subsequent performance* of .35 ($p$ < .0005), which consisted of a direct effect of .30 ($p$ < .005), and an indirect effect of .05 ($p$ < .025) by way of a path through interest to effort to subsequent performance.

*"Effects" of Exogenous Predictors on Interest and Effort*

*Achievement orientation* had a total effect on *interest* of .33 ($p$ < .005), which consisted of a direct effect of .27 ($p$ < .005), and an indirect effect of .06 ($p$ < .025) by way of a path through initial performance to interest. Achievement orientation had a total effect on *effort* of .53 ($p$ < .0005), which consisted of a direct effect of .31 ($p$ < .0005) and an indirect effect of .22 ($p$ < .005). The indirect effect encompasses a path through initial performance to interest to effort (.04), combined with a path straight through interest to effort (.18). *Learning orientation* had a direct effect on *interest* of .17 ($p$ < .05), and a marginal indirect effect on *effort* of .11 ($p$ < .10) by way of a path through interest to effort. *Performance orientation* had a direct effect on effort of .19 ($p$ < .01). Finally, *cognitive ability* had an indirect effect on *interest* of .06 ($p$ < .025) by way of a path through initial performance to interest, and an indirect effect on *effort* of .04 ($p$ < .05) by way of a path through initial performance to interest to effort.

*"Effects" of the Exogenous Predictors and Interest on Subsequent Performance*

*Achievement orientation* (.23, $p$ < .0005) and *performance orientation* (.06, $p$ < .025) had indirect effects on subsequent performance, whereas *learning orientation* (.03, $p$ < .10) had a marginal indirect effect. The effect of *achievement orientation* on subsequent performance existed by way of paths straight through effort to subsequent performance (.09), straight through initial performance to subsequent performance (.08), through interest to effort to subsequent performance (.05), and, finally, through initial performance to interest to effort to subsequent performance (.01). The effect of *performance orientation* on subsequent performance existed by way of a path straight through effort to subsequent performance (.06). The marginal effect of *learning orientation* on subsequent performance existed by way of a path through interest to effort to subsequent performance (.03).

*Cognitive ability* had a total effect of .30 ($p$ < .0005) on subsequent performance, which consisted of a direct effect of .21 ($p$ < .01) as well as an indirect effect of .09 ($p$ < .01). The indirect effect of cognitive ability on subsequent performance existed by way of a path straight through initial performance to subsequent performance (.08), combined with a path through initial performance to interest to effort to subsequent performance (.01). Finally, *interest* had an indirect effect on subsequent performance of .20 ($p < .005$) by way of a path through effort to subsequent performance.

# DISCUSSION

## Strengths of This Study

This study offers a greater understanding of how approach-goal orientations contribute to performance-enhancing adjustments (after an initial period of experience) in a naturalistic learning endeavor, as well as how each contributing orientation promotes performance improvement. Two aspects of the results indicate that improved performance reflected adaptive responses to somewhat challenging circumstances. First, a relatively strong relationship existed between initial and subsequent performance. This relationship suggests that mastery of the course material for the second performance episode extended upon that for the initial episode. Further, such a circumstance makes it difficult for other predictors to explain unique variance in subsequent performance, which thereby underscores the indirect effects of the goal orientations on subsequent performance. Second, cognitive ability predicted an improvement in performance, suggesting that an improvement in performance was at least somewhat difficult in that it was facilitated by greater cognitive resources.

We believe that the time lapses between measurements of different sets of study variables, in combination with when the variables were measured, contribute to the importance of the results. Whereas the goal orientations were measured four weeks before initial performance, interest and effort were measured in the middle of the period in which individuals would have been making performance-enhancing adjustments in response to their initial performance. Given that interest and effort were assessed two weeks prior to the second exam, their relationships with performance on the second exam are notable. In contrast to our timing of measurement, other studies have measured mediating motivational states either a short time span before or after a performance episode. For example, VandeWalle et al. (2001) measured exam-specific self-efficacy and goal level in the class session before the second exam, and assessed exam-specific effort in the class period following the second exam (a retrospective report of effort by respondents). Future research might explore such timing issues, with the intent of determining the extent to which they affect observed relationships.

## Implications of Results

Our results have several meaningful implications, as explained below. First, they support the efficacy of general approach-goal orientations as predictors of responses to specific circumstances. Second, they support a *multiple goal orientation* perspective, which holds that different goal orientations may jointly engender adaptive responses. As explained further below, our findings represent a combination of the *specialized* and *additive* goal patterns (see Barron & Harackiewicz, 2000). Third, our results highlight the importance of achievement orientation as a predictor of performance-enhancing motivational states. Fourth, they

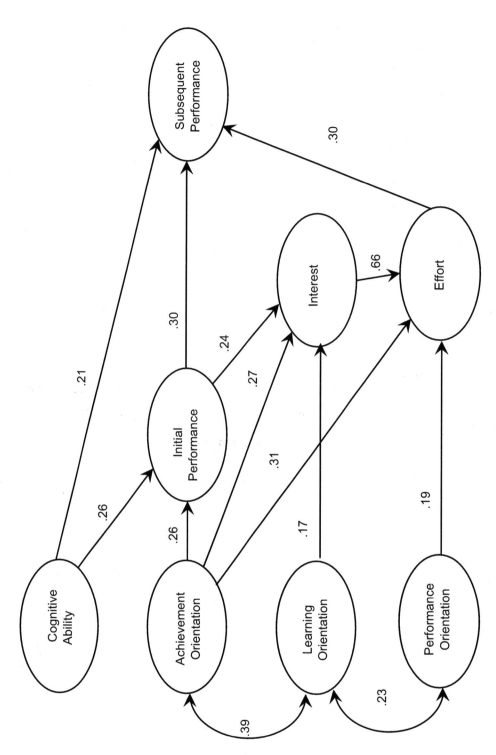

*Figure 2.* Final model with standardized path coefficients; all coefficients are significant at $p < .05$ (one-tailed).

**Table 2**

*Direct and Indirect "Effects" of Exogenous Predictors on Endogenous Factors*

| Endogenous factors | Exogenous Predictors | | | | | | | |
|---|---|---|---|---|---|---|---|---|
| | Cognitive ability | | Achievement orientation | | Learning orientation | | Performance orientation | |
| Initial performance | .26 | — | .26 | — | — | — | — | — |
| Interest | — | .06 | .27 | .06 | .17 | — | — | — |
| Effort | — | .04 | .31 | .22 | — | .11 | .19 | — |
| Subsequent performance | .21 | .09 | — | .23 | — | .03 | — | .06 |

*Note.* For each exogenous predictor, direct "effects" are located in the left column, whereas indirect "effects" are located in the right column. Dashes signify no effect.

underscore the relevance of interest for promoting adaptive processes. Finally, our findings underscore the ultimate importance of effort in performance improvement.

*General approach-goal orientations.* The results of our study suggest that general approach-goal orientations have relevance for predicting performance in learning endeavors, although their effects are mediated by proximal motivational variables. These results are consistent with other research that has found general traits to be related to important self-regulatory and behavioral outcomes, and thus provide additional support for the argument that general propensities have utility as predictors (Fleeson, 2001; Funder, 2001; Payne et al., 2007). In light of the potential predictive efficacy of general goal orientations, we advocate that future research continue to investigate them as predictors of adaptive responses.

*Multiple goal orientation perspective.* Our results provide additional evidence that goal orientations are not necessarily competing propensities, insofar as they may complement each other in engendering positive responses among individuals in a learning endeavor. Specifically, we found that each of the goal orientations tested contributed to improved performance, yet did so by way of different mediators. Learning orientation contributed by way of its association with interest, performance orientation contributed through its relationship with effort, and achievement orientation contributed via its links to both interest and effort. Thus, our results support Baron and Harackiewicz's (2000) *specialized* goal pattern, in that learning and performance goal orientations were directly related to different outcomes. Further, our results suggest that learning and achievement orientations are not redundant, as they each made unique contributions to positive motivational states. As a whole, the results provide initial evidence that expands current conceptions of which approach-goal orientations are salient and of the potential roles of those different orientations in promoting adjustment. That is, our results argue for a complementary, and more inclusive, perspective on approach-goal orientations and adaptive performance.

The underlying premise for our study was the *specialized* goal pattern (see Barron & Harackiewicz, 2000). The pattern of results indicated that, indeed, each of several approach-goal orientations promoted a different experiential consequence. As such, a specialized goal pattern does apply to framing our findings. However, some of the findings also support an *additive* goal pattern, such that two approach-goal orientations were independently advantageous for the same outcome. For instance, achievement and learning orientations additively combined to make direct, and unique, contributions to interest. Further, achievement and performance orientations each made unique contributions to effort, while learning orientation had a unique indirect contribution to effort through interest. As such, our findings represent a combination of the *specialized* and *additive* goal patterns (see Barron & Harackiewicz, 2000).

*Contributions of achievement orientation.* Our results support the notion that individuals' approach-goal orientations are not completely captured by learning and performance orientations (a notion that is consistent with Kanfer and Ackerman, 2000). Specifically, achievement orientation was found to be a viable predictor of both initial performance and an improvement over initial performance. In fact, among the exogenous predictors, achievement orientation had the most pervasive "effects" on the four endogenous variables (see Table 2). As hypothesized, achievement orientation complemented learning orientation and initial performance in predicting interest. Moreover, the relationship of achievement orientation with interest actually overshadowed the relationships of the remaining goal orientations with interest. Although we had initially proposed that the relationship of achievement orientation with effort would be explained completely by interest, our results indicated that this was not the case. That is, achievement orientation had a direct, as well as indirect, relationship with effort. This unanticipated result suggests that achievement orientation promotes a portion of overall effort that is not explained merely by interest.

The results involving achievement orientation together suggest that it engenders adaptive types of effort that stem from a sense of purpose, in addition to intrinsic interest. It is possible that a high level of achievement orientation encourages people to not only maintain interest in learning and improving, but also to identify actions that are more directly conducive to performance and to channel their efforts to those actions. Perhaps achievement oriented individuals not only exert a high level of effort toward performance in an endeavor, but also allocate their time and effort to performance-relevant actions such that their use of time and effort is more productive or efficient. Of course, these are issues to be empirically addressed by future research.

In addition to capturing a tendency to exert effort, achievement orientation may embody tendencies to develop and utilize cognitive self-regulation strategies that promote greater performance. These strategies may involve approaches such as initiating one's own goals, visualizing the attainment of a high level of competence, considering what would be the best approach to use, formulating appropriate plans, focusing specifically on those activities or tasks that are most likely to elevate one's level of proficiency, and using cognitive tactics such as mental rehearsal. In turn, such strategies may promote timely and appropriate adjustments to shifting task demands. Future research exploring achievement orientation as a predictor of adaptive performance would benefit from including these types of cognitive self-regulation strategies, as proximal predictors of performance. Doing so would enable researchers to test the extent to which such strategies explain relationships between achievement orientation and various types of adaptive performance.

*Interest as an explanatory mechanism.* A fourth implication of our results centers on their support of interest's pivotal role in linking achievement and learning orientations to improved performance. Thus, our results suggest that achievement and learning orientations promote an interest in exploring and learning new things within a specific endeavor (Ryan & Deci, 2000). Given that previous research has typically not explored interest as a mechanism through which general approach-goal orientations are linked to effort and performance, our results provide additional understanding of how such orientations shape important outcomes. As well, Sansone and Smith (2000) have suggested that the extent to which some individuals may use interest-regulating tactics in everyday life has been underestimated by researchers who have emphasized situational conditions. Nevertheless, relationships of achievement and learning orientations with the phenomenon of flow (i.e., individuals' actions being experienced as relatively effortless) were not directly tested, and remain a viable topic for future research.

*Effort as an ultimate explanatory mechanism.* In our study, effort was the ultimate mechanism through which approach-goal orientations and interest facilitated performance improvement. This is consistent with the proposition that effort provides the mediating linkage between psychological involvement in a domain of activity and actual performance in that domain (Brown & Leigh, 1996). It is advisable that researchers include effort as a key explanatory mechanism in models of performance improvement.

*Additional Points of Relevance for Future Research*

The three goal orientations included in this study represent forms of "approach" motivation, in that they encompass self-regulation toward attaining some measure of success. Future research on general goal orientations might benefit from also including "avoidance" propensities, which would encompass self-regulation toward avoiding expressions of incompetence (see Elliot, 1999; Higgins, 1997; Hirschfeld, Thomas, & Lankau, 2006; Kanfer & Heggestad, 1997; Payne et al., 2007). The present study was conducted in an academic setting using a sample of undergraduate students. The setting and sample afforded us the opportunity to measure a number of relevant predictor variables, obtain objective measures of performance, and observe a change in performance in a naturalistic setting with inherent incentives to perform well. As such, the setting offered a strong test of the hypotheses (Cook & Campbell, 1979). Yet, although many characteristics of academic settings parallel those of workplace training programs (Chen et al., 2000; Noe, 2002), the use of an undergraduate student sample may limit the generalizability of the findings to other types of settings such as those that do not involve learning. Future research should perhaps explore whether our results generalize to individuals engaged in other performance-related endeavors.

## CONCLUSION

Whetten (1989) has suggested that in developing a theory, researchers must strike a balance between comprehensiveness on the one hand, and parsimony on the other. Whereas comprehensiveness would entail all relevant constructs being included, parsimony would involve including only those constructs that are most useful in explaining the phenomenon of interest. A number of recent studies have used a parsimonious typology of general approach-goal orientations by including two such constructs: learning and performance orientations. Our study's results suggest that achievement orientation should be included in future research on goal orientations, and that a multiple goal orientation perspective may well reflect the potentially positive contributions of different orientations. Only after a number of studies have assessed the contributions of various goal orientations, will scholars have the necessary evidence from which to formulate a parsimonious theory of goal-related propensities and adaptation that includes only those constructs offering the greatest utility in predicting adaptive behavior.

## REFERENCES

Bandura, A. (1997). *Self-efficacy: The exercise of control.* New York: W. H. Freeman and Company.

Barron, K. E., & Harackiewicz, J. M. (2000). Achievement goals and optimal motivation: A multiple goals approach. In C. Sansone & J. M. Harackiewicz (Eds.), *Intrinsic and extrinsic motivation: The search for optimal motivation and performance* (pp. 229–254). San Diego: Academic Press.

Bell, B. S., & Kozlowski, S. W. J. (2002). Goal orientation and ability: Interactive effects on self-efficacy, performance, and knowledge. *Journal of Applied Psychology, 87,* 497–505.

Blanton, H., Buunk, M. P., Gibbons, F. X., & Kuyper, H. (1999). When better-than-others compare upward: Choice of comparison and comparative evaluation as independent predictors of academic performance. *Journal of Personality and Social Psychology, 76,* 420–430.

Brett, J. F., & VandeWalle, D. (1999). Goal orientation and goal content as predictors of performance in a training program. *Journal of Applied Psychology, 84,* 863–873.

Brown, S. P., & Leigh, T. W. (1996). A new look at psychological climate and its relationship to job involvement, effort, and performance. *Journal of Applied Psychology, 81,* 358–368.

Browne, M. W., & Cudeck, R. (1993). Alternative ways of assessing model fit. In K. A., Bollen & J. S. Long (Eds.), *Testing structural equation models* (pp. 136–162). Newbury Park, CA: Sage.

Button, S. B., Mathieu, J. E., & Zajac, D. M. (1996). Goal orientation in organizational research: A conceptual and empirical foundation. *Organizational Behavior and Human Decision Processes, 67,* 26–48.

Chan, D. (2000). Understanding adaptation to changes in the work environment: Integrating individual difference and learning perspectives. *Research in Personnel and Human Resources Management, 18,* 1–42.

Chen, G., Gully, S. M., Whiteman, J., & Kilcullen, R. N. (2000). Examination of relationships among trait-like individual differences, state-like individual differences, and learning performance. *Journal of Applied Psychology, 85,* 835–487.

Cook, T. D., & Campbell, D. T. (1979). *Quasi-experimentation: Design and analysis issues for field settings.* Boston: Houghton Mifflin.

Csikszentmihalyi, M. (1990). *Flow: The psychology of optimal experience.* New York: Harper & Row.

Dweck, C. S. (1986). Motivational processes affecting learning. *American Psychologist, 41,* 1040–1048.

Dweck, C. S. (1989). Motivation. In A. Lesgold & R. Glaser (Eds.), *Foundations for a psychology of education* (pp. 87–136). Hillsdale, NJ: Erlbaum.

Dweck, C. S. (1999). *Self-theories: Their role in motivation, personality, and development.* Philadelphia, PA: Psychology Press.

Dweck, C. S, & Leggett, E. L. (1988). A social–cognitive approach to motivation and personality. *Psychological Review, 95,* 256–273.

Elliot, A. J. (1999). Approach and avoidance motivation and achievement goals. *Educational Psychologist, 34,* 169–189.

Elliot, A. J., & Church, M. A. (1997). A hierarchical model of approach and avoidance achievement motivation. *Journal of Personality and Social Psychology, 72,* 218–232.

Ericsson, K. A., Krampe, R. T., & Tesch-Römer, C. (1993). The role of deliberate practice in the acquisition of expert performance. *Psychological Review, 100,* 363–406.

Fisher, S. L., & Ford, J. K. (1998). Differential effects of learner effort and goal orientation on two learner outcomes. *Personnel Psychology, 51,* 397–420.

Fleeson, W. (2001). Toward a structure- and process-integrated view of personality: Traits as density distributions of states. *Journal of Personality and Social Psychology, 80,* 1011–1027.

Ford, J. K., Smith, E. M., Weissbein, D. A., Gully, S. M., & Salas, E. (1998). Relationships of goal orientation, metacognitive activity, and practice strategies with learning outcomes and transfer. *Journal of Applied Psychology, 83,* 218–233.

Funder, D. C. (2001). Personality. *Annual Review of Psychology, 52,* 197–221.

Goldberg, L. R. (1999). A broad-bandwidth, public-domain, personality inventory measuring the lower-level facets of several five-factor models. In I. Mervielde, I. J. Deary, F. De Fruyt, & F. Ostendorf (Eds.), *Personality psychology in Europe,* Vol. 7 (pp. 7–28). Tilburg, The Netherlands: Tilburg University Press.

Gottfredson, L. S., & Crouse, J. (1986). Validity versus utility of mental tests: Example of the SAT. *Journal of Vocational Behavior, 29,* 363–378.

Harackiewicz, J. M., & Sansone, C. (2000). Rewarding competence: The importance of goals in the study of intrinsic motivation. In C. Sansone & J. M. Harackiewicz (Eds.), *Intrinsic and extrinsic motivation: The search for optimal motivation and performance* (pp. 79–103). San Diego: Academic Press.

Henderlong, J., & Lepper, M. R. (2002). The effects of praise on children's intrinsic motivation: A review and synthesis. *Psychological Bulletin, 128,* 774–795.

Herold, D. M., & Fedor, D. B. (1998). Individuals' interaction with their feedback environment: The role of domain-specific individual differences. *Research in Personnel and Human Resources Management, 16,* 215–254.

Hidi, S. (2000). An interest researcher's perspective: The effects of extrinsic and intrinsic factors on motivation. In C. Sansone & J. M. Harackiewicz (Eds.), *Intrinsic and extrinsic motivation: The search for optimal motivation and performance* (pp. 309–339). San Diego: Academic Press.

Higgins, E. T. (1997). Beyond pleasure and pain. *American Psychologist, 52,* 1280–1300.

Hirschfeld, R. R., Lawson, L., & Mossholder, K. W. (2004). Moderators of the relationship between cognitive ability and performance: General versus context-specific achievement motivation. *Journal of Applied Social Psychology, 34,* 2389–2409.

Hirschfeld, R. R., Thomas, C. H., & Lankau, M. J. (2006). Achievement and avoidance motivational orientations in the domain of mentoring. *Journal of Vocational Behavior, 68,* 524–537.

James, L. R., Mulaik, S. A., & Brett, J. M. (1982). *Causal analysis: Assumptions, models, and data.* Beverly Hills, CA: Sage.

Kanfer, R. (1990). Motivation theory and industrial and organizational psychology. In M. D. Dunnette & L. M. Hough (Eds.), *Handbook of industrial and organizational psychology* (Vol.1, pp. 75–170). Palo Alto, CA: Consulting Psychologists Press.

Kanfer, R., & Ackerman, P. L. (1989). Motivation and cognitive abilities: An integrative/aptitude–treatment interaction approach to skill acquisition. *Journal of Applied Psychology, 74,* 657–690.

Kanfer, R., & Ackerman, P. L. (2000). Individual differences in work motivation: Further explorations of a trait framework. *Applied Psychology: An International Review, 49,* 470–482.

Kanfer, R., & Heggestad, E. D. (1997). Motivational traits and skills: A person-centered approach to work motivation. *Research in Organizational Behavior, 19,* 1–56.

Kozlowski, S. W. J., Gully, S. M., Brown, K. G., Salas, E., Smith, E. M., & Nason, E. R. (2001). Effects of training goals and goal orientation traits on multi-dimensional training outcomes and performance adaptability. *Organizational Behavior and Human Decision Processes, 85,* 1–31.

Krapp, A. (2005). Basic needs and the development of interest and intrinsic motivational orientations. *Learning and Instruction, 15,* 381–395.

Landis, R. S., Beal, D. J., & Tesluk, P. E. (2000). A comparison of approaches to forming composite measures in structural equation models. *Organizational Research Methods, 3,* 186–207.

Larson, R. W. (2000). Toward a psychology of positive youth development. *American Psychologist, 55,* 170–183.

Lee, S., & Klein, H. J. (2002). Relationships between conscientiousness, self-efficacy, self deception, and learning over time. *Journal of Applied Psychology, 87,* 1175–1182.

Lee, F. K., Sheldon, K. M., & Turban, D. B. (2003). Personality and the goal-striving process: The influence of achievement goal patterns, goal level, and mental focus on performance and enjoyment. *Journal of Applied Psychology, 88,* 256–265.

Linnenbrink, E. A., & Pintrich, P. R. (2000). Multiple pathways to learning and achievement: The role of goal orientation in fostering adaptive motivation, affect, and cognition. In C. Sansone & J. M. Harackiewicz (Eds.), *Intrinsic and extrinsic motivation: The search for optimal motivation and performance* (pp. 195–227). San Diego: Academic Press.

London, M., & Mone, E. M. (1999). Continuous learning. In D. R. Ilgen & E. D. Pulakos (Eds.), *The changing nature of performance: Implications for staffing, motivation, and development* (pp. 119–153). San Francisco: Jossey-Bass.

Mulaik, S. A., James, L. R., Van Alstine, J., Bennett, N., Lind, S., & Stilwell, C. D. (1989). Evaluation of goodness-of-fit indices for structural equation models. *Psychological Bulletin, 105,* 430–445.

Noe, R. A. (2002). *Employee training and development.* Boston, MA: McGraw-Hill.

Payne, S. C., Youngcourt, S. S., & Beaubien, J. M. (2007). A meta-analytic examination of the goal orientation nomological net. *Journal of Applied Psychology, 92,* 128–150.

Phillips, J. M., & Gully, S. M. (1997). Role of goal orientation, ability, need for achievement, and locus of control in the self-efficacy and goal-setting process. *Journal of Applied Psychology, 82,* 792–802.

Pinder, C. C. (1998). *Work motivation in organizational behavior.* Upper Saddle River, NJ: Prentice Hall.

Pintrich, P.R. (2000). Multiple goals, multiple pathways: The role of goal orientation in learning and achievement. *Journal of Educational Psychology, 92,* 544–555.

Renninger, K. A. (2000). Individual interest and its implications for understanding intrinsic motivation. In C. Sansone & J. M. Harackiewicz (Eds.), *Intrinsic and extrinsic motivation: The search for optimal motivation and performance* (pp. 373–404). San Diego: Academic Press.

Ryan, R. M., & Deci, E. L. (2000). Self-determination theory and the facilitation of intrinsic motivation, social development, and well-being. *American Psychologist, 55,* 68–78.

Ryan, R. M., & La Guardia, J. G. (1999). Achievement motivation within a pressured society: Intrinsic and extrinsic motivations to learn and the politics of school reform. *Advances in Motivation and Achievement, 11,* 45–85.

Sansone, C., & Smith, J. L. (2000). Interest and self-regulation: The relation between having to and wanting to. In C. Sansone & J. M. Harackiewicz (Eds.), *Intrinsic and extrinsic motivation: The search for optimal motivation and performance* (pp. 341–372). San Diego: Academic Press.

Schiefele, U. (1999). Interest and learning from text. *Scientific Studies of Reading, 3,* 257–279.

Schmidt, F. L., & Hunter, J. (2004). General mental ability in the world of work: Occupational attainment and job performance. *Journal of Personality and Social Psychology, 86,* 162–173.

Shiner, R. L. (2000). Linking childhood personality with adaptation: Evidence for continuity and change across time into late adolescence. *Journal of Personality and Social Psychology, 78,* 310–325.

Spence, J. T., & Helmreich, R. L. (1983). Achievement-related motives and behaviors. In J. T. Spence (Ed.), *Achievement and achievement motives: Psychological and sociological approaches* (pp. 7–74). San Francisco: W. H. Freeman.

Spence, J. T., Pred, R. S., & Helmreich, R. L. (1989). Achievement strivings, scholastic aptitude, and academic performance: A follow-up to "Impatience versus achievement strivings in the Type A pattern." *Journal of Applied Psychology, 74,* 176–178.

The College Board (1998, September). *Score change when retaking the SAT I: Reasoning test* (RN-05). New York, NY: Author.

Van Yperen, N. W. & Hagedoorn, M. (2003). Do high job demands increase intrinsic motivation or fatigue or both? The role of job control and job social support. *Academy of Management Journal, 46,* 339–348.

VandeWalle, D., Cron, W. L., & Slocum, J. W. (2001). The role of goal orientation following performance feedback. *Journal of Applied Psychology, 86,* 629–640.

Whetten, D. A. (1989). What constitutes a theoretical contribution? *Academy of Management Review, 14,* 490–495.

Zusho, A., Pintrich, P.R., & Coppola, B. (2003). Skill and will: The role of motivation and cognition in the learning of college chemistry. *International Journal of Science Education, 25,* 1081–1094.

In: Applied Psychology Research Trends
Editor: Karl H. Kiefer, pp.183-210

ISBN 978-1-60456-372-6
© 2008 Nova Science Publishers, Inc.

*Chapter 9*

# THE SOCIAL PERCEPTION OF THE 2006 FOREST FIRES IN THE NORTHWEST REGION OF SPAIN: INFORMATION, TRUST, EDUCATION AND PARTICIPATION[1]

## *Ricardo García-Mira[1], Carmela García González[2] and Xosé Luis Barreiro Rivas[3]*

[1] University of Corunna, Spain
[2] IES Val Miñor de Nigrán – Pontevedra, Spain
[3] University of Santiago de Compostela, Spain

## ABSTRACT

A social approach to the study of fires is very necessary in the design and implementation of natural environment and forest programs and policies. Forest fires, and the risk they generate to the ecosystem and to human beings, are not only technical problems that can be solved solely by technical experts and the evaluation they make; they also involve environmental understanding, active commitment of citizens and their participation in land management.

The dramatic situation that was the result of the Galician forest fires, in the summer of 2006, revealed the weakness of this region's ecosystem when exposed to one of the most serious risks affecting this community. Also, it made visible the fact that a complex problem – one that has many causes, among which the most important are perceived to be the intentional and irresponsible actions of people - requires multidimensional strategies.

This chapter analyses the subjective perception that the citizens have of the forests fires, and tries to contribute to the development and improvement of efficient public policies in the fight against fires. The necessity to integrate technical and objective criteria, along with the more subjective ones, in the analysis of fires is discussed; also, the reader is provided with an analysis of the social representations of fires, which contain key information for evaluations related to the decision-making process.

---

[1] The authors would like to express their gratitude to the Galician Committee for Culture (CCG) and to the Caixa-Galicia Foundation. The work reported here is based on the results of a wider study on forest fires in the Autonomous Region of Galicia (Spain), promoted by the CCG and carried out under the direction of F. Díaz-Fierros, X. Balboa and X.L. Barreiro Rivas (2007).

**Keywords**: Social Perception, Forest Fires, Environmental Policy, Participation.

# INTRODUCTION

When studying forest fires, as with any other environmental problem, the social perspective is an essential angle from which to establish programmes and lines of action and to implement risk prevention policies. Environmental policies and risk management are more than just technical problems that can be resolved simply be having recourse to expert assessment and guidance. The putting into practice of public policies to deal with risk contains a fundamental element involving the understanding of, participation in and active commitment to a change in the way the environment is seen and land managed on the part of the population. For this reason when managing risk it becomes necessary, in addition to the technical processes of assessment and management, to have a well-defined strategy of social communication and education that will guide the debate and enable a deeper insight into the complexity and scope of environmental intervention. A strategy of this nature should foster participation in discussions and favour a much-needed change in people's attitudes, values and awareness with a view to the adoption of good practices in risk prevention, working towards a model of development that is both socially and environmentally sustainable. In the case of forest fires, especially when most of them appear to have been caused intentionally, social prevention through communication and awareness-raising amongst the population becomes a top priority, albeit one that is by no means easy to achieve. When determining the direction that this process of communication and education should take, the analysis of public opinion and its habits provides an extremely interesting guide to the detection of deficiencies in the representation of problems, elements that create resistance and difficulties in evaluation and understanding that hinder the introduction of desirable changes. Public opinion surveys provide the opportunity to:

> ➤ Obtain a more precise definition of images, difficulties and deficiencies, of gaps along the way between knowledge, intentions and actions, of the transition from words to active response.
> ➤ Visualise people's social representations with regard to environmental problems and the perceptive aspects associated with them.
> ➤ Systematise an on-going monitoring of opinion, as a basic element in the design of communication and social prevention strategies.
> ➤ To collect and establish relevant information that favours the strengthening of social processes that are reflective, deliberative and support decision-making.

A large proportion of studies dealing with the relationship between awareness of the problem of the environment, attitudes and responses point out that more information and greater knowledge do not immediately translate into better actions; information and awareness of the consequences do not immediately determine a change of behaviour towards responsible actions with regard to the environment and the taking of measures to prevent risk. Complex psychological mediations, habits and other social aspects influence individual behaviours. In this context, the importance of the processes of communication and social participation becomes apparent, not only because of their ability to promote expert knowledge and the opinions of the general public and those with management responsibilities, but because they also facilitate the appearance of active frameworks that favour change in environmental practices and shared responsibility in environmental actions. It is important not to overlook the value of mechanisms that stabilise communication and bring the various levels at which measures are taken closer to the public: risk assessment, the setting of goals and timescales, the analysis of potential responses, the implementation of responses and the evaluation of outcomes.

## Social Concern Over Forest Fires

The dramatic situation arising from the wave of forest fires in the summer of 2006 highlighted on the one hand the vulnerability of the land in the Autonomous Region of Galicia (Spain), and therefore of its ecosystems, in the face of one of the most serious risks affecting the region, and on the other the multiple strategies required to deal with a multifactorial problem for which a wide range of causes has been identified, with intentional and irresponsible actions being those to which the greatest importance is attached.

The number of fires and the surface area affected by them, particularly the wooded surface area, over several decades have put Galicia in the limelight in this respect, even more so during the year in question, in which a considerable number of people and amount of property were exposed to the flames (which came dangerously close to residential areas, causing the death of four people). There is therefore indubitable concern over this problem, and apart from the necessary technical evaluation of the situation, the analysis of other factors which can only be discovered by evaluating the subjective perception of the local population is a relevant aspect which should be taken into account when designing any system of evaluation.

The study that appears in this chapter aims to analyse and evaluate this subjective perception of the inhabitants of Galicia with regard to the forest fires of the summer of 2006, in order to contribute to the creation of a vision that will favour the enhancement and development of public policies designed to combat them. When local programmes are being developed, the need to integrate technical and objective criteria with those of a different and more subjective nature, namely how the people of Galicia (Northwest Spain) see the problem of forest fires, is a topic to which the social sciences have paid particular attention, given its seriousness. In this respect, the model being followed is that applied in the Western world in general, and more specifically in Europe, when evaluating and assessing the damage caused by disasters, whether these arise from natural causes or as a result of technological progress.

The relevance of this study, which explores the dimensions that explain the subjective perception of the inhabitants of Galicia with regard to forest fires, is that it aims to contribute to revealing the keys to interpretation that will make it possible to understand the conception that the local population has of non-arable land and the value they attach to it, which may well be of interest for the planning of forestry policy. This is also justified by the increasing lack of coincidence between assessments based on the vision of technical experts and those based on lay perception. By bringing together the two visions, which are complementary, a full overview can be obtained that will throw some light on the strengths and weaknesses of policies directed at non-arable land, landowners and local residents in a region in which forest fires may constitute a threat for safe cohabitation in certain residential areas close to zones at risk.

The study reported in this chapter, therefore, sets out to mitigate the lack of public perception studies on social representations of forest fires, the evaluation of the latter being seen from a social perspective in which people are seen as containers of useful information which should be made known, and of subjective experiences that should be taken into account during the decision-making process.

## A Framework for Analysis: Risk Society and Perception

The roots of perception and the acceptance of risk lie in cultural and social factors, the response to danger normally being mediated by social influences transmitted by others in one's environment (neighbours, friends, colleagues, etc.), as well as by institutions and the mass media. In many cases the perception of risk may be formed after an act of reasoning by the person concerned, and is closely linked to environmental awareness. With regard to forest fires, culture is a decisive factor when it comes to conceptualising risk. The attitude adopted by those concerned when confronted by a fire will vary according to the perception of the risk it entails, within any given social and cultural framework. These attitudes are moulded by a series of factors (see Tretting and Musham, 2000) such as: a) the feeling of involvement in the community and in the decision-making process; b) the degree of satisfaction with the information received; c) the degree of trust in institutions and government; d) their own beliefs regarding health risks; and e) their awareness of state-of-the-art fire prevention and extinction technologies.

In order to achieve a better understanding of the framework in which environmental crises are problematised, reference must be made to one of the most suggestive characterisations of modern societies that have been proposed in the field of sociology: that of a risk society. These proposals consider "risk" to be the characteristic element of post-modern or late modern societies, "risk societies", as Ulrich Beck puts it. Even if one thinks it excessive to take risk as being the single element that best defines modern society, it is also true to say that risk lies at the core of many debates on environmental policy. And in the present case, namely the social contexts in which the effect of forest fires should be understood, this proposition is revealing indeed.

"Risk", as Bechmann (2004, cf. Luján and Echeverria, 2004) warns us, rather than being the direct opposite of "safety", is defined in contrast to the concept of "danger". Danger is something that affects a possible victim of harm, a victim with no responsibility or decision-making capacity with regard to the origins and causes of that harm; risks are something that are faced by a human being who is defenceless against the forces of nature, or in situations that lie beyond collective responsibility. Risk, therefore, is concomitant with responsibility. It is the vision of danger from the point of view of a decision-making process in which the decisions are associated with situations of uncertainty. These decisions are numerous, taken at different levels and in different strata, and impossible to attach to a single event or moment; they are actions in which, as some sociologists of risk indicate, a collective responsibility, or in other words, an "organised irresponsibility" (Beck, 2002) can be descried. The framework of risk is, therefore, a question of the attributability of responsibility for the numerous prior human actions that generate consequences that at times could never have been imagined or foreseen beforehand, decisions remote in time and space but having undesired effects in the present. The language of risk reformulates in terms of responsibility, and, naturally, in the language of politics, matters which previously were only governed by chance, far removed from any human responsibility. Proof of all this is the new angle from which Galician society's relations with the environment are now beginning to be focused and the way in which the relationship between land use and practices and the risk of fires or floods is gradually starting to be perceived. Part of the results of the way in which the environment has been managed in the past, the reflection of previous interventions and transformations of the natural environment, is now becoming apparent; damage as a result of previous human actions or omissions. And these are the lines along which the change in social perception detected in the population after the summer forest fires can be understood.

## The Process of Amplification of Risk

Another process connected with the understanding of risk is the phenomenon of *amplification*, based on the thesis that some events or dangers create an impact with secondary effects that go beyond the immediate effect they produce, by interacting with psychological, social, institutional and cultural processes that enhance or lessen the perception of individual or social risk, thereby possibly moulding the consequent behaviour of the population (Renn, Burns, Kasperton, Kasperton and Slovic, 1992).

Risk, in this theoretical framework, has partly been contextualised as a social construct, and partly as the physical property of a danger or event (Short, 1989). The process of its social amplification describes how individuals perceive and interpret this risk in accordance with their mental schema, which they then communicate to other individuals or groups (Renn, 1991). Social amplification occurs when communicative and behavioural responses generate secondary effects that impinge on people outside the ranks of those initially affected by an event, in this case a forest fire. A peculiarity of this process is that amplification may have several different outcomes: an increase in the intensity of the perceived risk, a call for a response to the event on the part of the institutions responsible for combating it, or even an attenuation of the perceived risk (Renn *et al.*, 1992). The resulting outcome depends on the way in which the psychosocial, institutional or cultural processes referred to above interact.

One of the objectives of the present study is to examine the reasons why there was a greater perception of risk in the summer of 2006. Several variables that may provide an explanation for this phenomenon of amplification deserve comment:

*Physical consequences for the terrain.* The devastation of the hillsides, wooded or otherwise, is a clear example of this phenomenon of amplification occurring when the public becomes aware of the full magnitude of the consequences of a forest fire.

*Media coverage.* The mass media are a major factor in the amplification or attenuation of the public response to risk, since they seek to respond to, as well as reflect on, social concerns and adopt the role of active interpreters that mediate between the risk of fire and the fires themselves. This notwithstanding, the general public is more than a mere passive receiver of this transmission of knowledge, since people draw on multiple sources of information and comprehension (e.g. personal experience, the mass media, informal conversation or the Internet). The mass media, on the other hand, are not necessarily a negative influence on risk perception. The general public is perfectly capable of understanding the sensationalism, intentions and style of the media from which they obtain their information. Thus, when people want information on important topics or need to verify the facts, they look for different versions, having recourse to a variety of media, thus increasing their level of media consumption when a story interests them. The media undoubtedly set the agenda for public concern, but this selective attention acquires greater importance when people lack direct personal experience of the risks concerned: in other words, when the fragmented coverage of an event by the media coincides with non-experiential knowledge of the topic, this information may reinforce public uncertainty (Petts, Horlick-Jones & Murdock, 2001).

*Social perception of government and institutional intervention.* In this dimension, trust and credibility are two essential factors when it comes to understanding the perspectives of the population with regard to the environmental risk posed by forest fires (see García-Mira & Lema, 2008; García-Mira et al. 2005, 2006). Trust depends on cultural and economic circumstances, experiences and needs. Subjective factors (personal experiences, public involvement) and circumstances such as living in neighbourhoods threatened by fires, where the population lives in a situation of real environmental risk, can make some residents extremely untrusting.

Nevertheless, some studies (Williams, Brown & Greenberg, 1999) indicate that citizens show great trust in the ability of scientists to resolve situations of danger or risk, strongly supporting scientific competence in resolving conflictive situations relating to risk resulting from fires.

*Socio-economic and political consequences.* Some authors have highlighted the influence of socio-economic status on risk perception (Moffatt, Hoeldke & Pless, 1992), this consisting of the perception on the part of local inhabitants of the cost or economic benefits of the circumstance causing the risk, in this case that of fire, or of the importance it has for them, their environment, the local economy or the productive sector.

On the other hand, with regard to political impact, Peters *et al.* (1997) hold that the role of institutions and the information received by the public with regard to risk are major determiners of credibility and perceived trust. When faced by possible environmental risks from forest fires, people look for information and assistance from those institutions that they believe have the experience, power or responsibility to help (politicians and leaders).

The attribution of responsibility generates a feeling of control over events, since there is an awareness of who is assuming responsibility for the problem and who is responsible for finding a solution to it. It is by no means an easy matter to assign responsibility in the case of environmental problems, particularly when they pose the problem of a multiplicity of causes, as is the case of forest fires. In their efforts to lay the blame on somebody people blame the government, for failing to protect them (Hallman & Wandersman, 1992). For many people who belong to the least favoured socio-economic groups, those responsible for managing environmental risks are not perceived as being people who work to protect their interests (Petts, Horlick-Jones & Murdock, 2001), and this finding can be generalised to include forest fires.

To sum up, the study of public perception, together with that of people's social representations, is a factor of basic interest that will make it possible to: a) have access to a store of information on the perception of the Galician population, which will provide support for the decision-making process affecting local fire-fighting policy; b) know which aspects citizens take into account with regard to the policies and actions designed to guarantee safety in the Galician countryside; c) improve the quality of decisions by integrating the perspective of the local population in the public information and decision-making processes; d) provide better training for the professionals involved by integrating the psychosocial perspective in educational programmes dealing with fire prevention.

## OBJECTIVES

The principal objective of the present study is therefore to analyse the social perception of the wave of forest fires that swept through Galicia in the summer of 2006 in order to obtain a better understanding of the public perception of their consequences and the damage they caused, of the attribution of responsibilities for and causes of the disaster, and of the current level of trust in public institutions together with a projection of the same for the future, which will give the reader an idea of the social impact caused by these fires.

This overall objective was sub-divided into a set of specific objectives, as follows:

> - Determine the attributions given by the population with regard to the causes that led to the situation and its associated effects, as well as how responsibility was attributed.
> - Identify differential elements influencing the situation experienced in the summer of 2006.
> - Identify and estimate the principal damage perceived by the population of Galicia, both individually and collectively, evaluating the scope of each.
> - Evaluate the response coming from the various levels of government, public institutions and social agents.
> - Determine the degree of trust in institutions and social agents, as well as the level of efficacy attributed to current legislation in the matter of preventing and combating forest fires.
> - Determine the main sources of information consulted by the local population and their evaluation of the information received.
> - Determine the degree of protection afforded to the population, or their expectations, in future years.
> - Identify the main measures to be taken, from the point of view of the local population.

## METHODOLOGY

The nature of the evidence required by the study led to the adoption of a *survey* format, this survey being conducted among a representative sample of the population of Galicia, for the purpose of obtaining the information needed to pursue the objectives outlined above.

## Characteristics of the Sample

The universe of reference consisted of all persons over the age of 18 living in the Autonomous Region of Galicia (Spain). A multistage sampling technique using clusters was chosen to select the first level units (municipal districts in which the interviews were to be carried out), whilst stratified random sampling with proportional allocation by province, gender and age group was used when selecting the second level unit (individuals). The technical specifications are shown in Box 1.

| Scope | Galicia |
|---|---|
| Universe | Infinite (N approx.:2,378,005). Persons over the age of 18 living in Galicia |
| Sampling technique | Multistage sampling using clusters to select municipal districts and stratified random sampling with proportional allocation by Province, Gender and Age Group to select respondents |
| Worst-case hypothesis | p=q=50 |
| Desired overall maximum error | ±3.84% |
| Significance level | α= 0.05 |
| Sample size | 651 subjects |
| Information gathering | Computer-assisted telephone interview (CATI) |
| Field work | 11-23 April 2007 |

**Box 1.** Technical specifications for the study

## Procedure

The data were collected be means of computer-assisted telephone interviews (CATI), with calls being made to a total of 37 different municipal districts. These municipalities were selected with a view to ensuring that the variable Environment (Inland *vs*. Coastal) was proportionally distributed with regard to population, as was the Area of Residence. In the latter case three categories were established: (1) Urban (municipalities with a population of over 50,000 inhabitants); (2) Semi-urban (municipalities of between 10,000 and 15,000 inhabitants); and (3) Rural (municipalities with fewer than 10,000 inhabitants). The reference used for this purpose were the data corresponding to the 2006 census published by the Galician Institute of Statistics (IGE).

The interviews were conducted on the basis of a questionnaire specifically designed for this study, which began with a short introduction aimed at ensuring the participation of the respondents in the survey, not always an easy task, and the highest degree of sincerity possible in their replies to the questions. A series of socio-demographic questions were also included, and interviewers were also able to include comments or observations on any incident that might have led to any individual questionnaire being excluded from the survey.

The interviews varied in length, depending on the age and educational level of each person interviewed, the average time taken being from 10 to 15 minutes. Interviewers attended a training session on how to handle and conduct the interview, with a view to unifying criteria and procedures to be applied when obtaining information. A field coordinator was also appointed to supervise data collection on a daily basis and check the questionnaires as they were completed, before coding them.

The field work was done from April 11-23 2007. The initial number of interviews was 672, of which 21 were later eliminated, either because they contained an excessive number of blank answers or because they distorted the previously established sampling quotas.

## Data Analysis

Both descriptive and graphic analyses were undertaken, with variables being crossed to form contingency tables that enabled the results to be analysed, discussed and visualised by means of the corresponding frequency polygons relating to the variables of interest for the study.

# RESULTS

## 1. Attributions of Causes and Responsibilities

The results of the study show that the majority of those interviewed in 2007 considered intentional criminal actions and irresponsible behaviour as the main immediate causes of the fires (see Figure 1). This coincides with the findings of Varela (2005) regarding the attribution of causality in the case of the forest fires of the summer of 2005. Nevertheless, caution must be applied when comparing the results of different surveys of causality, because the precise definition and cataloguing of the multiple causes and the wording of the questions used to determine these are not homogeneous. The high percentage attributed to intentional criminal actions can be seen as a consequence of the state of emotional agitation, or the social and media-related atmosphere, in which the attribution of responsibilities was discussed during the crisis.

It can also be observed that those interviewed in the present study see little relation between the fires and change of land use or the wood-processing industry, factors that are mentioned with relative frequency as being behind the fires (see Figure 1). This is not the case in the study by Varela (2005), in which economic and financial interests were seen as one of the major causes. Nor do political causes, in the opinion of the local population, appear as one of the principal factors explaining causality, although the percentage of respondents citing this cause is slightly higher than in 2005.

Some comparisons can be made with other surveys, for example the results of the Autumn Barometer carried out by Sondaxe in 2002, which, as the regional newspaper *La Voz de Galicia* indicated, pointed out that "*the generally-held opinion amongst the population is that, when it comes to finding an explanation for the fires, financial and economic motives are considered to be much more important than the carelessness of day-trippers and farmers and the occasional actions of deranged people*". Land transactions and property speculation were two of the most frequently cited factors in discussions and debates at the time, as was the wood-processing industry. Similarly, the 2003 and 2004 Barometers of opinion, carried out at national level, showed that a significant percentage of citizens considered financial and economic reasons to be more important, in comparison with the *General Statistics on Forest Fires* published by the Ministry of the Environment. These studies, on a comparative basis, show a general tendency towards an increase in the perception of intentionality as opposed to the natural or accidental causes to which the causal relations of the fires had previously been attributed (Doiz Reus, 2005 and APAS & IDEM, 2003).

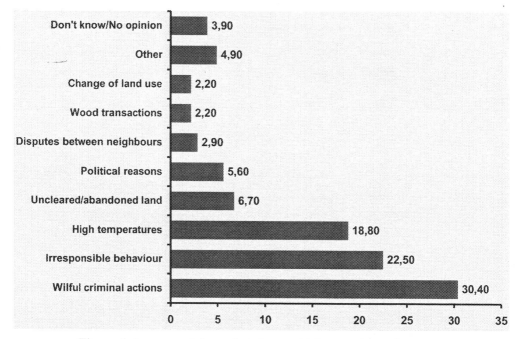

**Figure 1.** In your opinion, what do you think were the main causes of the wave of forest fires last summer?

When asked about the factors and practices that they considered either as causes of, or having some relation to, the fires, 78.7% of those interviewed said that forest fires had "Quite a lot" or "A lot" to do with the current state of abandon of non-arable land in Galicia. 67.7% considered that the manner in which non-arable land is exploited and the current use of land are also relevant factors (see Table 1 and Figure 2). This evaluation by the local population is interesting, since it reveals a certain degree of sensitivity to the problem that relates land management to risk, thus making it easier to guide social discussion towards territorial planning and changes in land use that may help to decrease combustibility and the intentional lighting of fires. This reveals that public opinion is closer to the complex network of practices and situations regarding non-arable land, which are structural problems that influence the problem and which had previously not been clearly seen. This is the case of the study on the forest fires of 2005 (Varela, 2005), in which a high degree of relevance was not attached to uncleared or abandoned land.

**Table 1.** In your opinion, the difficulties with forest fires
and their consequences are related to...

|  | NOT RELATED | RELATED TO SOME EXTENT | QUITE HIGHLY RELATED | HIGHLY RELATED | DON'T KNOW/NO OPINION |
|---|---|---|---|---|---|
| The manner in which non arable land is exploited and the current use of land | 6.50 | 21.20 | 41.30 | 26.40 | 4.60 |
| Abandoned non-arable land | 5.40 | 14.70 | 34.60 | 44.10 | 1.20 |
| The nature of property development in the area | 16.40 | 26.90 | 32.30 | 19,00 | 5.40 |
| Controlled fires and forest clearances | 15.50 | 27.30 | 35.20 | 18.60 | 3.40 |
| The predominant form of ownership | 13.40 | 24.6 | 32.10 | 18,00 | 12,00 |

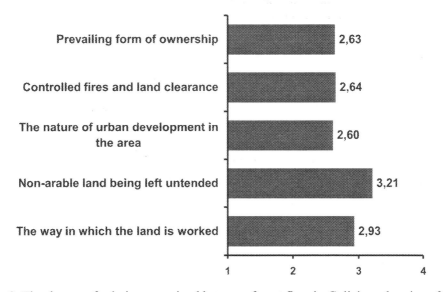

**Figure 2.** The degree of relation perceived between forest fires in Galicia and various factors.

When respondents were asked about the attribution of responsibilities, a large proportion cited the Regional Government of Galicia. On adding together the percentages attributing responsibility to the various levels of government, local, regional and central, 36.2% of those interviewed allotted responsibility to the authorities, a much higher percentage than those citing social institutions and agents (see Figure 3). This finding, compared with the low perception of responsibility being attributable to private land owners, communal land owners or local residents, will be discussed later.

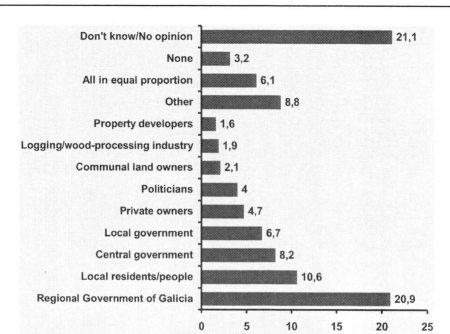

**Figure 3.** In your opinion, who do you think was mainly responsible for the serious situation experienced in Galicia last summer?

## 2. Differential elements in the situation experienced

A series of questions enabled the way in which respondents experienced the 2006 forest fires, and how they compared them to those of previous years, to be calibrated. For over 85% of respondents both the number of fires and the surface area affected by them were greater than in previous years (see Table 2 and Figure 4).

**Table 2.** What do you think changed in comparison with previous years?

| | LESS | THE SAME | GREATER | DON'T KNOW/NO OPINION |
|---|---|---|---|---|
| Number of fires | 3.40 | 6.60 | 87.60 | 2.50 |
| Surface area affected | 3.80 | 7.10 | 86.50 | 2.60 |
| Extent to which people and property were exposed to fire | 5.10 | 20.40 | 70.70 | 3.80 |
| Means of prevention and extinction | 15.80 | 36.30 | 41.30 | 6.60 |
| Involvement of the Regional Government of Galicia | 13.70 | 43.60 | 34.30 | 8.40 |
| Involvement of Municipal Councils | 12.10 | 44.20 | 33.20 | 10.40 |
| Regulations and Laws | 7.70 | 48.50 | 23,00 | 20.70 |

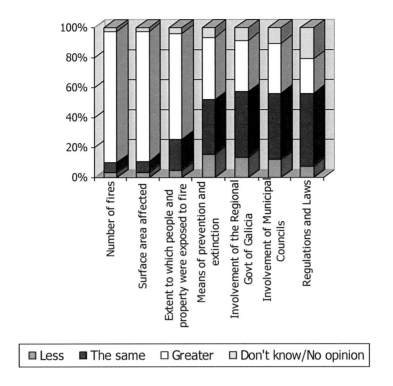

**Figure 4.** What do you think changed in comparison with previous years?

70.7% of those consulted thought that people and property were exposed to fire to a higher degree than before (Table 2, Figure 4). This proximity, whether experienced directly or at one remove, through the media, is what marked a change in the experience of the perception of risk. The awareness of the population with regard to the 2006 fires appears to be greater, even though in other years, e.g. 1989, the number of hectares affected by forest fires was double that of 2006. In the present study, the proximity and intensity "experienced" is clearly reflected in the results, whether this was brought home by the media or by the real proximity to the flames that many respondents cited.

On the other hand, there does not appear to be a generalised perception in this case of an improved response with regard to the means used by the authorities or on paper, as reflected in laws and the courts. Opinions regarding these factors were very similar to those expressed in previous years (see Figure 4).

## 3. Individually or collectively perceived damage, and scope

The perceived impact on the ecosystem, on the lives of the people in the affected areas and on some spheres of their working lives, amongst other aspects, was considered to be quite high (see Table 3 and Figure 5). The scope of the damage was considered to be high for all the elements taken into consideration (*soil, vegetation, estuaries, rivers*, with the greatest effect being on the *landscape*). The *ecosystem, life in the affected areas, the economy* and *the image of Galicia* were seen by a high percentage of the sample as having been "quite badly" or "very badly" affected (see Table 3).

When compared to the data from the 2005 study referred to above (Varela, 2005), the two coincide with regard to perceived damage to the ecosystem being one of the main effects. Furthermore, there is a trend towards an increasing perception of the damage to, and consequences for, the population and the life of those living in the affected areas.

**Table 3.** To what extent do you think the fires last year affected...?

| | NOT AFFECTED | SOMEWHAT AFFECTED | QUITE BADLY AFFECTED | VERY BADLY AFFECTED | DON'T KNOW / NO OPINION |
|---|---|---|---|---|---|
| Ecosystem | 0.90 | 7.10 | 30.90 | 59.80 | 1.40 |
| Land owners | 3.80 | 11.20 | 37.90 | 45.60 | 1.40 |
| Tourism | 10.80 | 22.30 | 31.30 | 33.50 | 2.20 |
| Life of those living near the affected areas | 2,00 | 9.80 | 36.10 | 50.70 | 1.40 |
| The Galician economy | 3.40 | 17.50 | 38.20 | 37.60 | 3.20 |
| The image of Galicia | 3.70 | 14.70 | 34.90 | 45.80 | 0.90 |
| The image of Spain abroad | 9.10 | 27.20 | 31.60 | 26,00 | 6.10 |
| Employment in certain sectors | 4,00 | 21.40 | 41.30 | 29.50 | 3.80 |
| Society and public awareness | 5.20 | 23.50 | 37.60 | 31.30 | 2.30 |

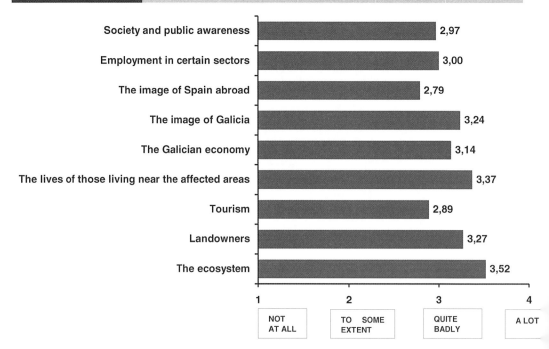

**Figure 5.** To what extent do you think the fires last year affected...?

With regard to the psychological impact of the fires, the feelings felt by most respondents were "*sadness*" (almost 30%) and "*indignation*" (almost 30%), followed by "*nervousness*" (18%) and "*fear*" (10.8%) (see Figure 6). Nevertheless, the normal daily activities of 92.9% of respondents were not affected. Further research is needed into this question, but there are no big differences in this psychological perception between the percentages of people living in rural, semi-urban or urban areas, with different educational levels or with different relations to non-arable land, when assessing the impact, effect and causality of the fires.

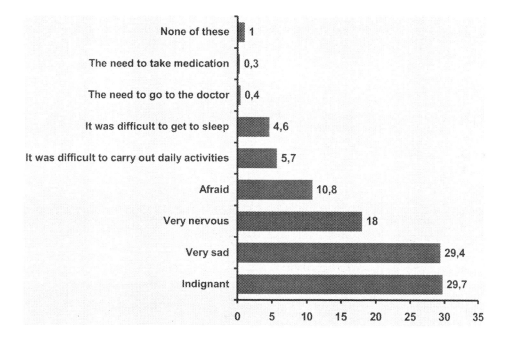

**Figure 6.** Personally, did you feel ...?

To sum up the findings so far, respondents considered that the intensity of the fires in the summer of 2006 was greater than in previous years, and that their impact was also greater. The population did not undervalue the effect of the fires, which were considered to be something that affected them closely, regardless of the damage suffered personally, and the impact on awareness appears to be high.

## 4. The response of the authorities, public institutions and social agents.

Generally speaking, those interviewed valued the response of those living nearby and the population in general higher than that of the authorities (see Figure 7). This result, when crossed with those already analysed for responsibility, reveals a very low level of trust shown by the local population in public policy and the action taken by the authorities.

The fact that the response of the general population was evaluated higher than that of the authorities may be related to the growing active support given to volunteering and social mobilisation in answer to environmental crises and risks in recent times.

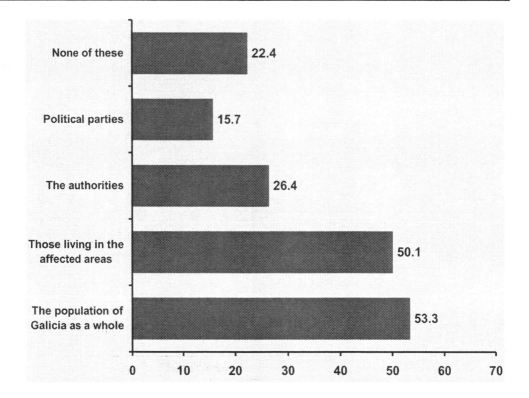

**Figure 7.** The percentage of respondents who considered there
to have been an adequate response from...

## 5. The degree of trust in institutions and social agents, and the level of efficacy attributed to the relevant legislation

The degree of trust shown by respondents in institutions and social agents once again reveals that the authorities are valued less highly than those living in the affected areas or the population as a whole (see Table 4). It is important to note the degree of trust shown in *ecologists* (see Figure 8), which is indicative of a greater social awareness and knowledge, as well as a change in values regarding the public exposure of environmental problems and the social agents that carry this out.

If once again the results of the present study are compared with those of Varela (2005), it can be seen that there has been an increase in the lack of trust in the authorities regarding the management of non-arable land. Two years ago, according to this author, opinion was divided almost equally: 1 in 3 gave a positive opinion, 1 in 3 a negative opinion and 1 in 3 were undecided.

**Table 4.** At present, with regard to the way in which non-arable land is currently being managed, how much trust do you have in each of these categories?

| | NO TRUST | SOME DEGREE OF TRUST | QUITE A HIGH DEGREE OF TRUST | A LOT OF TRUST | DON'T KNOW / NO OPINION |
|---|---|---|---|---|---|
| The Spanish government | 31.3 | 42.4 | 15.7 | 2.5 | 8.1 |
| The Galician government | 24.6 | 45.2 | 21.8 | 3.1 | 5.4 |
| Local councils | 27.6 | 45.2 | 20 | 2.8 | 4.5 |
| Local residents, the population in general | 8.3 | 31.2 | 44.4 | 12.7 | 3.4 |
| Ecologists | 16.3 | 36.6 | 31.5 | 10.9 | 4.8 |
| Private land owners | 16.7 | 45.5 | 26.6 | 5.7 | 5.5 |
| Communal land owners | 16.3 | 45 | 23.8 | 3.7 | 11.2 |

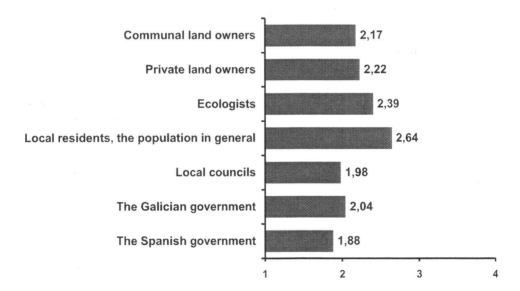

**Figure 8.** Level of trust in various institutions and social agents

A low opinion on the part of the population of the efficacy of current legislation with regard to combating forest fires was also observed (see Figure 9). Further research is needed to determine which aspects of the legal framework receive a negative evaluation: the laws themselves, investigation and the search for evidence in order to present charges, the resources allocated for this purpose, or the resulting trials. Popular opinion tends not to take into account the legal guarantees the characterise a democratic society, nor the complexity of trying to find evidence at the scene of the fires.

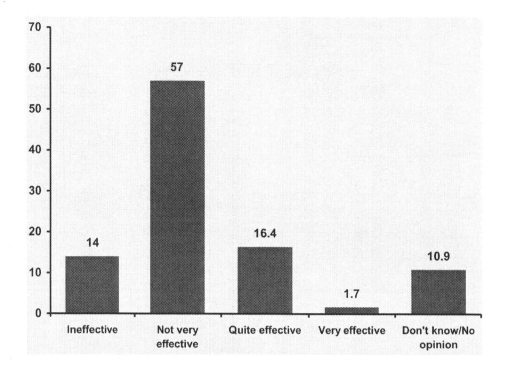

**Figure 9.** How do you assess the effectiveness of Galician
laws in the prevention of forest fires?

## 6. Sources of information consulted and evaluation of the information received

According to the study, the main source of information about the forest fires of summer 2006 for people in Galicia (see Figure 10) was the *television* (47.7%), followed by the *press* (33.9%). With regard to how they valued the quality of the information provided by the various mass media, only 48.4% of those interviewed considered that the information they received was *good* (see Figure 11). Furthermore, when asked their opinion of information on specific aspects (preventive measures, causes, impact, extinction) only 30% thought it was *good*. The social perception of events is closely linked to the way in which these are presented in the media. The greater receptiveness of the population to environmental problems, and basically to risks, is related to the coverage given to these topics by TV channels and the press. The visualisation of catastrophes is important, as is the media debate and discussion that heighten public awareness of the complexity of the problems surrounding risk.

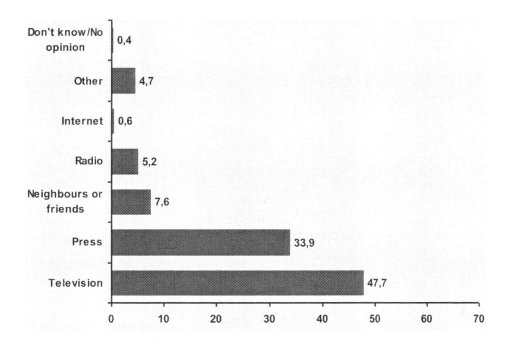

**Figure 10.** What was your main source of information about the fires?

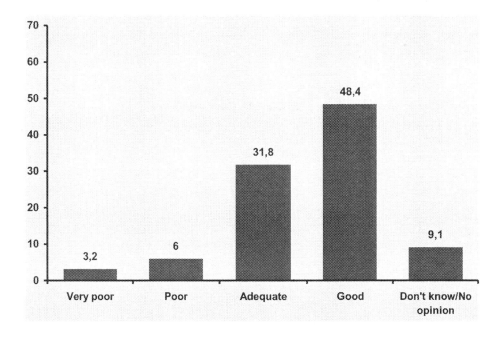

**Figure 11.** What is your opinion of the information about the fires in general?

## 7. Future projections and expectations

The opinion of a large majority of those interviewed with regard to the possibility of a similar situation arising in the future is that this may well be the case (see Figure 12), and that this was no one-off or isolated event. When this result was crossed with that obtained for the evaluation of the seriousness of the damage caused and that for the expression of the psychological impact of the experience, it can be deduced that forest fires are seen as a problem of the first order, there being a high probability of repetition, with considerable damage resulting.

**Figure 12.** Do you think the situation could repeat itself this year?

## 8. Measures to be taken, from the standpoint of the local population

The majority of those interviewed think that more preventive measures (27.5%) and more police surveillance and intervention (27.8%) are necessary. It is curious to note that respondents attach little importance to education and information, without which the necessary change referred to earlier on will never come about, or that they show little trust in current policing measures (see Figure 13). The results in this section are similar to those of the 2005 study, although there are some differences between the two. The two main measures suggested are the same: surveillance and prevention (clearance of undergrowth). In the present study, however, greater importance is attached to policing measures, which is consistent with the finding of the present study that the main cause attributed to the fires is wilful criminal action, as has been explained above.

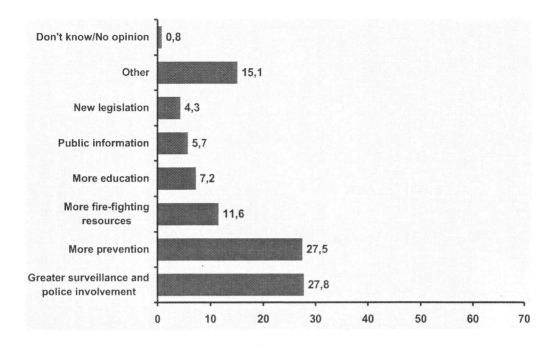

**Figure 13.** What do you think are the most important measures to be taken
now to prevent damage caused by forest fires?

In short, the finger of accusation in the case of these fires points to the hand of man,
basically to criminal actions or carelessness, with the responsibility for prevention then being
seen to rest on the authorities. There is a demand for further surveillance and policing
measures in order to combat criminal behaviour, and further preventive policies are seen as
necessary, but there seems to be little appreciation of the responsibility of society as a whole
and the importance of raising not only the awareness, but also the level of commitment of the
population, regarding the fight against forest fires and the changes required from the
standpoint of risk prevention. People are highly critical and demanding of the relevant
authorities, and have very little trust in the way in which the non-arable land in Galicia is
currently managed, particularly when this corresponds to the authorities, at whatever level,
with more government intervention being required. On the other hand, they are far less
demanding and critical when it comes to the role played by the population as a whole, local
residents and land owners in the response to these forest fires.

Finally, the findings of the survey are extremely revealing: although 57.4% of those
interviewed or members of their family own land, 4.5% belong to communal associations that
own non-arable land and only 17.2% have no relationship with non-arable land, responsibility
is basically perceived to correspond to the authorities. This is evidence of a lack of social co-
responsibility with the problems of managing one's own environment.

## DISCUSSION

In the light of the above, what lessons can be learnt? What kind of guidelines can be applied to the policies and management of risk communication in the case of forest fires?

### The Relationship between Trust and Communication

A major concern is the development of public trust in sources of information and in the institutions or organisations that manage crisis intervention, because risk perception determines the way people react to different kinds of risk. Trust in institutions and their products decreases the perceived risk (Frewer, 2003). Trust is of particular importance in those circumstances in which people feel they have little control over any potential damage (e.g. fires that are fanned by high temperatures or wind, drought or the risk deriving from natural causes).

Trust in institutions can only develop through the implementation of transparent decision-making processes in the sphere of risk management, which in turn implies that the values held by society should in no way be excluded from risk analysis, this being due to the fact that society operates on the basis of a rationality that is essentially social in nature, contextualised in a situation of risk and conditioned by cultural and local factors. People prefer to have information that they can then use to determine the personal relevance of a given risk (Frewer, 2003).

So how can greater trust on the part of society be achieved? A key factor in this regard is the communications policy adopted. To this end a system of coordination is needed, which will largely depend on the work of the people involved, particularly those responsible for making decisions. Regardless of the strategy adopted, if goals are to be reached the person or persons in charge of communication must respect three basic principles that apply to any communications strategy:

*Credibility*: Since this concerns official information, there must be a relationship of trust between the source from which the information proceeds and the target or general public receiving it;

*Context*: The characteristics of the environments in which the information is transferred must be respected. In the case of an emergency resulting from a forest fire, prompt and accurate public information is the key to reducing uncertainty in the population and organising operational tasks in the most efficient way possible without public pressure demanding to know what is going on or what has happened.

*Continuity*: Public information should not be a one-off or occasional event. Permanent links need to be set up between the authorities and the general public or target community, using the channels selected for this purpose.

Furthermore, when designing communication campaigns one of the factors that need to be taken into account is time, i.e. when communication with the public should be established. In this respect, communication initiatives can largely be categorised as being reactive or preactive (McComas, 2004):

*Reactive communication* occurs when the public or the mass media focus their attention on a specific topic, or in response to a sudden outbreak of fire. One of the problems of reactive communication is that it may come too late to protect people from the risk in question.

*Preactive communication* calls attention to a potential or existing risk and proposes an agenda for discussion, makes recommendations and suggests a format for the exchange of information. Preactive communication provides the wherewithal for deeper discussion and debate. Nevertheless, preactive communication can also alert people to a risk of which they were unaware, which may be a disadvantage, particularly in the case of risks that pose no significant threat to human health or the environment. Generally speaking, preactive communication is more efficient in obtaining the trust of the general population and that of risk managers, whilst at the same time satisfying any ethical and legal requirements. This kind of communication could be used to establish a debate into land planning and the definition of land use that is more in line with forest fire risk prevention policies.

## Directing Communication

Communication can be channelled in various ways, including:

- ➢ *"Face-to-face"*: by means of meetings, the viewing of films or videos about managing or combating forest fires, etc. This format allows for direct interaction with those concerned and a high degree of control over the message being delivered.
- ➢ *"Public forums"*: this involves organising and participating in seminars, talks, informational sessions and meetings. It allows for interaction with the audience and shares the same advantages as personal communication, but in both cases it should be noted that this audience will always be a limited one.
- ➢ *"Mass media"*: through interviews, press conferences, announcements and advertisements in the press, etc. The main advantage of this form of communication is the size of the audience that can be reached, but effectiveness can be reduced if control over the message is lost.
- ➢ *"Internet"*: e-formats (web-pages, e-mailing, etc.) reach a wide audience and control over the message is higher than through the mass media, but effective communication depends on the trust and credibility that the communicator is able to create (see McComas, 2004).

## Reviewing Action Plans and Crisis Coordination

Institutions need to carry out an in-depth review of their action plans and coordination strategies for crisis situations in order to provide a rapid response to the demand for information, rethinking their criteria and attitudes towards communication to ensure that this will be immediate and visible to those affected by the crisis in question. Communication in crisis situations requires a high degree of agility in order to respond to the demands of the media, as well as a particular sensitivity towards individuals or groups of people negatively affected by the situation. Whenever a serious and negative event or unforeseen situation arises, the tendency is to commit certain mistakes from the point of view of institutional communication, this resulting in the loss of trust and credibility on the part of the society concerned, which once lost is extremely difficult to regain.

In this regard, although in the initial stages of the crisis situation there is little information or quantifiable data available, information should always be provided about what is known and about the decisions made with a view to solving the problem. People expect answers and solutions, and the situation can become socially stressful if there is a perception that not enough is being done in the face of a risk situation, or if what is being done is inappropriate. Care should be taken to avoid speculating with undocumented hypotheses: what is needed is a response, which should be swift but considered when rumours or erroneous information abound. Anticipation and preparation are also of the essence. Perceptions are important, and so, therefore, are the words and gestures that help to form them (Laureau, 2003).

An oft-repeated mistake in these cases is to apply a policy of "*news blackout*". If the authorities do not provide the necessary information, the mass media will try to obtain it from other sources, the ensuing consequence being a loss of control over the message. This, however, was clearly not the case with the way in which information was handled in the forest fire crisis of 2006, when the efforts of the authorities, mindful perhaps of how previous crises had been managed, may well have exceeded the level of attention and information that any citizen could reasonably demand.

## Encouraging the Participation of the People in Environmental Matters

In the literature dealing with the social management of risks and the relationships between science, technology and society (López Cerezo & Luján, 2000), various procedures for ensuring deliberation and social participation are described, which bring together managers, technical assessors, interest groups and the general public. Although they differ in status with regard to the crisis, according to whether they are decision-making, consultative or information-gathering and disseminating in nature, public hearings, opinion surveys, negotiated management, citizen and expert panels, consensus meetings, hearings or public advisory committees are some of the formulae used for the purpose of analysis and decision making in matters concerning the management of the environment and the application of technology. People are informed, debate and give their verdicts, recommendations or considerations, or reach consensus and establish a degree of co-responsibility, according to the extent to which the chosen formula for participation allows for involvement in the matter. These formulae, even at the least participative level, when they serve only to provide information, nevertheless enable the general public to become aware of the discourse and opinions of the experts, stimulate interest in the problem or problems, systematise discussion and exchange points of view with the authorities, and may even go so far as to stimulate cooperation between the parties concerned. They each demand a different level of education and information from those participating in them, and the content and nature of this participation also varies, but there can be no doubt that they all provide access to the problems in question and favour reflection on them, whilst at the same time enhancing visibility of the topics under discussion, promoting debate and the rigorous evaluation of any proposals put forward. They allow for the inclusion in this debate of not only expert knowledge and opinion, but also the personal experience of the people taking part in it and the proposals of different interest groups. They promote the visibility and evaluation of the facts and values involved, as well as of the possible options and responses. In this way they can also be seen as a form of social learning.

This type of formulae, two of the most well-known being the *Consensus Conference* and the *Citizens' Panel*, have had a successful history since their origin in Denmark and Northern Europe. They have brought the problems surrounding the applications of technological and scientific advances closer to the general public, and have endowed socio-political participation with a totally new concept (López Cerezo, Méndez Sanz & Todt, 1998).

Of interest too are the experiences in the Autonomous Region of Andalusia (Spain) with their so-called *Ecobarometers*, programmes which since 2001 have given a stable format to surveys on perception, attitudes and behaviour in environmental matters. *Public opinion studies* on the perceptions, sensitivities, attitudes, knowledge and appraisals of the general public, as well as making the communication process more effective, also help to structure debate and organised deliberation.

In the framework of democratic societies any measure taken to drive forward the processes of citizens' participation not only possesses the instrumental goal of reducing resistance and making it easier for the authorities to achieve their objectives, but also has the value of being a formula that enhances the cohesion of society and cements ideas of citizenship by means of a commitment to making decisions that affect the future of the population as a whole and of the environment. The analysis of the opinions and perceptions of the population by means of surveys provides data that enable problems to be identified, concerns to be detected, evaluation criteria to be determined and the impact of specific measures to be appraised, as well as facilitating the design of strategies for communicating with the population and responding to their concerns.

The question arises, in the present case, of what could be the possible ways of structuring public participation in the process of managing the risks deriving from forest fires. If the associations of communal owners of non-arable land, interest groups in the forestry sector and experts already take part with certain frequency in discussion forums with the authorities, then it would seem to make sense to include the opinions of other social groups and members of the general public concerned about the future of no-arable land by making them possible participants in the process.

The members of the general public and their views have to be incorporated into the discussion on territorial planning and the uses and functions of land, a discussion which is not only aimed at reducing the risk of forest fires, but can also be used to direct attention to other problems: floods, town planning or the economic revitalisation of rural areas along sustainable lines.

## Bringing the Debate to the Schools

The educational system is responsible for establishing the framework in which members of the school community can gain awareness of the immediate problems of their environment. Schools have to enable a global approach to local problems, and in the specific case with which this study is concerned, this means an approach to forest fires in which preventive measures are placed within the context of sustainable management of the environment. Programmes, projects and activities dealing with the specific problem in question may be an appropriate platform from which to undertake an analysis of forest fires, floods or other environmental risks affecting the area. Environmental problems demand a global approach.

The educational approach to the problem of forest fires should take into account, amongst others, the following aspects:

Encourage reflection on territorial planning and organisation and risk prevention, with attention being paid to all the various facets involved: legislation, awareness-raising and changes in people's customs and habits, structural measures such as the organisation and planning of non-arable land and the territory, limitations on certain land uses, economic aspects to increase the value of non-arable land, and the socio-cultural aspects involved.

Promote a forestry culture, which at present is lacking in the region, and a culture of the land that will guarantee a reduction in the wilful starting of forest fires and the combustibility of non-arable land.

Form part of the general debate on the land and what would constitute a sustainable line of development with regard to territorial planning and organisation and specific practices. Sustainability in this case is understood as being ecological sustainability with uses that do not exhaust resources and conserve the environment; economic sustainability that make prosperity possible whilst at the same time restricting and preventing actions causing an irreversible impact, with bearable sacrifices; and social sustainability that channels participation and social consensus with regard to the making of decisions.

Cover all the various elements that constitute risk. An understanding of the technical language of risk is one of the pre-requisites for successful communication and participation in social debates. The technical analysis of risk involves concepts such as the dangerousness of possible events, vulnerability and the exposure of people, property and ecosystems. It attempts to evaluate and establish the most appropriate measures and guidelines for the preventive management of risk. Dangerousness is determined by analysing the probability of the event, its causes and its potential intensity or seriousness, whilst the definition of zones and moments of risk enable risk maps to be produced. From the point of view of the social understanding of risk, however, the most interesting concept is that of vulnerability or the degree of susceptibility and proneness to damage or losses, whether of lives or of the economic or environmental goods exposed to risk. This a concept that facilitates consideration of possible responses, actions and measures designed to reduce the level of risk; it makes it possible to consider the importance of the degree of awareness and knowledge of the populations exposed to risk. It is a concept with a markedly social content that incorporates the idea of protection and the response measures that society is prepared to adopt in order to reduce the possibility of suffering damage. It also enables concepts of social responsibility in the field of prevention to be introduced, and to differentiate between spheres of action in the natural and social environment.

# REFERENCES

APAS & IDEM (2003). *Estudio sociológico sobre la percepción de la población española hacia los incendios forestales* [A sociological study on the perception of the Spanish population towards forest fires] An on-line publication that can be downloaded from the Association's webpage: www.idem21.com/descargas/pffs/IncendiosForestales.pdf.

Beck, U. (2002). *La Sociedad del riesgo* [Risk society]. Madrid: Siglo XXI.

Bechmann, G. (2004). Riesgo y sociedad postmoderna [Risk and post-modern society]. In J.L. Luján and J. Echeverría (Eds.), *Gobernar los Riesgos. Ciencia y Valores en la Sociedad del Riesgo* (pp. 17-34). Madrid: Biblioteca Nueva (OEI).

Díaz-Fierros, F.; Balboa, X. & Barreiro Rivas, X.L. (Eds.) (2007). *Por unha Nova Cultura Forestal fronte aos Incendios. Informes e Conclusións* [For a New Forest Culture regarding Fires. Reports and Conclusions] . Santiago de Compostela, Spain: Consello da Cultura Galega.

Doiz Reus, M.L. (2005). Percepción de la sociedad ante el problema de los incendios forestales [Society's perception of the problem of forest fires]. Presented at the summer school *"Paisaje, Sociedad e Defensa contra Incendios"* organised by the Universidad Internacional de Andalucia in August 2005.

Frewer, L.J. (2003). Consumer science implications for the interface of risk assessment and risk management. *Supplement, Human and Environmental Risk Assessment, The Interface between Risk Assessment and Risk Management.*

García Mira, R. & Lema Blanco, I. (2008). The role of information and trust in the process of risk perception. In E. Edgerton, O. Romice & C. Spencer (eds.), *Environmental psychology: Putting research into practice.* Newcastle upon Tyne, UK: Cambridge Scholars Publishing.

García-Mira, R.; Real, J.E.; Uzzell, D.; Blanco, G. & Losada, M.D. (2005). Exploring cognitive representations of citizens in areas affected by the Prestige disaster. In B. Martens and A. Keul (eds.) *Exploring Social Innovation: Planning, Building, Evaluation (pp. 137-145).* Göttingen, Germany: Hogrefe & Huber.

García-Mira, R.; Real, J.E.; Uzzell, D.; San Juan, C. & Pol, E. (2006). Coping with a threat to quality of life: the case of the 'Prestige' disaster. *Revue Européenne de Psychologie Appliquée, 56(1),* 53-60.

García-Mira, R.; García González, C. & Varela Mallou, J. (2007). *La percepción social dos incendios forestais 2006 na poboación galega* [The social perception of the 2006 forest fires amongst the Galician population] . Unpublished report. Department of Methodology and Social Psychology. University of Santiago de Compostela, Spain.

Hallman, W.K. & Wandersman, A. (1992). Attribution of Responsibility and Individual and Collective Coping with Environmental Threats. *Journal of Social Issues, 48 (4),* 101-118

Laureau, C. (2003). *Acción, reacción y emoción ante la catástrofe del "Prestige"* [Action, reaction and emotion in the face of the "Prestige" catastrophe]. In: http://www.bursonmarsteller.es/pdf/Prestige.pdf

López Cerezo, J.A.; Luján, J.L. (2000). *Ciencia y Política del Riesgo* [Science and Risk Policy]. Madrid: Alianza Editorial.

López Cerezo, J.A.; Méndez Sanz, J.A. & Todt O. (1998). Participación pública en política tecnológica. Problemas y perspectivas [Public participation in Technological Policy. Problems and Perspectives], *Arbor,* CLIX, 627 (March), 279-308.

Luján, J.L. & Echeverría, J. (Eds.) (2004). *Ciencia y valores en la sociedad del riesgo* [Science and values in the risk society]. Madrid: Biblioteca Nueva.

McComas, K. *(2004).* When even the 'best-laid' plans go wrong: Strategic risk communication for new and emerging risks. *European Molecular Biology Organization, 5 (Special Issue),* 61-64.

Moffatt, S.; Hoeldke, B. & Pless-Mulloli, T. (2003). Local environmental concerns among communities in North-East England and South Hessen, Germany: the influence of proximity to industry. *Journal of Risk Research, 6 (2),* 125-144.

Peters, R.; Covello, V.T. & McCalumm, D.B. (1997). The determinants of trust and credibility in environmental risk communication: An empirical study. *Risk Analysis,* 17(1), 43-54

Petts, J. ; Horlick-Jones, T. ; Murdock, G. (2001) *Social Amplification of Risk. The Media and The Public.* Research report 329/01. London: Health and Safety Executive.

Renn, O. (1991). Risk communication and the social amplification of risk. In J. Kaspeston and P. J. Stallen (Eds), *Communicating risk to the public* (pp. 287-324). Dordrecht, The Netherlands: Kluwer.

Renn, O.; Burns, W.J.; Kasperton, J.; Kasperton, R. & Slovic, P. (1992). The Social Amplification of Risk, Theoretical Foundations and Empirical Applications. *Journal of Social Issues, 48 (4),* 137-160.

Short, J. F. (1989). On defining, describing and explaining elephants (and reactions to them): Hazards, disasters, and risk analysis. *Mass Emergencies and Disasters,* 7, 397-418

Tretting, L. & Musham, C (2000). Is Trust a Realistic Goal of Environmental Risk Communication? *Environment and Behaviour,* 32 (3), 410-425.

Varela Mallou, J. (2005). *Percepción social dos incendios forestais* [The social perception of forest fires]. Unpublished study. Department of Methodology and Social Psychology. University of Santiago de Compostela, Spain.

Williams, B.L.; Brown, S. & Greenberg, M. (1999). Determinants of trust perceptions among residents surrounding the Savannah River Nuclear Weapons Site. *Environment & Behavior,* 31, 354-371.

In: Applied Psychology Research Trends
Editor: Karl H. Kiefer, pp.211-228

ISBN 978-1-60456-372-6
© 2008 Nova Science Publishers, Inc.

*Chapter 10*

# FARMERS AND THE ENVIRONMENT: OF THE INDIVIDUAL PRACTICE TO THE SOCIAL PRACTICES

## *Elisabeth Michel-Guillou**

Center for Psychological Research, University of Bretagne Occidentale, Brest (France)

## ABSTRACT

We are currently witnessing a growing concern regarding lifestyle and a raised awareness in relation to preserving the threatened natural environment. Through its modes of production and its particular relationship with nature, agriculture is directly affected by these concerns. Farming is not the only source of some environmental matters, but because of this particular relationship with natural environment, the media has held it largely responsible, and therefore, so has society. Out of concern for the environnement as well as to restore public confidence in agricutlure or agricultural practices, pro-environmental approaches have appeared and/or developed (organic farming, integrated farming, territorial farming contracts, watershed operations....). A feature that these voluntary actions in favour of the environment have in common is that they are officially referenced, checked and socially recognized. However, despite the rapid development and improvement of these approaches, changes in farming practices seem difficult to bring about and remain a minority.

In that sense, a psychosociological and environmental study was conducted to understand the sociocognitive processes which would allow to distinguish farmers committed in pro-environmental action from farmers not committed in this kind of action. To understand these processes, we were attempting to identify how farmers (committed or not committed in pro-environmental approaches) perceived their environment and their profession. These phenomena were analyzing through the study of the social representations which are defined as modalities of knoledges constructed and

---

* Elisabeth.Michel@univ-brest.fr

shared by a social group. This theoretical approach was privileged especially because of the close relationship between social representations and practices.

In this chapter, we would like to show the interest of a collective approach in the explanation of pro-environmental behaviours which takes into account indivduals as "social subjects" (in contrast to an individual approach based on emotions, responsability, individual values…). Thus, after a short presentation of the agriculture-environment relationship to introduce the context of the study, we will present the theoretical approach of social representations and its interest to answer our objective. Finally, we will stress on the main results which highlight that the representation of the environment remains basically identical between farmers, and it is closely bounded to the definition of the profession. In fact, the commitment in pro-environmental action appears to be more reasoned by the need to restore a positve social image of the profession than by the need to protect a threatened natural environment. And in turn, this is this commitment which seems to trigger a more important interest in the environment.

# INTRODUCTION: FRAMEWORK OF THE RESEARCH: THE SOCIAL AND INSTITUTIONAL REQUEST

In 1996, the transmissibility of BSE[1] ("Mad cow" disease) to humans was announced by the media. This phenomenon triggered a process of doubts and controversies regarding the system of agricultural production. French consumers have become mistrustful and demand more openness in agricultural practices Beyond the controversy about the health and gustative quality of the agricultural products for humans or animals, non respectful practices towards the environment are also called into question, and even more that they can be at the root of a deterioration of products quality (Jollivet, 2001).

With regard to this statement of fact, an experimental program of quality and environment management, which entilted "*Garanties of quality in crop farms of Picardie*" (*Qualit'Terre®*), is implemented. This project has been put in place by the *Chambers of Agriculture of Picardie* in collaboration with *INRA*[2] and *Agro-transfert*[3]. It aimed to make recognize aptitudes of farmers for satisfy requirements of a "good agricultural practices" guideline and their commitment to apply it. In the end, it allowed farmers to qualify the global running of their farm, in other words, the recognition by a third organization that their competencies were in accordance with the specified requirements (*i.e.*, guaranty of farm quality). This program is one of the first recent applications implemented with the aim of restoring the link of confidence between farmers and society (Aubry, Galan, & Mazé, 2005).

Within the framework of this program, the *INRA* constituted a pluridisciplinary team of researchers with economists, agronomists, zootechnicians, ergonomists, managers and psychosocologists. The role of the *INRA* was to help to adapt international standards of quality and environment management to crop farms, and to take part in the conception of advice and accompanying methodologies to support adoption by farmers and their economic surrounding (*e.g.*, suppliers, customers). More specifically, the role of the psychosociologists

---

[1] Bovine Spongiform Encephalopathy

[2] National Institute for Agronomic Research

[3] Organisation aiming to enhance the status of research for agricultural development.

was to analyze the motivation and the interest of farmers to commit themselves to pro-environmental practices. Consequently we have directed our research towards the field of perceptions, evaluations and representations of the natural environment by farmers. The application of the social representation theory to this study could be a relevant approach in so far as, by definition, social representation is a form of socially elaborated, shared and practical knowledge that allows for the construction of a reality that is common to a social group (Jodelet, 1999). Because of this practical knowledge, the study of social representation of the environment and of their profession by farmers themselves could be relevant to understanding the farmer-environment relationships.

Among environmental matters, water quality is a major environmental problem (*e.g.*, by its geographical and humans consequences) which justifies our interest. Agriculture is really involved in water pollution by nitrates, phosphates and/or pesticides. Therefore, the media and society have held it largely responsible. So, understanding the farmer-water relationships was unavoidable to understand the relationships between farmers and the environment.

Finally, nowadays, there are various pro-environmental actions (*i.e.*, actions aimed at changing agricultural practices in favour of the environment) such as *Quali'Terre®*. Consequently, we have had to take into account and to compare various pro-environmental actions (*e.g.*, organic farming, integrated farming, watershed operations, territorial farming contracts), and therefore, to compare different levels or different forms of commitments.

This chapter aims to present the issue of the relationship farmers-environment from a psycho-sociological and environmental approach. Thus, the first section will be devoted to a historic presentation of this relationship in the French context. The second section will present the content of the social representation of the environment. This second part will show us that when we talk ecology to farmers, they answer in terms of profession. Then, the third section will introduce the representation and the evaluation that farmers have about the own professional activity. Thus, we will show the importance of the social image in the choice that farmers make in terms of agricultural and pro-environmental practices. This choice has, in turn, an impact on the perception of environmental problems; we will consider that in the section four.

# I. HISTORIC AND ISSUE OF THE RELATIONSHIPS FARMER - ENVIRONMENT

Nowadays, the environment is an increasing social preoccupation. Society is more and more concerned by its lifestyle and its quality of life. Thus, there is a raised awareness in relation to preserving the threatened natural environment. This growing interest for ecological problems is bounded to the fear that non respectful practices towards the environment provoke. Through its intensive modes of production, through its function of providing food, and through its specific use of ecological resources, agriculture is directly concerned by theses preoccupations.

Historically, since the end of World War II, the necessity of feeding the population and of remaining competitive at an international level have encouraged farmers to produce more and at a lower cost. The increase in productivity has led to physical alterations of the countryside, such as the levelling of banks, the removal of hedges and the draining of wet zones which, twenty years later, have proved to be dramatic for the ecosystem. Before awareness of consequences of intensives practices of modern agriculture for the environment, agriculture was considered as "protector" of landscape. But as farmers have defined themselves as "industrialists" through an over production, they have opened a space to be thought as "polluters" (Kalaora, 1997). Furthermore, these unfavourable practices towards the environment are even more called into question that they are at the root of a degradation of product quality and consequently become a growing concern for human health (Jollivet, 2001).

Moreover, because of its privileged relationship with nature, and more especially with water, soil, biodiversity and the landscapes (Jollivet, 2001), the responsibility and the role of agriculture have clearly come to the forefront of public debate (Kalaora, 1997; Katerji, Bruckler, & Debaeke, 2002). It is thus the impact that farming can have on these interdependent elements that is being questioned.

Sensitization about the imperilled water resource has taken place under media pressure. Though their evaluation of water problem is sometimes biased, the majority of farmers are aware of this matter (Michel-Guillou, 2005). Water is a major environmental problem in terms of quality as well as quantity. In terms of quantity, agricultural sector is one of the first consumers of water; it is thus essentially a problem of irrigation (Katerji et al., 2002). Concerning quality of the resource, it deals with nitrates and pesticides levels. Farming is only one cause of water pollution; urban areas and industries are also actors of this degradation; but because of its particular relationship with nature, it is largely held responsible (Katerji et al, 2002).

France and the larger European community can be credited with a number of measures aimed at preserving the environment quality. But the persistence of environmental problems shows the limits of regulations and operating standards. Beyond regulations and other legislative of normative texts, several farmers and farming-related organizations have decided to take additional voluntary steps (Sebillotte, 1999). In the concern to respect the environment and health quality of products, as well as to offset the image of "farmer-polluter", pro-environmental efforts has developed and taken hold in the farming world (*e.g.*, integrated agriculture, territorial farming contracts). However, despite the rapid development and improvement of these approaches in the face of economic constraints, changes in farming practices seem difficult to bring about and remain a minority (Mazé, Aubry, & Papy, 2000). Thus, as so far as some external barriers are removed (*e.g.*, economic or material), we postulate that psychological or social factors are likely to prevent the evolution of agricultural practices because of a pro-environmental policy involves a sacrifice of values and interests (Montada & Kals, 2000), and more especially, it frequently entails abandoning one's own interests in favour of the common interest (Hardin, 1968).

This research, then, is carried out within the context of the opposing methods of conventional farming, bounded to intensive practices, and "pro-environmental" farming, socially committed[4] to new practices which promote a greater respect for the environment. This categorization allowed us to distinguish farmers who maintained conventional practices

---

[4] The expression "socially committed" refers to socially recognized behaviours, in contrast with those of farmers who maintained traditional practices. They may in fact individually adopt certain environmentally respectful behaviours but they do not credit them with social recognition.

from farmers who adopted pro-environmental practices, committed in pro-environmental actions which are officially indexed and socially recognized[5].

With regard to this review, this research aims to compare farmers' social representations of the environment, and their attitudes and beliefs towards water quality, according to the practices implemented. It aims to highlight sociocognitve processes which would allow us to distinguish committed farmers to pro-environmental actions from not committed farmers to this kind of actions. In the following section, after a short presentation of the social representations theory, we begin the analysis of farmer-environment relationships by a presentation of the content of farmers' social representation of the environment.

## II. FARMERS' SOCIAL REPRESENTATION OF THE ENVIRONMENT

### 2.1. The Theory of Social Representations

Because of it exists different agricultural practives towards the environment (*e.g.*, organic agriculture, integrated agriculture), we have supposed that it could exist different social representation of the environment.

The theory of social representations has been developed in first by Moscovici (1961)[6]. By definition (Abric, 2001a, 2001b; Jodelet, 1999; Moscovici, 1961, 1988, 1998), social representations correspond to a specific form of knowledge conveyed by society which allows individuals to understand their social and physical environment; they give them a vision of the world. They do not correspond to an objective representation of reality but to a social construct of a common reality (Jodelet, 1999; Moscovici, 1988, 1998, 2001). They are social because they are the product and the reflection of a social process (*e.g.*, interactions, communication), and they are shared by individuals belonging to the same group. Thus, social representations constitute the public image of the members of a specific group. They provide the group members with their specificity and identity (Guimelli, 1994; Rateau, 2000). Furthermore, the representational process develops in a particular context of social interaction (Doise, 1985). Therefore, the representations are highly linked to context: their signification depends on the context in which they occur (*i.e.*, the immediate context) and their elaboration depends on the context in which they circulate (*i.e.*, the social and ideological context) (Abric & Guimelli, 1998).

Social representations have several functions. According to Moscovici (1961), two main functions are linked to social representations: they contribute both "to the processes of formation of behaviours, and to the orientation of social communications" (p.75). For Grize, Vergès and Silem (1987), they allow us to organize our conducts and our views by sharing ideas, values and norms. They preserve the social link in which they develop and evolve (Farr, 1984). They also allow individuals to interpret and to explain the world as well as to be situated in an environment and to control it (Jodelet, 1999). Consequently, social

---

[5] Pro-environmental actions are defined as "actions which contribute towards environmental preservation and/or conservation" (Axelrod & Lehman, 1993, p.153). The following actions are taken into account in this study: organic agriculture, integrated agriculture and *Quali'Terre*®, watershed operations, charter quality systems and local groups such as protection of the wildlife, group of cynegetic interest, association of water, etc.

[6] A second edition has been published in 1976.

representations mediate our relationship with the external world. Finally, they allow groups to preserve their specificity and they allow individuals to justify their standpoints and their behaviours (Doise, 1999).

Taking into account this latter point, representations can be subjected to individual variability (Doise, 1985; Doise, 1999; Doise, 1992; Clémence, Doise & Lorenzi-Cioldi, 1994). In this sense, social representations are viewed as generating and organizing principles of individual standpoints which. Thus, they provide individuals with common points of reference which allow them to regulate symbolic relations. But according to the importance of the object of representation for people, and according to their social integration, individual standpoints towards the object will vary (Clémence et al., 1994).

Finally, various authors (Abric, 2001c; Flament, 1987, 2001b; Guimelli, 2001, 1998; Jodelet, 1989) have shown that practices and social representations influence each other. The nature of their connection is determined by the characteristics of the situation, in other words, by the autonomy of actors and the effective charge of the situation (Abric, 2001c). Social representations determine behaviours when the effective charge is strong or when the individuals have certain autonomy. On the contrary, when individuals are in a highly constrained situation, either socially or materially, practices and representations begin to interact. If the new practices appear to contradict the value system and representations of individuals, they will be led to determine the reversibility of the situation in order to adapt their behaviours. In this case, practices will determine representations. If the situation is judged irreversible, social representation will be led to change (Flament, 2001a).

Consequently, understanding the various representations between the given actors allows us to identify the different ways of managing and reacting to environmental issues, and the subsequent potential conflicts. So in a first time, we sought to know if it might have different representations of the environment which would explain that there are different agricultural practices towards the environment.

## 2.2. The Social Representation of the Environment

The social representation of the environment is in complete evolution. For farmers, the environment has always been a part of their day-to-day practices but nowadays, the relationships between agriculture and environment are evolving[7]. Farmers, who are seen as "nature's gardeners" (Thiébaut, 1994), are held more and more responsible for the environment. Agricultural practices towards landscape management or the protection of natural resources have been very controversial for a number of years; the were called into question with the Common Agricultural Policy (CAP) in 1992, and consequently, they have sometimes changed in favour of a greater respect for the environment. This has led to a progressive transformation of the social representation (Michel-Guillou, 2006a; Michel-Guillou & Moser, 2006).

The social representation of the environment is structured and organized on the natural environment. Thus, it is link with words such as "water", "respect", "land", "nature" and "landscapes" (Michel-Guillou, 2006a; Michel-Guillou & Moser, 2006). It could be a

---

[7] In the pragmatic relationship between agriculture and the environment, or in the view thate the society has of this relationship which involves an evolution of agricultural practices and attitudes (Thiébaut, 1994).

collective representation, shared by all groups of society. However, the absence of words which refer to "built environment" and the presence of words like "land" make us think that it is not only stereotyped cognitions but also a specific way of thinking of farmers. "Love of land" is a fundamental value of farmer's work (Mendras, 1995). This author explains this valorisation by affective and socio-economic factors. Thus, the social representation of the environment conveys not only a relation to the nature which would be linked to the pleasure of the living surrounding but it is also a relation to the land which induces an utilitarian function. In this case, the environment is not only perceived as natural surroundings to be respected but also as a personal and economic resource to be preserved (Weiss, Moser, & German, 2006). This consensus amongst farmers concerning their representation, regardless of the practices implemented, makes it difficult to conclude that the adoption of pro-environmental farming practices is specifically related to ideologies that promote respect for the environment.

According to Flament (1999), two groups of a same population can have a representation of a given object basically identical, but for circumstantial reasons, for example different individual practices, some elements of the representation (*i.e.*, non fundamental elements) can differ. In our population, differences can be observed according to the farming practices implemented. First, farmers who committed to pro-environmental actions evoke more often the expression "integrated agriculture"[8] in relation to the environment than farmers who maintained traditional practices. Instead of "integrated agriculture", the latter prefer talk about "protection" (*i.e.*, protecting the environment instead of reasoning the practices towards the environment), a term with a more general and pragmatic connotation. Second, the evocation of "pollution" appears more important in the representation of "pro-environmental" farmers than in the representation of "conventional" farmers. Quite obviously, awareness of all forms of pollution seems to be more prevalent for farmers who adopt pro-environmental practices than for farmers who are still engaged in conventional practices. Thus, each type of practices infers different references, specific for some farmers (*i.e.*, pro-environmental) and conversely, normative or of common sense for the others (*i.e.,* conventional). In the first group, a functional dimension of the representation is more particularly activated; in the second group without specific practices socially recognized towards the environment a normative dimension, referring to norms or ideological positions, is predominant (Michel-Guillou, 2006a).

More precisely (*see*, figure 1), we have shown that according to the type of pro-environmental actions, different standpoints towards the environment appear. For example, farmers who committed to "*integrated agriculture*" talk about their own practices which refer to their identity. Farmers who committed to "*organic agriculture*" evoke "ecology" which traduces the ideology of this group (Giraudel & Caplat, 1995). This action exists for the beginning of the 20th century. Thus, the environmentalist conception, based on respect of the environment, takes root for a long time in the group, and anchor through the agricultural practices. Farmers who committed to "*local groups*" refer to "pollution" and "public image". Referring to pollution is not surprising because these farmers are committed to this type of actions to deal with particular problems at a local level (*e.g.*, water pollution in the case of

---

[8] This expression does not specifically refer to the pro-environmental action called "*Integrated agriculture*", but to an expression in fashion which indicates the new practices which take into account the needs of the environment and its natural resources.

watershed operations). Finally, Farmers who committed in *"charter quality system"* talk about general aspects of the environment and its resources (*i.e.*, landscape, wildlife, plants). These conventional evocations can be explained by the fact that, conversely to the other pro-environmental actions, not many practices distinguish these farmers from conventional farmers. Thus, the identification to specific practices and the elaboration of a particular professional identity are difficult to implement. This is why these farmers refer to common values, beliefs and cognitions of the representation. Finally, this analysis allow us to identify individual variations in the social representation of the environment according to the social anchoring (Doise, 1992) and the socio-historic relationships with it (Roussiau & Bonardi, 2002 ; Roussiau & Renard, 2003).

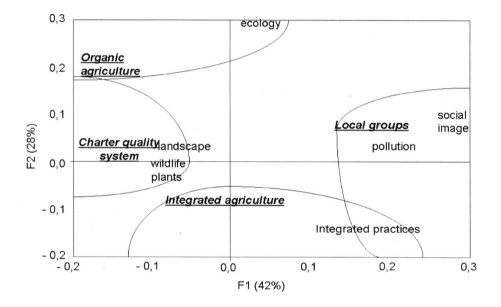

Figure 1 – Simultaneous representation of pro-environmental actions and associations of words to the environment

However, even there are different standpoints towards the environment, the social representation appears basically identical for all farmers. Environment will be a natural element to be respected. Thus, as we have ever said, this representation can not explain the commitment or the lack of commitment of farmers to pro-environmental actions. But, these results show that this representation partly refers to the definition of the profession. It is what we present in the following section.

## III. Evaluation and Representation by Farmers of their Own Professional Activity

### 3.1. The Farming Profession: A Changing Work

In the context in which agriculture evolves, we must take into account social pressure on farmers to understand their perception and definition of the profession. Professional characteristics seem to constitute a key factor in order to understand the relationships between farmers and their environment (Michel-Guillou & Weiss, in press).

The representation of the farming profession, by farmers themselves, is organized on three main thematics: 1) mechanisation, 2) low incomes, 3) the love of nature, of the land and of life (*see*, figure 2).

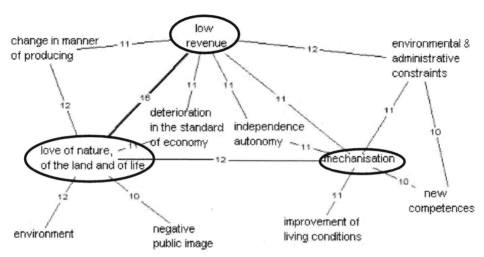

Figure 2 – Representation of the farming profession

Farmers say that: 1) the agricultural practices are improved (*e.g.* mechanisation, change in the manner of producing, acquiring new compences); 2) the economic conditions are deteriorated (*e.g.* deterioration in the standard of economy, low revenue, increase of investments); 3) the professional activity is based on a relationship with land anchored for generations (*e.g.*, the love of nature, of the land and of life). These three aspects of the profession refer to the three dimensions which constitute a professional representation (Blin, 1997): the *functional dimension* through all that refers to the production and farming practices, 2) the *contextual dimension* through all that refers to the social and economic conditions; 3) the *identity dimension* through all that refers to the fundamental values.

Most of farmers are agree with this representation of the farming profession, but on the basis of these three dimensions, individual standpoints can appear according to the importance of the issue for farmers and according to their social integration (Clémence et al., 1994; Doise, 1985). Thus, for most of farmers, the image of the work is more defined in negative terms than in positive terms. In postive terms, the image refers to the main and enhanced function of the profession: "feeding the individuals". This fucntion is evoked by a majority, and it can not be called into question because it is the first function of farmers since the origin (Savy, 1999). Furthermore, the dynamis, the technicity and the exprertise of the profession are hightlighted. In negative terms, the negative social image is evoked. This image induces a malaise for farmers. Moreover, they denounce the economic, social and political dependency. With regard to this image and the evolution of farming profession, some of farmers seem to be more optimistic than the others. This vision of the profession can have an impact on the commitment to pro-environmental actions (Michel-Guillou & Weiss, in press; Weiss et al., 2006).

These different standpoints towards the farming profession can be explained by the differences of social integration which partly depends on the commitment or the non commitment of farmers in pro-environmental actions. One reason is that belonging to these subgroups is related to various behaviours, which can be socillay valued or not (Flament, 2001b). The consecutive social image of the group can then be modified. Thus, despite a negative vision of the profession, the commitment in pro-environmental actions seems to contribute to the valorisation of the public image and the restoring the link of confidence between agriculture and society (Michel-Guillou & Moser, 2006).

### 3.2. The Representation of Farming Profession according to the Practices Implemented

Then, the interest that farmers show for pro-environmantal actions seems to be linked to a search for social approbation (Michel-Guillou & Moser, 2006). And against all the evidence, ecomomic factors, such as income improvements, are not determinant factors of the commitment. They play a role but they are not decisive. On the contrary, the improvement of the social image could be perceived as a powerful determinant of the commitment. In that sense, some results showed that actions completed in the defense of farming profession, and principally in defense of identity or social cohesion, can have a greater impact on farmers than actions that invoked environmental degradation (Weiss et al., 2006). Because, the environment is linked to the profession, as we ever said, it constitutes a personal and economic resource to be preserved and maintained, before constituting a natural surrounding to be protected.

Moreover, Stern and colleagues (Stern, 2000; Stern & Dietz, 1994) have shown that the attachment ot egocentric values which are reelated to personal interests can generate a positve attitude towards the environment. This positive attitude can appear because the ecological behaviour finds its source in individual values as well as in specific beliefs about the consequences of environmental problems. The egocentric justification of the pro-environmental efforts of the farmers cannot be denied: 43,5% of the farmers justify their efforts with somme personal reasons like the imporvement of their social image, the support of agricultural advisers or economic profit. This proportion goes up to 61% if we add people who justify their behaviour at the same time with eco-centred reasons (i.e., protection of the environment and of natural resources) and human-centred ones (i.e., to allow the transmission of fertile land to future generations). It then seems that the interest people have for themselves as well as for the biosphere depends on a general attitude for the objects they value. In this case, the protection of a positive social image seems to be more important than the protection of the environment.

Finally, all farmers agree that pro-environmental efforts can improve the public image. But as we pointed before, the representation of the profession is not the same among farmers. Some of them are more optimistic than the others. It appears that farmers who maintain conventional practices have a more negative vision of the professional activity than farmers who commit in pro-environmental actions (Michel-Guillou, 2006b). For example, for these farmers, the evolution of the profession is connected with weakening of the economic situation, fall in the number of farmers, etc. Whereas, for "pro-environmental" farmers, the evolution of the work is linked to the environment, acquiring new competences, change in the manner of producing, etc. Moreover, in terms of social image, conventional farmers talk more about the negative social image. Pro-environmental farmers who talk bout the work describe the capacity of adaptation of agriculture, its dynamism, etc. They evoke more the positive side of the profession. Thus, the vision of the profession, and precisely, of the professional future can play a role in pro-environmental commitment (Weiss & al, 2006), "optimistic" farmers being likely to defending their work and so to commit in pro-environmental efforts which are more likely to improve the public image.

Protecting the environment is not a main determinant of the commitment, but it plays a role. In the last section, we consider the consequences of this commitment on environmental conscience. More precisely, we are interested on water pollution according to the practices implemented.

## IV. Farmer and Water Pollution

The media coverage of the problem of water pollution and the attribution of a major responsibility to farmers are important (Katerji et al., 2002). In this sense, the mass media want to inform and to heighten public awareness of environmental problems. But for farmers, the converse effect is observed. Most of the farmers recognize that there is a problem of water pollution, and 64% think it is a really worrying question. However, this percentage is not as high as it should be because some farmers deny the existence of this kind of problem, as a farmer says: *"I would like to say "water pollution" to you, but immediately, you are going to think: "it is agriculture which pollutes". So, I'm sorry, but I shall not say it. Certainly, it is a problem, and I am quite aware of it"*. This attitude of denial is clearly a strategy that aims to protect a positive image of their profession. These farmers do not identify with or do not want to be identified with the question of water and soil pollutions. By denying the problem, farmers protect themselves from uncomfortable feelings (Gardner & Stern, 1996) with regard to a social and environmental situation judged hard to control. And it is not really the question of the preservation of the water resource which is judged difficult to control but it is more the social and media situation with which they are confronted (*e.g.*, 70% of the farmers questioned consider that the issue is given bad coverage). Thus, conversely to some studies (Kaiser & Shimoda, 1999), the attribution of responsibility cannot explain the attitudes of farmers towards water (Michel-Guillou, 2006c).

Indeed, the awareness of a water problem and of a possible action towards it does not necessary lead to face up to their responsibilities. We have shown that there is no difference in attribution of responsibility among farmers, regardless the practices implemented (Michel-Guillou & Moser, 2006). Thus, although farmers judge important the problem water and although they partly recognize their responsibility, farmers minimize the impact of their own practices regardless industry and households. In other words, no matter which farming practices are adopted, farmers clearly see themselves as less responsible for water pollution than industry or households. According to several studies (Fransson & Gärling, 1999; Gärling, Fujii, Gärling, & Jakobsson, 2003), this seems to be an indispensable factor in adopting pro-environmental behaviour insofar as it allows one to become aware of one's acts. However, it is a matter of determining the type of personal responsibility. Kaiser and Shimoda (1999) distinguished between moral responsibility and conventional responsibility. This latter goes back to a type of responsibility that depends on norms and social expectations. This responsibility does not need a genuine awareness of the causes and consequences of one's acts. Perhaps, this is how farmers conceived their role and responsibility.

However, if the level of responsibility cannot vary according to the practices implemented, it can vary according to the level of pollution of settings (Michel-Guillou, 2005). Perception and attitudes of farmers regarding pollution are closely linked to the level of nitrates in the ground water. Farmers recognize a problem of water pollution when the level of nitrate is low. They attribute a shared responsibility to industry, households and agriculture. But this attitude does not really commit them because, at this level, the pollution is low. On the other hand, when the level of pollution increases, more than half of farmers deny the problem. As we pointed before, the deny would be explained by a lack of perceived control on the environment and it would allow farmers to protect from uncomfortable feelings (Gardner & Stern, 1996). It was a mechanism of defence or protection against an uncontrollable social situation. But this process decreases with the aggravation of the problem. Thus, as soon as the level reaches a critical threshold, they have to recognize the pollution and subsequently feel involved. In other words, they are prone to act in favour of the resolution of the problem of water quality. In conclusion, even most of farmers recognize a problem of water pollution at a local level, more than half of them do not feel involved by this problem. Thus, it is not the recognition of the problem that is determinant pour the action but, its level of gravity and the involvement of farmers regarding the problem. Furthermore, it seems exist a link between the personal implication towards water quality and the commitment in pro-environmental actions.

Farmers who adopt pro-environmental practices feel more involved towards water pollution than farmers who maintain conventional practices (Michel-Guillou & Moser, 2006). Moreover, they consider that intervention regarding this current problem is still possible and they feel personal more capable of acting towards solving it. Thus, one's evaluation of one's capacity for action seems to play an important role with regard to commitment. Even though this feeling might be conceived as a rationalization for commitment (Joule & Beauvois, 1998), it is nonetheless a powerful determinant in developing environmental awareness (Moser et al., 2004; Rouquette, 1997).

# CONCLUSION : TO RESTORE THE BEHAVIORS IN THEIR CONTEXT

Our actions depend on individual factors as well as contextual factors, linked to the social or environmental context and to the manner in which we collectively perceive and evaluate this context. We depend on a social context which involves us in a system of reference with values, norms, beliefs and ideologies that we share with the members of our groups. The question of evaluation takes us back to the idea that the way in which we perceive our environment does not correspond to an objective representation of reality but to a social construct of reality which is based on information received from the environment (Ittelson, 1973). This social construct also depends on the experiences, motivations, values, expectations and needs of the individuals or of the groups. In that sense, several studies have highlighted an inherent link between pro-environmental commitment and ideological conceptions (Poortinga, Steg, & Vlek, 2002, Steg & Sievers, 2000). These authors have shown the link between individuals' conception of nature (*e.g.*, values, beliefs) and adoption of strategies of environmental management. These beliefs are implemented through social representations which correspond to a social construct of reality (Jodelet, 1999) which provide a guide for action (Moscovici, 1961).

More particularly, as far as water is concerned, Moser and colleagues (2004) show that the implementation of preservation behaviours towards water resources depends on the awareness of the matter and on the elaboration of a diagnosis built as a function of the perception of an evolution of the state of water from a quantitative and qualitative point of view. This awareness depends on representations of the problem which are influenced by contextual characteristics and the value system of individuals and of society. Thus, adopting pro-environmental behaviours does not seem to depend on the objective perception of the problem; instead, it seems to be linked to the representation that the individuals have. Thus, in the case where the pollution is diffuse and not directly perceptible, in function of the representations and implicit norms established by the group, the individuals judge water of good quality as being polluted and polluted water as being of good quality (Moser, 1984). In the same way, we have shown that farmers are more aware of pollution if the level is low or very high, but they deny it exists if the level is average (Michel-Guillou, 2005). All these results highlight a gap between the farmers' evaluation of water quality and the reality such as she is defined in terms on standards or thresholds of pollution. Thus, analyzing the social representation of the environment and the farming profession allowed us to understand the manner in which individuals perceive and evaluate their environment, and to understand the justification of their actions or strategies of actions.

In conclusion, we postulate that the pro-environmental commitment depends on various ideological conceptions, giving value every bit as much to the environment as to personal interests. The consensual meaning that the farmers share of the environment, the general valuing of the environmental problems and the low rate of taking personal responsibility towards the water problem suggest that the farmers' commitment to pro-environmental efforts does not depend on an ideology that promotes respect for the environment. It appears that this commitment depends more on social pressure which has, as a consequence, made farmers aware of the seriousness of environmental problems, allowing them to examine the impact of their practices and of their possibility for action. In addition, the integration of "integrated practices" into their conception of the environment shows an effort to change in their relationship with nature. However, despite this social pressure, we can suppose that the commitment in pro-environmental actions also depends on different ideologies. This will explain the different kinds or levels of commitment among "pro-environmental" farmers. This could be related to the various ideological conceptions of nature (Poortinga, Steg, Vlek, 2002; Steg & Sievers, 2000). Consequently, a radical, moderate or weak commitment towards actions in favour of the environment would depend on the lifestyle of the farmers, in association with their conceptions of nature and of its resources (Douglas & Wildavsky, 1983). A conception of nature as "*ephemeral*" (*i.e.*, with degraded and precarious resources) would suppose both a high interest and a high environmental commitment. Conversely, a conception of nature as "*benign*" or "*capricious*", corresponding to an under-evaluation or a denial of environmental problems, would lead to a very weak environmental commitment. The application of the cultural theory would help explain some differences which sometimes distinguish some farmers who belong to the same group, but who act in various ways (Michel-Guillou, 2006a).

Furthermore, this study allowed us to highlight that some farmers would be ideologically more predisposed to adopt pro-environmental behaviours (*i.e.*, organic farmers). In that sense, it seems inconceivable to incite conventional farmers to become organic farmers if these ones are not quite ready to accept these efforts. In the current agricultural context, external constraints (*i.e.*, social, political and economic) make pressure on farmers to incite them to "voluntary" involve in actions which advocate a larger respect of the environment. This commitment would be more induced by the need to restore a negative social image than by the necessity to improve purchasing power or to restore the environment. However, this commitment might consequently modify the attitudes and opinions of farmers who became "pro-environmental", towards the environment and its natural resources. These ones appear to be more predisposed to act in favour of the resolution of environmental problems. This might be conceived as a rationalization of their action, which can induce increase awareness towards the environment. In this context, the adoption of new practices will have, in turn, an impact on the farmers' representations. This might explain the different standpoints towards the environment despite a fundamental common conception of it. The environment is commonly perceived as a natural element to be protected but according to the practices implemented it can be differently evaluated (*e.g.*, associated to the professional activity through integrated practices, associated to an ecologically threatened element, associated to constraints, etc.).

Finally, this study shows that the relationship between farmer and the environment is in complete evolution. This relation is dependent on the perception of farming profession. Thus, some farmers define the environment as a necessary element of their profession, as a function of the profession (*i.e.*, pro-environmental farmers and particularly organic farmers), whereas, for the others, it is linked to the quality of production (*i.e.*, taking care of the environment is making products of quality) which is declared to be the main function of their profession (Michel-Guillou & Ehrlich, 2005). Thus, not only the representation of the environment but the farming profession is just being in complete change. Although the environment, in its historical and natural dimension, is a fundamental value for all farmers, its incorporation into the work as a function is yet partly controversial. In essence, farmer has a liking for nature, the land and the life. But until the present day, nobody told him to make it his job. And whatever people say about the "nature's gardeners", the main function of farmers is first to be producers. The environmental function officially and explicitly appears in the text in 1995, in the framework of the Agricultural Guidance Law (Savy, 1999). Regarding the evolution of the values, this function remains relatively new.

# REFERENCES

Abric, J-C. (2001a). A structural approach to social representations. In K. Deaux, & G. Philogène (Eds.), *Representations of the social: Bridging theoretical traditions* (pp. 42-47). Malden: Blackwell Publishing.

Abric, J-C. (2001b). Les représentations sociales: Aspects théoriques [Social representations: Theoretical aspects]. In J-C. Abric (Ed.), *Pratiques sociales et représentations* (pp. 11-35). Paris: Presses Universitaires de France.

Abric, J-C. (2001c). Pratiques sociales, représentations sociales [Social practices, social representations]. In J-C. Abric (Ed.), *Pratiques sociales et représentations* (pp. 217-238). Paris: Presses Universitaires de France.

Abric, J.-C., & Guimelli, C. (1998). Représentations sociales et effets de contexte [Social representations and context effects]. *Connexions, 72,* 23-37.

Aubry, C., Galan, M-B., & Mazé, A. (2005). Garanties de qualité dans les exploitations agricoles : Exemple de l'élaboration du référentiel Quali'Terre® en Picardie [HACCP methodology and quality/environmental specifications for crop farms. Implications for the design of good agricultural practices guidelines], *Agricultures, 14*(3), 313-322.

Axelrod, L. J., & Lehman, D. R. (1993). Responding to environmental concerns: What factors guide individual action? *Journal of Environmental Psychology, 13,* 149-159.

Blin, J-F. (1997). *Représentations, pratiques et identités professionnelles* [Representations, practices and professional identities]. Paris : L'Harmattan.

Clémence, A., Doise, W., & Lorenzi-Cioldi, F. (1994). Prises de position et principes organisateurs des représentations sociales [Standpoints and organizing principles of social representations]. In C. Guimelli (Ed.), *Structures et transformations des représentations sociales* (pp. 119-152). Paris: Delachaux et Niestlé.

Doise, W. (1985). Les représentations sociales : Définition d'un concept [Social representations : Definition of the concept]. *Connexions, 45,* 243-253.

Doise, W. (1992). L'ancrage dans les études sur les représentations sociales [Anchoring in the studies of social representations]. *Bulletin de Psychologie, 45,* 189-195.

Doise, W. (1999). Attitudes et représentations sociales [Attitudes and social representations]. In D. Jodelet (Ed.), Les représentations sociales (6th ed., pp. 240-258). Paris : Presses Universitaires de France.

Douglas, M., & Wildavsky, A. (1983). *Risk and culture: An essay on the selection of technical and environmental dangers.* Berkeley: University of California Press.

Farr, R. M. (1984). Les représentations sociales [Social representations]. In S. Moscovici (Ed.), *Psychologie sociale* (pp. 379-389). Paris: Presses Universitaires de France.

Flament, C. (1987). Pratiques et représentations sociales [Practices and social representations]. In J-L. Beauvois, R-V. Joule, & J-M. Monteil (Eds.), *Perspectives cognitives et conduites sociales. Théories implicites et conflits cognitifs* (Vol. 1, pp. 143-150). Cousset: DelVal.

Flament, C. (1999). Structure et dynamique des représentations sociales [Structure and dynamic of social representations]. In D. Jodelet (Ed*.), Les représentations sociales* (6th ed., pp. 204-219). Paris: Presses Universitaires de France.

Flament, C. (2001a). Aspects périphériques des représentations sociales [Peripheral aspects of social representations]. In C. Guimelli (Ed.), *Structures et transformations des représentations sociales* (pp. 85-118). Neuchâtel: Delachaux et Niestlé.

Flament, C. (2001b). Pratiques sociales et dynamique des représentations [Social practices and dynamics of representations]. In P. Moliner (Ed.), *La dynamique des représentations sociales* (pp. 43-58). Grenoble: Presses Universitaires de Grenoble.

Fransson, N., & Gärling, T. (1999). Environmental concern: Conceptual definitions, measurement methods, and research findings. *Journal of Environmental Psychology, 19,* 369-382.

Gardner, G. T., & Stern, P. C. (1996). *Environmental problems and human behavior.* Boston: Allyn & Bacon.

Gärling, T., Fujii, S., Gärling, A., & Jakobsson, C. (2003). Moderating effects of social value orientation on determinants of proenvironmental behaviour intention. *Journal of Environmental Psychology, 23*, 1-9.

Giraudel, C., & Caplat, G. (1995). *L'agriculture biologique et la qualité: Approche juridique et normative* [Organic farming and quality : Legal and normative approach]. Limoges: Centre de Recherche en Droit de l'Environnement, de l'Aménagement et de l'Urbanisme.

Grize, J.-B., Vergès, P., & Silem, A. (1987). *Salariés face aux nouvelles technologies : Vers une approche socio-logique des représentations sociales* [Employees with regard to technological innovations : Towards a socio-logical approach of social representations]. Paris: Editions du CNRS.

Guimelli, C. (1994). Introduction. In C. Guimelli (Ed.), *Structures et transformations des représentations sociales* (pp. 11-24). Neuchâtel: Delachaux et Niestlé.

Guimelli, C. (1998). *Chasse et nature en Languedoc: Etude de la dynamique d'une représentation sociale chez des chasseurs languedociens* [Hunting and nature in Languedoc. Study of the dynamics of a social representation among hunters from Languedoc]. Paris: L'Harmattan.

Guimelli, C. (2001). La fonction infirmière: Pratiques et représentations sociales [Function of a nurse: Practices and social representations]. In J.-C. Abric (Ed.), *Pratiques sociales et représentations* (pp. 83-107). Paris: PU.F..

Hardin, G. (1968). The tragedy of the commons. *Science, 162*, 1243-1248.

Ittelson, W. H. (1973). Environment perception and contemporary perceptual theory. In W. H. Ittelson (Ed.), *Environment and cognition* (pp. 1-19), New York: Seminar Press.

Jodelet, D. (1989). *Folies et représentations sociales* [Mental illness and social representations]. Paris: Presses Universitaires de France.

Jodelet, D. (1999). Représentations sociales: Un domaine en expansion [Social representations: An expanding domain]. In D. Jodelet (Ed.), *Les représentations sociales* (6th ed., pp. 47-78). Paris: Presses Universitaires de France.

Jollivet, M. (2001). *Pour une science sociale à travers champs: Paysannerie, ruralité, capitalisme* [For a social science through fields: Farming community, rurality, capitalism]. Paris: Arguments.

Joule, R-V., & Beauvois, J-L. (1998). *La soumission librement consentie. Comment amener les gens à faire librement ce qu'ils doivent faire? [*Compliance without pressure. How make people do without pressure what they have to do?*]* Paris: Presses Universitaires de France.

Kaiser, F. G., & Shimoda, T. A. (1999). Responsibility as a predictor of ecological behaviour. *Journal of Environmental Psychology, 19*, 243-253.

Kalaora, B. (1997). Quand l'environnement devient affaire d'Etat [When environment becomes affair of state]. In M. Abélès, & H-P. Jeudy (Eds.), *Anthropologie du politique* (pp. 179-196). Paris : Armand Colin/Masson.

Katerji, N., Bruckler, L., & Debaeke, P. (2002). L'eau, l'agriculture et l'environnement. Analyse introductive à une réflexion sur la contribution de la recherche agronomique [Water, agriculture and environment. Thoughts about the contribution of agronomic research]. *Courrier de l'Environnement de l'INRA, 46*, 39-50.

Mazé, A., Aubry, C., & Papy, F. (2000). La certification des exploitations agricoles [The certification of farms]. *Economie rurale, 258*, 134-139.

Mendras, H. (1995). *Les sociétés paysannes: Eléments pour une théorie de la paysannerie* [Peasant societies: Element for a theory of the peasantry]. Paris: Gallimard.

Michel-Guillou, E. (2005). Qualité des eaux souterraines: Attribution de responsabilité et implication personnelle des agriculteurs [Quality of groundwater: Attribution of responsibility and personal involvement of farmers]. *Psychologie et Société, 8*, 157-167.

Michel-Guillou, E. (2006a). Représentations sociales et pratiques sociales : L'exemple de l'engagement pro-environnemental en agriculture [Social representations and social practices: Example of the pro-environmental commitment in agriculture]. *Revue Européenne de Psychologie Appliquée/European Review of Applied Psychology, 56*(3), 157-165.

Michel-Guillou, E. (2006b). The environment: A new function of the farmer's profession? Paper presented at *The 19th Conference of the International Association for People-Environment Studies (IAPS): Environment, Health and Sustainable Development*. Alexandria (Egypt): Bibliotheca Alexandrina, September, 11-16, 2006.

Michel-Guillou, E. (2006c). Les agriculteurs et l'eau: Evaluation de la prise de conscience d'un problème [Farmers and water: Evaluation of the awareness of the problem]. Paper presented at the *Entretiens de la Psychologie II*. Boulogne-Billancourt: Institut de Psychologie (Paris 5), 2-4 novembre 2006.

Michel-Guillou, E., & Ehrlich, M. (2005). Proximité d'appartenance mentale des individus: Les réseaux de relations professionnelles dans l'agriculture [Proximity of mental belonging: Professional networks in agriculture]. In A. Torre & M. Filippi (Eds.), *Proximités et changements socio-économiques dans les mondes ruraux* (pp. 215-233). Paris : INRA.

Michel-Guillou, E., & Moser, G. (2006). Commitment of farmers to environmental protection: From social pressure to environmental conscience. *Journal of Environmental Psychology, 26*(3), 227-235.

Michel-Guillou, E., & Weiss, K. (in press). Representations and behaviours of farmers with regard to sustainable development: A psycho-environmental approach. In B. A. Larson (Ed.), *Sustainable development research advances*. New York: Nova Science Publishers.

Montada, L., & Kals, E. (2000). Political implications of psychological research on ecological justice and pro-environmental behaviour. *International Journal of Psychology, 35(2)*, 168-176.

Moscovici, S. (1961). *La psychanalyse, son image, son public* [Psychoanalysis, its image and its public]. Paris: Presses Universitaires de France.

Moscovici, S. (1988). Notes towards a description of social representations. *European Journal of Social Psychology, 18*, 211-250.

Moscovici, S. (1998). The history and actuality of social representations. In U. Flick (Ed.), *The psychology of the social* (pp. 209-247). New York: Cambridge University Press.

Moscovici, S. (2001). Why a theory of social representations? *In* K. Deaux, & G. Philogène (Eds.), *Representations of the social: Bridging theoretical traditions* (pp. 8-35). Malden: Blackwell Publishing.

Moser, G. (1984). Water quality perception, a dynamic evaluation. *Journal of Environmental Psychology, 4*, 201-210.

Moser, G., Ratiu, E., & de Vanssay, B. (2004). Water use and management in the light of sustainable development: Social representations, ideologies and practices in different societal contexts. *IHDP Update, 4*, 13-15.

Poortinga, W., Steg, L., & Vlek, C. (2002). Myths of nature and environmental management strategies. A field study on energy savings in traffic and transport. In G. Moser, E. Pol, Y. Bernard, M. Bonnes, J. Corraliza, & V. Giuliani (Eds.), *Places, people & sustainability / Sustainability, people & places* (pp. 280-290). Göttingen: Hogrefe & Huber.

Rateau, P. (2000). L'approche structurale des représentations sociales [The structural approach of social representations]. In N. Roussiau (Ed.), *Psychologie sociale* (pp. 79-88). Paris: Press Editions.

Rouquette, M-L. (1997). *La chasse à l'immigré: Violence, mémoire et représentations* [Immigrant hunting: Violence, memory and representations]. Sprimont: Pierre Mardaga.

Roussiau, N., & Bonardi, C. (2002). Quelle place occupe la mémoire sociale dans le champ des représentations sociales ? [Which is the place of social memory in the approach of social representations?] In S. Laurens & N. Roussiau (Eds), *La mémoire sociale. Identités et représentations sociales* (pp. 33-49). Rennes : Presses Universitaires de Rennes.

Roussiau, N., & Renard, E. (2003). Des représentations sociales à l'institutionnalisation de la mémoire sociale [From social representations to the institutionalisation of social memory]. *Connexions, 80,* 31-41.

Savy, H. (1999). L'activité agricole, les fonctions de l'agriculture et le modèle d'exploitation. L'agriculture à travers les lois d'orientation agricole de 1960 à 1999. *POUR. Produire, entretenir et accueillir. La multifonctionnalité de l'agriculture et le contrat territorial d'exploitation, 164,* 17-24.

Sebillotte, M. (1999). Agriculture et risques de pollution diffuse par les produits phytosanitaires: Les voies de la prévention et les apports de l'expérience Ferti-Mieux [Agriculture and the risks of diffuse pollution caused by phytosanitary products: Prevention and the benefits of the Ferti-Mieux experiment]. *Courrier de l'Environnement de l'INRA, 37,* 11-22.

Steg, L., & Sievers, I. (2000). Cultural theory and individual perceptions of environmental risks. *Environment and Behaviour, 32,* 250-269.

Stern, P. C. (2000). Toward a coherent theory of environmentally significant behaviour. *Journal of Social Issues, 56,* 407-424.

Stern, P. C., & Dietz, T. (1994). The value basis of environmental concern. *Journal of Social Issues, 50,* 65-84.

Thiébaut, L. (1994). L'évolution de la relation agriculture-environnement [Evolution of the relationship agriculture-environment]. *POUR. Agriculture, environnement, 141,* 13-30.

Viaud, J. (2003). Mémoire collective, représentations sociales et pratiques sociales [Collective memory, social representations and social practices]. *Connexions, 80,* 13-30.

Weiss, K., Moser, G., & Germann, C. (2006). Perception de l'environnement, conceptions du métier et pratiques culturales des agriculteurs face au développement durable [Perception of the environment, professional conceptions and cultural behaviors of farmers in favor of sustainable development]. *Revue Européenne de Psychologie Appliquée, 56,* 73-81.

In: Applied Psychology Research Trends
Editor: Karl H. Kiefer, pp.229-238

ISBN 978-1-60456-372-6
© 2008 Nova Science Publishers, Inc.

*Chapter 11*

# UNDERSTANDING FACE PROCESSING IN CHILDREN AND ADULTS USING EYEWITNESS METHODOLOGY

## *Joanna D. Pozzulo[1], Julie Dempsey, Rayna House, and Alberta Girardi*

Department of Psychology, Carleton University, Ottawa, Ontario, Canada

## ABSTRACT

For adults, faces encoded using trait judgments (e.g., friendliness of the face) are more likely to be accurately recognized than faces encoded using featural judgments (e.g., the distance between one's eyes). Trait judgments can be likened to holistic encoding whereas, feature judgments can be likened to featural encoding. Thus, adults are likely to use holistic encoding for faces. The research on children's facial processing abilities remains equivocal. It has been argued that children are unable or unlikely to process faces holistically. The current study found that both children (6- to 9-years-old) and adults demonstrated higher identification accuracy rates using eyewitness methodology when making either a single trait judgment or no imposed judgements, compared to single featural judgments. Moreover, making two feature judgments produced accuracy rates at a level comparable to single trait judgments and no imposed judgments for children and adults. These data suggest that children are capable of holistic processing and may be using such a strategy when encoding a face "naturally", similar to adults.

[1] Correspondence to: Department of Psychology, Carleton University
1125 Colonel By Drive, Ottawa, Ontario, K1S 5B6, Canada
Joanna_pozzulo@carleton.ca

Research has suggested that facial recognition and identification is affected by an individual's ability to encode facial information as well as his/her ability to retrieve that information from memory (Baddeley & Woodhead, 1982; Wells, 1993; Wells & Hryciw, 1984). Encoding refers to "the dual process of forming a representation of a new face and storing that representation in memory" (Carey, Diamond, & Woods, 1980, p. 257). Retrieval or recognition abilities refer to "matching a representation of a new instance with a representation already stored in memory" (Carey et al., 1980, p. 257).

Generally, two types of face processing are mentioned in the literature: featural processing and holistic (or trait) processing. Schwarzer (2000) pointed out that most researchers agree that featural processing involves focussing on a single facial feature. However, two different definitions of trait processing have been presented. The term *holistic encoding* usually refers to a face being represented by a template that takes into account the entire face; in other words, the face is not represented by its parts (Farah, Wilson, Drain, & Tanaka, 1998). This is the definition that will be used in the present study. On the other hand, *configurational* encoding does involve specific features of the face, but the features are used only to determine spatial relationships (de Heering, Houthuys, & Rossion, 2007). For example, when processing a new face, an individual might judge the distance from the forehead to the eyes (de Heering et al., 2007).

While it is generally accepted that adults are capable of encoding faces holistically (Mueller, Carlomusto, & Goldstein, 1978; Winograd, 1976), less is known about children's encoding abilities (Carey & Diamond, 1977). Some researchers believe that children encode faces featurally until approximately age 10 and then switch to a holistic encoding strategy (Carey & Diamond, 1977; Hay & Cox, 2000, Schwarzer, 2002). Others believe that even young children are capable of holistic processing of faces (Blaney & Winograd, 1978; Pellicano & Rhodes, 2003, Tanaka, Kay, Grinnell, Stansfield, & Szechter, 1998). The present study will examine both children's and adults' face processing abilities using an applied paradigm; eyewitness methodology.

### Age Differences in Facial Encoding and Facial Recognition

Early facial recognition work by Hochberg and Galper (1967) suggested that adults were able to accurately recognize upright photographs of faces at a significantly higher rate than inverted photographs. The researchers concluded that adults do not merely use pattern storage and pattern recognition when trying to recognize faces, because simply inverting a face does not change the pattern. It is generally accepted that adults can recognize a large number of individual faces even if the faces are physically similar, if facial characteristics change, or if the angle of the view is different in the encoding condition than in the recognition condition (Carey & Diamond, 1977; Laughery, Alexander, & Lane, 1971).

The majority of research on children's facial recognition abilities has suggested that younger children are more likely to pay attention to (and thus, encode) specific features of the face (Sharwarzer, 2000). Results of one study indicated that 6- to7-year-old children are better at identifying individual features of a face (especially the eyes) than 9- to 10-year-old children (Hay & Cox, 2000). Researchers who support the notion that younger children are not capable of holistic encoding often cite empirical evidence on the effects of delay, paraphernalia, and upright/inverted faces on children's facial recognition abilities (Baenninger, 1994; Carey et al., 1980; Carey & Diamond, 1977; Diamond & Carey, 1980;

Ellis & Flin, 1990; Hay & Cox, 2000). The results of these studies indicate that younger children (6- to 8-years-old) are not affected by delay (i.e., time from exposure of target to recognition task). Also, they appear to rely on paraphernalia (i.e., cues not associated with the face itself) for recognition. Furthermore, they do not differ in their ability to recognize upright versus inverted faces. These findings support the idea that young children pay attention to the features of a face; in other words, they encode faces featurally.

### *Manipulating Encoding Instructions*

Some researchers, however, have suggested that even young children are capable of processing faces holistically (Blaney & Winograd, 1978; Tanaka et al., 1998). While the research that supports this notion is limited, this issue has been examined by manipulating encoding instructions provided to children. Blaney and Winograd (1978) found that while older children have superior recognition abilities when compared to younger children, the recognition abilities of all children benefited from the presentation of holistic encoding instructions.

Courtois and Mueller (1979) manipulated encoding instructions to compare holistic processing with single feature encoding and multiple feature encoding. Single feature encoding involved asking the participants to make a decision about a single facial feature (i.e., distance between the eyes or thickness of lips). Participants in the multiple feature encoding condition were asked to identify the person's most distinctive facial feature. In contrast, participants in the holistic encoding condition rated the face on its friendliness or honesty. The results suggested that facial processing with multiple features was superior to single feature processing, and that both featural conditions were inferior to holistic encoding. In other words, participants were more likely to recognize a face if they were given holistic encoding instructions rather than featural encoding instructions.

With research that directly examines children's holistic encoding abilities (i.e., by providing them with holistic encoding instructions) being very limited, and a vast body of research suggesting that children are, in fact, more likely to attend to the individual features of a face, the exact encoding capabilities of children remain ambiguous.

### *A Specific Form of Facial Recognition: The Lineup*

Bradshaw and Wallace (1971) raised an important point concerning an individual's everyday usage of facial recognition. Normally, people attempt to locate a familiar person among unfamiliar faces. It is unusual for a person to have to locate an unfamiliar face from among other unfamiliar faces that are similar in appearance. This latter situation, however, is likely to be encountered by eyewitnesses to crimes. While it is important to understand how children process faces, it is equally important to understand how children encode and recognize unfamiliar faces, especially in the context of being an eyewitness.

In an overview of the empirical research on eyewitness identification, Wells (1993) hypothesized that eyewitness identification is a holistic process. Poorer lineup identification accuracy has been observed when *adults* attempt to process faces featurally as opposed to holistically. A conclusion on how children's processing abilities affect eyewitness identification has yet to be developed. However, Wells (1993) suggested that the process of facial recognition may be different for child witnesses because, unlike adults, they may process faces featurally. Moreover, Wells (1993) argued that eyewitness lineup identification represents a different task from what most participants experience in facial recognition experiments.

The present study, therefore, implemented eyewitness methodology in order to further understand children's encoding capabilities. One reason for using eyewitness methodology was to avoid the problem of portrait recognition. Thus, the target face was presented in video-tape format, while the recognition task was presented in photograph format. The recognition task did not involve a photograph of the target (i.e., target-absent lineup) because it is a more informative test to determine which processing strategy was used. More specifically, if the recognition task contained the target, it would not have been possible to determine why a correct decision occurred (i.e., a featural or holistic match). Thus, recognition accuracy was measured using the rate of false positive/correct rejection.

### The Present Study

Children and adults were given encoding instructions manipulating featural processing (e.g., size of the eyes) and holistic processing (e.g., friendliness of the face). In addition, a group of children and adults were given no encoding instructions (control condition) to examine how participants encode faces "normally." It was predicted that adults would have a lower false positive rate (i.e., make fewer errors)/higher correct rejection rate when given holistic or no encoding instructions compared to featural instructions. If children are unable process faces holistically, we would expect no differences in false positive/correct rejection rate across the three instructional conditions (feature vs. holistic vs. control).

## METHOD

### Participants

Ninety elementary school children, ($M_{age}$ = 7.66, $SD$ = 1.03, age range = 6- to 9-years-old) from grades one, two, or three, were recruited from an elementary school in Central Newfoundland, Canada. In addition, 90 adults ($M_{age}$ = 36.07, $SD$ = 12.77, age range = 18- to 64-years-old) were recruited from the First Year Psychology Participant Pool at a University in Eastern Ontario, Canada. The children received a small token for their participation (a colourful pencil). The adults received course credit for their participation.

### Measures

**Exposure to target face**. Participants were shown a five-second video clip of a male confederate's face (i.e., target). The confederate looked directly into the camera for the length of exposure.

**Facial Processing Task**. In a procedure adapted from Blaney and Winograd (1978), participants were asked to make yes/no judgements concerning the target's face as it was displayed on screen. Each participant made one type of judgement: feature, holistic/trait, or control (no specific judgement requested). A featural judgement involved asking the participant if s/he thought the person's eyes were small. In contrast, a trait judgement involved asking the participant if s/he thought the person on the video was fun. Participants in the control condition, who made no judgements of the target face, watched the video and were not asked any questions. The judgement questions were pre-tested with 6-year-old children to ensure that the children understood the task.

**Description Form**. Participants were asked to describe the target using a free recall format (i.e., *"please tell me everything you can remember about the person in the video"*). This task was a filler to allow a brief time delay between encoding and identification. Responses to this task were not coded and will not be discussed further.

**Lineup Task.** Head and upper body photographs were taken of male undergraduate students who resembled the confederate. From this pool of photographs, a six-person, target-absent (i.e., target's photo not included) lineup was constructed.

**Lineup presentation**. A simultaneous lineup was used to display the photographs. All photos were displayed at the same time in a three-column by two-row arrangement. Participants were informed that the person in the video may or may not be present in the lineup. Participants were asked to examine the photographs and indicate whether one of the photographs was of the target.

**Experimental design**. A 3 x 2 between-subjects factorial design was employed. Three facial processing instruction conditions were examined: feature, holistic/trait, and control. Two age conditions were included: child and adult. Participants in both the holistic and featural encoding conditions were told that they would watch a short videotape of a person and would be asked questions about the person while they were watching the videotape. Participants in the control condition were told that they were going to watch a short videotape. One third of the children, and one third of the adults were presented with featural judgement instructions. Another third of the children and another third of the adults were presented with trait encoding instructions.

## Procedure

**Children.** Children who had parental/guardian consent were asked if they would like to help the researcher with her project. Children who were agreeable to participate were shown the videotape of the target for five seconds. Prior to the start of the video, participants in the holistic/trait and featural encoding conditions were given the appropriate encoding instructions. While the target's image was on the screen, these participants completed as many judgements (either holistic or featural) as possible during the 5 seconds. Participants in the control encoding condition were asked to watch the video. None of the participants were informed they would later need to recognize the face in a recognition task. Upon completing the encoding task, all participants were asked to describe the target (i.e., free recall). Lastly, participants were asked to examine a six-person lineup, and to determine whether the target's face was present. Once participation was complete, participants were debriefed.

**Adults.** An identical procedure was used with adults.

## RESULTS

### Identification Accuracy

For the purpose of examining the effect of age (child vs. adult) and encoding instruction (holistic vs. featural vs. control) on identification accuracy, a subtype of loglinear analysis, hierarchical analysis, was used. The 3-way association between age, encoding instructions, and lineup identification accuracy was not significant, indicating that if lineup identification accuracy was regarded as the dependent variable, the interaction of age and encoding instructions on identification accuracy was not reliable, partial $\chi^2(2) = 3.52$, $p = .17$. See Table 1 for identification accuracy rate as a function of age and encoding instructions. The 2-way association between age and identification accuracy was not significant, partial $\chi^2(1) = 2.36$, $p = .12$. However, the 2-way association between encoding instructions and identification accuracy was significant, partial $\chi^2(2) = 8.42$, $p = .01$. Thus, there was a main effect of encoding instructions.

**Table 1. Rates of identification accuracy (n) as a function of age and encoding instructions.**

| Age | Type of Encoding Instructions | | |
| --- | --- | --- | --- |
| | Trait | Featural | Control |
| Child | | | |
| Correct Rejection | .43(13) | .17(5) | .57(17) |
| Adult | | | |
| Correct Rejection | .53(16) | .43(13) | .53(16) |

In order to determine where differences existed with respect to the encoding instructions variable, post hoc analyses were conducted. All three types of encoding instructions (holistic, feature, and control) were compared using three chi square tests with an alpha set at .016 (.05/3). Significant differences were observed between the correct rejection rates of participants receiving feature encoding instructions ($M = .30$) and participants receiving no encoding instructions ($M = .55$), $\chi^2 = 7.673$, $p = .01$. Comparisons between the correct rejection rates of featural and holistic encoding instructions ($M = .48$), and holistic and no encoding instructions approached significance ($\chi^2 = 4.232$, $p = .06$, and $\chi^2 = .534$, n.s.). Thus, participants who received featural encoding instructions produced the lowest accuracy rate; they were least likely to correctly indicate that the target's picture was not present in the lineup.

## Single Feature Judgements versus Multiple Feature Judgements

One surprising result emerged from the hierachical analysis; namely, adults who made feature judgements did not produce lower identification accuracy compared to adults who made holistic judgments or who received no encoding instructions. A review of the data indicated that participants differed in the number of judgements made across conditions, which may have obscured the results. See Table 2 for identification accuracy rate as a function of age and number of judgements made per encoding condition.

A second hierarchical log linear analysis was conducted involving participants who made only one trait encoding judgement, one feature encoding judgement, or who received no encoding instructions. The 3-way association between age, encoding instructions, and identification accuracy was not significant, indicating that if identification accuracy was regarded as the dependent variable, the interaction of age and encoding instructions was not reliable, partial $\chi^2(2) = 1.41$, $p = .50$. The 2-way association between age and identification accuracy was not significant, partial $\chi^2(1) = .58$, $p = .45$. However, the 2-way association between encoding instructions and identification accuracy was significant, partial $\chi^2(2) = 20.15$, $p < .001$. Thus, there was a main effect of encoding instructions on identification accuracy.

**Table 2. Rates of identification accuracy (n) as a function of the number of judgements made and age.**

Identification (ID) Accuracy

|  | Correct Rejection | Incorrect ID |
|---|---|---|
| **Adults** | | |
| One Feature Judgement | .15(2) | .85(11) |
| Two Feature Judgements | .65(11) | .35(6) |
| One Trait Judgement | .61(14) | .39(9) |
| Two Trait Judgements | .29(2) | .71(5) |
| No Encoding Instructions | .53(16) | .47(14) |
| **Children** | | |
| One Feature Judgement | .12(3) | .88(23) |
| Two Feature Judgements | .50(2) | .50(2) |
| One Trait Judgement | .41(9) | .59(13) |
| Two Trait Judgements | .50(4) | .50(4) |
| No Encoding Instructions | .57(17) | .43(13) |

In order to determine where differences existed with respect to encoding instructions, post hoc analyses were conducted. All three types of encoding instructions (holistic, feature, and control) were compared using three chi square tests with an alpha set at .016 (.05/3). Significant chi square tests were observed for the comparison between the correct rejection rates of feature encoding instructions ($M = .13$) and no encoding instructions ($M = .55$), $\chi^2 = 17.70$, $p < .001$, and between the correct rejection rates of feature encoding instructions and holistic encoding instructions ($M = .51$), $\chi^2 = 13.79$, $p < .001$. The comparison between the correct rejection rates of those who received holistic and no encoding instructions was not significant, $\chi^2 = .16$, n.s. Thus, unlike in the first analysis, receiving holistic encoding instructions or no encoding instructions led to better accuracy than receiving featural encoding instructions. This was true for both children and adults. When two feature judgements were made, identification accuracy rates resembled those for the holistic/trait encoding instructions and no encoding instructions for children and adults.

## DISCUSSION

The purpose of the present study was to examine children's facial recognition abilities compared to the abilities of adults using eyewitness methodology. First, we examined whether children would be more accurate in recognizing the target's picture if they received holistic compared to featural encoding instructions versus no specific instructions. We were further interested in determining whether children and adults would differ in their ability to recognize or identify faces across the three encoding conditions.

It was predicted that children would show a comparable identification rate across encoding instructions conditions: feature, holistic, and no instruction. Such a pattern would indicate that children between 6- and 9-years tend to use feature processing when encoding an unfamiliar face. In contrast, it was predicted that adults would demonstrate a higher accuracy rate with holistic encoding instructions or no instructions compared to feature instructions.

Children and adults who made holistic judgements or who used their own form of encoding were more likely to make a correct rejection than those who made feature judgements. This finding is consistent with previous research suggesting that trait encoding leads to more accurate recognition than featural encoding (Carey & Diamond, 1977; Courtois & Mueller, 1979). With the similar correct rejection rates in the control and holistic encoding conditions, it may be that all participants were utilizing an encoding style similar to that of trait encoding. Thus, it seems plausible that children are indeed capable of holistic encoding, as suggested by Blaney and Winograd (1978) and Tanaka et al. (1998).

The notion by some that children under the age of 10 process faces featurally (Carey & Diamond, 1980; Hay & Cox, 2000) did not receive support in the present study Children in the present study had a mean age of 7 years and ranged from 6- to 9-years. It is possible that feature encoding is predominant for younger children under 6 years of age. Future research should examine the processing abilities of younger children and how they compare to older children and adolescents.

Another issue that emerged from the results of the present study concerns the non-significant finding for the main effect of age. Previous research using an eyewitness paradigm has indicated that while children's ability to correctly identify a target from a *target-present* line-up is comparable to adults, their identification accuracy rates with a *target-absent* lineup, such as the one utilized in the present study, results in a lower identification accuracy rate (Pozzulo & Lindsay, 1998). In the present study, children and adults produced comparable correct rejection rates across the respective encoding conditions.

One possible explanation for this inconsistent finding is the extreme age range of adults used in the present study. Adult participants ranged in age from 18 to 64 years, with a mean age of 36 years. In fact, many of the participants were above the age of 40. The older age of the adult participants could have affected the identification accuracy rate of the adult group, possibly lowering it. As suggested by Adams-Price (1992), there is a moderate negative relationship between age and identification accuracy. Moreover, in the present study, older adult participants may be more likely to have a low level of education; whereas, in previous research  younger adult participants are usually obtained from a university setting representing a higher educational bracket. The complete educational background of the adults in the current study is not known; however, some of the participants were teachers (i.e., high education level), whereas other participants were from rural Newfoundland and may be less likely to have attained post high school education. Thus, the accuracy rate of the adults in the current study could be lower than that of younger adult participants in comparable studies.

It is interesting to note that participants making two feature judgements produced accuracy rates similar to those who made holistic judgements or those who were given no encoding instructions. This result was present for both children and adults. Similarly, Courtois and Mueller (1979) demonstrated that multiple feature encoding led to better recognition than single feature encoding; with multiple feature encoding resulting in only slightly inferior recognition than holistic encoding. Consistent with the configurational conception of holistic encoding, it is possible that participants who made more than one featureal judgement also were more likely to make comparisons among the features of the face, leading them to encode the face holistically.

The goal of the present study was to extend the knowledge of children's facial encoding and recognition abilities, and to merge the methodology of both the facial recognition literature and the eyewitness identification literature. Children as young as 6 years of age seem capable of holistic encoding both when provided with holistic encoding instructions and when encoding a face using their own methods. Future research should examine the encoding abilities of younger children (children aged 4- to 5-years-old) to delineate the developmental trajectory of holistic encoding.

# REFERENCES

Adams-Price, C. (1992). Eyewitness memory and aging: Predictors of accuracy in recall and person recognition. *Psychology and Aging, 7,* 602-608.

Baddeley, A., & Woodhead, M. (1982). Depth of processing, context, and face recognition. *Canadian Journal of Psychology, 36,* 148-164.

Baenninger, M. (1994). The development of face recognition: Featural or configurational processing? *Journal of Experimental Child Psychology, 57,* 377-396.

Blaney, R. L., & Winograd, E. (1978). Developmental differences in children'srecognition memory for faces. *Developmental Psychology, 14,* 441-442.

Bradshaw, J. L., & Wallace, G. (1971). Models for the processing and identification of faces. *Perception & Psychophysics, 9,* 443-448.

Carey, S., & Diamond, R. (1977). From piecemeal to configurational representation of faces. *Science, 195,* 312-314.

Carey, S., Diamond, R., & Woods, B. (1980). Development of face recognition: Amaturational component? *Developmental Psychology, 16,* 257-269.

Courtois, M. R., & Mueller, J. H. (1979). Processing multiple physical features in facial recognition. *Bulletin of the Psychonomic Society, 14,* 74-76.

De Heering, A., Houthuys, S. & Rossoin, B. (2007). Holistic face processing is mature at 4 years of age: Evidence from the composite face effect. *Journal of Experimental Child Psychology, 96,* 57-70.

Diamond, R., & Carey, S. (1977). Developmental changes in the recognition of faces. *Journal of Experimental Child Psychology, 23,* 1-22.

Ellis, H. D., & Flin, R. H. (1990). Encoding and storage effects in 7-year-olds' and 10-year-olds' memory for faces. *British Journal of Developmental Psychology, 8,* 77-92.

Farah, M. J., Wilson, K. D., Drain, M., & Tanaka, J. N. (1998). What is "special" about face perception? *Psychological Review, 105,* 482-498.

Hay, D. C., & Cox, R. (2000). Developmental changes in the recognition of faces and facial features. *Infant and Child Development, 9,* 199-212.

Hochberg, J., & Galper, E. (1967). Recognition of faces: 1. An exploratory study. *Psychonomic Society, 9,* 619-620.

Laughery, K.R., Alexander, J.F., & Lane, A.B. (1971). Recognition of human faces: Effects of target exposure time, target position, pose position, and type of photograph. Journal *of Applied Psychology, 55,* 477-483.

Mueller, J. H., Carlomusto, M., & Goldstein, A. G. (1978). Orienting task and study time in facial recognition. *Bulletin of the Psychonomic Society, 11,* 313-316.

Pellicano, E., & Rhodes, G. (2003). Holistic processing of faces in preschool children and adults. *Psychological Science, 14,* 618-622.

Pozzulo, J. D., & Lindsay, R. C. L. (1998). Identification accuracy of children versus adults: A meta-analysis. *Law and Human Behavior, 22,* 549-570.

Schwarzer, G. (2000). Development of face processing: The effect of face inversion. *Child Development, 71,* 391-401.

Schwarzer, G. (2002). Processing of facial and non-facial visual stimuli in 2- to 5-year-old children. *Infant and Child Development, 11,* 253-269.

Tanaka, J. W., Kay, J. B., Grinnell, E., Stansfield, B., & Szechter, L. (1998). Face recognition in young children: When the whole is greater than the sum of its parts. *Visual Cognition, 5,* 479-496.

Thompson, L. A., & Massaro, D. W. (1989). Before you see it, you see its parts: Evidence for feature encoding and integration in preschool children and adults. *Cognitive Psychology, 21,* 334-362.

Wells, G. L. (1993). What do we know about eyewitness identification? *American Psychologist, 48,* 553-571.

Wells, G. L., & Hryciw, B. (1984). Memory for faces: Encoding and retrieval operations. *Memory & Cognition, 12,* 338-344.

Winograd, E. (1976). Recognition memory for faces following nine different judgements. Bulletin of the Psychonomic Society, 8, 419-421.

In: Applied Psychology Research Trends
Editor: Karl H. Kiefer, pp.239-256

ISBN 978-1-60456-372-6
© 2008 Nova Science Publishers, Inc.

*Chapter 12*

# AWARENESS OF SELF, IMITATION, AND LINGUISTIC COMPETENCES IN YOUNG CHILDREN WITH AUTISM

*R. Pry[1], A.F. Petersen[2], and A. Baghdadli[3].*
[1]Departement of Psychology, University .Montpellier III,
[2]187, Draye du Marbre, F-34170 Castelnau-le-Lez,
[3]Child & Adolescent Psychiatry, CHU-Montpellier, France.

## ABSTRACT

The present longitudinal study focuses on interactions between self-awareness, imitation, and language development in young children with autism. 30 children aged 5 years on average participated. The sample was divided into two groups according of a scale-evaluation regarding the variable 'recognition of being imitated' (*Group 1*: observant children; *Group 2*: indifferent children). An evaluation of interactions between competences of imitation and of language was then carried out for the two groups. The results show that the children of the two groups develop almost identically with respect to imitation but with important differences regarding language. The results are discussed with a view to typical psychological development.

**Keywords:** Autism, Self-Awareness, Imitation, Language.

## INTRODUCTION

Autism is a pervasive developmental disorder which was first described in 1943 by the American psychiatrist Leo Kanner. The disorder appears in early childhood and presents a variety of symptoms depending on the stage of development and the chronological age of the

---

[1] Correspondence to: rene.pry@wanadoo.fr
[2] Correspondence to: afpetersen@free.fr
[3] Correspondence to: a-baghdadli@chu-montpellier.fr

child.  Autism restrains the child's ability to communicate with others, and it is often accompanied by other problems such as mental retardation, epilepsy, behavioural disorders, sensory-motor and perceptual deficits.  The progression of the disorder is influenced by a number of heterogeneous factors of a genetic, biochemical, biological, and developmental nature, but its manifestation is also differentiated by such factors as the child's cognitive abilities, the date of the appearance of language and by not yet well-known influences from the sex of the individual, his or her age when the first signs of the syndrome appeared, and various external influences (Aussilloux, Baghdadli, Bursztejn, Hochmann and Lazartigues, 2001).

Epidemiological studies calculate the rate of children with autism to be 2 to 5 among 10.000 persons, and estimations and surveys testify that autism attains boys for the major part and that it is found in all populations and social strata (Fombonne, 1998).

According to the latest version of the diagnostic manual of the American Psychiatric Association (DSM-IV, 1994) the diagnostic criteria of autism are the following:  qualitative impairment of social interaction, verbal and nonverbal communication, and limitations of activities and interests.

As both verbal and nonverbal communication (imitation, joint attention, intersubjective understanding etc.) are disturbed it is notably problems of interchange with others which constitute the core difficulty encountered by children with autism.  In most cases language fails to appear or develops in a peculiar way and with considerable delay.  There is a great heterogeneity in this domain:  some children remain mute their whole life while others develop a rudimentary jargon, using occasionally a few isolated words or finally beginning to speak with an extended vocabulary and syntax (Rey, Tardif, Vol, Thomas and Bondil, 2002).


## II. REVIEW OF THE LITERATURE

### 1. Consciousness of Self and Recognition of Self

An important distinction is here to be made between *consciousness of self* and *recognition of self*. Consciousness of self implies necessarily a recognition of self, since one may very well be able to recognize oneself without having yet developed a consciousness of self. From everyday experience we know that our bodily awareness is nourished by mirror reflections, by our respiration and heartbeat, and more so from the sensations we get from moving around.

Although babies do not move around by themselves they seem to have a knowledge about themselves from early on, and research during the last decades supports the view, often expressed by parents, that *self-recognition* in babies develops progressively with age in tempo with activities of increasing complexity. By storing traces of such perceptions and actions, the baby gradually develops knowledge about his body and realizes that he has an effect on the world (distinction between himself as an entity among others), and as he interacts with others as a social partner (distinction between self and others) he arrives at distinguishing himself from other persons.  To arrive at that the baby must have some *awareness of self* as well as a certain understanding of the existence of an environment of objects and other living beings.

Meltzoff (1990) demonstrated that if an infant is left the choice between someone who imitates him and someone who does different things, the infant (from the age of 9 months) shows more interest for the person who imitates him. He also showed that 14 month old babies can make quick modifications of actions which adults find difficult to reproduce. This sort of behaviour shows that babies already at that age recognise that others are imitating them.

Different techniques have been designed to demonstrate self-recognition in babies. One such method is a mirror technique which allows the child to recognise himself and to differentiate his own body from its mirror image. Judging from the child's reactions in front of his mirror image one can deduce that he has a representation of his own body, and therefore knows what he looks like. The first study of this kind was done by Zazzo (1985) with his own children as subjects. He also pioneered the hypothesis that the child's reactions in front of the mirror reveal the beginning of self-awareness, and he lanced the idea that the child's verbalisation of his own name is a criterion of self-recognition.

Other self-awareness techniques have since been introduced, like that of an altered image with which one may study the development of the concept of self by evaluating visual self-recognition after, say, some red colour has been put on the child's nose (Amsterdam, 1972). Here it turned out that children less than 15 months rarely touched their nose whereas the majority of the 2 year olds saw a difference between their coloured nose and what they knew it should look like. Babies thus seem to develop a visual concept of self between 15 and 24 months of age.

Self-recognition in children with autism has not been much explored until now. According to Nadel and Decety (2002) autistic children generally do recognise that they are being imitated even if they don't express it. They also showed that repeated imitation of the child by an adult, using pairs of attractive objects, increased their awareness of being imitated. Like normal children, children with autism are capable of recognising that they are being imitated, and they may even initiate imitation behaviour and provoke reactions in their imitating partner. For Nadel (2003) the recognition of being imitated and the different types of imitations are related processes.

## 2. Imitation

According to some authors, imitation is present right from birth. The new-born is capable of imitating facial movements like tongue protrusion, opening of the mouth (Meltzoff and Moore, 1977), eye blinking (Kugiumutzakis, 1999) and various facial expressions (Field, Woodson, Cohen, Greenberg, Garcia and Collins, 1983). The ability to imitate enables children to reproduce other's actions and to integrate the representation of this action. This capacity was considered essential for the development of the child's awareness of himself and of others by Piaget as early as the 1930s.

Piaget later described imitation as a precursor of the symbol function (Piaget, 1936). Subsequent research has confirmed this association between imitation and development of language in normally developing children (Bates, Benigni, Bretherton, Camaioni and Volterra, 1979; Snow, 1989). According to other authors, imitation has different functions and is not only considered a tool for learning but also for communication: 'Imitation offers a unique opportunity to perceive what the other feels by reproducing his actions, to learn what our own actions look like when they are reproduced by another and to observe our intentions in action through the behaviour of others' (Nadel and Potier, 2005, p. 78).

Imitation develops gradually: the first imitations may be observed a few hours after birth, and around 9 months, children are capable of imitating actions with objects (immediate and delayed); they even begin to notice when they are imitated and progressively become capable of spotting imitation as intentional. Recent studies show that imitation and recognition of being imitated is present in children at 14 months, and after 18 months, children use imitation as a tool of communication. At this age they also begin to understand turn-taking and to use imitation for communicating with their peers (Meltzoff, 2002; Decety, 2002).

While typically developing children show an ability to imitate right from birth, children with autism have great difficulty in imitating body movements of others and delayed imitation of actions where objects are used (Toth, Munson, Meltzoff and Dawson, 2006).

## 3. Imitation and Autism

There is no agreement in the literature on the imitative skills of children with autism. Some authors claim that they are not capable of imitation, while others (Nadel and Potier, 2002) maintain that the only deficit they suffer from is that they just imitate later than normal children do; indeed, Nadel (1999) suggests that difficulties with imitation in children with autism can be among the first signs of the disorder itself. However this may be we notice that children with autism have a poor motor repertoire, probably a consequence of their limited capability for spontaneous actions.

A frequent shortcoming of studies on the capacity of imitation in autistic children is that they deal mostly with *induced imitation*, which demands of the subject to employ executive functions in order to look beyond his own needs at any given moment and follow what is being proposed by the experimenter or his confederate, despite the fact that it is one of the things children with autism have difficulty of doing (Nadel and Potier, 2005). Nonetheless it is important to realise that imitation is a simple operation which autistic children are capable of performing. Nadel and Butterworth (1999) has shown that some low functioning autistic children have a certain imitation capacity and that they react to being imitated by directing their attention towards the adult and showing a social behaviour that indicates their expectations to the adult. Stone, Ousley and Littleford (1997) compare the different abilities of imitation in children with autism, mentally retarded children and normally developing children; the results reveal poor imitation abilities in children with autism, their body imitation being more impaired than object imitation, and meaningless imitation more impaired than meaningful imitation. Rogers, Hepbrun, Stackhouse and Wenher (2003) studied imitation (motor, verbal and object imitation) in autistic children, children presenting Fragile-X syndrome and other developmental disorders; the results of this study also show that children with autism are less good at imitation than others.

The literature on imitation recommends two types of research: (i) studies of imitation deficits in children with autism with a special view to imitation being a possible factor for early detection of autism; (ii) studies of imitative skills as predictive for subsequent linguistic activity.

## 4. Is Imitation a Predictive Factor for Language Development?

For the last twenty years research on autism has searched for predictive factors of development in all domains, and more especially in language development. Certain authors (Roy, Elliot, Dewey and Square-Stoner, 1990) have defended the view that difficulties in imitation are not specific to autism but to a category of language disorders. They believe that the difficulty related to gestures and sequences of action are frequent in many types of atypical development. According to Cermack, Coster and Drake (1980), children with dysphasia also have difficulties in imitation and physical gestures which supports Smith and Bryson's (1994) premise that the deficit in imitation attributed to autism could include a broader category of language disorders. However, Rogers, Bennetto, McEvoy and Pennington (1996) do not support this hypothesis; in their study high functioning autistic adolescents were compared to dyslexic adolescents of the same chronological age and verbal standard, and they found that the performances of young persons with autism are inferior irrespective of the type of movement, simple or sequential, facial or bodily, symbolic or non-symbolic. Stone *et al.* (*op.cit.*) elaborate the concomitant and predictive relationships between abilities of body imitation and language skills; according to them, imitation of body and facial movements is related to language development while imitation with objects is related to the development of play. Moreover, the deficit in imitation is associated with echolalia (which is atypical repetitions of vocalizations; Charman and Baron-Cohen, 1994) and with echopraxia (which is imitations of atypical gestures; Libby, Powell, Messer and Jordan, 1997).

Toth *et al.* (*op.cit.*) studied the correlations between imitation, joint attention and language in 60 children with autism 3-4 years old. They found that proto-declarative joint attention and immediate imitation are strongly associated with language capacities and that delayed imitation contributes to the growth of language and communication.

## 5. Language

Language development reveals itself during the first months of life and proceeds rapidly, as children by the age of 4 already master everyday language to a considerable extend. Right from birth children show predispositions for communicating with the world around them. Around 4 months, babies begin to babble and this form of vocalisation comprises sounds which are close to those used in speech. At about 12 months babies combine vocalisation with pointing and gazing. This kind of communication behaviour spurs on the development of joint attention, turn-taking, and other social behaviour, and is also considered an important precursor to language development (Tomasello, 1992). The production of the first word takes place at about one year of age, however, with large inter-individual variations.

A veritable verbal explosion occurs at about 18 months as between 16 to 20 months, the child is typically able to produce from 50 to 170 words and more than 200 words after 20 months of age (Boysson-Bardies, 1996). 2 year old children learn several words a day and when linking them their communication efficiency increases considerably.

From the first stages of language development, normal children are capable of using prosody, intonation, words and grammatical constructions accurately to express their feelings and moods (Ochs, 1993).

## 6. Language and Autism

In autism language remains heavily affected and distorted, ranging from absence of language to a functional language which is idiosyncratic. Characterised by a peculiar prosody, an absence of reaction to name calling (Charman, Drew and Baird, 2003), and confusion of personal pronouns (I, you…), children with autism often use third-person constructions which shows an absence of consciousness of self. The language of children with autism is typically marked by echolalia – of which there are two kinds:

> ➢ Immediate echolalia which consists of immediate repetition of what has just been said;
> ➢ Delayed echolalia consists of repeating a sentence after a certain delay like nursery rhymes, public messages… (Courtois-du-Passage and Galloux, 2004).

Immediate echolalia is part of language development in autistic children, and its presence shows that communication as a function of language is not really understood. Most children who attain language pass through this stage where they repeat what others say instead of taking a complementary role as partner of communication (Prizant and Duchan, 1981). These authors showed furthermore that echolalia could have different functions such as demand or protest. Echolalia may thus represent an emergence of communication which the child can use for acquiring a functional communication system later on. Even though children who use echolalia the most are also the ones who use spontaneous language to the least, we also notice that echolalia decreases with age as shown by Coutois-du-Passage *et al.*, *op.cit.*). It seems these children use language more in order to ask for things than to communicate or share with others.

Some children with autism do develop language but it is often peculiar in a number of ways. Compared to typically developing children, they are also slow in learning words, which is not surprising considering that children learn the meaning of words by interacting with other people (Bartolucci, Pierce & Streiner, 1980) and, as mentioned above, this capacity is deficient in children with autism. Autistic language is disturbed not only in the way it is expressed but also in its reception (Aaron and Gittens, 1999), as can be seen from the difficulties these children have in comprehending gender distinction (masculine/feminine) and metaphors. Moreover, it is difficult for children with autism to grasp fluctuations in tone and voice accentuations used by the speaker while these aspects are essential for comprehending the different meanings which one and the same sentence may have (Mathews, 1990).

As far as grammar is concerned, studies of autistic language at a certain level of functionality have shown that the employed grammar and syntax are governed by rules which resembles those used by typically developing children (Fay and Schuler, 1980). However, in a recent study Courtois-du-Passage *et al.* (*op.cit.*) found that children with autism, well knowing, do not use certain grammatical rules and morphemes because of discursive and syntactic problems.

Even if we admit that linguistic efficiency can be intact in some forms of Asperger's Syndrome or high functioning autism, these children do still have difficulty comprehending social situations, humour and implied meanings. Several studies have compared comprehension in children with autism and mentally retarded children with results showing that the level of comprehension in autistic children is inferior to that of the others (Paul and Cohen, 1984; Barta, Rutter and Cox, 1975).

# III. OBJECTIVE

The present study addresses questions of awareness of self in children with autism and its possible interrelations with the development of interactive competences: does consciousness of self facilitate the development of imitative abilities and linguistic competences in children with autism, or is it rather the other way round (as proposed in Pry, Petersen and Baghdadli, 2005), that means of interaction, including language, help the child to develop self-recognition and consciousness of self?

# IV. Methodology

The study has been coordinated by the 'Autism Resource Center' (*Centre de Ressources Autisme*) of the Region of Languedoc-Rousillon, France, situated in a child psychiatric ward, directed by Professor Ch. Aussilloux, at CHU-Montpellier (*Centre Hospitalier Universitaire* of Montpellier).

## 1. Population Sample

### 1.1. Inclusion Criteria

> ➢ Diagnosis of Infantile Autism or atypical Autism according to the ICD 10 diagnostic criteria and the revised version of the Autistic Diagnostic Interview;
> ➢ Developmental age greater than or equal to 18 months in the two principal domains of the revised version of the Brunet-Lézine: hand-eye coordination and posture coordination;
> ➢ Chronological age between 3 and 5 years;
> ➢ Written agreement from parents.

### 1.2. Data Collection
Data collection was done over the span of 1 year. The data concerning imitation and language were collected at three stages (T0, T2, and T4); each evaluation was done with a time interval of 6 months. The imitation scale concerns a standardised procedure in which an adult seeks the participation of the child  letting the child act and intervene spontaneously with him or her. Each 20 minutes session is filmed so that the adult can score the presence or absence of expected behaviour.

## 2. Imitation

Imitation skills were measured by an Imitation Scale created by Nadel and Butterworth (1999) – a scale of 31 items which assesses the ability of the child to imitate spontaneously, on request, and to recognise being imitated.

> ➤ The first step is to the explore the ability of the child to imitate spontaneously which requires that the confederate suggests attractive play activities with available objects to arouse the child's the desire to imitate. These activities cover a fixed panel of simple or complex, familiar or new, functional or unusual actions, with or without objects.
>
> ➤ The second procedure consists of estimating the capacities of the child to recognise that he is being imitated. The confederate imitates the postures and the new or familiar, simple or complex activities of the child with or without an identical object.
>
> ➤ The third step concerns assessment of the child's ability to imitate upon request: having asked the child to 'do as I do', the confederate presents once again a fixed panel of familiar, new, simple or complex actions… but always playing the role of the designated model.

## 3. Scoring

For spontaneous imitation and imitation on request, each act of imitation is scored from 0 to 3:

- 0 = no imitation
- 1 = partial imitation
- 2 = successful imitation after 2 or 3 trials
- 3 = successful imitation upon 1$^{st}$ trial

For the recognition of being imitated, the scoring is 0 or 1:

- 0 = the child does not react to being imitated
- 1 = the child reacts to being imitated

In view of the data obtained for 'recognition of being imitated' the sample can be divided into two groups: *Group 1* consists of children, who recognise that the adult is imitating them, and *Group 2* comprises children, who do not react to the fact that they are being imitated by the adult.

## 4. Language

The data concerning language consist of observations made from video-recordings used for scoring imitations. To begin with, we phonetically transcribe all utterances made by the children. Then, applying CHILDES, a detailed analysis of the recorded linguistic activity is carried out, thereby obtaining information not only about the number of phonemes and morphemes but also about the number of nouns, grammatical words, and other paralexical words used by the child during his interaction with the adult.

## 5. Statistical Analysis

A repeated ANOVA-measure is done in order to certify if the development in the two groups ('observant' *versus* 'indifferent' children) are significant according to the chosen variables of language and imitation ('spontaneous' and 'on request')

# V. RESULTS

## 1. Description of the Sample

The sample consists of 30 children: 2 girls and 28 boys; the sex-ratio is thus 1/14.
The chronological age at T0 is 50 months on average.
The two groups were formed according to the variable 'recognition of being imitated', a scale established by Nadel *et al.* (1999). Children scoring more than '3' were considered as 'observant' (*Group 1*) and those scoring below or equal to '3' were considered as 'indifferent' (*Group 2*); '3' is taken as the determining criterion as it is the median. Each group counted 15 children.

## 2. Relations Between the Variables

### 2.1 Interactions Between Type of Imitation and Recognition of Being Imitated.
We note that imitation skills (spontaneous as well as on request) increase with time in both groups even if there is a difference in the rate of increase between spontaneous imitation than with imitation on request.

### • Spontaneous Imitation
Children in *Group 1* imitate more than the children in *Group 2*. *Group 1* attains a score of 6 in T0 compared with 2.6 for children in *Group 2*. Despite this variation between the two groups, there are no significant difference between them.

**Table 1: Spontaneous imitation**

|  | T0 | T2 | T4 |
|---|---|---|---|
|  | Mean | Mean | Mean |
|  | Standard deviation | Standard deviation | Standard deviation |
| GROUP 1 | 6 | 6,8 | 10,1 |
|  | 5,7 | 4,7 | 6,3 |
| GROUP 2 | 2,6 | 4,2 | 5,2 |
|  | 4 | 5 | 8,7 |

The ANOVA shows no significant relationship between the development of spontaneous imitation in the different stages, which means that the two groups develop in a similar way resulting in a $p = 0.35$ (not significant).

- **Imitation on Request**

*Table 2* shows that children of *Group 1* have better imitation skills (on request) than children of *Group 2*. The results also show an increase in this behaviour through the year (between T0 and T4) for the two groups.

**Table 2: Imitation on demand**

|  | T0 | T2 | T4 |
|---|---|---|---|
|  | Mean | Mean | Mean |
|  | Standard deviation | Standard deviation | Standard deviation |
| GROUP 1 | 6,6 | 9,8 | 14,6 |
|  | 6,8 | 6,8 | 9,7 |
| GROUP 2 | 3,5 | 5,5 | 7,3 |
|  | 5,9 | 6,6 | 10,5 |

The results of ANOVA indicate that the two groups develop similarly between T0 and T4 (p=0.32). The results also show that the standard deviation increases which means that there is heterogeneity within the groups.

## 2.2 Relationship/Interactions Between Language and the Recognition of Being Imitated

### • Phonemes

Children of *Group 1* do have better linguistic skills when compared to children of *Group 2* at all three stages. Children of *Group 2* develop progressively regarding the number of phonemes used, but children of *Group 1* seem to remain stable throughout the one-year observation period (around 25 phonemes).

**Table 3: Phonemes**

|  | T0 | T2 | T4 |
|---|---|---|---|
|  | Mean<br><br>Standard deviation | Mean<br><br>Standard deviation | Mean<br><br>Standard deviation |
| GROUP 1 | 25,9<br><br>10,9 | 27,2<br><br>5,6 | 25,8<br><br>7,9 |
| GROUP 2 | 18,4<br><br>11,0 | 19,5<br><br>9,5 | 21,6<br><br>8,4 |

The ANOVA results show that the two groups develop differently between T0 and T4; however, $p=0.09$ is at the limit of significance.

### • Nouns

The children of *Group 1* use more nouns on an average than the children of *Group 2* in all three stages of the observation period. Even though a development in the number of nouns used between T0 and T4 is observed in the children of *Group 1*, this development is minimal.

**Table 4: Nouns**

|  | T0 | T2 | T4 |
|---|---|---|---|
|  | Mean<br><br>Standard Deviation | Mean<br><br>Standard Deviation | Mean<br><br>Standard Deviation |
| GROUP 1 | 9,5<br><br>7,7 | 9,3<br><br>7,4 | 11,7<br><br>9,8 |
| GROUP 2 | 4,3<br><br>8,8 | 2,5<br><br>3,0 | 5,0<br><br>6,2 |

For the children of *Group 2*, we note that no development has taken place between T0 and T4. These children use approximately the same number of nouns throughout the year of observation, even though there is a slight decrease at T2 (between 4 and 5 on an average).

The ANOVA results confirm the results from the descriptive data, implying that the two groups develop differently from T0 and T4 (p=0.02).

● *Grammatical Words*

The children of *Group 1* use more grammatical words than the children of *Group 2*. Moreover, they improve between T0 and T4, from using 25 grammatical words to 38, whereas the children of *Group 2* remain stable. It is also important to note that the standard deviation increases in the children of *Group 1*, thereby showing that the differences deepen between these children.

**Table 5: Grammatical words**

|  | T0 | T2 | T4 |
|---|---|---|---|
|  | Mean<br><br>Standard Deviation | Mean<br><br>Standard Deviation | Mean<br><br>Standard Deviation |
| GROUP 1 | 25,08<br><br>24,14 | 29,08<br><br>19,56 | 38,08<br><br>40,84 |
| GROUP 2 | 9,43<br><br>12,9 | 4,81<br><br>6,47 | 8,25<br><br>11,16 |

The results of the ANOVA indicate that there are interactions between the variables. This shows that the children of *Group 1* and *2* develop differently between T0 and T4 (p=0.00).

# VI. DISCUSSION

## 1.Limitations of the Study

This study is strained by certain limitations. A first one concerns the scoring of the variable 'recognising being imitated'. As it was not obvious which reactions of the child could be considered representative of this kind of recognition, we did not have precise criteria for the scoring. We therefore selected one or more criteria to indicate, in a non-ambiguous manner, that the child recognises his own image - emotional and verbal expressions (verbalising name), as well as movements directed at himself or towards another person or object). Admittedly, the reactions of children with autism are not always very expressive, which add to the subjectivity of this scoring. However, reactions easily observable by the adult were taken into account (such as addressed smile, re-initiation of action by the child to be imitated once again…).

A second limitation of the study has to do with the language scoring, especially for those children who manifest very little language as they use only a few comprehensible words, and since the articulation is often distorted the analysis of the expressions may be difficult.

## 2.Discussion of Results

In general, the children of *Group 1* have better linguistic and imitative efficiency than the children of *Group 2*.

### 2.1 Imitation

It seems that, in children with autism, spontaneous imitation, imitation on request, and the ability to recognise being imitated develop in the same way (but not at the same rate).

Three variables which describe imitation behaviour seem to be strongly correlated, since the developmental pathways for the two groups are parallel as can be seen from the ANOVA curves. The results from our sample confirm those of Nadel (2003), who has put forward the hypothesis that the recognition of being imitated brings about and improves other imitation behaviour. Nadel (*op.cit.*) maintains also that the recognition of being imitated generates reciprocal imitation and this, in turn, induces social behaviour towards the imitator such as a smile or a gaze. Our results reveal a similar tendency, thus supporting the hypothesis that those children, who are aware that they are being imitated, are also those who imitate more than the other children. According to Nadel (*op.cit.*), the different forms of imitation stimulate recognition of the partner allowing the child to perceive his own actions through the other.

Despite that different forms of imitation develop in the same manner, it is important to note that there are also differences: children perform better with spontaneous imitation than with imitation on request. This may be explained by the fact that while spontaneous imitation is a voluntary action with an intention to communicate and interact with somebody else, imitation on request demands of the child to be interested in the other and his activity in order to be able to repeat his actions.

### 2.2 Grammatical Words

Regarding grammatical words there is a large difference between the two groups throughout the three stages. We may therefore deduce that the usage of grammatical words requires a certain level or standard that the children of *Group 2* have not yet reached.

While the stock of grammatical words increases in some of the children of *Group 1* the children of *Group 2* remain at the same level. We notice that, at T4, the confidence interval increases with respect to the other two stages, which indicates that there is an increase in diversity within the group.

The two groups use more grammatical words than nouns. The fact that utilisation of language in children with autism is primarily to ask for something might explain their usage of more grammatical words than nouns. These results are surprising and go against what we would find in normally developing children. The distribution of words produced by normal children is characterised by the domination of nouns, then predicates and finally grammatical words. In normal children nouns appear earlier and are used more than verbs (Caselli, Casadio and Bates, 1999; Fenson, Dale, Reznick, Thal, Bates, Hartung, Tethick and Reilly, 1993; Gentner, 1982)

Besides, the standard deviation is large between the different stages suggesting that the gap between children with a good level of language and those with a less good level of language is widening. This further supports the heterogeneity often found in autism.

## 2.3 Phonemes

There is little difference in the production of phonemes between *Group 1* and *2* at all three stages. This explains that p = 0.09 is not significant but only 'leans towards' significance.

Children who have a sense of self recognition seem to show less development in their linguistic activity as compared to children in *Group 2* whose development is slight yet progressive.

The French language is composed of 38 phonemes. We note that even the children of *Group 1*, who are supposed to have a normal language level, have not acquired all the phonemes. 'Normal children', as we often call them, possess all the phonemes of their mother tongue at the age of 5. Here, at T0, children of *Group 2* produce 18.4 phonemes on average and those of *Group 1* produce 25.9.

## 2.4 Interaction

The interrelations between the variables 'recognition of being imitated' and 'nouns' indicate that the two groups develop differently regarding the number of words they use during the evaluation period.

In a recent study by Smith, Miranda and Zaidman-Zait (2007) on the predictors of vocabulary development in children with autism, the authors point to four predictive factors in language development: (i) the number of words present at the beginning of the study; (ii) verbal imitations; (iii) pretend play with objects, and (iv) joint attention.

The present study shows that children, who imitate the most, are also those with the highest level of language. This has also been found in typically developing children. Some authors argue that imitation plays an important role in the child's social development and that imitation is a predictor of the language capacities in normally developing children. Other recent studies of children with autism have demonstrated that the different forms of imitation are correlated with future language capacities (Toth *et al.*, 2006), as, for example, immediate imitation was found firmly associated with language capacities of these children 3-4 years old. A study by Stone *et al.* (1997) showed that immediate imitation with objects in 20 month old autistic children is correlated with their receptive language at 42 months, and that motor imitation at 24 months predicts expressive language capacities at 48 months.

These results agree with the present results, and other things being equal children, who use more imitative behaviour, are also those who develop a better language level.

## 2.5 Imitation, Joint Attention, and Language Capacities

The present study shows that the different types of imitation seem to be related and that self-recognition generates reciprocal imitation, all of this facilitates the child's communication and interaction with other people. Recognition of being imitated by others is firmly associated with good imitation capacities and language development. There is a heterogeneity regarding the standard of language within the two groups, which is characteristic of children with autism.

Recent studies has mostly dealt with the predictive factors of language. In a study by Toth *et al.* (*op.cit.*), an initial hypothesis that joint attention and the different types of imitation are predictive for future language capacities of children with autism was corroborated. They also found that proto-declarative joint attention and immediate attention are strongly associated with language capacities in children with autism 3-4 years old. Furthermore, delayed imitation and imaginative play in these children at 4-6 years are associated with the rapidity of the acquisition of communicative abilities.

In future studies it would therefore be of interest to consider findings like those of Toth *et al.* (*op.cit.*) in applying their hypothesis to a population like the present one, in order to see if similar results can be obtained. Moreover, it would be interesting to increase the sample so as to examine how the variables, imitation, joint attention and language develop on a larger scale. - Will a larger population render the same results?

## VII. CONCLUSION

As implied in the findings discussed above there seems to be degrees of consciousness: a simple comparison of the early sensations that a baby may enjoy of his body with the explicit self-identity that a two-year old may manifest so unequivocally suggests that we are dealing with self-awareness on different levels. It is tempting to think that babies are born with the ability to unite perceptual information which renders them different from other entities, and that this first kind of self is probably determined by such direct perception and action - self-exploration and self-contemplation seem to reveal that. Recognition of self in the mirror, on the other hand, is the result of reflection, a veritable mental reflection. With the arrival of language the young child will reach another level of self-consciousness, more conceptual, and in referring to himself verbally he gradually arrives at identifying himself in relation to others and in making himself an object of thought.

In this developmental process imitation is probably a strong mechanism which facilitates this comprehension. Phenomena like motor resonance, emotional resonance, mimicry or spontaneous imitation which are present from birth participate, in all likelihood, to this differentiation of 'own body' from other bodies. Equipped with capacities for simulation of his own actions by repetition (self-imitation) it only takes a couple of months before the child arrives at distinguishing self-recognition in the mirror from his concept of self in general. The results obtained and discussed in this study, that interactive competences such as imitation and language tend to develop synchronously, might suggest that they also contribute to the formation of the self.

## VIII. BIBLIOGRAPHY

APA - *American Psychiatric Association : Diagnostic and statistical manual of mental* disorders (4<sup>th</sup> ed., International version, Washington DC, 1995). French translation by Guefi, J.-D. *et al.*; Paris: Masson, 1995.

Amsterdam, B.K. (1972). Mirror self-image reactions before age two. *Developmental Psychobiology*, 5, 297-305.

Aarons, M. & Gittens T. (1999). *Handbook of autism. A Guide for Parents and Professionals.* 2<sup>nd</sup> Edition, London & New York: Routledge.

Aussilloux, C., Baghdadli, A ., Bursztejn, C., Hochmann, J . & Lazartigues, A. (2001). Recherche sur les facteurs d'évolution de l'autisme : caractéristiques initiales d'une cohorte de 193 enfants autistes de moins de sept ans, *Neuropsychiatrie de l' enfance et de l'adolescence,* 49, 96-107.

Bartak, L., Rutter, M. & Cox, A. (1975). A comparative study of infantile autism and specific developmental receptive language disorder. I. The children, *British Journal of Psychiatry,* 126, 127-145.

Bartolucci, G., Pierce, S. J. & Streiner, D. (1980). Cross-sectional studies of grammatical morphemes in autistic and mentally retarded children. *Journal of Autism and Development Disorders,* 10, 39-50.

Bates, E., Benigni, L., Bretherton, I., Camaioni, L. & Volterra, V. (1979). *The emergence of symbols: Cognition and communication in infancy.* New York: Academic Press.

Boysson-Bardies, B. (1996). *Comment la parole vient aux enfants.* Paris: Odile Jacob.

Caselli, C, Casadio, P. & Bates, E. (1999). A comparison of the transition from first words to grammar in English and Italian. *Journal of Child Language* 26(1), 69-109.

Cermak, S., Coster, W. & Drake, C. (1980). Representational and non-representational gestures in boys with learning disabilities. *Journal of Occupational Therapy,* **37**, 466-473.

Charman, T. & Baron-Cohen, S. (1994). Another look at imitation in autism. *Development and Psychopathology,* 6, 403-13.

Charman, T., Drew, A., Baird, C. & Baird, G. (2003) Measuring early language development in preschool children with autism spectrum disorders using the MacArthur Communicative Development Inventory (Infant Form), *Journal of Child Language,* 30, 213-236.

Courtois-du-Passage, N. & Galloux, A.-S. (2004). Bilan orthophonique chez l'enfant atteint d'autisme: Aspects formels et pragmatiques du langage. *Neuropsychiatrie de l'enfance et de l'adolescence,* **52**(7), 478-489.

Decety, J. (2002). Neurobiologie des representations motrices partagées. In: Nadel, J. & Decety, J. (eds.), *Imitez pour découvrir l'humain.* Paris: PUF; 105-126.

Fay, S. & Schuler, L. (1980). *Emerging language in autistic children.* Baltimore: University Park Press.

Fenson, L., Dale, P., Reznick, S., Thal, D., Bates, E., Hartung, J.,Tethick, S. & Reilly J. (1993). *MacArthur Communicative Development Inventories: User's guide and technical manual.* San Diego: CA Singular Publishing Group.

Field, T. M., Woodson, R., Cohen, D., Greenberg, R., Garcia, R. & Collins, E. (1983). Discrimination and imitation of facial expressions by term and preterm neonates, *Infant Behavior and Development,* 9, 415-421.

Fombonne, E. (1998). Epidémiologie de l'autisme en France. *Psychologie Française,* 43-2.

Gentner D. (1982). Why nouns are learned before verbs: Linguistic relativity versus natural partitioning. In: Kuczaj, S. (ed.), *Language, culture and cognition.* Hillsdale, NJ: Lawrence Erlbaum, 56-67.

Kugiumutzakis G. (1999). Genesis and development of early infant mimesis to facial and vocal models. In: Nadel, J., & Butterworth, G. (eds.), *Imitation in infancy.* Cambridge: Cambridge University Press, p.36-59

Libby, S., Powell, S., Messer, D. & Jordan, R. (1997). Imitation of pretend play acts by children with autism and down syndrome. *Journal of Autism and Developmental Disorders,* 4, 365-83.

Matthews, A. (1990). *Making friends : a guide to getting along with people*. Singapore: Media Masters.

Meltzoff, A. N. (1990). Foundations for developing a concept of self : The role of imitation in relating self to other and the value of social mirroring, social modeling, and self practice in infancy. In: Ciccheti, D. B. M. (ed.), *The Self in Transition : Infancy to Childhood*, Chicago: University of Chicago Press,139-164.

Meltzoff, A. N. (2002). La théorie du "like me", précurseur de la comprehension sociale chez le bébé: imitation, intention et intersubjectivité. In: Nadel, J., Decety, J. (eds.) *Imitez pour découvrir l'humain*. Paris: PUF; 33-54.

Meltzoff, A. N. & Moore, M. K. (1977). Imitation of facial and manual gestures by human neonates. *Science*, 198, 75-78.

Meltzoff, A., & Decety, J. (2003). What imitation tells us about social cognition: a rapprochement between developmental psychology and cognitive neuroscience. *Philosophical Transactions of the Royal Society, London. B. Biological Science.* 358, 491-500.

Nadel, J. (1999). The evolving nature of imitation. In: Nadel, J., Butterworth, G. (eds.), *Imitation in Infancy*, Cambridges: Cambridge University Press, 209-234.

Nadel, J. (2003). Imitation et autisme. *Cerveau & Psycho*, 4, 68-71.

Nadel, J., & Butterworth, G. (1999). *Imitation in infancy*. Cambridge: Cambridge University Press.

Nadel, J. & Decety, J. (2002). *Imiter pour découvrir l'humain : psychologie, neurobiology, robotique et philosophie de l'esprit*. Paris: PUF.

Nadel, J. & Potier, C. (2002). Le statut développemental de l'imitation dans l'autisme. *Enfance*, 1, 76-85.

Nadel, J. & Potier, C. (2005). Imiter et être imité dans le développement de l'intentionnalité. In : Nadel, J. & Decety, J. (eds.), *Imiter pour découvrir l'humain*. Paris: PUF; 83-104.

Ochs, E. (1993). Constructing social identity : A language socialization perspective. *Research on Language and Social Interaction*, 26, 287-306.

Paul, R., & Cohen, D., (1984) responses to contingent queries in adults with mental retardation and pervasive developmental disorders, *Applied Psycholinguistics,* 5, 349-357.

Piaget, J. (1962). Le rôle de l'imitation dans la formation de la représentation, *l'Evolution psychiatrique,* 27(1), 141-150.

Prizant, B. & Duchan, J.F. (1981). The functions of immediate echolalia in autistic children, *Journal of Speech and Hearing Disorders*, 46, 241-249.

Pry, R., Petersen, A.F. & Baghdadli, A. (2005) The relationship between expressive language level and psychological development in children with autism 5 years of age. *Autism*, 9(2), 179-189.

Rey, V., Tardif, C., Vol, S., Thomas, K. & Bondil, M. (2002). Autisme et trouble du langage: étude exploratoire des capacités phonologiques. In: Pech-Georgel, C. & George, F. (eds.), *Approches et remédiations des dysphasies et dyslexies*. Marseille: Solal; 59-79.

Rogers, S. J., Bennetto, L., McEvoy, R. & Pennington, B. F. (1996). Imitation and pantomime in high-functioning adolescents with autism spectrum disorders. *Child Development*, 67, 2060-2073.

Rogers, S.J., Hepbrun, S.L., Stackhouse, T. & Wehner, E. (2003). Imitation performance in toddlers with autism and those with other developmental disorders. *Journal of Child Psychology and Psychiatry*, 44(5), 763-781.

Roy, E., Elliot, D., Dewey, D. & Square-Storer, P. (1990). Impairments to praxis and sequencing in adult and developmental disorders. In: Bard, C., Fleury, M. & Hay, L. (eds.) *Development of eye-hand coordination across the life-span*. New York: Columbia University, 358-384.

Smith, I., & Bryson, S. (1994). Imitation and action in autism: A critical review, *Psychological Bulletin*, 116, 259-273.

Smith, V., Miranda, P. & Zaidman-Zait, A. (2007). Predictors of expressive vocabulary growth in children with autism. *Journal of Speech, Language & Hearing Research*, 50, 149-160.

Snow, C. E. (1989). Imitativeness : A trait or a skill ? In: Speidel, G. E. & Nelson, K. E. (eds.), *The many faces of imitation in language learning*. New York: Springer-Verlag; 73-90.

Stone, W. L., Ousley, O. Y. & Littleford, C. D. (1997). Motor imitation in young children with autism: what's the object? *Journal of Abnormal Child Psychology*, 25(6), 475-485.

Tomasello, M. (1992). *First verbs: a case study of early grammatical development.* Cambridge: Cambridge University Press.

Toth, K., Munson, J., Meltzoff, A. N. & Dawson, G. (2006). Early predictors of communication development in young children with autism spectrum disorder: joint attention, imitation, and toy play. *Journal of Autism and Developmental Disorders*, 9, 11-29.

Rogers, S. J., Hepbrun, S. L., Stackhouse, T. & Wenher, E. (2003). Imitation performance in toddlers with autism and with other developmental disorders. *Journal of Child Psychology and Psychiatry*. 44(5), 763-781.

Zazzo, R. (1985). Conscience de soi et méthode des doubles perceptifs. *Comportements*, 3, 199-211.

# INDEX

## J

## K

## N

## O

## P

## T

## U

## V

## W